MW01630153

Robert Motherwell on Paper

I knew who had sent them in those
green cases.
Who doesn't lose his mind will receive
like me
That wire in my neck up to the ear.

RM

Robert Motherwell on Paper

Drawings • Prints • Collages

Edited by David Rosand

Essays by David Rosand, Arthur C. Danto, Stephen Addiss, and Mary Ann Caws

Harry N. Abrams, Inc., Publishers

in association with the Miriam and Ira D. Wallach Art Gallery, Columbia University

Published on the occasion of the exhibition "Robert Motherwell on Paper: Drawings, Prints, Collages" at the Miriam and Ira D. Wallach Art Gallery, Columbia University, New York, organized by David Rosand, Meyer Schapiro Professor of Art History, Columbia University

EXHIBITION ITINERARY

Miriam and Ira D. Wallach Art Gallery, Columbia University, New York • January–March 1997
Marsh Art Gallery, University of Richmond, Virginia • September–November 1997
Spencer Museum of Art, University of Kansas, Lawrence • March–May 1998

Editor: James Leggio • Designer: Judith Michael

LIBRARY OF CONGRESS CATALOGING-IN-PUBLICATION DATA
Motherwell, Robert.
Robert Motherwell on paper / edited by David Rosand ; with essays
by David Rosand . . . [et al.].
p. cm.
Exhibition catalog.
"In association with the Miriam and Ira D. Wallach Art Gallery."
Includes bibliographical references and index.
ISBN 0–8109–4294–1 (clothbound)
1. Motherwell, Robert—Exhibitions. 2. Motherwell, Robert—
Criticism and interpretation. I. Rosand, David. II. Title.
N6537.M67A4 1997
760.092—dc20 96–19574

Published in 1997 by Harry N. Abrams, Incorporated, New York
A Times Mirror Company

Printed and bound in Japan

FRONTISPIECE: *Elegy to the Spanish Republic No. 1*, 1948. India ink on paper, 10¾ x 8½" (27.3 x 21.8 cm).
The Museum of Modern Art, New York. Gift of the artist. Cat. no. I.1
PAGE 8: Robert Motherwell in his studio, Greenwich, Connecticut, 1991. Photograph © Renate Ponsold Motherwell
PAGE 12: Robert Motherwell with *Black Mountain (State I)* on the wall
of his studio, Greenwich, Connecticut, 1983. Photograph © Renate Ponsold Motherwell
PAGE 81: Robert Motherwell in his collage studio, Greenwich, Connecticut, 1976.
Photograph © Renate Ponsold Motherwell
PAGE 93: Robert Motherwell at the installation of the exhibition "Robert Motherwell and Black,"
The William Benton Museum of Art, University of Connecticut, Storrs, 1979. Photograph © Renate Ponsold Motherwell

To Renate Ponsold Motherwell in friendship and gratitude

Contents

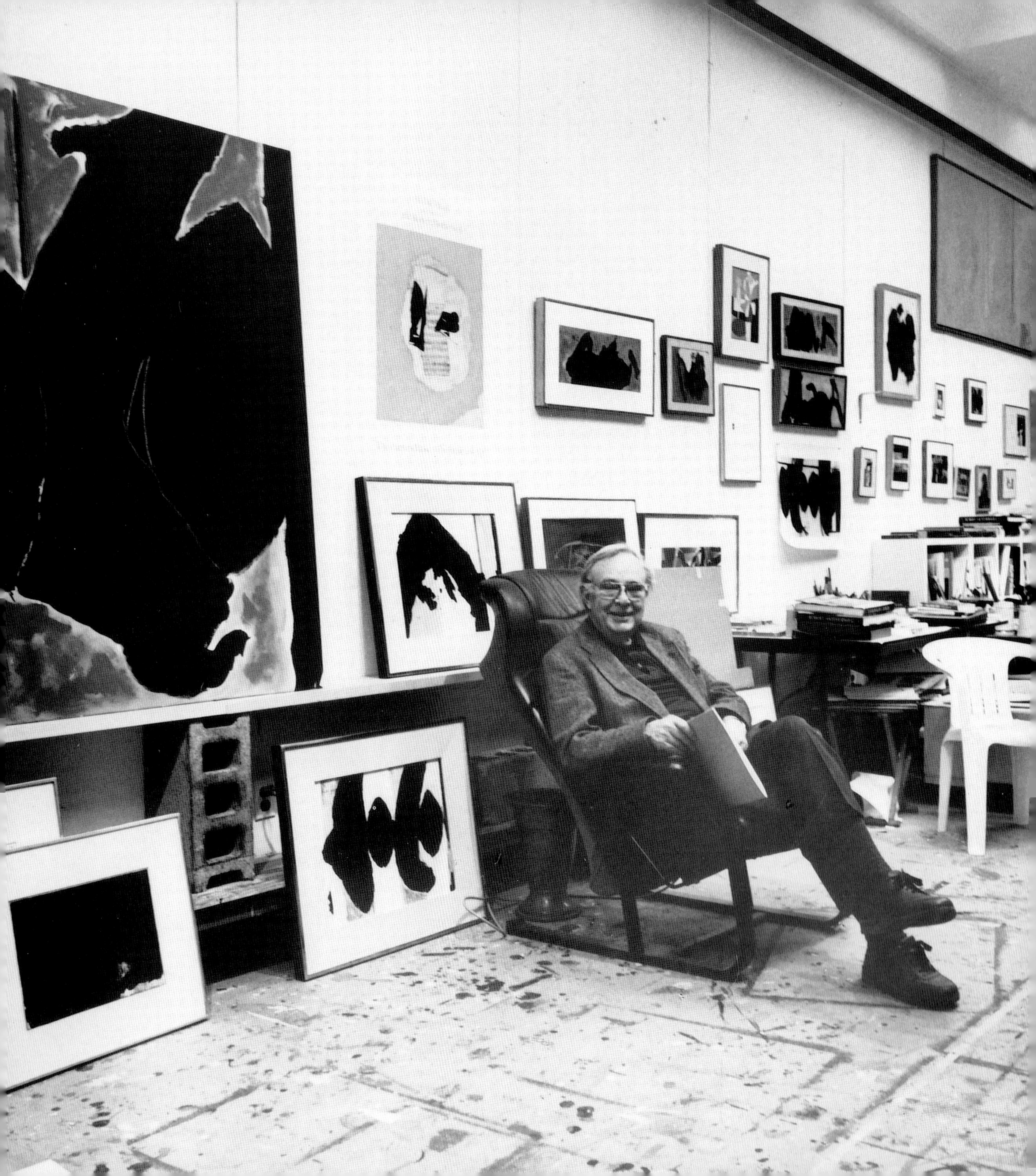

Preface

Gesture, Variation, Continuity

The idea for this exhibition of drawings, prints, and collages by Robert Motherwell was born in the artist's studio; it was conceived and developed in conversations with him during the year before his death, on July 16, 1991, at the age of seventy-six. Presenting mediums and supports that were central to Motherwell's creative development, it focuses on the products of his continuing fascination with paper and with working in series. Despite their obvious status as independent works of art as well as their importance for the fullest understanding of the artist's achievement, Motherwell's works on paper have rarely received the kind of sustained critical attention or public display they deserve; they were, the artist himself felt, neglected in his gallery exhibitions in New York. When Stephen Addiss and I proposed an exhibition of this body of work, he responded immediately with enthusiasm; he was especially happy at the prospect of an exhibition that would travel to university galleries, bringing his art to a younger generation of viewers.

The project itself is, as Motherwell might have said, the result of "studio chance." Addiss had chosen to conclude his book on Zen painting with an illustration of one of Motherwell's etchings from the *Hollow Men* suite, juxtaposing it with the famous image of a circle, triangle, and square by Sengai. Motherwell was pleased by the juxtaposition; he thought it revealed certain basic values of his art. During our visits to the artist's Greenwich, Connecticut, studio—especially our final one, a few weeks before his death—the conversation often turned to paper, which he called "the most sympathetic of all painting surfaces." And, of course, to the marking implement: "In the beginning was the brush," as he had declared with scriptural authority on another occasion. In reviewing his own work with us in his studio, Motherwell delighted in rediscovering himself in those images, reviving and renewing the energies that created them.

"Robert Motherwell on Paper" is organized around two determining coordinates: serial creation and thematic continuity. The first focuses on actual series—that is, groups of works created on single themes or inspired by single initial gestures—in drawing, printmaking, or collaging. Traditionally, at least since the Renaissance—paper has lent itself to such a process, inviting the dialectic of invention and variation in drawing and, especially, printmaking. Motherwell reclaimed that dialectic and exploited the potential of the material, whether as support or medium; paper, in his hands, was both. Responding to his own initial inventive gesture, whether an actual stroke of the brush or a peculiar tear of the paper in collage, to both the accidental and the deliberate, he pursued that suggestive potential.

The second organizing coordinate of the exhibition, thematic continuities, traces creation over a longer duration. Along this line, the innate quality of an initial creative gesture is confirmed by repetition or rediscovery; basic pictorial structures emerge as natural identifying marks of the artist. The gestures of the *Elegy* configuration offer the most obvious, and significant, example; beginning in an almost casual drawing in 1948, the motif follows Motherwell throughout the rest of his life, codified, as it were, in prints and transfigured finally in the grand canvas of the *Hollow Men*.

"Robert Motherwell on Paper" demonstrates the complex relationship between abstraction and figuration, the phenomenology of the mark and of marking, and the capriciousness of artistic invention. The exhibition aims to present the creative gesture in its various manifestations—as immediate impulse, as dialectic response, as deliberate variation—and also in its different temporal dimensions, whether as a concentrated sequence of moments or as the retrieval and revival of latent content from the artist's past. Intended to explore one artist's ongoing cycles of creativity, the exhibition has, unhappily, become a memorial to that artist, the last and the most articulate of the heroic generation of Abstract Expressionists; it remains a tribute to his creative example.

Motherwell's work raises important questions about the values of art in our time. The painter, like the art historian who effectively set him on his course, Meyer Schapiro, affirmed the essential humanity of abstract painting. The professor's responsiveness to painting and painters opened the way for the graduate student in art history at Columbia to discover his true path, in 1940. The human qualities that Schapiro discerned in modern art—as, indeed, in medieval art and in art-making in general—were precisely those that Motherwell was to embody in his work as a painter. "The humanity of art lies in the artist and not simply in what he represents," Schapiro professed in his lectures on abstract art. "It is the painter's constructive activity, his power of impressing a work with feeling and the qualities of thought that gives humanity to art. . . . For the most part, what we see on the canvas belongs there and nowhere else. But it calls up more intensely than ever before the painter at work, his touch, his vitality and mood, the drama of decision in the ongoing process of art. Here the subjective becomes tangible."

Attentive to the nuances of the painting process, Schapiro was particularly sensitive to the decisions of the painter and to his dialectic rapport with his painting. "The power of the artist's hand to deliver constantly elements of so-called chance or accident, which nevertheless belong to a well defined, personal class of forms and groupings, is submitted to critical control by the artist who is alert to the rightness or wrongness of the elements delivered spontaneously, and accepts or rejects them." In championing the abstract art of his time, including the art being produced by a former student, Schapiro spoke as a painter himself, to and for other painters; he celebrated in that art "the presence of the individual, his spontaneity and the concreteness of his procedure." "This art is deeply rooted," he knew, "in the self and its relation to the surrounding world."

Motherwell's own academic training in philosophy and, probably more important, his own passionate reading of poetry and poetics made him the most articulate of painters. He was able to talk from and to experience, as maker and viewer of images. Despite his occasional reticence of tone, he knew the value of words: ". . . there is some sense—one that I cannot adequately formulate—in which the statements of artists themselves constitute the literature that is most inspiring to others," he wrote with regard to his editing the Documents of Modern Art series. And his own words do indeed constitute the very best commentary on his art.

From the beginning of his career, Motherwell talked about the "felt-content" of experience. The "inner world" of the artist was a complicated human affair, "and consequently difficult to express. That is why I invented my art. In this sense art is a necessity, a natural outgrowth of man's life." "Pictures are vehicles of passion," he declared in a talk called, significantly, "A Painting Must Make Human Contact" (1955). He was keenly aware of the paradox of subjective objects, of the awkward but necessary relationship between the private image-maker and the public image. "The relation to the audience is a social matter," he said in 1954. "And it is our pictures, not ourselves, that live the social life and meet the public. . . . It is interesting that the creations of solitary individuals should turn out to have such a gift for sociability!"

The personal urgency of these statements, their pathos and psychological imperative, transcends any easy equation with the existentialism that dominated the intellectual life of the 1940s and early 1950s. To reduce the paintings to mere expressions of the time is a misleading critical strategy, one that closes off the communication that the images themselves demand. And it is surely a worse mistake to interpret the eventual institutional acceptance and support of Abstract Expressionism as evidence that the notions of individual freedom built into that art were merely part of Cold War rhetoric. This can only be the thesis of historians insensitive to an art of "felt-content," who remain closed to the voice of the artist and refuse the dialogue initiated by paintings.

"Robert Motherwell on Paper" insists on that dialogue. Motherwell always affirmed the living qualities of his mediums, the sensuousness of paint and canvas, ink and paper: "An artistic medium is the only thing in human existence that has precisely the same range of sensed feeling as people themselves do." These strong words only underscore the affective character of the imagery. The gesture of the artist is more than a motion of his arm; it is that, indeed, but it is more—a genuine reaching out.

In the exhibition and in the accompanying essays, we have kept the focus on the images and, through them, on the artist, who remains present, vitally so, in his work. Motherwell thought of himself as "mainly a lyrical artist, a 'poet,' " and, in asking a poet, Frank O'Hara, to be the curator of his exhibition at the Museum of Modern Art in 1965, he imagined something "more like a poetry recital than a retrospective." We can only hope that "Robert Motherwell on Paper," with its many drafts and redactions on his favorite material, might have satisfied the artist.

•

I must acknowledge the help and example of those colleagues without whose counsel and support this exhibition could not have been realized, friends and colleagues of Robert Motherwell who worked closely with him over many years. First and foremost, I wish to thank Joan Banach, his longtime curator and now curator of the Dedalus Foundation; with her unsurpassed knowledge of the artist's work, she was an essential guide through studio and warehouse and an invaluable curatorial advisor and collaborator. Next, the art historians who have established the foundations for our understanding of the art of Motherwell: Dore Ashton's writings have taken us closest to the core of meanings of that art and the New York world of Abstract Expressionism; her friendly criticism served to refine the shape of our project. Jack Flam, whose intimate knowledge of the artist and of the modernist tradition informs every page of his own work on Motherwell, not only helped in that refinement but also played a crucial role in preserving it. John Elderfield's support and encouragement at critical moments in the development of the project were essential and gratefully appreciated.

The contributors' dedication of this volume to Renate Ponsold Motherwell is our way of acknowledging friendship and thanking her for the warm hospitality we have all enjoyed in Greenwich, Provincetown, and New York. Her photographs, recording two decades of life with Robert Motherwell, have become precious historical documents of the artist and the man.

When first conceived, the exhibition was designed to draw exclusively on material in the artist's studio and collection; since his death, that collection has become part of the Dedalus Foundation, which he established. Some of the pictures have been acquired subsequently by public museums, and we would like to thank them for lending these works to the exhibition. In addition, certain key works were graciously lent by private collectors. We thank Helen Frankenthaler, in particular, for her ready response in lending *At Five in the Afternoon*, and Renate Ponsold Motherwell for lending *Torn Elegy*.

At Columbia University, I would like to acknowledge the support of Sarah Elliston Weiner, the Director of the Miriam and Ira D. Wallach Art Gallery, and her staff, and the support of members of the Advisory Council of the Department of Art History and Archaeology, whose continuing enthusiasm has made this exhibition possible.

—D.R.

All quotations of the artist are from *The Collected Writings of Robert Motherwell*, ed. Stephanie Terenzio (New York and Oxford: Oxford University Press, 1992). Meyer Schapiro's essays "Recent Abstract Painting" (1957) and "On the Humanity of Abstract Painting" (1960) are republished in volume two of his selected papers, *Modern Art: Nineteenth and Twentieth Centuries* (New York: George Braziller, 1978).

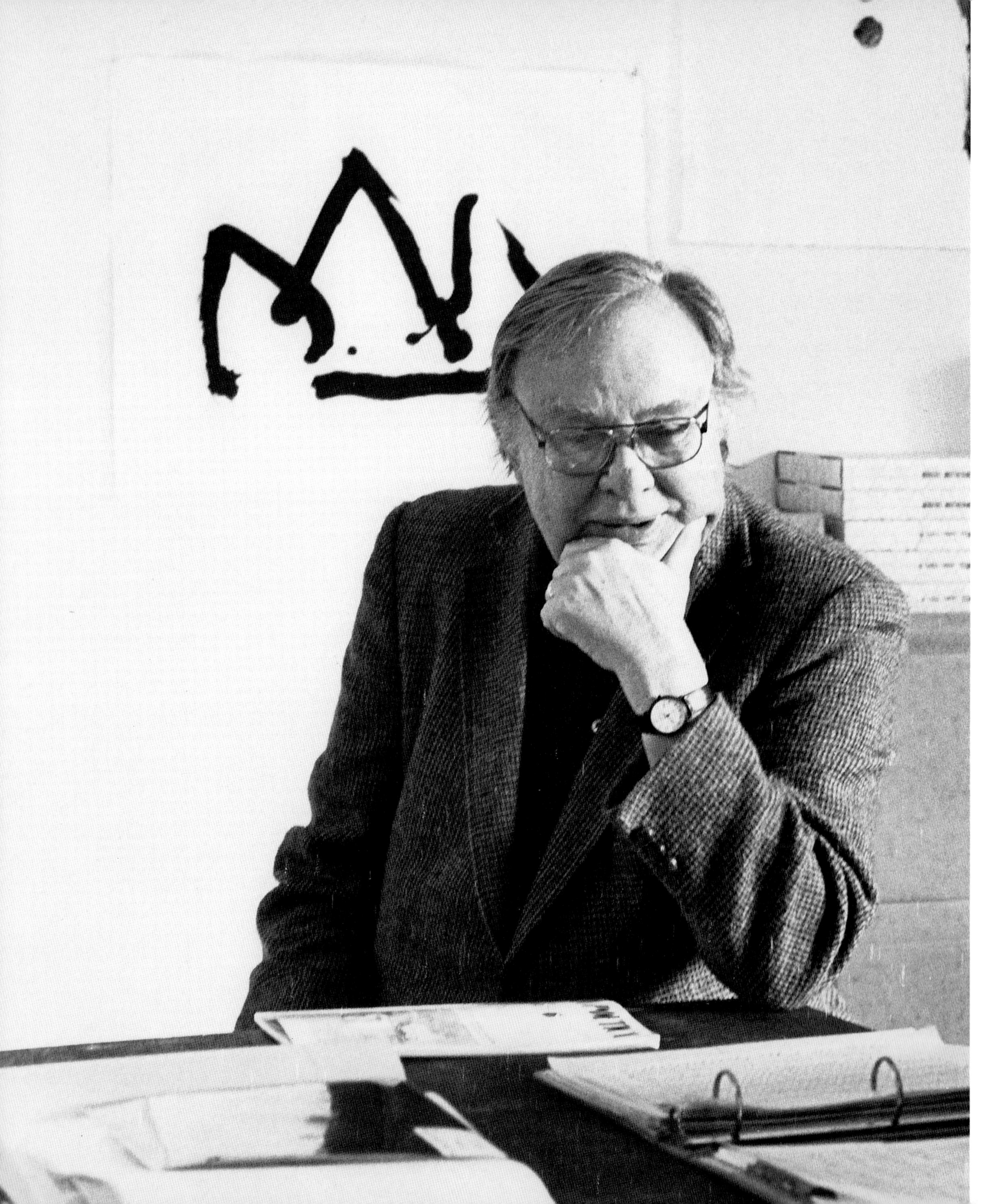

"My I": Toward an Iconography of the Self

David Rosand

We find that the question,—What is Art? leads us directly to another,—Who is the artist? and the solution of this is the key to the history of Art.

—Ralph Waldo Emerson[1]

The Invention of the Artist

Robert Motherwell made himself a painter. Against the inertia, if not outright opposition, of upbringing and then against the odds of American society, he willed himself a modern artist. In his feat was recapitulated, for the nth time, a quintessential chapter in the history of art in this country. Through his determination to define himself as artist, to claim space for his professional self—that is, for his *self*—Motherwell was the distant heir of great predecessors on this continent, of eighteenth-century masters like John Singleton Copley. Faced with a "people entirely destitute of all just Ideas of the Arts,"[2] Copley finally abandoned his Beacon Hill farm in Boston for a more cultured Old World. For Motherwell, as for his companions in New York, the proving of art had—for many reasons—to be here, in America. Determinedly modern, abstract, that art took strength from the very incomprehension, not to say hostility, of its early audience.

The story of the New York School, of the emergence and triumph of Abstract Expressionism, has been narrated often enough, and not even the recent revisionist twists on the tale can diminish its epic scale. A younger generation of art historians may be appropriately questioning the mythic proportions attained by that story, but the essence of the achievement withstands even such historicizing skepticism.[3] That essence was expressed, under different but hardly unrelated circumstances, early in the American tradition by Emerson, in the lines quoted above. Affirming an intimate bond of identity—between art and artist, between what and who—he articulated the dialectic that lies at the heart of America's most impressive pictorial achievement. No more than Copley—or Thomas Cole or Thomas Eakins—could painters in the New York of the 1940s take for granted their position as artists. Since, in this country, as Copley put it, "a taste for painting is too much Wanting,"[4] art itself could claim no secure place within the social world; it could establish neither its foundation nor its credentials by an appeal to tradition. Every strong American painter has had to reinvent the art of painting for himself, "to start from scratch, to paint as if painting had never existed before."[5] Only by affirming art through the act of making pictures could any one of them affirm himself. The reinvention of painting means the invention of the artist.

Emerson's existential tautology was enacted with renewed force and conviction by artists of the New York School, who modified the equation only by insisting that both art and artist be modern, of their time. Motherwell spoke for a generation of American painters when he observed that "in choosing to become an artist . . . one discovers who one is, more exactly, invents oneself."[6] To be a painter—to cease the academic circling of art in aesthetics and the history of art and enter the arena of its making—was the decisive act. Once taken, that decision in turn challenged the newly self-defined artist to define his self, by his art.

Born in 1915 in Aberdeen, Washington, Motherwell grew up in California, where he studied art briefly at the Otis Art Institute in Los Angeles and at the California School of Fine Arts in San Francisco. As an undergraduate at Stanford he majored in philosophy, receiving his A.B. in 1937, and it was in philosophy that he continued his graduate education at

Harvard. He spent the academic year 1938–39 in France, developing a dissertation on the *Journals* of Delacroix. In Paris he translated Paul Signac's *D'Eugène Delacroix au néo-impressionisme*, studied for a while at the Académie Julien, and began painting on his own. Upon returning to the United States, he taught art at the University of Oregon; the following year, 1940, he moved to New York, where, on the advice of the composer Arthur Berger, he entered the graduate program in art history at Columbia University to study with Meyer Schapiro. One of the rare art historians of the time who understood and valued the achievements of modernism, who saw beyond the surface formalism of modern art to its individual expressiveness and social meaning, Schapiro confirmed Motherwell's studio inclinations.[7] He introduced the aspiring painter to the European artists in exile, a group of émigrés of primarily Surrealist orientation. Through this group, Motherwell found the possibility of identifying himself as an artist, a committedly modern artist.

In his involvement with the Surrealists, Motherwell encountered the "creative principle" that was to serve him, in practice and in theory, throughout his career: "psychic automatism"—"what the psychoanalysts would call 'free association,' " as he later described it, ". . . what in its most common visual form in everyday life would be called 'doodling.' "[8] He never considered himself a Surrealist painter, however, "because I reject their sense of what a picture is."[9] He rejected the illusionism of Surrealist imagery and its literary dependency. Motherwell's modernism, from the beginning, was predicated on "the cubist idea of what a picture is . . . plastically; but the conventional subject was to be replaced by an automatically invented subject matter." Automatism offered him "an active principle for painting, specifically designed to explore unknown possibilities. A voyage to the Now, in Baudelaire's metaphor."[10]

The very volubility of the Surrealist movement encouraged Motherwell to articulate his personal search for a principle, and his own intellectual bent and academic preparation assured the clarity of his voice. It is striking how early in his experience the young artist found the concepts that were to accompany what he might have called his own plastic development. The meaning of Surrealism, as he tried to explain it in a letter to William Carlos Williams in 1941, involved "a. stimulation of the imagination . . . , the invention of new objects of perception within reality . . . ; b. the preservation of the dignity and value of personal feelings . . . ; c. . . . revolution in the sense of increased *consciousness*, of consciousness of the *possibilities* inherent in *experiencing*."[11] *Experiencing* for Motherwell involved art as well as life; from early on the two were bound, the one giving form to the other. "To express the felt nature of reality is the artist's principal concern."[12]

In automatist practice, the first fortuitous mark—line or drip or stain—on the surface initiates a creative dialogue between the artist and his medium; that dialogue, in which the emerging work is both self and other, increasingly finds voice in the course of Motherwell's development. His earliest preserved drawings, in the *Mexican Sketchbook* (figs. 1–4), already attest to that particular creative dynamic.[13] Even as these designs betray the linear structures of Surrealist space—in their orthogonal focus and suggestive natural detail—the India-ink blackness of the brush imposes a different pictorial order: in dialectic response to the field, to its shape and its initial linework, the brush declares its own dominant surface marking.

Motherwell's Mexican sojourn of 1941 was a period of intense Surrealist involvement; he traveled there with the Chilean-born Roberto Matta Echaurren and worked with Wolfgang Paalen, contributing to the Surrealist journal *DYN*. The drawings made during this period, however, may testify as much to the young American's discomfort with his continental friends. The *Mexican Sketchbook* suggests an effort to overcome those aesthetic surroundings, to counter Surrealist

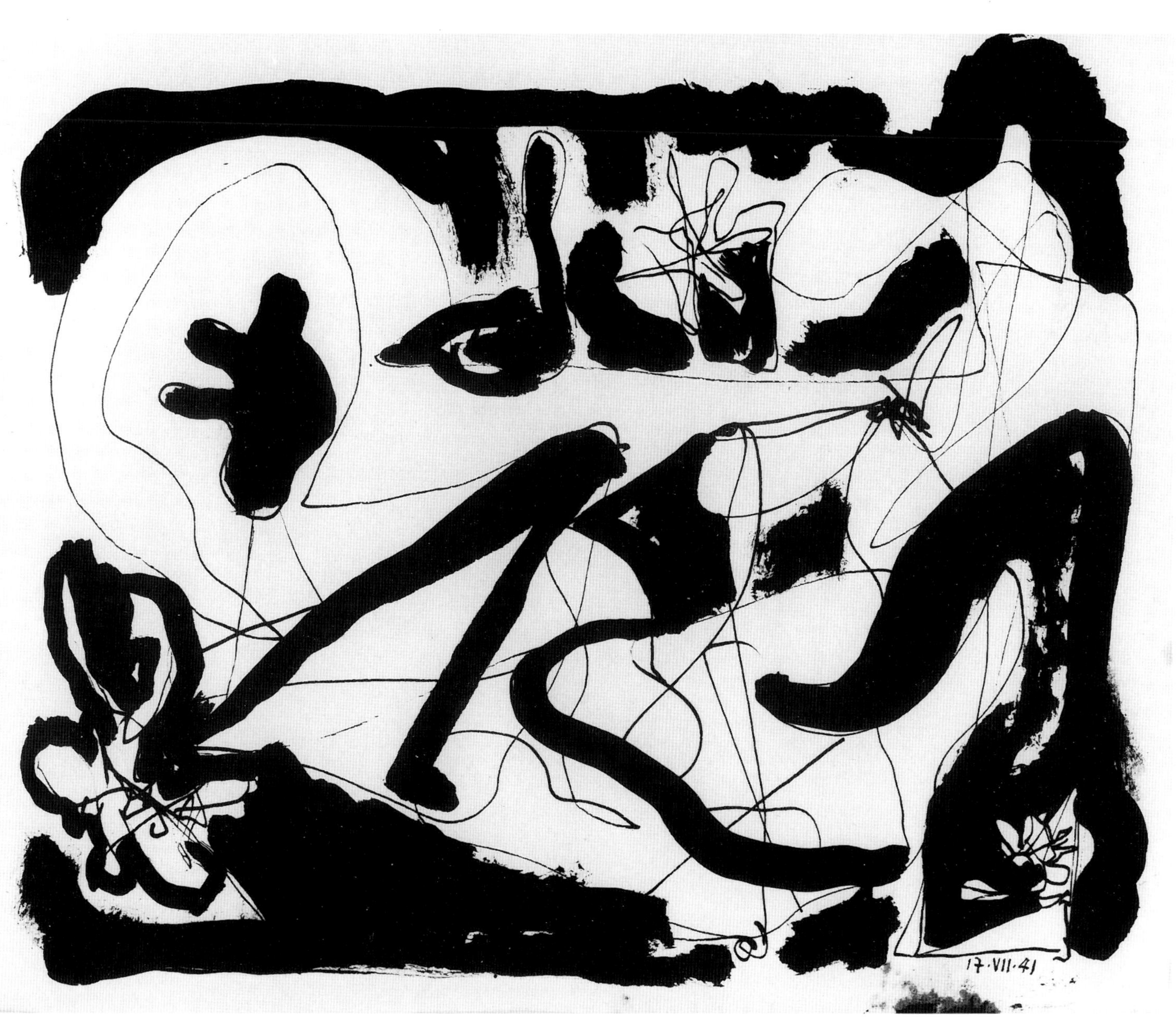

1. Robert Motherwell. *Mexican Sketchbook*, 1941, page one. India ink on paper, 9 x 11½" (22.8 x 29.2 cm). The Museum of Modern Art, New York. Gift of the artist

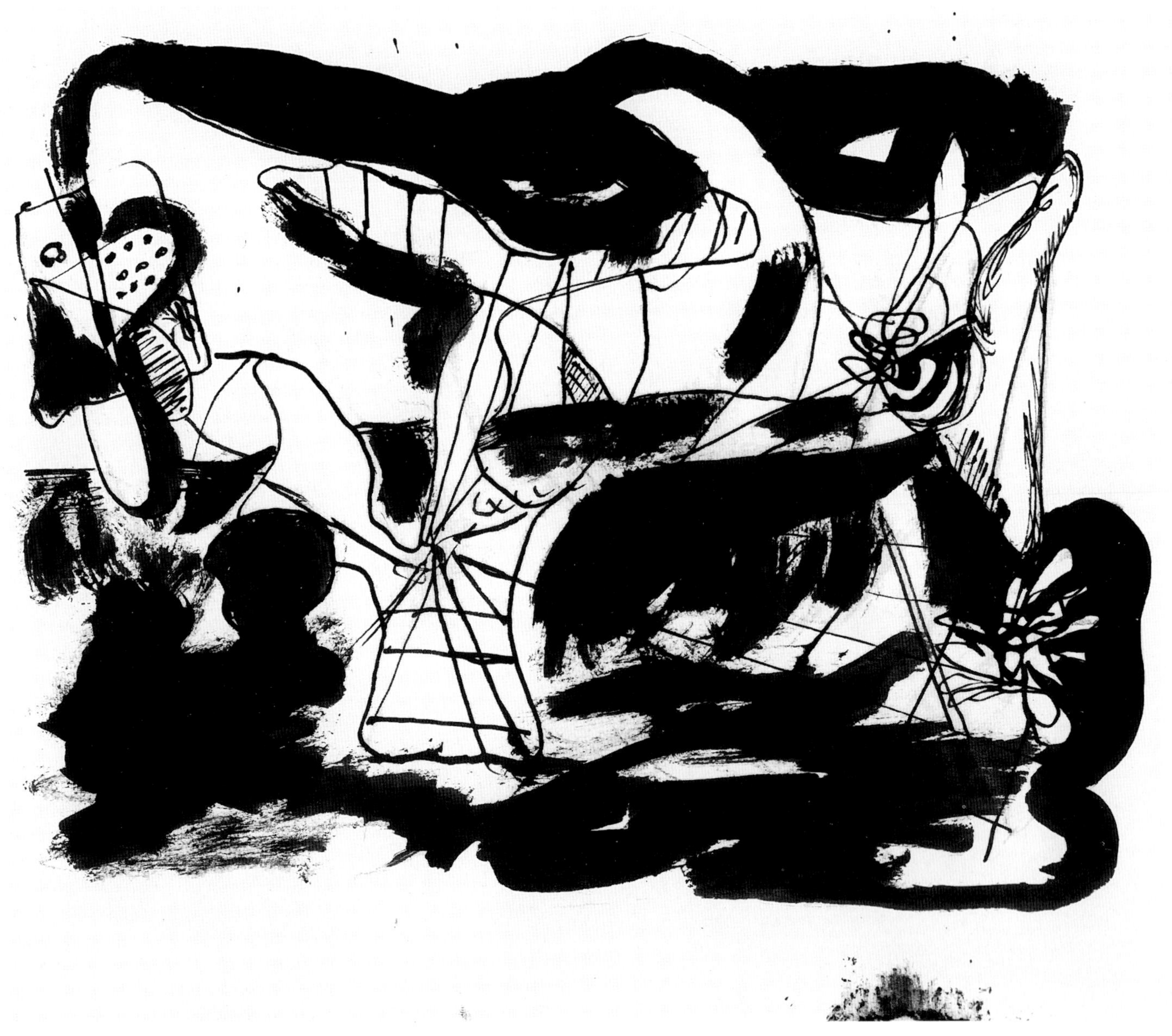

2. Robert Motherwell. *Mexican Sketchbook*, 1941, page two. India ink on paper, 9 x 11½″ (22.8 x 29.2 cm). The Museum of Modern Art, New York. Gift of the artist

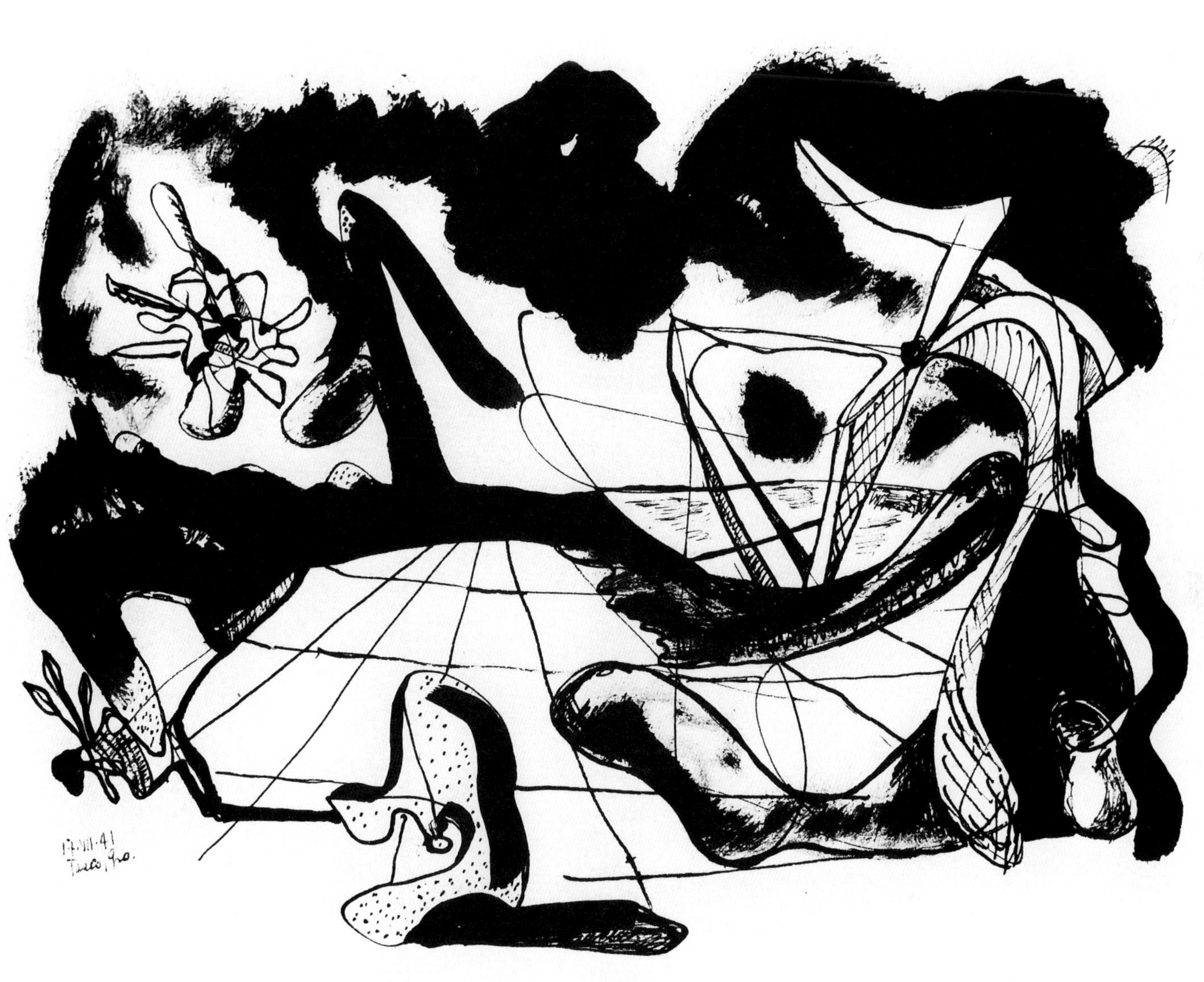

3. Robert Motherwell. *Mexican Sketchbook*, 1941, page three. India ink on paper, 9 x 11½" (22.8 x 29.2 cm). The Museum of Modern Art, New York. Gift of the artist

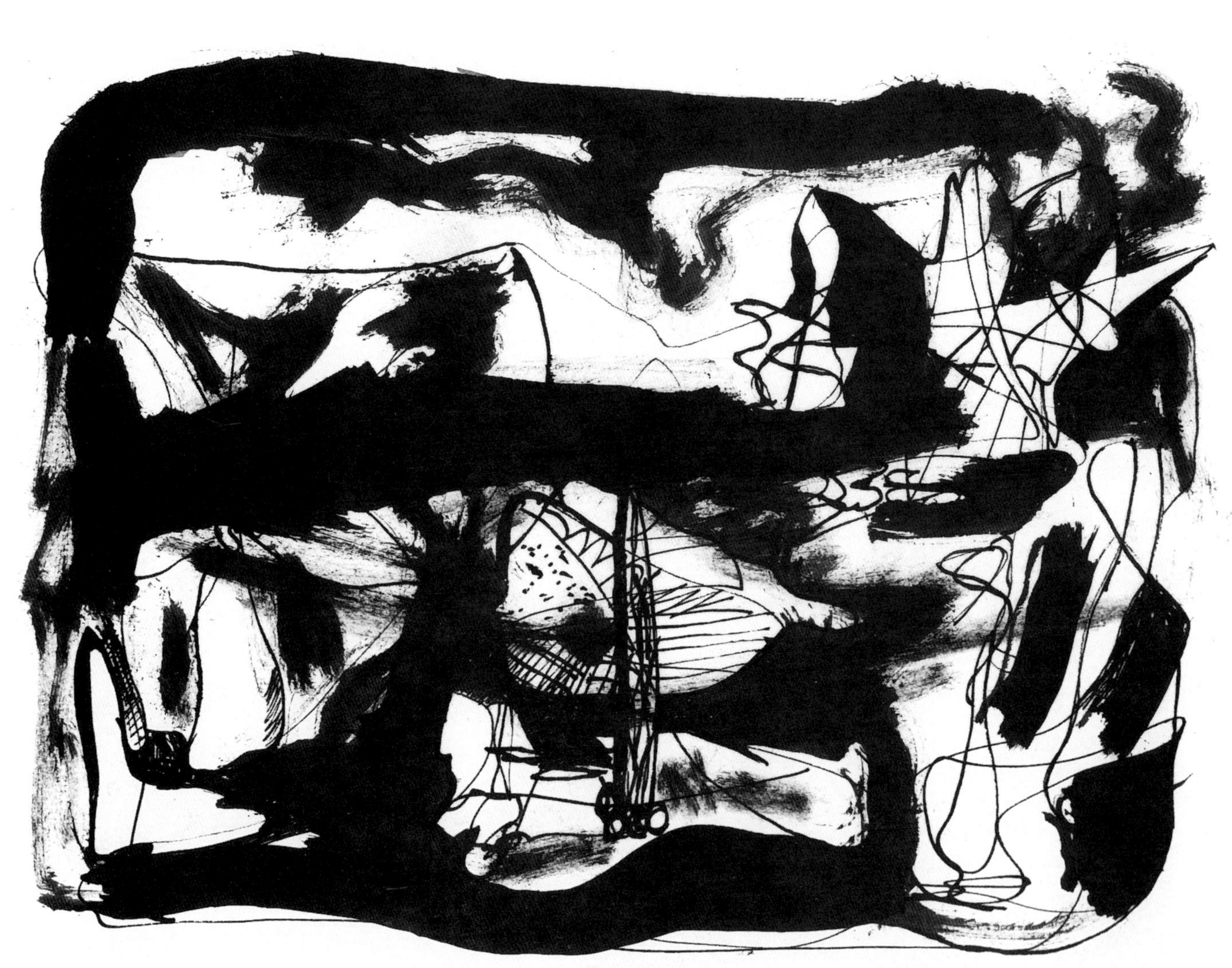

4. Robert Motherwell. *Mexican Sketchbook*, 1941, page four. India ink on paper, 9 x 11½" (22.8 x 29.2 cm). The Museum of Modern Art, New York. Gift of the artist

illusions with its own aesthetic alternative—in effect, "the cubist idea of what a picture is." In every sense, Motherwell was seeking to make his own mark.

Automatism served Motherwell not only in the beginning, as a means of conception, a way into the work; it could also assume a determining role in establishing a subsequent, postpartum relationship to the finished work. "I could not find a title for possibly my single most important 'figure' painting," he recalled of a picture of 1948. "Then I remembered a Surrealist custom, viz., to take a favorite book and place one's finger at random in it. In *Finnegans Wake* my finger rested on the words 'the homely protestant,' and I thought, 'Of course, it is a self-portrait.' "[14] The aleatory element kept experience open to new possibilities, and yet the very gesture of pointing, while extending the ethos of automatism, remains just that: a movement of the artist's body, the physical extension of his self.

"Man is his own invention; every artist's problem is to invent himself," Motherwell wrote in a preliminary notice to the first English translation of D.-H. Kahnweiler's *The Rise of Cubism* (1949). "Cubism," he insisted, "invented Picasso as much as he invented cubism; it revealed himself to himself, as painting does to every true painter."[15]

Motherwell's modernist aesthetic had its roots in the poetics of Charles Baudelaire and Stéphane Mallarmé—the sense of voyaging into the unknown, of finding the new—which inspired the titles of several of the painter's most significant works. His commitment to his own moment, however, is clearest in his essential existentialism. During an interview in 1974 he was asked, "Do you think your paintings are related to the way Mallarmé used symbolism? Would you consider yourself an abstract symbolist . . . ?" His answer was resolute: "No. An existentialist."[16] Indeed he was.

"Art is a form of action, a drama, a process," Motherwell declared in 1949. "One enters the studio as one would an arena. One's entire character is revealed in the action. . . . From one point of view, the artist's function is to give each risk its proper style."[17] These, of course, are the notions and values that were to inform Harold Rosenberg's influential essay of 1952, "The American Action Painters," which gave controversial currency to a concept of, and a title for, the phenomenon of Abstract Expressionism.[18] Motherwell's pronouncements, however, were those of a painter; his talk of action and risk arose from and was validated by a precision of experience, concrete experience in the studio. For the painter, questions of self-revelation, of self-identity, were hardly abstract.

Elegiac Discoveries

One might say that the School of New York tries to find out what art is precisely through the process of making art. That is to say, one discovers, so to speak, rather than imposes a picture. What constitutes the discovery is the discovery of one's own feeling, which none of us would dare to propose before the act of painting itself. . . .[19]

In 1944 Motherwell had his first solo show in New York, at Peggy Guggenheim's Art of This Century gallery, and, in a further effort to translate the modernist tradition to America, he began his direction of the Documents of Modern Art series, published by Wittenborn, Schultz. He moved easily between the worlds of art and literature, indeed was anxious to bring them together under the auspices of a shared modernism. In the winter of 1947–48 appeared the first (and only) issue of *Possibilities*, "a magazine of artists and writers who 'practice' in their work their own experience without seeking to transcend it in academic, group or political formulas," as Motherwell wrote in his editorial statement, announcing the conviction of individual responsibility that distinguished this generation.

Such practice implies the belief that through conversion of energy something valid may come out, whatever situation one is forced to begin with.

> The question of what will emerge is left open. One functions in an attitude of expectancy. As Juan Gris said: you are lost the instant you know what the result will be.[20]

For the second, never published number of *Possibilities*, Motherwell prepared an "illumination" for a poem by his co-editor Harold Rosenberg, "The Bird for Every Bird" (see frontispiece). In the page he designed, the final lines of the poem are written in a band of white framed above by a heavy weight of India ink and by a more complex image below. That lower image fills more than half the sheet, claiming a horizontal space of its own within the larger vertical field. In it a sequence of dark vertical bars holds another of pressed ovals in a declamatory A-b-A-b-b-A rhythm; in the second measure, the final two oval notes are conjoined by a horizontal slur above. It seems natural to adopt the language of musical notation in describing the patterns of this starkly inked sketch, which, in the apparent intention of its graphic juxtapositions, seems to imply text setting. Surely, we are tempted to conclude, the tensile vertical dividing the twin ovals, even as it modifies their relationship as a further bar line, responds to the concluding line of the poem: "that wire in my neck up to the ear." Rejecting this possibility, Motherwell insisted, "It has literally nothing to do with the poem—except for them both having a brutal quality—certainly not its images."[21]

Motherwell, who had never accepted the literary dependency of much Surrealist imagery, respected the independence of the arts; although he appreciated their analogies and explored the correspondences between them, he guarded against possible mutual contamination. This most verbal of painters knew well the power of the word and the hegemonic instinct of language to claim experience for itself. Against such claims he argued the unique concreteness of his own art: "Painting is a medium in which the mind can actualize itself; it is a medium of thought. Thus painting, like music, tends to become its own content."[22]

That thesis was to be proved in the artist's subsequent evolving relationship with his unpublished design for *Possibilities*. Months later, he returned to the page and rehearsed the lower horizontal image in a slightly larger format (plate 1), and in this act of retrieval he (re)discovered a thematic motif that was to become essential to his identity. Fusing formal meaning into a highly charged iconic format of expressive latency, this pictorial structure, once acknowledged by the artist, will continue to engage him for the rest of his career. The original ink sketch was ultimately to be known as *Elegy to the Spanish Republic No. 1* (frontispiece). The particular dynamics of this image—the tension between the tectonic and the organic, between the precariously held stability of its structural relationships and the narrative impulse of its notational sequence—recall still earlier expressions in Motherwell's work, especially *The Little Spanish Prison*, begun in 1941, his first year as a full-time painter. There, the artist already realized something like a heroic struggle in the entrapment of a short horizontal unit within a system of modulated verticals. From the beginning, too, he evoked through titles the moral and political experience that epitomized the frustrated idealism of the 1930s. More than a merely political response, Motherwell's evocation of the Spanish Civil War acquired a growing resonance as it became increasingly identified with his own personal iconography, appropriated as experience.

Titling is a key to identity. Motherwell called his second essay in the elegiac mode, the casein of 1949 (plate 1), *At Five in the Afternoon*, the words of the tympanic refrain of García Lorca's poem "Lament for Ignacio Sánchez Mejías." Typically, the title arose from the artist's dialogue with his own finished work, from his own response to his own invention. Drawing upon his involvement with Lorca's lament on the death of a bullfighter, Motherwell appropriated the refrain, which, through his reading, had become part of his own experience. The title represented a dedication of the image, "consecrated to a

Spanish sense of death, which," as he later recalled, "I got most from Lorca, but from other sources as well—my Mexican wife, bullfights, travel in Mexico, documentary photographs of the Mexican revolution, Goya, Santos, dark Hispanic interiors."[23] As he developed the motif on a larger scale, Motherwell continued to assign Spanish titles to the pictures—*Spanish Drum Roll*, *Granada*, *Barcelona*, *Sevilla*, and so on. Only in 1950, when he showed them in the exhibition "Black or White" at the Samuel Kootz Gallery, were they gathered under the collective title of *Elegies to the Spanish Republic*. And with that titling, itself a product of the artist's continuing dialogue with and meditation on his own work, Motherwell recognized the larger meaning of that work, its dialectic between public statement and personal feeling.

> I take an elegy to be a funeral lamentation or funeral song for something one cared about. The "Spanish Elegies" are not "political," but my private insistence that a terrible death happened that should not be forgot. They are as eloquent as I could make them. But the pictures are general metaphors of the contrast between life and death, and their interrelation.[24]

The bold blackness of India ink in the first *Elegy* sketch—anticipated in the *Mexican Sketchbook* drawings—established a chromatic theme as well. This was an imagery born in and committed to black—and, inevitable chromatic corollary, white. Insisting that abstract painting has meaning ("I never met an outstanding artist not interested in ideas as well as sensuality"), Motherwell affirmed the associative values of his colors. "Black is death, anxiety; white is life, éclat," he suggested, without, however, limiting the signifying options of his palette;[25] ochre, he reminded, is the color of the sand of the Spanish bullring and of the adobe houses of Mexico, and the invitation of Motherwell's Mediterranean blues is to the openness of sky and sea. But black and white constitute the essential palette of the *Elegies*, an imagery that is fundamentally graphic.

In the course of his career, Motherwell may have painted close to two hundred *Elegies* and produced hundreds more in drawings and prints (plates 2–7; fig. 5). The image became, in a number of literal senses, second nature to him, the form his doodling hand produced automatically, an alter ego in which he saw himself reflected. More than any other image in his art, this one came to represent the man; the rhythms of the *Elegies* are those of Motherwell himself, deliberate, even ponderous. "It has to do with one's sense of life: is it airy enough or is it leaden? It has to do with one's own inner sense of weights: I happen to be a heavy, clumsy, awkward man, and if something gets too airy—probably though I admire it very much—it doesn't feel like my *self* to me. . . ."[26] (I once characterized the forms in some of his later drawings, forms evoking Lascaux as well as the *Elegies*, as "pachydermous"; he smiled and accepted, in self-recognition.)

The rhythms of this image type, invented by this artist's gestures and repeated so often, reciprocally condition the creating body. "When you've done something a lot, it gets built into your arm and wrist and just comes out—in the way you might use a certain phrase habitually, though in wholly different contexts." He was talking of the *Elegies* and his recurrent engagement of the theme and the reasons for such return: "To say it better and to understand it better. Some viewers might think, 'Oh, he's doing another *Spanish Elegy*.' But to this day, I really don't know how that vocabulary functions. . . . Yet, if it's any good, I recognize myself."[27]

In the dialectic relationship with his own work, Motherwell returned to confront himself. On that familiar ground, as he said in 1951, "the strain of dealing with the unknown, the absolute, is gone." Liberated, for the moment, from the anxiety of the blank canvas, the artist could take refuge in the known. "When I need joy, I find it only in making free variations on what I have already discovered, what I know to be mine. We modern artists have no generally accepted subject matter, no inherited iconography. . . . An existing subject for me—even though I

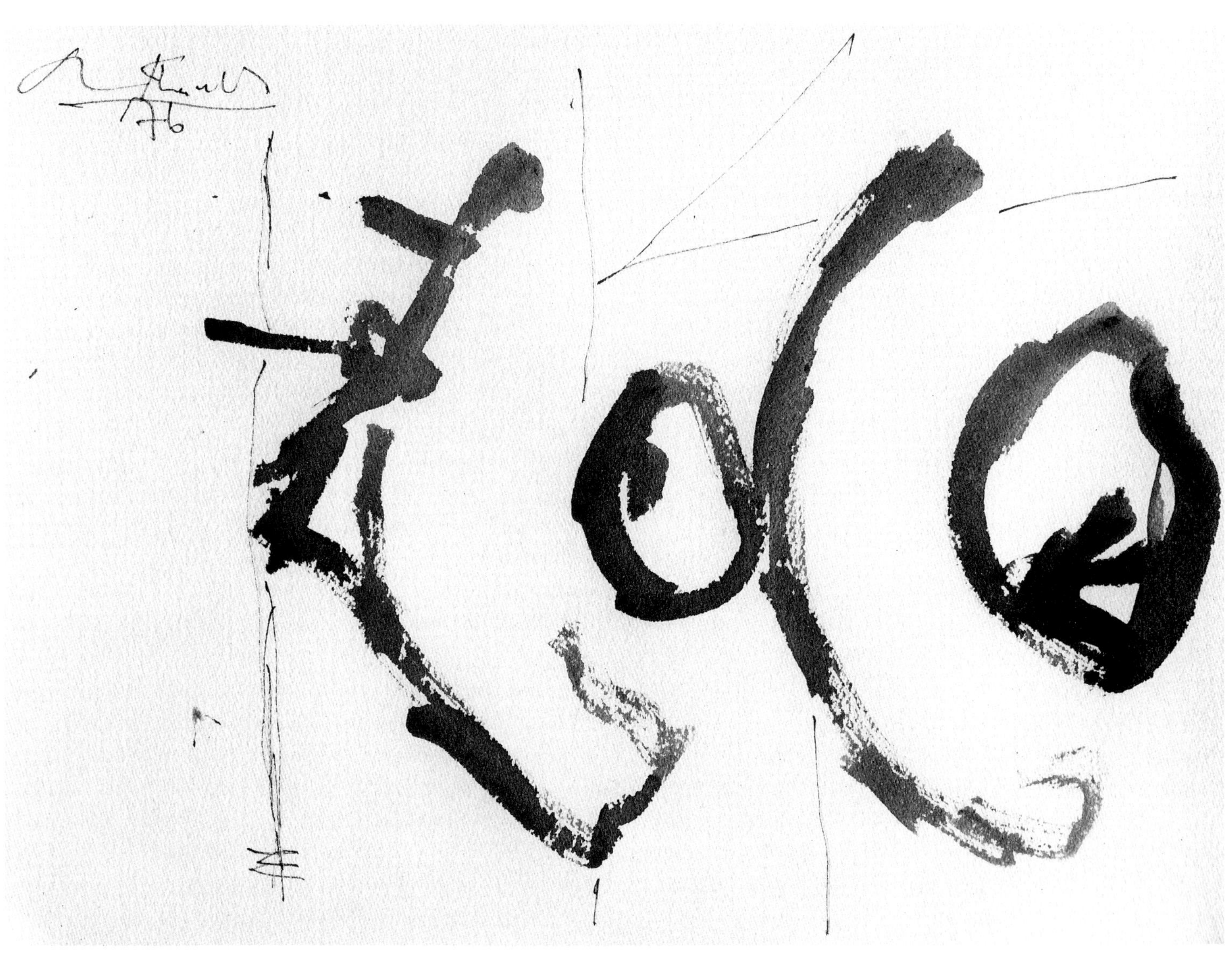

5. Robert Motherwell. *Elegy Drawing No. 13,* 1976. Ink on paper, 11¾ x 15¾" (29.9 x 40 cm). Private collection. (Dedalus no. D76–1052)

had to invent it to begin with—gives me moments of joy."[28] His modernist parochialism notwithstanding, Motherwell might have been speaking universally, for all artists. Even those predecessors who enjoyed the comfort of "inherited iconography" had turned for inspiration to themselves. In the suggestive openness of their own sketches earlier painters too had sought new inventions—Leonardo da Vinci, most famously and articulately.[29] It is, we might say, the self-reflexive condition of creativity, the artist confronting himself and/in his art: "A subject emerges out of an interaction between my self, my I, and my medium. . . ."[30]

Motherwell insisted that the *Elegies* were "abstract" images—although viewers have traced the etiology of their alternating forms in earlier "figural" work, such as *Pancho Villa, Dead and Alive* (1943)—and he eventually came to regard them as "public statements."[31] And yet, so completely had he internalized those rhythms, which came so naturally to his drawing hand, that he was able to give them a new and quasi-independent lease on pictorial life, culminating in the image that was eventually to be baptized as *The Hollow Men* (see plates 99, 100, 102, 105). Taken from T. S. Eliot, the title acknowledges the volumetric opening of these ovals. No longer of solidly massed black, no longer internally generated by the heavy brush, they are now more circumscribed, drawn rather than painted, shaped initially by charcoaled contours whose repeated strokes enhance their mobile plasticity. These open forms are further articulated axially or biaxially, according them a distinctive anatomy, and often by dots that seem calculated to confirm such physiognomic implication. No longer contained by controlling verticals, these figures congregate chorally, stringing themselves across the stage, with suggestions of spatial overlapping. It is as though the dancers have reclaimed a certain freedom of motion, affirming buoyancy—a lightness of touch that we may imagine tested Motherwell's sense of his *self*, his *I*.[32]

Body-and-Mind Gestures

> The painter "takes his body with him," says Valéry. Indeed we cannot imagine how a *mind* could paint. It is by lending his body to the world that the artist changes the world into paintings. To understand these transubstantiations we must go back to the working, actual body—not the body as a chunk of space or a bundle of functions but that body which is an intertwining of vision and movement.
>
> —Maurice Merleau-Ponty[33]

In *The Hollow Men* and its progeny, graphic as well as painted, Motherwell had discovered new life in his own "inherited iconography"; an "existing subject" had given him the "joy" of new discovery. An alternative mode of self-renewal was afforded by his "original creative principle," automatism, which required him to confront the unknown. Turning him back upon himself, to face the artist not the art, this too was a way out of a creative impasse—a "throw of the dice," as he liked to say, invoking Mallarmé.

Such was the experience of the *Lyric Suite*, the remarkable series of ink paintings on rice paper that Motherwell produced in sustained bursts of desperate energy in 1965 (plates 14–37). Four years later he recalled the situation. His account begins with musing on automatism and pays tribute to "my wife, Helen Frankenthaler, and our closest friend, David Smith, both prolific artists whose fecundity moved me more than I was aware of then." He continues:

> On an impulse one day in a Japanese shop in NYC, where I was buying a toy for a friend's child, I bought 10 packets of 100 sheets each of a Japanese rice paper called "Dragons & Clouds" . . .
>
> Some weeks later—early in April, 1965, it came to me in a flash: PAINT THE THOUSAND SHEETS WITHOUT INTERRUPTION, WITHOUT A PRIORI TRADITIONAL OR MORAL PREJUDICES OR A POSTERIORI ONES, WITHOUT ICONOGRAPHY, AND ABOVE ALL WITHOUT REVISIONS OR ADDITIONS UPON CRITICAL REFLECTION AND JUDGMENT.* GIVE UP ONE'S BEING TO THE

ENTERPRISE AND SEE WHAT LIES WITHIN, WHATEVER IT IS. VENTURE. DON'T LOOK BACK. DO NOT TIRE. EVERYTHING IS OPEN. BRUSHES AND BLANK WHITE PAPER!

Something like that, but intuited, not thought out.

Like the first stage of a passionate affair. With paper!

So I began, in early April, 1965.

No Japanese brushes, no Japanese ink. Was already using ink and Japanese paper, so no calligraphy either. No fake Oriental work for me.

Sable watercolor brushes, Pelikan (German), Parker, and Sheaffer inks. (India ink turned out to be too leathery on rice paper.)

Anywhere from ten to fifty a day, on the floor, sweat dimming my spectacles on hot days.

Unable to control spread of ink, which varied according to heat and humidity—never knew what one would end as, until "set"; *each picture would change before my eyes after I had finished working it*, sometimes for hours—as the ink spread, like a spot of oil.† Was tempted to use blotting paper at a miraculous moment on some of them, but never did. A few spread until a square inch or two of white was all that was left of the original blank white paper.

That some of the inks bled was wholly unexpected, and did not show until the ink was nearly set, so never could exploit bleeding: couldn't see it while actually painting.

Part of the experience was like those speeded up botany films that show you months' growth in several minutes, the bud becoming a flower.

Most made in seconds, not minutes.

The rhythm of my wrist became freer and broader and unself-conscious.

The strokes were made with as much violence as possible without tearing the paper. . . .

Most groups of the same color were made on the same day—can't remember the sequence, but the very first were black. Some later ones were, too.

Am still astounded with their freshness, four years later.

Was anxious that they were not complex enough. Now prefer the barest ones.

Ventured about 600.

Then one Sunday late in May, Kenneth Noland telephoned from Bennington (as we were finishing dinner in NYC) that David Smith was seriously hurt, and in the hospital at Albany. My car was delivered from the garage immediately, and I drove Helen at ninety miles an hour in the dark night to the hospital where Tony Caro met us at the door and quietly told us David had died a few minutes before.

I never made another of the *Lyric Suite* series.[34]

The account—beginning, significantly, "On an impulse"—is especially moving as testimony to the intimate relationship between life and art for Motherwell, as an articulation of the feeling that he has always insisted was central to art. So, too, does the title itself record the life surrounding creation; it alludes to the suite for string quartet by Alban Berg, "which I listened to again and again as I worked."[35] The phenomenology of painting means an engagement in the world. "The function of the artist is to express reality as *felt*," Motherwell had declared in 1944. "By feeling is meant the response of the 'body-and-mind' *as a whole* to the events of reality."[36] His own subsequent development affirmed that thesis.

In this exercise in what he called "unadulterated automatism," Motherwell deliberately abandoned himself to his medium, in which he always placed his deepest faith and trust, and to his own body, his own physical self. And the thousand movements comprising the *Lyric Suite* justify that faith. Individually and collectively, these inked images prove the creative potential of Motherwell's modernist aesthetic. Their graphic response to his gesture, spreading beyond anticipation in chromatic transformation, adding auras of new color, rewarded the artist's belief in the creative dialogue with his medium. Individually, they confirm the sure pictorial instinct that always modifies, and undermines, automatism's pretension of innocence.

Even though he knew its limitations—"that the unconscious cannot be *directed*, that it presents none of the possible choices which, when taken, constitute any expression's form"—automatism continued to serve the artist well. What, by 1944, he was distinguishing as "plastic automatism" was "a weapon with which to invent new forms."[37] To invent new forms: that was the task of the artist. "To give oneself over completely to the unconscious is to become a slave." It would mean ignoring your partner in creativity, your materials, your medium; it would mean ignoring your physical self, the performing body. But medium and motion are precisely what inform Motherwell's deliberate exercises in automatic drawing (plates 8–12)—an "activity of bodily gesture serving to sharpen consciousness."[38]

Sensitive to his medium, acknowledging his dependence on it, the painter knows the material stuff of his art; he knows his art is a physical act. The experience of automatic drawing taught Motherwell to trust his own body, its motions both natural and acquired, the gestures "built into your arm and wrist." He liked to talk about "doodling," always careful to acknowledge its professional credentials: "doodling can be, in the proper hands, *as high a mode of drawing as any*. By nature doodling is one of the generic modes of drawing and, when elaborated, of painting in general."[39] He quite naturally acknowledged the ancient status of drawing as the foundation of painting, the rich Renaissance concept of *disegno*, of drawing as ideating process as well as structural foundation: "Drawing is faster than painting, perhaps the only medium as fast as the mind itself."[40] "Doodling," he wrote, quoting Saul Steinberg, "is the brooding of the hand."[41] It is the prelude to and provocation of artistic thought. Motherwell's sense of the imaginative adventure of automatic drawing relives Leonardo's Renaissance enthusiasm for discovering new inventions in one's own rough sketches, in the chaotic scribbling of the hand.

"The essential thing was to let the brush take its head and take whatever we could use from the results."[42] Letting the work " 'pour out,' so to speak, without critical intervention or editing," was how he recalled, with real pleasure, the creative process that yielded the *Lyric Suite*. "Fourteen years later, in a larger format and with oil paint mixed with turpentine to, roughly, the consistency of ink, I had a similar 'outpouring,' though I made less than a hundred works which I call the *Drunk with Turpentine* series [plates 91–94], a title that no matter how evocative, is also literal. I might add that I deeply regret the Occidental prejudice against painting on paper, which to me is the most sympathetic of all painting surfaces."[43] The title is indeed evocative and literal, descriptive of a state of being and acting that is self-defining—as Hokusai had recognized himself as "the old man mad with painting."

Although insistent about the essentially abstract character of his art, Motherwell was fully responsive to the world around him. He recognized the natural elements in his imagery, whether figural reflections, the motions of his body, or the light, color, and textures of a particular place. At Provincetown during the summer of 1962, he recalled, "I used to be struck by the beauty, the force and the grace, at high tide with a strong southwest wind of the sea spray spurting up, sometimes taller than a man, above the sea wall" (see fig. 6). In the barn studio at Days Lumberyard,

. . . I began experimenting with *painting* the sea spray. . . . I quickly discovered that I could not imitate the spray satisfactorily—as Arp says, "I like nature, but not its substitutes." It then occurred to me to use nature's own process: after all I was using liquid oil paint mixed in a bucket, not much more viscous than salt water. So, with dripping brush, I hit the drawing paper with all my force. There was indeed painted spray, but the physical force with which it was produced split the rag paper wide open. The next day, at Jim Forsberg's marvelous Studio Shop, I bought a package of five-ply (that is, paper sheets made of five sheets laminated together, tougher to tear than playing cards) Strathmore one hundred percent rag paper. I also made yard-long handles for my brushes. I hit the laminated paper with the full force of my one hundred eighty pounds, with the painting brush moving in a six

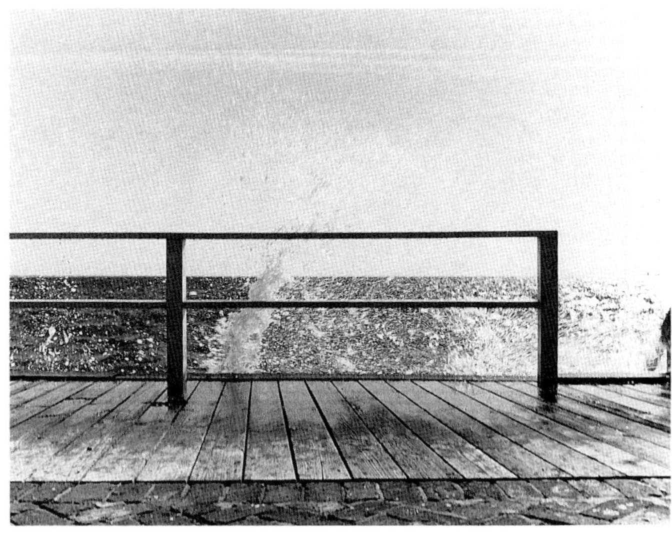

6. High tide, Provincetown; view from the Motherwell house. Photograph © Renate Ponsold Motherwell

foot arc—I remember the sensation as that of cracking a bull whip. An adequate equivalent of the pounding summer sea spray appeared, in deep sky blue, on that lovely kid finish, creamy white laminated paper, *without* splitting or tearing, to my delight.[44]

"To paint not the thing, but the effect it produces"—a favorite quotation from Mallarmé. In the series he called *Beside the Sea* (plates 53–55), Motherwell achieved just that effect by, as he said, using "nature's own process"—reconfirming Leonardo's observation that the painter is indeed "like a second nature."[45]

In that gesture of imitating sea spray, Motherwell reenacted an ancient studio anecdote, regarding "the uses of fortune" in pictorial representation: the Greek painter Protogenes, unable to imitate with his brush the foam on the muzzle of a panting dog, threw his sponge at the panel in frustration, and the marks left by the sponge produced exactly the desired effect; "chance thus became the mirror of nature."[46] Motherwell acknowledged the element of chance in his imagery in the Mallarméan title he assigned to a related series of recorded gestures, *A Throw of the Dice* (plates 56–62).

Motherwell's fond appreciation of paper and its responsiveness and his awareness of the viscosity of ink were qualities he recognized as sharing with Japanese Zen painting. Above all, he knew that his own brushmanship related to East Asian calligraphy, "in the sense of the hand taking off by itself." Surrealist automatism seems to find renewed articulation, refined through association with a more established creative tradition. "You learn from Japanese calligraphy to let the hand take over; then you begin to watch the hand as though it is not yours, but as though it is someone else's hand, and begin to look at it critically. . . . It becomes a kind of critical self-analysis, of how your body is functioning in relation to a plane surface." In interviews, musing on his practice, Motherwell rehearsed the physicality of his art, always respecting the partnership of his medium in creation, the determining role of viscosity. "If the medium is thick and you want to move quickly, it will not move quickly enough—it will be too inert. If the medium is too thin, it will drip or run. But if it is exactly right, my hand just flies and I do not even have to think; my hand just does it, as though I am not there."[47]

Remembered Lines

. . . he never draws a line without remembering whether he has ever drawn it before. . . .

—Ascanio Condivi[48]

But he always *is* there; the artist is always there, in the work, in his mark. This is a truth established at the very beginning of the Western tradition—when Protogenes recognized the presence of Apelles in a single line, the beginnings of connoisseurship[49]—and it is central to the aesthetics of Chinese and Japanese calligraphy. Out of the movements of the drawing hand, movements that get "built into your arm and wrist," come those phrases that get used "habitually, though in wholly different contexts." Gestures and fragments of gestures, those phrases come to constitute the vocabulary of a graphic language, the basic units of a pictorial poetry. "Drawing is a form of rhyming," Motherwell recalled Picasso saying somewhere. "If you use gestures, you instinctively make forms rhyme" (see fig. 5). Motherwell had been speaking of the recognition of himself in his pictures, the "shock of recognition"—"what Baudelaire refers to as 'mon frère, mon semblable.' "[50] Calling it style, perhaps, we too, as connoisseurs, recognize Motherwell in the tracing of his habitual rhythms.

One very characteristic movement of his hand is a sequence of diagonal impulses that yields a pattern like the letter M (plates 71–78). Like the alternating forms that constitute the basic *Elegy*, the pattern of the M, block or cursive, appears in Motherwell's earliest work and, of course, in the uniqueness of his signature—the most repeated habitual graphic gesture of a life. The artist confronted and, understandably, resisted the reductive critical explanation of simple self-reflexivity. Speaking of the etching *Dance I* (plate 76), for example, he insisted on the openness of meaning:

> Again, the imagery is full of ambiguities, mountains, massive blacks against pure white paper, rhythms of my arm-mind, immediacy yet not intimate. The "M" that some critics read into some of this series is unintentional, and when looked at so, detracts from the essential tone meant to be sounded. But it could be that the letter is indeed a conditioned reflex in my arm; but from my standpoint, I begin these works as a random but knowing scribble, allowing them to complicate and turn in on themselves as they will. I also have almost pre-history associations with these images. In any case, for several years now they seem to become increasingly dominant among my various motifs.[51]

Appropriating his own gestures, retrieving and reviving earlier discoveries, the artist creates a cumulative corpus, a body of work that comes to represent him. That process of recollection involves more than a formal recall, however, more than the exploitation of his own received visual constructs. Each of these patterns is part of memory in a still deeper sense; each carries with it an aura of experience that may lie beyond the threshold of articulation—except through a kind of visual replay.

In Madrid in 1958, on a honeymoon trip, Motherwell made a series of drawings on paper taped to the hotel wall (figs. 7, 8). Rubbing against its rough surface, the crayon or graphite recorded the texture of the wall behind, which became an integral part of the image. Some years later, in 1965, the artist relived that experience in a series of lithographs that he called the *Madrid Suite* (plates 39–48). Using the grained wall of the print studio, he recaptured the "mural" texture of the Madrid drawings and a memory—"a transfer of feeling from Madrid to Tenth Street."[52] Elaborating on the physiognomy of the triangular figure that is the protagonist of the design and on its setting, the images of the *Madrid Suite*, individually and collectively, become elaborations on the memory of a past moment as well.

One theme in particular carries the emotional charge of memory most movingly, that is, of the link between the artistic gesture and the life lived. "It is one thing to think and another *to exist in what is thought*," Motherwell wrote in 1956, quoting Kierkegaard. "For the last two years I have been making a series of paintings with *'je t'aime'* written across them in calligraphy of the painting, sometimes tenderly, sometimes in a shriek. . . . I am sure in part it is some kind of emphasis or *existing in* what is thought. . . ."[53]

Without indulging in the biographical knowledge of a failed marriage, we recognize the urgent gesture of these images. That desperation is most evident in the formal structures themselves, pictorial compositions in a precarious state of control.[54] The sudden imposition of writing seems a desperate effort to hold the center, a physical action punctuated by the

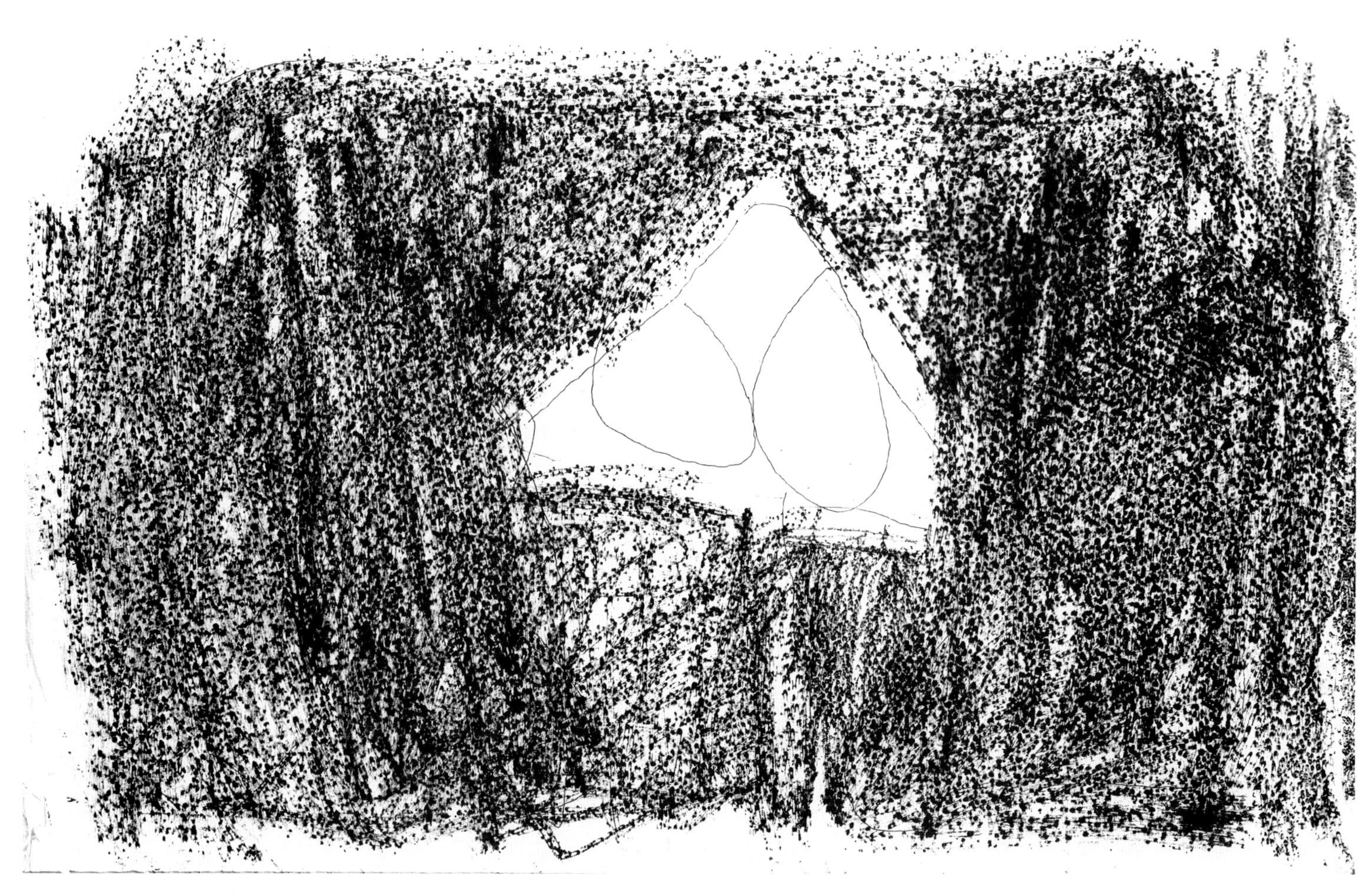

7. Robert Motherwell. *Madrid No. 1*, 1958. Crayon and ink on paper, 15¼ x 24¼" (38.1 x 61 cm). Collection Prof. and Mrs. Robert Gutman, Princeton

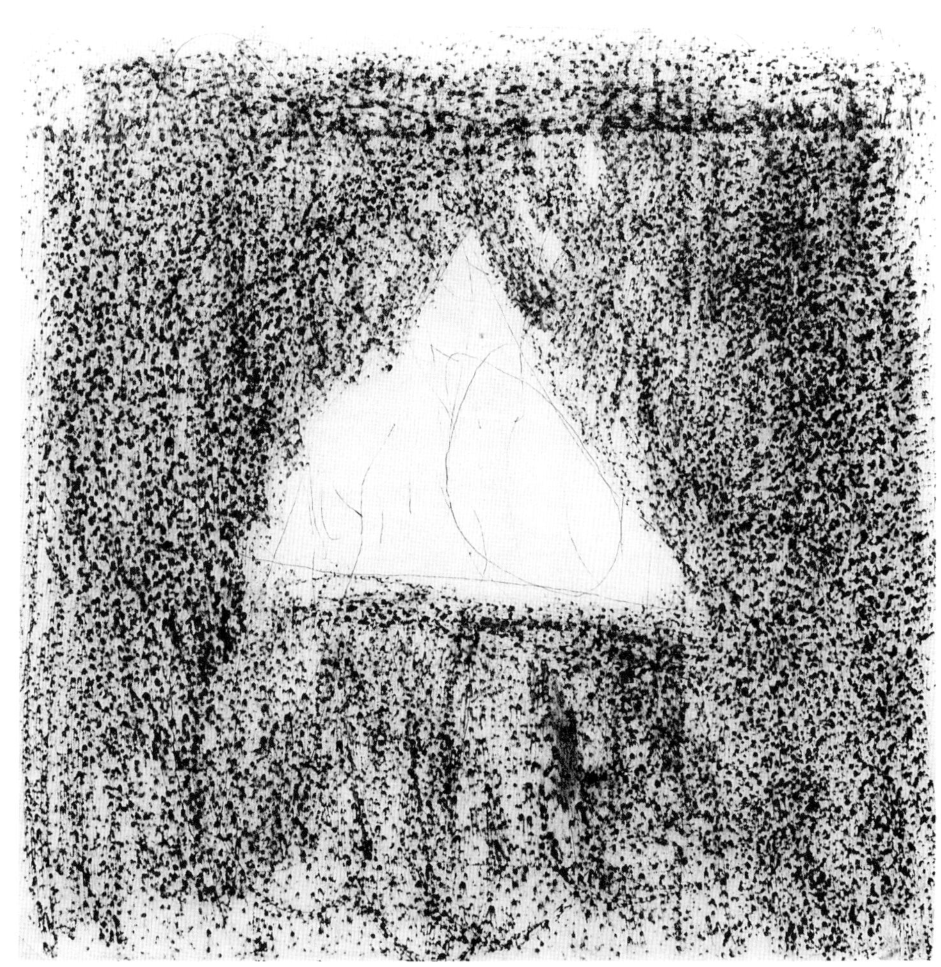

8. Robert Motherwell. *Madrid No. 2,* 1958. Graphite on paper, 14½ x 14½" (36.8 x 36.8 cm). Collection Elaine Lustig Cohen, New York

exclamatory emotional force of its literal message. From the paintings themselves we do indeed come to understand a sense of personal crisis. The paintings are autobiography; they are the life of the artist, pictorial worlds in which he continues to reside. It is their pathos, their humanity—the fragility of relations, the desperate need for contact and communication, the assertion of love—that moves us.

Motherwell, in almost confessional moments, actually addressed the emotional complexities of the situation. "My suspicion is that an artist begins as a person with an enormous capacity for love who cannot, in the beginning anyway, direct his love toward another person satisfactorily, and consequently directs it toward a medium instead," he allowed in a seminar on "The Creative Use of the Unconscious by the Artist and by the Psychotherapist" at the Eighth Annual Conference of the American Academy of Psychotherapists in 1963.[55] He always found it easier to confess his love for (and to) his medium.[56] "Je t'aime" may be a cry affirming a capacity to love. Like other gestures of the drawing hand, however, the phrase becomes habitual, an extension of the artist. Redirected to his medium, it becomes part of his pictorial arsenal as well as of his personal iconography. Early on, in 1956, it is repeated in a drawing with a revealing addition, in parentheses: "ce dessin me plait" (plate 38)—a design that will be revived over twenty years later in a lithograph (plate 49). The drawing itself becomes the beloved object; the phrase has been appropriated by and for art (plates 49–52).[57]

"Drawing is dividing the surface plane," Motherwell declared, with a kind of Albertian authority, in his letter to Frank O'Hara on the occasion of his retrospective in 1965. Part of a litany of pronouncements constituting a kind of artistic credo, it was followed by another: "Color is a question of quantity, i.e., extension in space."[58] Together, the two definitions adumbrate the working principle of the pictorial motif which was to become as important to Motherwell as that of the *Elegies*, what he called the *Open*. Recalling the discovery of that motif, he elaborated on the dicta of his letter in light of practice:

> It used to cross my mind from time to time that it would be much more intelligent to go the other way—*to begin with unity* and then, within unity, create (through dividing) disparate elements. An idea floating around in my mind for maybe a decade. Now, one day I had a vertical canvas about seven by four feet; I had decided not to use its white ground, and had painted it flat yellow ochre. By studio chance, leaning against it was a smaller canvas with its back side showing—the wooden stretchers—and in looking at the wooden chassis of the smaller rectangle against the larger one, the two together struck me as having a beautiful proportion. . . . So I picked up a piece of charcoal and just outlined the smaller canvas on the larger one. At the time, I had the notion of either putting imagery outside the smaller space or within it. One day it occurred to me that it really didn't need imagery, that it was a picture in itself, a lovely painted surface plane, beautifully, if minimally *divided, which is what drawing is*. The image association was "an opening," and as I made more, the series came to be called the *Open* series; *cf.* the Random House unabridged dictionary entry "open."[59]

The discovery of the *Open* motif in 1967—"by studio chance"—quite literally opened new prospects for the painter. On one fairly obvious level, it relates to the window motif, the self-referential frame-within-the-frame, so important to the traditions of Western painting—and reclaimed for modernism most relevantly by Matisse. For Motherwell, the motif simultaneously acknowledged the integrity of the surface (assigning new expressive weight to the chromatic ground) and of the marking (more precisely considering the function of the drawn line and its spatial inflection) (plates 63–66, 70). Placement in the field became decisive. Charcoal in particular, a most friable medium, assumed an interesting role in Motherwell's development of the motif. Leaving a varied line that is itself a spreading trace of particles, charcoal at once marked and modified the surface, covering and revealing, participating in its already activated texture. As he worked with the basic rectilinear U, the drawn motif became another habitual gesture to Motherwell, lending itself to development "in wholly different contexts." The Euclidean clarity of the original intention—division—yielded to its process, to the motion of its making. Under the pressure of stronger graphic impulse, line became more differentiated, itself subject to division. From the Platonic being of the *Open* motif Motherwell arrived at the controlled energies of imagery like *Shem the Penman* (plates 67–69). One discovery leads to another.

In titling this particular graphic character *Shem the Penman*, Motherwell again had recourse to his favorite author's *Finnegans Wake*, identifying his own imagery with the artistic twin son of H. C. Earwicker. It was as a twenty-year-old in Paris that Motherwell first bought a copy of Joyce's *Ulysses*, "at a time," he recalled, "when I was searching for the key to a vaguely perceived modernist aesthetic that I knew I had to make my own."[60] *Ulysses* became a constant companion, to be dipped into "the way one might look through the Bible," reading a dozen pages or so at random. From early on, Joyce became a major inspiration for titles and a major theme in Motherwell's work. *Ulysses* became part of the fabric of his experience, part of his own memory, to be drawn upon actively. The great M-shape of the painting called *Stephen's Iron Crown*, for example, "looked like a crown, and in my mind I associated it with James Joyce's use of the iron crown and Stephen Dedalus."[61] Together, gesture and association establish meaning. Both are recapitulated in *Stephen's Iron Crown Etched* (plate 95); if the "context" here is not "wholly different," new scale and different medium necessarily inform the gesture with new and different resonance.

It was in the summer of 1982, involved in organizing the International Joyce Society symposium to be held the following summer, that Motherwell began the rapid doodling in two sketchbooks which were to become his albums of Joycean iconography.[62] Several of these sketches were translated into etchings with titles like *Mulligan's Tower, Athena*, and *Wind* (plates 96–98).[63] In 1985 the artist was invited to design images for an edition of *Ulysses*; his response was hesitant and understandably fraught with ambivalence, but the book did finally appear three years later with twenty-two etchings by him.[64] He referred to them as "modest illuminations." Unlike his other *livres d'artiste*, which were conceived essentially as portfolios, with prominence given to the lithographs,[65] the *Ulysses* is very much a book for reading. Motherwell wanted to make "a beautiful book *that can be read*. I also wanted to be—as I should be—very modest in proximity to maybe the greatest text in English since Shakespeare."[66]

"The problem was iconography," as he had said of his first *livre d'artiste*, Rafael Alberti's *A la pintura*.[67] How does a resolutely modernist artist create text-related images without falling into illustration? Although he did indeed allow himself a portrait of Joyce as frontispiece and some of the designs are clearly architectural in reference, in the *Ulysses* "illuminations" Motherwell again responded to the challenge of the text by "sticking to my own iconography." The etchings were chosen from hundreds of sketches, random doodles that filled small pads like the one that came to be called the *Joyce Sketchbook* (plates 107–127). "Very often, when I'm resting during a [painting] session, I'll pick up a pad, begin to draw on it—only half looking—and sometimes do this very rapidly, maybe make ten sketches in a half an hour."[68] The drawing gestures were habitual; the results, almost inevitably, were variations on the artist's own previous inventions. In these sketchbooks we recognize the graphemes of Motherwell's art, the basic units that constitute his own iconography: double ovals, split by a line; the triangle (with or without accompanying square and circle); the chorus of ovals depending from a line; "je t'aime," and so on. Deep recollections of their own original invention, these forms recombine to suggest new possibilities—even stumbling into figural and physiognomic structures[69]—as the drawing hand maintains its unconscious, automatic momentum.

A Passionate Affair with Paper

I have always been excited by the quality of various papers since childhood. . . .[70]

Motherwell's insistence on the priority of the aesthetic—"which is the sensuous aspect of the world"[71]—always accommodated the emotional complexities of his relationship to the art he loved. In retrospect, then, it seems only natural that his serious engagement with printmaking, which began in the sixties, should have been born out of a certain psychological need. At a time of "almost metaphysical loneliness" and depression he found a certain solace in a new medium, in its technical challenge and in the satisfaction of working with people whose craft he respected. "And though my approach was in many ways primitive, it was then that I began to get deeply interested in printmaking. I had always instinctively loved working on paper, but it was the camaraderie of the artist-printmaker relationship that tilted the scale definitively, a phenomenon that I think often happens when artists grow older and more isolated."[72] The collaborative activity of making prints opened prospects for him that were both social and artistic, and his tribute to his colleagues in his introductory note (1984) to the catalogue of his prints is explicit and touching: "What earthy and lovely characters these printers are! My respect for such artisans has no limits. . . . To work with such craftsmen has been a joy and a welcome break from the essential solitude in which an artist works. I hope this book succeeds in expressing what I wanted most: a clear recognition that no modern artist is an island—individual as he is—that he works and lives owing, in part, to the givingness—and skills of others."[73]

These skilled artisans introduced Motherwell to the possibilities of new mediums, which meant the excitement of new adventures—passionate affairs with inks and papers. An art of multiples that disseminates an image to a broader public, printmaking enabled Motherwell to extend his art, and himself, back into a larger world. The imagery of the prints participates fully in his own iconography, modified by his response to the viscosity of tusche, the grain of stone, the fabric of paper.

Motherwell had dabbled in intaglio printmaking as early as 1943 in Stanley William Hayter's Atelier 17, where he admitted to having been intimidated as a young painter surrounded by older, established artists. "What was practiced in popular American printing," he recalled in 1980, "was like pencil drawing, while I am an ink man."[74] Irwin Hollander, with whom Motherwell began working in 1965, after his major exhibition at the Museum of Modern Art, has described the artist's fascination with the various blacknesses of greasy lithographic crayons and of different inks, and his approach to the plate, a probing and testing of possibilities:

He's *played* first. He's been looking at the plate. And on it he sees a Conté crayon line indicating the paper's size. And all the time he's looking at the plate, he's mixing tusche in this bowl with whatever brush he's going to use. He's *chosen* a brush. He's blending it into the tusche. He's feeling the viscosity. And each time it's a different viscosity for each of those grades of whatever he's mixing. So he's doing a watercolor of *sumi* ink, and he's getting into *that* brush. Then he makes his stroke. He watches what happens to it. And *then* there are some things that he can do.[75]

The legendary Tatyana Grosman tried to lure Motherwell into printmaking shortly after she established Universal Limited Art Editions in 1957, proposing a *livre d'artiste*, a collaboration between artist and poet; she eventually did publish *A la pintura*, which Motherwell worked on between 1968 and 1972. Before that project, she had in effect seduced

Motherwell into lithography by letting him get to know the stones. To them he brought his painter's sensibility, a vigorous brush that seemed determined to challenge the values of the printer's craft. In translating the energetic gesture that created *Beside the Sea* (plates 53–55) into a new medium, thinned oil paint was traded for lithographic ink in *A Throw of the Dice* (plates 56–62); without the spreading halo of oil, the resulting mark was of black intensity, every blot and spray of the generating motion recorded with indelible graphic finality. In some way these gestures—originally imitative of sea spray but now only of the dancing hand of the artist—failed to satisfy the professional printmaker. Grosman thought "they were not for publishing," and no editions were pulled.[76]

As Motherwell worked with graphic possibilities, a mutual accommodation was achieved between the painter and the medium. The gestures of his brush adapted to and exploited the conditions of ink, and the painter's own sense of field and surface discovered the varieties of paper with joy. He mastered the various techniques of etching—aquatint and lift-ground, in particular—to preserve the open quality of his brush mark (plates 71–78, 100–106). He got the print to adapt to the force of his gesture. In the printing of multiples he saw the possibility of new variations on a theme: for example, the color notes in the three states of *Running Elegy II* (plates 5–7). In *Samurai* (plate 80), the fluidly brushed image—set in stabilizing tension with the floating thin vertical—was printed on handmade Japanese Suzuki paper cut to different sizes; the image itself was not fixed with lacquer, and so each impression varies—an "edition of proofs."[77] In *Samurai II* (plate 86), another monumental lithograph, the overlapping of two distinctive papers complicates the surface of this hanging scroll; the resulting transparency situates the grand stroke of the image in a transcendent space.

The superimposition of papers became a favorite mode of both toning the ground and, as important, locating the image within a larger space. Controlling the field was essential to the painter. "For me the margins are the proper wall or the proper space for the image to be in. That has a lot to do with how the page comes to be the way it is. I make the etchings self-matting: there are margins that are right for a given image."[78]

That sense of adjustment—of setting a piece right in the field, refining its relationship with its neighbors and with the margins—is critical to Motherwell's longest passionate affair with paper: collage. No other American painter took up the Cubist example and worked so creatively with what Motherwell always considered the greatest discovery of modern art. From very early in his career, he was articulating and modifying the painting surface by pasting on it fragments of other surfaces, most famously, perhaps, in *Pancho Villa, Dead and Alive*.

Although he was quite clear in distinguishing the act of collaging from painting or drawing or printmaking, the boundaries remained permeable. Collage offered an opening to a world outside, as opposed to the internal pressures of painting. "To pick up a cigarette wrapper or wine label or an old letter or the end of a carton is my way of dealing with those things that do not originate in me, in my I."[79] Collage seemed to take the pressure off, as the artist worked with papers that were usually things "familiar to me, part of my life . . . autobiographical material. I do feel more joyful with collage, less austere."[80] Compared to the demands of painting, collage was "a form of play." *The Best Toys Are Made of Paper*, as he titled a collage of 1948.[81]

Most of the materials in Motherwell's collages came directly from the studio, often pieces of paper that arrived by mail. "In these cases I was indeed aware of Meyer Schapiro's emphasis on the cubists having used studio life as a main subject, but tried to make it more fluid, a matter of 'chance.' That is, I had a much less stable studio life."[82] The most readily available studio material, however, was provided by the artist's own work. The comfort of the studio comes from being surrounded by one's own work, and, in this regard Motherwell was, as he admitted, quite "homely." From his earliest collages the papers readiest to hand were those he himself had marked, and the cannibalizing of previous work, especially discarded print impressions, adds a peculiar aesthetic frisson to such works. Much of the expressive power of Motherwell's collages derives from the traces of the torn edge, with its sensate graphic eloquence (see plate 2). He considered the torn edge part of his personal contribution to the art—epitomized in a title of 1957, *The Tearingness of Collaging*.[83] Motherwell's use of the verb form is significant: collaging for him was an act, an act of feeling.

> The sensation of physically operating on the world is very strong in the medium of papier collé or collage. . . . One cuts and chooses and shifts and pastes, and sometimes tears off and begins again. In any case, shaping and arranging such a relational structure obliterates the need, and often the awareness of representation. Without reference to likeness, it possesses feeling because all the decisions in regard to it are ultimately made on the grounds of feeling.[84]

The title he gave to his last great collage series, *Night Music* (plates 129–135), is partly an evocation of Mozart. And these moving images of darkly transparent illumination do indeed carry a classical sense of structure; they stand proud in their sensuousness, sure of their affect and the perfection of their balance—the quivering textures of rice paper on black, the dialogue of light and dark, of cut and torn edge. Individually, each is commandingly impressive; collectively, they are quietly overwhelming.[85] The opera of *Night Music* represent a magnificent climax and testament to an artist's passionate affair with paper—and with black.

Notes

1. "Thoughts on Art," *The Dial* 1 (January 1841), p. 368.
2. Letter of 1767(?), in John W. McCoubrey, *American Art, 1700–1960: Sources and Documents* (Englewood Cliffs, N.J.: Prentice-Hall, 1965), p. 17.
3. Skepticism may be too mild a characterization of the most infamous revisionist thesis: Serge Guilbaut, *How New York Stole the Idea of Modern Art: Abstract Expressionism, Freedom, and the Cold War* (Chicago and London: University of Chicago Press, 1983). For the literature on Abstract Expressionism, see the Bibliographical Note in the present volume.
4. Letter of 1767(?), in McCoubrey, *American Art, 1700–1960*, p. 18.
5. The words are Barnett Newman's, in "Jackson Pollock: An Artist's Symposium, Part I," *Art News* 66 (April 1967), p. 29.
6. "Reflections on Painting Now" (11 August 1949), in *The Collected Writings of Robert Motherwell*, ed. Stephanie Terenzio (New York and Oxford: Oxford University Press, 1992), p. 68.
7. Motherwell responded to the complexity of Schapiro's commitment to the essential humanity and social meaning of abstract art; the artist's own writings share those values and acknowledge the inspiration of the art historian. Two of Schapiro's most relevant papers were "Nature of Abstract Art," *Marxist Quarterly* 1 (January–March 1937), pp. 77–99 (reprinted in volume two of his selected papers, *Modern Art: Nineteenth and Twentieth Centuries* [New York: George Braziller, 1978], pp. 185–211), and "The Social Bases of Art," in *First American Artists' Congress* (New York, 1936), pp. 31–37 (reprinted in *Artists Against War and Fascism: Papers of the First American Artists' Congress*, ed. Matthew Baigell and Julia Williams [New Brunswick, N.J.: Rutgers University Press, 1986], pp. 101–13). Schapiro's position in the New York art world of the 1930s is discussed by Dore Ashton, *The New York School: A Cultural Reckoning* (Harmondsworth and New York: Penguin Books, 1979), pp. 56–61; see also Thomas B. Hess, "Sketch for a Portrait of the Art Historian Among Artists," *Social Research* 45 (Spring 1978), pp. 6–14.
8. Letter to Edward Henning (18 October 1978), in *Collected Writings*, p. 230. For further discussion, see Arthur Danto's essay, "The 'Original Creative Principle': Motherwell and Psychic Automatism," in the present volume.

9. "A Process of Painting" (5 October 1963), in *Collected Writings*, p. 140.
10. Interview with Bryan Robertson, *Addenda* (1965), in *Collected Writings*, p. 143.
11. On 3 December 1941, Motherwell wrote to invite the poet to participate in André Breton's new Surrealist magazine *VVV*; see *Collected Writings*, pp. 17–18. On *VVV* and its founding, see Martica Sawin, *Surrealism in Exile and the Beginning of the New York School* (Cambridge, Mass., and London: MIT Press, 1995), pp. 213–20.
12. "The Modern Painter's World" (10 August 1944), in *Collected Writings*, p. 31.
13. The *Mexican Sketchbook*, containing eleven drawings, was only rediscovered among the artist's papers in 1979 and published by Jack Flam in *Robert Motherwell: Drawings—A Retrospective, 1941 to the Present* (Houston: Janie C. Lee Gallery, 1979), cat. no. 1. For further illustrations, see Joan Banach et al., *Robert Motherwell 1915/1991: La Puerta Abierta/The Open Door* (Mexico City: Museo Rufino Tamayo, 1991), cat. no. 68.
14. The artist's comment on *The Homely Protestant* continues with a clarification: "'Homely' in 'the King's English' means a stay-at-home, a homebody—not what it means to us at all—and that's certainly what Joyce meant when he used it" (in H. H. Arnason, *Robert Motherwell*, 2nd ed., new and revised [New York: Harry N. Abrams, 1982], p. 111).
15. In *Collected Writings*, p. 55.
16. Interview with Richard Wagener (14 June 1974), in *Collected Writings*, p. 217.
17. "A Personal Expression" (19 March 1949), in *Collected Writings*, p. 61.
18. Originally published in *Art News* 51 (December 1952), "The American Action Painters" was included in Rosenberg's first anthology of criticism, *The Tradition of the New* (New York: Horizon Press, 1959), pp. 23–39.
19. "The New York School" (27 October 1959), in *Collected Writings*, p. 78.
20. *Possibilities* 1 (Winter 1947–48), p. 1; in *Collected Writings*, p. 45. The second part of the statement, more political in tone and content, was written by Harold Rosenberg, his co-editor and co-signatory.
21. Quoted in E. A. Carmean, Jr., "Robert Motherwell: The Elegies to the Spanish Republic," in *American Art at Mid-Century: The Subjects of the Artist* (Washington, D.C.: National Gallery of Art, 1978), p. 96.
22. "The Modern Painter's World" (10 August 1944), in *Collected Writings*, pp. 31–32. Originally delivered as a lecture at Mount Holyoke College, the text was published in *DYN* 1 (November 1944), pp. 9–14.
23. Quoted in Carmean, "Robert Motherwell: The Elegies to the Spanish Republic," p. 98.
24. Quoted in Frank O'Hara, *Robert Motherwell, with Selections from the Artist's Writings* (New York: The Museum of Modern Art, 1965), p. 54, from Margaret Paul, in *Robert Motherwell* (Northampton, Mass.: Smith College Museum of Art, 1963), cat. no. 16.
25. "Robert Motherwell: A Conversation at Lunch" (November 1962), in *Collected Writings*, p. 137.
26. "A Conversation with Students" (6 April 1979), in *Collected Writings*, p. 228.
27. Interview with David Hayman (12 and 13 July 1988), in *Collected Writings*, p. 288.
28. "Artists' Sessions at Studio 35 (1950)," in *Modern Artists in America*, ed. Robert Motherwell and Ad Reinhardt (New York: Wittenborn, Schultz, 1951), p. 20; reprinted in Ann Eden Gibson, *Issues in Abstract Expressionism: The Artist-Run Periodicals* (Ann Arbor and London: UMI Research Press, 1990), p. 339.
29. See E. H. Gombrich, "Leonardo's Method for Working Out Compositions," in *Norm and Form: Studies in the Art of the Renaissance* (London: Phaidon Press, 1966), pp. 58–63, and David Rosand, "On Drawing a Line," in *The Meaning of the Mark: Leonardo and Titian* (Lawrence: Spencer Museum of Art, University of Kansas, 1988), pp. 11–48.
30. Interview with Jack Flam (5 November 1982), in Flam, *Motherwell* (Oxford: Phaidon Press, 1991), p. 11.
31. In an interview with Jack Flam (22 October 1982), in Flam, *Motherwell*, p. 24. In a lecture delivered in October 1959, he referred to them as "'abstract' works without objects . . . [a] series of pictures with black ovals and stripes on white grounds" (*Collected Writings*, p. 122).
32. One senses the painter's ambivalence to this lightness in the great canvas: he has imposed a chromatic weight above the figures, a gravity to control their ebullience. Painted in 1983, *The Hollow Men* was the culminating picture in Motherwell's retrospective exhibition of that year, organized by the Albright-Knox Art Gallery in Buffalo: *Robert Motherwell* (New York: Abbeville Press, 1983), no. 93, ill. on p. 123. It is also illustrated in Flam, *Motherwell*, pl. 136, and in Marcelin Pleynet, *Robert*

Motherwell (Paris: Editions Daniel Papierski, 1990), pp. 170–171—who recalls as well Shakespeare's "hollow men" (*Julius Caesar*, IV.ii, ll. 21–26).

33. "Eye and Mind," trans. Carleton Dallery, in Maurice Merleau-Ponty, *The Primacy of Perception and Other Essays on Phenomenological Psychology, the Philosophy of Art, History and Politics*, ed. James M. Edie (Evanston: Northwestern University Press, 1964), p. 162.

34. From "Addenda to The Museum of Modern Art *Lyric Suite* Questionnaire—from Memory . . . with Possible Chronological Slips" (Fall 1969), in *Collected Writings*, pp. 170–73. The two footnotes added by Motherwell read: "*I violated this last on about ten sheets, always to their detriment." "†I repeat, because of the technical process of spreading and drying after I had ended my participation, the pictures literally continued to paint themselves as the ink spread in collaboration with the paper. . . ."

35. In Arnason, *Robert Motherwell*, text accompanying pl. 194.

36. "The Modern Painter's World" (10 August 1944), in *Collected Writings*, p. 28. Motherwell borrowed the notion from Bernard Bosanquet, "who goes on to say: 'When a "body-and-mind" is, as a whole, in any experience, that is the chief feature . . . of what we mean by feeling. Think of him as he sings, or loves, or fights. When he is as one, I believe it is always through feeling . . .' (*Three Lectures on Aesthetic*)."

37. "The Modern Painter's World" (10 August 1944), in *Collected Writings*, p. 34.

38. As Motherwell, indirectly invoking Paul Valéry, described the art of "The New York School" (27 October 1950), in *Collected Writings*, p. 78.

39. Interview with Bryan Robertson, Addenda (1965), in *Collected Writings*, p. 143.

40. "Thoughts on Drawing" (1970), in *Collected Writings*, p. 194.

41. Letter to Edward Henning (18 October 1978), in *Collected Writings*, p. 230. Although he eventually claimed to prefer the term "artful scribbling," which he took from the title of Howard Gardner's book on children's drawings (1980), Motherwell never really abandoned "doodling." See his comment in Arnason, *Robert Motherwell*, p. 116.

42. "Concerning the Beginnings of the New York School: 1939–1943" (January 1967), interview with Sidney Simon, in *Collected Writings*, p. 166. "And of course," Motherwell continued, "it was Pollock who became the most identified with this technique of working. In his dripping, one could see most clearly and nakedly the essential nature of the process." In *Partisan Review* (January 1944), reviewing Pollock's solo show at Peggy Guggenheim's Art of This Century, Motherwell recognized "one of the younger generation's chances" and, with a certain self-knowledge, articulated the great challenge confronting it: "His principal problem is to discover what his true *subject* is. And since painting is his thought's medium, the resolution must grow out of the process of painting itself" (in *Collected Writings*, p. 27).

43. In Arnason, *Robert Motherwell*, p. 221.

44. "Provincetown and Days Lumberyard: A Memoir" (1978), in *Collected Writings*, pp. 226–27.

45. Leonardo da Vinci, *Treatise on Painting [Codex Urbinas Latinus 1270]*, trans. A. Philip McMahon (Princeton: Princeton University Press, 1956), vol. 1, p. 49 (¶ 72).

46. Pliny the Elder, *Natural History*, XXXV.102–4; *The Elder Pliny's Chapters on the History of Art*, trans. K. Jex-Blake, ed. E. Sellers (London, 1896), p. 139.

47. Interview with Jack Flam (2 October 1982), in Flam, "With Robert Motherwell," in the Albright-Knox Art Gallery exhibition catalogue *Robert Motherwell*, p. 23; also in Flam, *Motherwell*, p. 16. Further on this issue, see Stephen Addiss, "Provisional Dualism: Robert Motherwell and Zen," in the present volume; see also the Zen reading of Robert C. Hobbs, "Robert Motherwell's Open Series," in *Robert Motherwell* (Düsseldorf: Städtische Kunsthalle, 1976), pp. 45–54.

48. Ascanio Condivi, *The Life of Michelangelo* (1553), trans. Alice Sedwick Wohl (Oxford: Phaidon Press, 1976), p. 107.

49. Pliny, *Natural History*, XXXV.81–83; *The Elder Pliny's Chapters on the History of Art*, pp. 121–23.

50. In Flam, *Robert Motherwell*, p. 11. The words of Picasso that Motherwell vaguely remembered may well have been: "Rhythm is a perception of time. The repetition of the pattern of the wicker chair is a rhythm. The fatigue of one's hand as one draws is a perception of time." Surely resonant for Motherwell, the passage appeared in Alexander Liberman's article on Picasso in *Vogue* (November 1, 1956) and was reprinted in Dore Ashton, ed., *Picasso on Art: A Selection of Views* (New York: Viking Press, 1972), p. 103.

51. *Robert Motherwell: Prints, 1977–1979* (New York: Brooke Alexander, Inc., 1979), n.p. For further comment on this motif, see E. A. Carmean, Jr., *Robert Motherwell: Stephen's Iron Crown and Related Works* (Fort

Worth: The Fort Worth Art Museum, 1985), cat. nos. 4, 7.

52. As Irwin Hollander, Motherwell's printer, observed. "It was a suite of ten. They were a simple exploration—the opportunity to work on the walls of my studio, on a French transfer paper. These walls reminded him of walls in Madrid during his honeymoon with Helen Frankenthaler. So by rubbing on these spackled walls, he could get a similar impression of texture that would be transferred to zinc and then printed. . . . These are rubbings! . . . a transfer of feeling from Madrid to Tenth Street." Interview in Stephanie Terenzio, *The Prints of Robert Motherwell* (New York: Hudson Hills Press, 1991), p. 32.

53. Letter (10 November 1956) in *Collected Writings*, p. 111.

54. For illustrations of the *Je t'aime* paintings, see O'Hara, *Robert Motherwell*, p. 38; Arnason, *Robert Motherwell*, pls. 29, 30, 32, 44, 142–44; Albright-Knox Art Gallery, *Robert Motherwell*, pp. 69, 70; Pleynet, *Robert Motherwell*, pp. 94, 95, 97.

55. "A Process of Painting" (5 October 1963), in *Collected Writings*, p. 139. After ascribing to the medium "precisely the same range of sensed feeling" as possessed by people, Motherwell observes: "And it is only when you think of the medium as having the same potential as another human being, that you begin to see the nature of the artist's involvement—as it appears to himself. . . ." Then, in a remarkable burst of self-revelation, he continues:

"Now, if a creative person in the arts is a person with an extraordinary capacity for love, who for whatever reason—say because of his early experience with his mother—as an example—cannot direct his love toward another person in full strength, but who nevertheless *must* love—he therefore directs his love toward the other thing in human existence as rich, sensitive, supple, and complicated as human beings themselves; that is to say toward an artistic medium, which is not an inert object, or conversely, a set of rules for composition, but a living collaboration, which not only reflects every nuance of one's being, but which, in the moments in which one is lost, comes to one's aid; not arbitrarily and capriciously (like the Greek goddesses intervening in man's fate), but seriously, accurately, concretely *with you*, as when a canvas says to you: this empty space in me needs to be pinker, or a shape says: the conception is too large or too small for me, all out of scale; or a stripe says: gouge me more—you are too polite or elegant; or a gray says: a bit more blue—my present tone is uncomfortable and does not fit with what surrounds me."

56. "We all have a thirst for love." Made somewhat casually in 1944 (in "The Modern Painter's World," in *Collected Writings*, p. 29), that declaration will continue to resonate. Although he liked to compare Abstract Expressionism to psychoanalysis—defined, with reference to Heinz Hartmann, as the unmasking of self-deception—Motherwell was uncomfortable with one significant critical foray into psychobiography: Jonathan Fineberg, "Death and Maternal Love: Psychological Speculations on Robert Motherwell's Art," *Artforum* 17 (September 1978), pp. 52–57.

57. The inscription may have been inspired by Matisse, who, in 1945, had added it to a drawing of a woman contemplating a drawing. It is of some relevance that in 1953 Motherwell was engaged in "a brief 'nude' series," which he abandoned, "destroyed most of the paintings, and began—all in 1955—the 'Je t'aime' series. . . ." See his foreword to William C. Seitz, *Abstract Expressionist Painting in America* (Cambridge, Mass., and London: Harvard University Press, 1983), p. xi. And yet another apparently casual observation may be revealing in this context. In his letter to Frank O'Hara dated 18 August 1965, Motherwell wrote: "Every artist needs a model. Not to paint, but as a beautiful living presence. Art that has no element of the erotic is like a life without the erotic, shrivelled" (in *Collected Writings*, p. 150).

58. O'Hara, *Robert Motherwell*, p. 67; also in *Collected Writings*, p. 151. Motherwell had already formulated this distinction in 1944, in "The Modern Painter's World": "The medium of painting is color and space: drawing is essentially division of space . . ." (*Collected Writings*, p. 32).

59. Barbaralee Diamonstein, "An Interview with Robert Motherwell," in Arnason, *Robert Motherwell*, p. 229. Motherwell's response began by rehearsing the problem of *unifying* "disparate and conflicting elements in painting. . . . (Part of the public's difficulty in apprehending Abstract Expressionism is an inability to discriminate order that is on the edge of chaos, but still order; e.g., Pollock)."

60. Interview with David Hayman (12 and 13 July 1988), in *Collected Writings*, p. 285.

61. On the back of the canvas, Motherwell inscribed: "Stephen's Iron Crown/(Joyce)." Further on the painting and the motif, see Carmean, *Robert Motherwell: Stephen's Iron Crown and Related Works*.

62. Some of these drawings, selected and edited by Constance and Jack Glen, have been published as *Robert Motherwell: The Dedalus Sketchbooks* (New York: Harry N. Abrams, 1988). Coinciding with the

symposium in June 1983 was an exhibition at the Hawthorne Gallery of the Provincetown Art Association and Museum, "Robert Motherwell: Tribute to James Joyce."

63. See *The Dedalus Sketchbooks*, pls. 21 (*Mulligan's Tower*), 23 (*Molly as Tower*), and 11 (*Untitled*).

64. Published by Arion Press: San Francisco, 1988 (*The Prints of Robert Motherwell*, "Catalogue Raisonné, 1943–1990" by Dorothy C. Belknap, nos. 384–405).

65. *A la pintura* by Rafael Alberti (1968–72; Belknap nos. 82–102), *El Negro Motherwell*, also by Alberti (1981–83; Belknap nos. 268–91); *Three Poems* by Octavio Paz (1987–88; Belknap nos. 354–80).

66. Interview with David Hayman (12 and 13 July 1988), in *Collected Writings*, p. 289.

67. "The Book's Beginnings" (1972), in *Collected Writings*, p. 213.

68. Interview with David Hayman, in *Collected Writings*, p. 287.

69. For example, the remarkable fullness of *Molly Bloom* or the sensitive face of *Stephen Dedalus* in *The Dedalus Sketchbooks* (pls. 22, 24).

70. "The Book's Beginnings" (1972), in *Collected Writings*, p. 211.

71. "Beyond the Aesthetic" (April 1946), in *Collected Writings*, p. 36.

72. Quoted by Stephanie Terenzio, "Introduction: Collaboration as Self-Transcendence," in *The Prints of Robert Motherwell*, p. 16.

73. *The Prints of Robert Motherwell*, p. 9.

74. Quoted in Robert S. Mattison, "Two Decades of Graphic Art by Robert Motherwell," *The Print Collector's Newsletter* 11, no. 6 (January–February 1981), p. 198.

75. Interview in *The Prints of Robert Motherwell*, p. 29.

76. On Motherwell's relationship with ULAE, see Esther Sparks, *Universal Limited Art Editions: A History and Catalogue—The First Twenty-five Years* (Chicago: The Art Institute of Chicago; New York: Harry N. Abrams, 1989), pp. 165–93. See also the interviews with Tatyana Grosman, Donn Steward, Tony Towle, and Bill Goldston in *The Prints of Robert Motherwell*, pp. 51–78.

77. Sparks, *Universal Limited Art Editions*, cat. no. 11.

78. Interview with David Hayman (12 and 13 July 1988), in *Collected Writings*, p. 288. In 1973, Motherwell acquired an etching press for his Greenwich studio, and Catherine Mousley became his master printer in that medium; see the interview with her in *The Prints of Robert Motherwell*, pp. 97–114.

79. Interview with Jack Flam (October 2, 1982), quoted in Flam, *Motherwell*, p. 18.

80. "Robert Motherwell: A Conversation at Lunch" (November 1962), in *Collected Writings*, p. 135.

81. Illustrated in Flam, *Motherwell*, pl. 19.

82. Conversation with E. A. Carmean, Jr. (15 July 1972), quoted in Carmean, *The Collages of Robert Motherwell: A Retrospective Exhibition* (Houston: The Museum of Fine Arts, 1972), p. 29.

83. See Arnason, *Robert Motherwell*, pl. 141; also Carmean, *The Collages of Robert Motherwell*, no. 15, pl. 7.

84. "Beyond the Aesthetic" (April 1946), in *Collected Writings*, p. 37.

85. For a fuller response to the *Night Music* series, see Mary Ann Caws's essay, "Robert Motherwell: Working Through the Night," in the present volume.

The "Original Creative Principle": Motherwell and Psychic Automatism

Arthur C. Danto

The circumstance of having had advanced training in philosophy before going on to become a painter, and indeed a great painter, is almost certainly unique to Robert Motherwell. But he carried his philosophical knowledge so casually that other than in the autobiographical mode that came easily to him in later years, when he was the subject of frequent interviews, or in the occasional title of a painting like *In Plato's Cave*—which in any case is so commonplace a cultural allusion that no inference from its use by someone to any special degree of philosophical education would be licit—one might have had no sense of him as ever having had a philosophical background or any great interest in the subject. In our numerous conversations, from 1985, when we met, until the year of his death, philosophy rarely came up in a way that made me feel that he brought with him from his graduate years any special grasp of the world that an exposure to philosophical discipline might explain. He loved talking about the Surrealists and their circle, and in the two public conversations we had, nothing seemed of greater interest to him than the memory of that extraordinary group of artistic intellectuals whom it fell to him to guide through the labyrinths of American, or at least Manhattan, life. He returned, again and again, to André Breton and Marcel Duchamp and Max Ernst, on whom he was always fascinating, but very much as if the ideas that drove them were a good deal less interesting and engaging than the personalities that embodied them, and his discourse a glittering stream of anecdotes, episodes, and portraits rather than a reflection on Surrealist theories and doctrines. Doubtless this was because those theories and dogmas had no great currency in the late eighties and early nineties, but it must also have been, it has come to me to seem, because Motherwell himself had no special concern for such theories. For someone who had a reputation as a thinker and an intellectual, this may seem odd, and suggest that his philosophical studies had not dyed, or at least not deeply dyed, the fabric of his mind. But it has recently begun to come home to me that Motherwell's philosophical spirit must be located elsewhere, in a set of critical attitudes that had an immense impact upon his own development as an artist and, through him, on the whole development of American modernism. His was the spirit one might say of critical, rather than of dogmatic, philosophy, to use the distinction through which Immanuel Kant sought to distinguish himself from his contemporaries and predecessors.

Motherwell's philosophical training shows up with particular vividness in the way that, in the 1940s, he saw painting itself as a problem, very much as the great philosophers of the past saw knowledge itself—or understanding, or truth—as a problem, or as, in the twentieth century, philosophers found philosophy itself a problem to which increasingly radical solutions were proposed. In an interview of 1977 with Barbaralee Diamonstein, he speaks of the task of finding a "creative principle"[1] as a problem and indeed as a crisis, as if painting, and especially American painting, could not go forward if the problem were not solved and the crisis overcome. The solution could not be discovered by simply continuing to paint, but rather by putting painting at a certain distance, and determining how it could be done. And this has the great sweep and methodological ambition we find in the master philosophers of the seventeenth and eighteenth centuries, whom Motherwell must have studied at Harvard as a graduate student, all of whom felt philosophy to be confronted by an intellectual crisis of one sort or other which required an ascent to a new level of knowledge, thought, and understanding, where knowledge, thinking, and understanding themselves became their own objects: René Descartes's *Discourse on Method*, Nicolas de Malbranche's *The Search for Truth*, Baruch Spinoza's *The Improvement of the Understanding*—or, as the climax of the great series of investigations into the foundations and limits of the human intellect, Kant's tremendous *Critique of Pure Reason*. "I know of no enquiries which are more important for exploring the faculty which we entitle understanding, and for determining the rules and limits of its employment, than those which I have instituted," Kant wrote in his preface, responding, as his predecessors did, to a sense of crisis in the old methods, and a sense of mission in finding a new method for leading philosophy out of "chaos and night [and] that ill-applied industry which has rendered them thus dark, confused, and unserviceable."[2] No painter—one is tempted to say no "mere painter"—could, like Motherwell, have conceived of painting as something that demanded a wholesale reconstructive methodological solution. It was this posture of philosophical address which set him apart from his peers. What is unique about him as thinker and artist is that he really did find the principle he sought, and then applied it in the great sequence of drawings, prints, collages, and paintings which stands as his life's work. The parallel with Descartes is intriguing, for Descartes not only hit upon the "Method of Rightly Conducting the Reason,"[3] but put it into application in a sequence of works on geometry, physics, optics, physiology, cosmology, and the like which, in his view, vindicated the validity of his method.

The creative principle—what we might call "The Method of Rightly Conducting the Brush"—was of course what the Surrealists called "psychic automatism," which, "in the case of painting . . . usually begins as 'doodling' or scribbling."[4] But before discussing this, I want to say a few words more on the philosophical nature of Motherwell's early investigations into the foundations of modernist art.

Kant distinguishes sharply between his own critical project and what he terms "dogmatism," which is "a procedure of pure reason *without previous criticism of its own powers*."[5] He speaks with a certain irony of "the celebrated Wolff, the greatest of all the dogmatic philosophers," who was "peculiarly well-suited to raise metaphysics to the dignity of a science, if only it occurred to him to prepare the ground beforehand by a critique of the organ, that is, of pure reason itself."[6] The Surrealists, and to an exaggerated degree Breton himself, were dogmatists through and through, not simply in the sense of being utterly convinced and, well, dogmatic in the articulation of their beliefs, but in the rather more strict Kantian sense of attempting to lay down deep metaphysical truths without first investigating the adequacy of their methods to do so. Motherwell, so far as I was ever able to tell, had no interesting theses to which he was committed about the nature of reality or of the mind: he was not a "dogmatist" at all. He was a pure painter in the Kantian sense of being interested purely in the act of painting,[7] without specific commitment to content. The Surrealists thought to use "psychic automatism" in order to reveal the underlying structure and contents of the unconscious mind, something in which, as a modern, Motherwell had a certain interest, but which did not, so far as I know, particularly motivate his appropriation of psychic automatism. Certain others in the Abstract Expressionist movement were, in the manner of Breton, dogmatists (and indeed dogmatism affects the art world to this day, whether as part of the Surrealist heritage or not I cannot say), and spoke of the Sublime, of the *Ding-an-sich*, and of Jungian archetypes with the assurance of "the celebrated Wolff." But Motherwell, in everything perhaps except the matter of the creative principle, was an exceedingly open person—pragmatic, flexible, diffident. I always thought in fact that his *Open* series was a monument to an openness that might easily have been a principle of his—as it almost had to be (as we shall see), given that psychic automatism leaves it open what is to emerge when one embarks upon it.[8]

We can, of course, press parallels too far, but the distinction between the critical and the dogmatic is a piece of philosophical structure, one to which a person who studied philosophy would have been alive in a way in which someone who came to philosophy from the outside, as a reader, might not. Barnett Newman was a dogmatist, Ad Reinhardt was a dogmatist, Mark Rothko and even Jackson Pollock were dogmatists, while Breton was a dogmatist raised to a higher power. But Motherwell was a criticalist in method and a pragmatist in everything else, a combination to which his employment of psychic automatism was perfectly suited.

Actions are considered "automatic" when they take place without their agents being conscious—or fully conscious—of their taking place. The term "action" excludes mere reflex motor responses, in the sense that a great many automatic actions begin as conscious actions to which the agent become habituated through repetition, whereas reflex responses have no history of explanation through consciousness at all, so that their causes are entirely mechanical or physical. Driving a car or riding a bicycle become "automatic" in the sense that we perform the various sub-actions involved in them without thinking about them, and without their ever breaking through to consciousness, and in much the same way the various sub-actions of playing a musical instrument get to be "second nature" to us in that we do not have to think of where, for example, we are to put our fingers. Playing a piece can get to be as automatic as moving one's fingers, especially when the piece has been completely learned and one plays it, like a theater musician, over and over again, without having to think, or think very much. And perhaps playing a role in a theatrical performance gets to be automatic in this sense, to the point, even, where one's effectiveness would be hindered if one in fact became overly conscious of what one was doing.[9] In the nineteenth century, there was a feverish interest in behavior that was automatic, in the sense that consciousness and premeditation played no particular role, but which was not in any obvious way rote or routinized. So-called automatic writing would be a case in point. "In a typical but simple case," Baldwin's 1901 *Dictionary of Pyschology* says, "a pencil placed in the hands of the automatist will begin to write apparently of its own accord; the automatic character of the result being indicated by the fact that the writing proceeds the more successfully the more the subject is distracted from the action . . . and frequently too by the content and character of the writing."[10] Creative writing is easily thought of as automatic in the sense that the poem or novel seems to write itself—which is more picturesquely characterized as having been dictated by the Muse. But automatic writing, as it is classified here, would rather rarely have much literary interest, and even more rarely a sustained literary interest: it would be marked by the fact that the writing seemed almost *physically* to have taken place without the intervention, or even against the will, of the agent—as if the pencil were driven by some source other than the one whose hand held it. And, with the high interest in "psychic" phenomena in the nineteenth century, automatic writing would most obviously have been explained with reference to some "spirit" communicating through the "medium" of a writer's hand. Needless to say, one's interest in what got written would almost certainly not have been literary, but in the information transmitted through automatism from the Beyond, viz., that "I am happy and I love you." (Motherwell's celebrated inscription "Je t'aime" has an uncanny affinity to a spiritualist's communication from an Absent Beloved; it would have been precisely the kind of message one would have wished to see formed "automatically" during a seance, validating the "medium's" powers.) Spiritualism was animated, if that term be allowed, by the thirst for evidence of immortality, and not simply the "intimations of immortality" with which the Romantics were content. The Romantics were defined by their disdain for science, whereas the spiritualists were defined by their fear that science might have cut the ground out from under hope in the Higher World and the Afterlife.

It is striking how the very phenomena that excited spiritualist hopes—dreams, visions, and of course automatic writing—were naturalized in the nineteenth century through complicating our picture of the mind. It is very much as if spiritualism was the obverse of positivism, the position that natural science and natural science alone is in a position to explain whatever takes place in the world. The corollary of positivism was a kind of materialism, according to which body and mind together are explainable through natural causes and covered by natural laws. Positivism meant that there was no "higher" revelation; materialism was taken to mean that the mind dies with the body; and spiritualism was an effort to find evidence that refuted the latter and enfranchised the former. "I hold it truth," Tennyson wrote in *In Memoriam*, "that men may rise on stepping stone / Of their dead selves to higher things." The postulation of what Baldwin's *Dictionary* designates "a subconscious personality, which has become dissociated from the main conscious stream of thought, a secondary personality split off from the main personality, and accessible only by psychological means like hypnotism or automatic writing which reveals as 'out of gear' the usual co-ordinating relationships of the highest cerebral center" replaces Tennyson's "higher thing" with a natural mechanism. And with the complication of our theories of the mind, through writers such as William James and Pierre Janet, and of course Freud, the explanation of automatic writing has come to be believed altogether endogenous. And with this, automatic behavior of whatever sort was transformed from a conduit to the supernatural into a diagnostic device for revealing inner mental structures themselves inaccessible to introspection, as of course the unconscious, or the "UCS System," in Freud necessarily was. The behavior was transferred from the psychic's parlor to the clinic, where Breton, who after all was a student of medicine—he worked at the Charcot clinic, where Freud had come to study the phenomenon of hysteria—discovered it and turned it to artistic ends. But those ends were, in important ways, tinctured with the psychological associations Breton learned about from psycho-analytical theory and practice. For him the unconscious was an exciting hidden world, to which automatism gave access.[11] But it was with a poet, Philippe Soupault, that he practiced automatic writing in 1919, which he clearly considered literature rather than clinical notation, since it was published as *Les Champs magnetiques* the following year.

In his first *Surrealist Manifesto* of 1924, Breton defined Surrealism methodologically. It was "pure psychic automatism by which one intends to express verbally, in writing or by other method, the real functioning of the mind. Dictation by thought, in the absence of any control exercised by reason, and beyond any aesthetic or moral preoccupation."[12] It is important to stress that Breton saw the unconscious from an epistemological perspective: it was like a cognitive organ that disclosed a world with which we have lost contact, a marvelous world that appears to us in dreams and to which automatic writing and drawing give us access. That is, automatism takes us not simply to the unconscious mind, but through that mind to the world with which it is in contact, past the real to the Sur-real. That world, through the mediation of the unconscious, speaks through the medium of automatic writing. To practice automatism means to disengage reason, calculation, and indeed everything component in "the highest cerebral center," to use Baldwin's expression. And since Breton found it imperative to identify automatism with art, the art he favored was an unpremeditated and uncontrolled pouring forth of language, without guidance or censorship—a kind of "speaking in tongues" that was, for the spiritualist, the

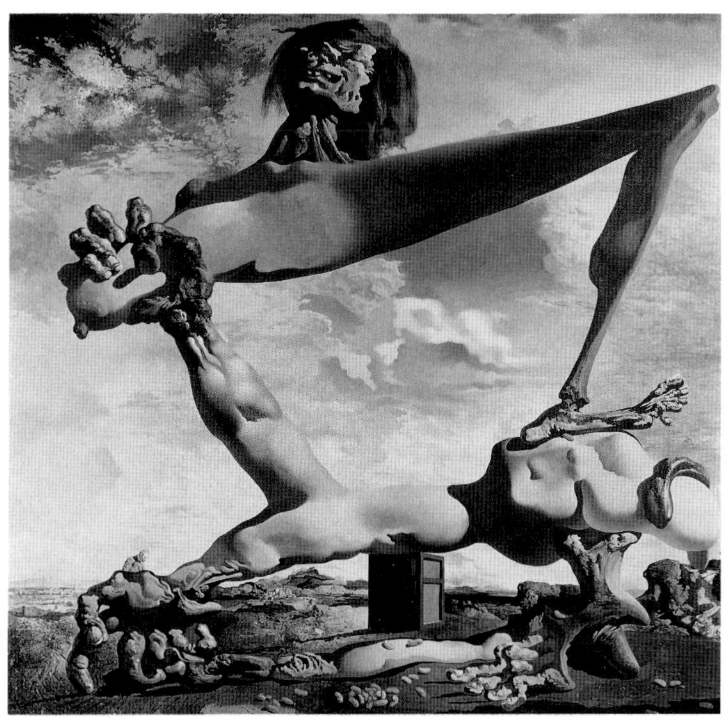

1. Salvador Dalí. *Soft Construction with Boiled Beans: A Premonition of Civil War,* 1936. Oil on canvas, 39½ x 39½" (100.3 x 100.3 cm). Philadelphia Museum of Art. Walter and Louise Arensberg Collection

mouthpiece, the persona, of the Holy Spirit. It is little wonder that the early Abstract Expressionists, who were profoundly affected by the tone of Surrealist thought, if not its substance, should have seen themselves as shamans through whom objective forces poured forth. Breton's marvelous world and his belief in the primitive mind are distantly present in the famous letter to the *New York Times* of 1943, written by Adolph Gottlieb and Mark Rothko, in which they say, "To us art is an adventure into an unknown world, which can be explored only by those willing to take risks."[13] And it could be conjectured that "pouring" itself should become among the means available to the true artist, as it did in Pollock at least, whose Jungian searchings into the archetypes of the unconscious made him an edgy heeder of Surrealist doctrine.

There is in truth very little "pouring forth" in the typical Surrealist canvases of the 1940s. They tended on the whole to use illusionistic pictorial space, and indeed, deep illusional space—with sharp, explicit perspective, as in the paintings of Salvador Dalí—became graphic shorthand for the space of dreams (fig. 1).[14] And Dalí, again, sought to convey the feeling of dreams by situating finely delineated objects in those spaces, exhibiting properties never encountered in ordinary experiences—like the celebrated limp watches—or juxtaposing objects in ways so incongruent with the conceptual schemata of ordinary life as to evoke uncanniness in the viewer's mind. Dalí, to be sure, deliberately exploited what he termed the "critical-paranoic" method, but this was a method of conjoining images whose facture was far from the uncontrolled gush and rush Breton evidently advocated. Breton had in mind words that spill from the mouth or the fingertips, rather than images built up

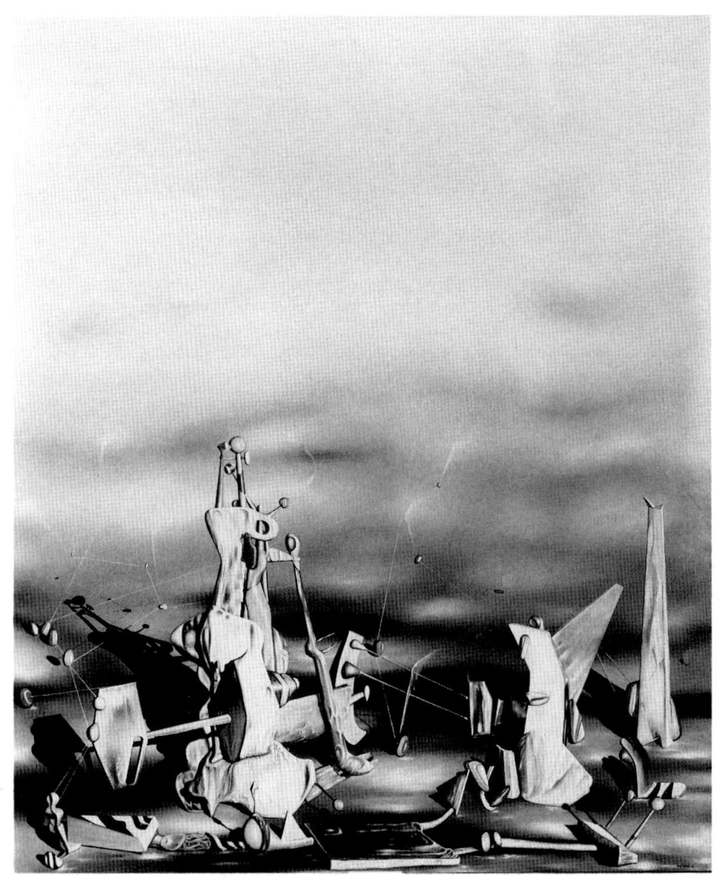

2. Yves Tanguy. *Palace with Rock Windows*, 1942. Oil on canvas, 64 x 52" (162.6 x 132.1 cm). Musée National d'Art Moderne, Centre Georges Pompidou, Paris

with glazes and cunningly shaded to elicit the sense of dramatic illuminations. But even the loosest of the Surrealist painters were more fixed on a kind of dream content than on a specific method of painting that was itself "automatic"—in the received sense of transpiring without being monitored by consciousness or directed by the representational capacities of the rational mind. With Breton, one dares to say, content and mode of utterance alike referred to the sub-rational mind. But with the Surrealist painters, it was content alone that was Surrealist: the method of painting remained traditional and even, in Dalí and in Yves Tanguy (fig. 2), academic. What Motherwell's automatism accomplished was to make the method itself congruent with Breton's way of writing, so that in effect painting could even be treated as a mode of writing—and either to eliminate recognizable content, or to treat content so abstractly that one could dash a figure or face across the space of canvas with the same unstudied urgency as with splashing paint. And the success of this change in the production of art has had the consequence—one among many in the subsequent history of art—of bumping the Surrealist painters onto a sidetrack of modernism.

It was precisely the illusionism of Surrealist treatments of space—not to mention, since it does not function in his criticism, the disjunction between writing, which does, and painting, which does not, lend itself to automaticity—which Clement Greenberg found incompatible witlh the very concept of modernist painting, whose essential principle required the exclusion from painting of everything alien to the medium. But, so Greenberg argued, illusional, three-dimensional space is proper to sculpture rather than to painting, which demands flatness. And the dominance of Greenberg's view has tended to keep Surrealist art very much on its sidetrack, much like that celebrated Surrealist photograph of an abandoned steam engine covered with vines. It is possible that, with the waning of Greenberg's influence, Surrealism will make a comeback, and, at least according to some writers, such as Hal Foster, it *has* made a comeback, even one "with a vengeance, the subject of many exhibitions, symposia, books, and articles."[15] Even so, Foster goes on to say, "surrealism is still often folded into discourses of iconography and style." And the symbols on which iconographical analysis is expended have cloyed over the years, while the hopeful belief that tapping into the unconscious, as if into an immense source of creative energy, has, along with the fourth dimension, lost its charm.

Stylistically speaking, the painter Matta has little to recommend him to someone who finds Surrealism wanting as a modernist paradigm (fig. 3). But he felt himself sufficiently apart from the governing body of Surrealism as a movement in the early 1940s to want to create what Motherwell described as a "palace revolution" in the movement, and it is possible that the crux of the revolution was precisely that change I have identified as Motherwell's. Motherwell did not admire Matta greatly as a painter—"For me [his paintings] were theatrical and glossy, too illusionistic for my taste"[16]—but thought highly of his colored pencil drawings: "His painting never compared to his drawings" (fig. 4). And drawing lends itself to "doodling" rather more readily than painting does; or painting has to be re-invented, so to speak, in order to make room for painterly doodles. (Dalí could make a splendid painting of a doodle, but it is difficult to picture him doodling as such.) "The fundamental principle that he and I continually discussed, for his palace revolution, and for my search for an *original creative* principle," Motherwell said in a letter to Edward Henning, written in 1978 (a little later than his public interview with Diamonstein), "was what the surrealists called psychic automatism, what a Freudian would call free-association, in the specific form of doodling."[17]

The "original creative principle," Motherwell said, more than once, was "the thing lacking in American Modernism."[18] It was to be something which, once discovered, would enable American artists to produce original modernist works, by contrast with what was the practice at the time, of attempting to be modernist by emulating European works which were by definition modernist. And it was in formulating this that Motherwell's philosophical training and sensibility come through. "*The American problem*," he emphasized in his discussion with Diamonstein, "was to find a *creative principle* that was not a style, not stylistic, not an imposed aesthetic."[19] He formulated this as a problem, on at least two occasions, with the painter Arshile Gorky specifically in mind.

> The enormously gifted Gorky had gone through a Cézannesque period and was, for the 1940s, in a *passé* Picasso period, whereas much lesser European talents were more in their own "voice," so to speak, because they were closer to the living roots of international modernism (in fact, it was through the Surrealists and, above all, personal contacts with Matta that Gorky shortly after would take off like a rocket . . .).[20]

Matta "shifted Gorky from copying *Cahiers d'art* to a full-blown development of his own."[21] So Gorky was the model of what the original creative principle could do. "With such a creative principle, modernist American artists could cease to be

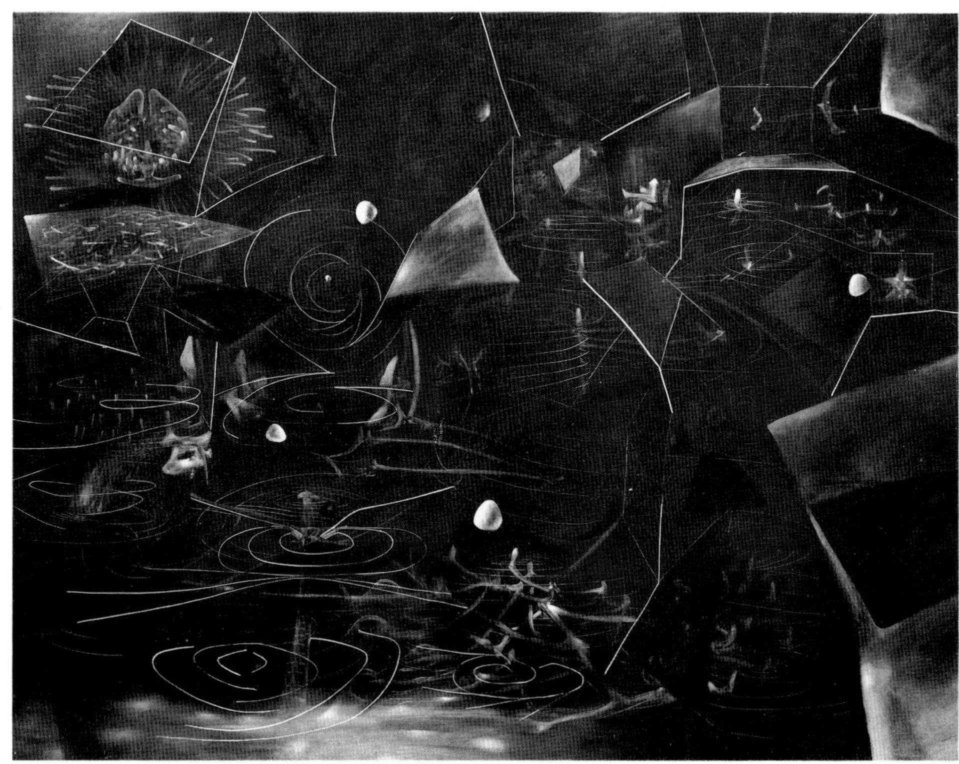

3. Matta. *The Vertigo of Eros*, 1944. Oil on canvas, 77 x 111" (195.6 x 251.5 cm). The Museum of Modern Art, New York. Given anonymously

mannerists," Motherwell told Henning. It transformed Gorky from a mannerist of modernist idioms to the original artist he became, realizing his native gifts through its means. Psychic automatism was an almost magical device for enabling each person to be at once artistically authentic to his or her true self, and at the same time to be modern. "And what was 'American' would take care of itself, as it did soon enough."[22]

Motherwell does speak of "the preconscious," but he sees this in a far different light than did Breton or, for that matter, Freud. For Motherwell it consists in that complex of causes, of influences, experiences, and circumstances, which make each of us the person we uniquely are: our *selves*. The same methods of automatism lead each of us to this rich and unique personal complex, but that to which we are led "differ[s] for everyone, to the exact degree that each person differs from another."[23] And he observes, in confirmation, not only how different each of the Abstract Expressionists who resorted to automatism are from one another—just as the Surrealists who resorted to it differ each from each—but how practitioners of the two movements differed generally from one another—"How different, in ultimate thrust, are each of these two movements." Motherwell, in personal conversation as well as in the interviews he granted, loved to describe the experiences which were peculiar to him, and which explained this or that feature of his paintings.

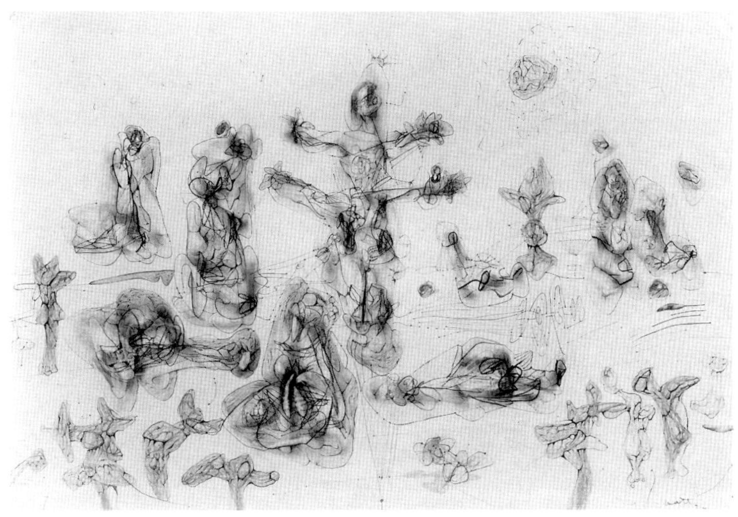

4. Matta. *Landscape*, 1940. Pencil and crayon on paper, 14¾ x 21½" (37.5 x 54.6 cm). Collection Lindy and Edwin Bergman, Chicago

The first time we met, after exchanging several letters, he took me to a restaurant he liked in Banksville, New York, where we spent some hours together talking, not about philosophy nor about art, but about our lives, about women, marriage, money, and children. He was immensely relieved, he told me afterward; he had had a kind of nightmare the night before about meeting me, and I think he must have feared that I was going to hold his feet to the fire of unremitting abstract discussion. Motherwell had reached a stage in his life where he was not anxious to talk abstractly about abstract ideas, having attained, as it were, to a philosophy of painting which served him admirably, as an artist of course, but also as someone who found himself increasingly called upon to talk about his art, and the history in which he had played a role: there was little reason for him to go back, so to speak, to the philosophical drawing board. Our conversations were always personal and delicious, and about what both of us, given our francophilia, would designate *les choses de la vie*. The difference was that in talking about himself he was talking about his art, for his art really was himself: "As for my lifelong interest in blue, it should be remembered that invariably I spend summers beside the sea."[24] "In some ways all an artist's past years remain intact, but particularly, as everybody knows, childhood impressions. [Dore Ashton] is the only one who has ever remarked how crucial was the fact that I grew up in pre-war California. . . . (The hills of California are ochre half the year)."[25]

Motherwell was singularly conscious of the contents of his preconscious. And his preconscious seems more to have been the scene of hills and oceans than that dank forest of Surrealist monsters and irrational fears, though he had plenty of his own private demons to deal with as well. It is the psychic compost of the daily experiences which form our characters and our work, and what automatism yields is continuous with our most common experiences. Matta evidently found this puzzling. In an essay for an exhibition of Matta's work at the Rose Art Museum at Brandeis University, Nancy K. Miller wrote that "the Americans Matta was intimate with . . . had never been completely comfortable with an art of images containing metaphorical ramifications."[26] The emphasis here should be on the word "images." For Matta's method was evidently close to a kind of game, consisting in making marks and then seeing what sort of image one could find in the mark, rather in the manner Leonardo describes in a famous and influential passage regarding the use of a mottled wall as an aid to invention. Matta is characteristically impish in describing what Leonardo did:

Leonardo da Vinci, as against the academic stillness that disturbed him in the work of Raphael and the classics, invented a new approach. He said that it was very boring to start with a white piece of paper and put a line on it, because all you are doing is putting what you know in the paper. He said you should start from a spot on the wall, humidity. If you look at a spot for a while, he said, something will start appearing by a funny process called hallucination. He would see whatever came in the hallucination, like we may see a horse in clouds. He said follow that image. When it comes to seeing things in the spot on the wall, you will be doing things you don't know—you will be discovering and inventing things. And you'll have more fun. That is my technique. If I see in the spot on the wall something I know, I erase it and wait until something else comes along. And then I see something which to me is fascinating because I don't know what it is. . . . I get amused. I get surprised. That's what I told the School of New York—I said "start like that and be very amusing."[27]

Being bored and having fun are hardly motivations we dare ascribe to Leonardo. Nor can we altogether imagine the serious young Americans as in the least driven by the desire to be amusing. Matta continued:

They made spots themselves—Pollock's spots, Motherwell's spots, etc. But then I told them to go the next step which is to get into the hallucination. I asked them to see things in the spot, because what they would see comes from our being, our social and emotional being. But they stopped there and didn't go into the next step.[28]

"Matta," Miller writes, "attributes the direction of Americans away from the poetic and philosophical toward an emphasis on the process of making pictures to American pragmatism."[29] As though it were practical considerations and concerns alone which made the Americans stop short with abstraction, and not go on into "hallucination." But in fact it was this refusal that was the entire crux of the "original creative principle." Motherwell, Miller goes on to say, "took his separate course in 1944 with a replacement definition for 'psychic automatism.' . . . He stated, 'Plastic automatism, as employed by modern masters like Masson, Miró, and Picasso, is actually very little a question of the unconscious. It is much more a plastic weapon with which to invent new forms.' "[30] But as we have seen, "new forms" was less the issue than not repeating, manneristically, old ways of being modern: was less an issue than enabling American artists to be modern without being sham Europeans. The new forms could come from whatever formed their spirits.

Abstraction was in some way internally connected with this. But abstraction, too, was something one could acquire, as an artist, and still be a mannerist. There was something infectious in Joan Miró, for example, and though Miró adamantly refused the label of abstract painter, the biomorphic blobs floating in thin space like amoeba under a cover glass lent themselves to abstract painting in America, as much so as did circles and triangles and squares. The "doodle" was neutral within what one might call the vocabulary of accepted abstract forms, but what was important about it, it seems to me, was the fact that it could be—perhaps had to be—done without being controlled by conscious mental process. But to have an identity of any kind, as a representation, would require conscious direction of the pen or brush. It would perhaps be unthinkable that someone could produce, say, the Ghent Altarpiece by doodling.[31] Even to draw the human torso requires some degree of conscious attention. So one has to disengage from the hand and let it find its way across the surface. In recollecting the meetings that took place between himself and the scarcely younger Americans—Pollock, Peter Busa, William Baziotes, Gerome Kamrowski, and Motherwell—Matta reported that he felt it important, if it was to be a group, that its members agree on a direction, find a vocabulary: "I remember that some of the first things we used to do were things like that—images of man. I felt we had to keep a degree of reference to reality. It couldn't be all explosion, you know."[32] And Matta spoke of going through a phase of "explosion," of "chaotic circles of drippings," which was "an expression of my anger in terms of the war," and then, afterward, his return to "anthropomorphic things," which "created a very definite divorce with the Americans, and especially with Motherwell. When he came to visit me, he would say, you are coming back to the figure." And Busa, in that same interview, added that Motherwell "had an abhorrence of the figure as I remember. As soon as we painted the figure it was as though it wasn't art."[33] It was as though the return to the figure meant a falling away from the universal creative principle. Memories differ. "Around 1943," Motherwell remembered in his letter to Edward Henning, "Matta abandoned us, as is his wont." "I became sort of the fellow who wasn't accepted," Matta remembered, in his conversation with Sidney Simon: "They were happy as long as my work expressed cosmic violence and whirlpools. I think it was a pity we didn't see more of each other. Because *action* is not necessarily the *hands*." But doodling, in Motherwell's sense, really was what the hands did, acting on their own. "It was a fratricidal situation in many ways," Busa recalled.

Motherwell gave every evidence of believing himself to have discovered what he set out to find, and in the retrospective mood more or less imposed upon him by the format of the increasingly frequent interview or historical inquiry of the seventies and eighties, he treated the "original creative principle" as a fait accompli. In his letter to Henning, he lays out the chief attributes of his discovery, very much as if he were describing a theorem that had been proved or a chemical breakthrough made. The letter is in numbered paragraphs, but paragraph 7, which treats of the original creative principle, is further broken down into lettered subsections. Rereading his letter, Motherwell expressed particular satisfaction with paragraph 7 as "worth the effort."

Here are the itemized attributes of psychic automatism from the letter to Henning, which I shall lay out serially and comment upon one by one.

A. Psychic automatism "cuts through any a priori influences—*it is not a style*." Because the psychic automatism of an artist *a* is not a style, one cannot speak of, or logically even think it sensible to look for, the influence of artist *b* on *a*. Hence in making art automatistically, it is logically not possible for an artist to be a "mannerist." In case what *a* does looks like what *b* has done, this is, if the former is automatistic, a strict coincidence. Hence, finally, in making use of psychic automatism, artists indemnify themselves against art-historical explanation of their work because their work, strictly, originates with *them*. Styles can be shared, so that it sometimes is difficult to tell which artist within a given style did which work, as in the case of Picasso and Georges Braque at a certain stage of Analytic Cubism, or Henri Matisse and André Derain at a certain moment in the history of Fauvism. With the first generation of Abstract Expressionists—and this is a confirmation of Motherwell's claim—there is no single style: Pollock, Willem de Kooning, Newman, Clyfford Still, Rothko, Motherwell himself, all look like no one other than themselves. One unquestioned truth is that de Kooning especially was easily mannerized, almost as though he had invented a vocabulary that other artists could use. Motherwell would explain this lapse from originality as due to the fact that those who followed de Kooning stood to him in the same relationship in which Gorky stood to Picasso or Miró: they were "mannerists." And the solution to this would have been issued like a prescription: psychic automatism!

B. Psychic automatism is "entirely *personal*." This means that the automatisms of artist *a* and of artist *b* are like the personalities of the two. They belong to them as native equipment, so to speak, and not as something acquired, by contrast with a manner or a style, or even a language. What emerges through automatism, since not acquired, cannot have been learned nor taught: an art school can give someone an opportunity to do things automatically, but cannot instruct anyone in what to do. Should the automatisms of two artists resemble each other, this again would be entirely accidental.

C. Psychic automatism "is by definition *original*, that is to say, that which originates in one's own being." This means that what one does automatistically stands in a very special kind of relationship to the artist who does it. Call this relationship "originary." Philosophers at one point sought to distinguish two kinds of causation, what they termed *immanent* from what they termed *transeunt* causation. The classic case of one billiard ball causing another to move by striking it would exemplify transeunt causation. The way in which an agent raises an arm voluntarily would exemplify immanent causation: there is no event which stands to the arm-raising in the relationship of cause to effect. The agent *simply* raises it.[34] One raises one's arm the way God creates the world, as an act of absolute beginning. This is what "originating" means in its deep metaphysical sense. Because there is no causal gap involved in immanent or originary causation, it is possible to say that the distinction between being and doing is overcome. One *is* what one *does*.

D. "It can be modified stylistically and in subject matter *at any point during the painting process*: for example the *same original primitive doodle* in the hands of, say, Paul Klee, Tanguy, Miró, Baziotes, Masson, and Pollock can end up as a Paul Klee, Tanguy, Miró, Baziotes, Masson, and Pollock, according to the aesthetic, ethic, and cultural values of each individual artist."

I must pause at this point, since I find this thought somewhat difficult to grasp: the modification of automatism, presumably, is not itself a further piece of automatism. This seems to imply that the modification of a doodle is not itself a doodle, and accordingly, that the higher cerebral processes—consciousness itself—must come in at this point. This may have been what Motherwell meant by "plastic" automatism, but since it involves the possibility of "stylistic" modification, it cannot itself be automatistic because automatism is not a style. Moreover, the very fact that the "same original primitive doodle" can be made by all the artists enumerated, suggests that their differences cannot be in automatism but in the modifications. I feel that this is where Motherwell should have borne down a little harder on his point. It suggests that the differences are not "original" but have to do with "aesthetic, ethic, and cultural values"—and these cannot be "personal," in a sense at least, that excludes their being shared. It sounds, in any case, as if the "modification" of the doodle is more important than the doodle itself.

E. Motherwell here expresses his belief that psychic automatism is "the most powerful creative principle—unless collage is—consciously developed in twentieth century art." He notes that collage too "is also partly free association," and it is instructive to recognize, through this bracketing together of collage and psychic automatism, that the word "principle" means in Motherwell's vocabulary "way of art-making." Both ways involve the conscious abandonment of consciousness, but then, at a certain point in the process, they both bring in conscious process, working consciously, as in the "modification" Motherwell brings in under D. It is the abandonment of consciousness in doodling and in tearing paper that is of most interest to him. My sense is that subsequent modification is not the originary upsurge of art that interested him. On the other hand, it may help explain why automatism led to the making of great art whereas it did not lead, in the hands of the Surrealist poets, to the making of great literature. It did not, at least to the degree that it was inconsistent with stream-of-conscious free association to rewrite, impose structure, control the final product. It is often observed that the way words relate to words in *Finnegans Wake*—as in the stream-of-consciousness passages of *Ulysses*—exemplifies to perfection what the Surrealists aspired to. But neither *Finnegans Wake* nor *Ulysses* were verbal doodles. Joyce controlled and shaped. And so, of course, did Motherwell. The only painter that at least on the surface seemed through and through automatist was Pollock in his drip phase, which raised the doodle to a transcendent power.

It is worth observing, after this, the degree to which Motherwell's automatism satisfies the conditions he lays down. There is an India-ink drawing on tracing paper of 1978 that is untitled, which fits, after all, with its status as a doodle (fig. 5). This work—when published as plate 129 in Arnason's *Robert Motherwell* (second edition)—elicited the following observation from the artist:

> I have been known as a proponent of "psychic automatism" in the form of what I used to call doodling, but following a recent book on children's art, I now prefer the usage "artful scribbling." But I am even better known for the imagery of my *Elegy to the Spanish Republic* series. It is still surprising to me that most persons have failed to see the connection between "artful scribbling" and the *Spanish Elegy* motif. The seeming contradiction disappears if one knows that nearly all the *Spanish Elegies* begin with "artful scribbling."

The untitled 1978 drawing has the feel of Japanese "grass-style" calligraphy, rapid and cursive, elegant and wiry. It traces the movement of the hand that inscribes it, the way we can imagine a line in the ice records the arabesque of a figure skater improvising a movement. At almost dead center of the paper, the line goes left, pivots and turns down and then curves right and, making two subcurves as it ascends, it reaches a point on the same level at which it began—whereupon it performs a small loop, curves slowly up, pivots, and then trails gracefully off as it descends. That is the main figure: to the left, it is touched by a sort of bell shape. There are two diagonals, one broken, with a line at about thirty degrees to the unbroken one. The artist has violated the grace of the basic figures by thickening the left sides of both main figures. It is very simple. One could count the strokes. There is nothing referential, but it is masterly and it could not easily be thought of as done by anyone but Motherwell. It is an abstract autograph of which the artist must have thought enough that he kept it and allowed it to be collected. It is about as basic an illustration as one might find of the "original creative principle" realizing itself through an artful scribble by a hand that conveys delicacy, sensitivity, and strength. One can see in it the history of unconscious decisions and reversals. I note that it is unsigned, as if the signature would introduce another element the drawing is too fragile to sustain.

I draw attention to the fact that this drawing has three verticals: the two left-hand curves, which the artist has drawn over to give them strength, and then the right-hand vertical. The two left-hand curves form a pair, and in an attenuated way one can see a nascent *Spanish Elegy* taking form. In his published comment on this sheet, Motherwell pointed to three drawings that build toward an *Elegy*, as if stages in a single emerging work. The first (fig. 6), pencil on mylar, has two continuous horizontal elements, as if the edges of a table. Between the edges, hence on top of the table, are some hesitant curves, suggesting the beginning of a still life, were the drawing identified as by Cézanne, preparatory for an array of apples and dishes. There is a dance of stronger verticals, like accents, five or six in all, depending upon how one is counting. These

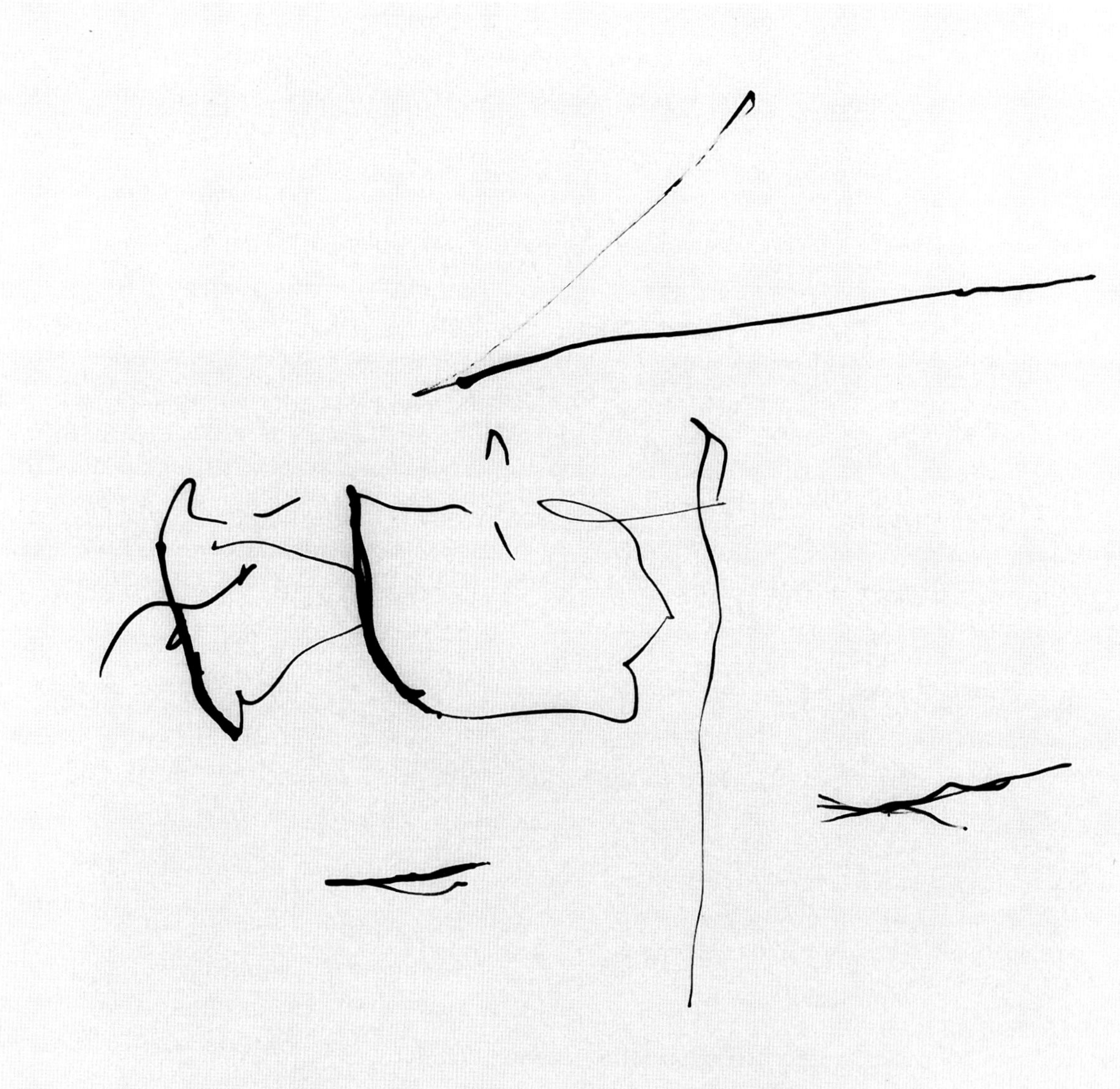

5. Robert Motherwell. *Untitled*, 1978. Ink on tracing paper, 13½ x 16¾″ (34.3 x 42.6 cm). Collection Dedalus Foundation, Inc. (Dedalus no. D78–2179)

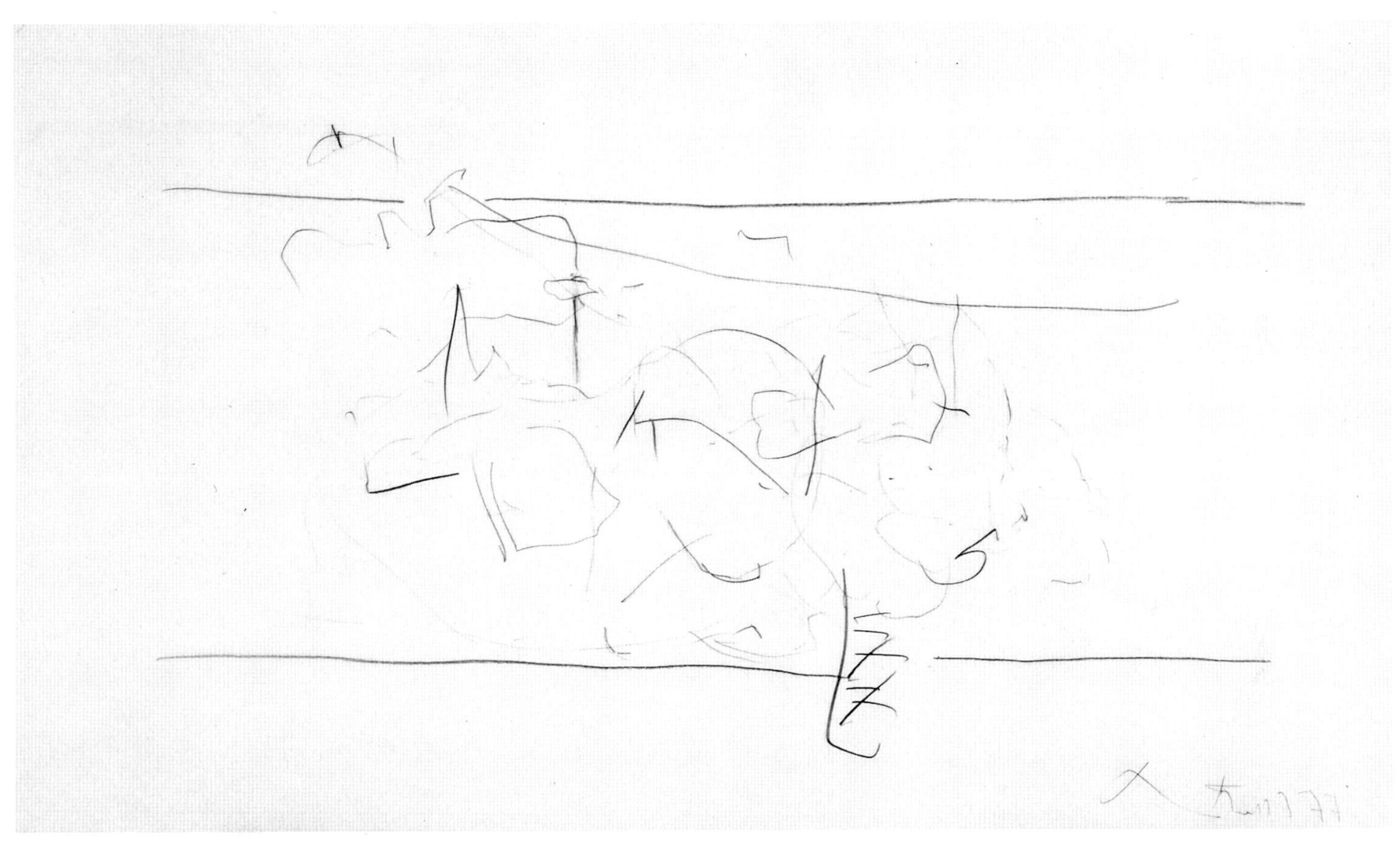

6. Robert Motherwell. *Untitled*, 1977. Pencil on mylar, 13½ x 23" (34.3 x 58.4 cm). Collection Dedalus Foundation, Inc. (Dedalus no. D77–1344)

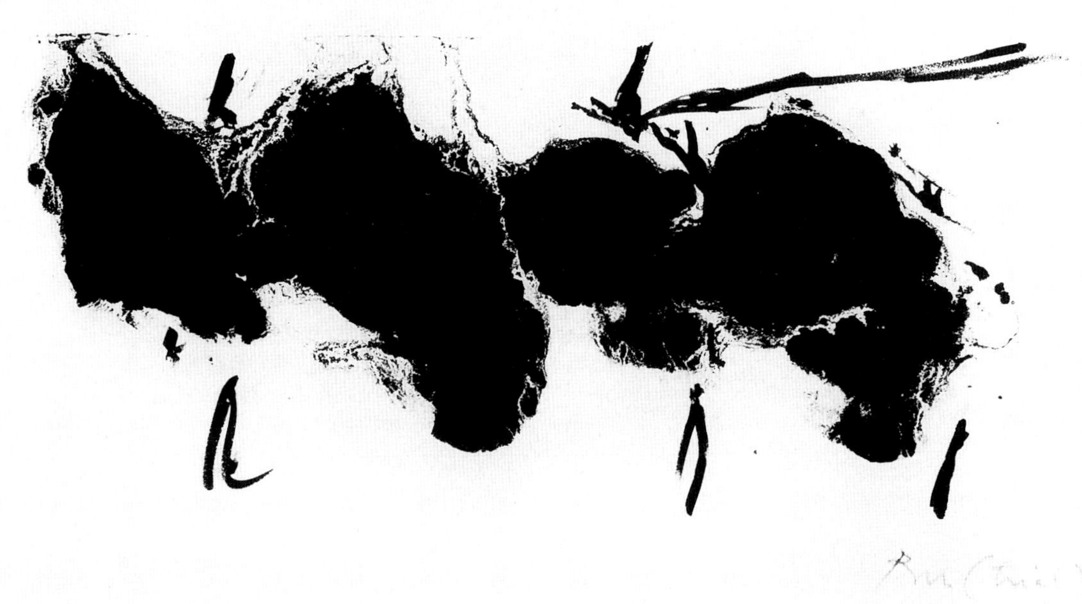

7. Robert Motherwell. *Altamira Elegy*, 1979–80. Lithograph from two aluminum plates; image: 4 x 9½" (10.1 x 23.5 cm); paper: 9⅜ x 11⅞" (23.8 x 30.2 cm). Collection Dedalus Foundation, Inc. (Belknap no. 229)

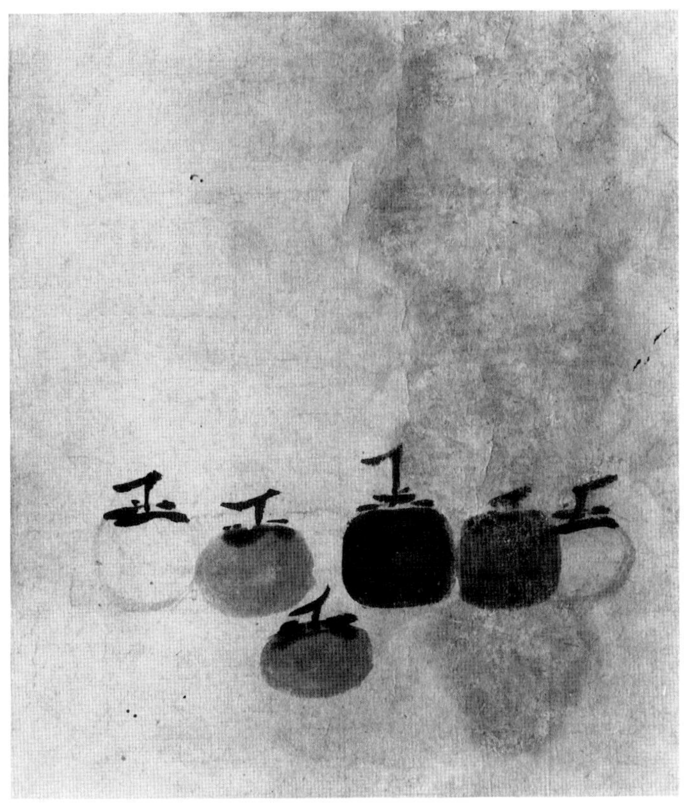

8. Mokkei (Mu-Ch'i, early 13th century). *Six Persimmons*. Ink on paper, 14 x 11½" (35.6 x 29.2 cm). Daitoku-ji, Kyoto

seem less *Elegy*-like than the nesting curves in our previous example. But in the lithographic *Altamira Elegy* (fig. 7), where the grass-style fibrillations have been exchanged for something heavy, as if deposited by a charged brush, there could be four shawled figures or four brooding trees, and there is a tense rhythm left and right and left. What gives it the elegiac feel is the heaviness, the downwardness of the forms, as if sorrow refused to let them rise. But perhaps one reads too much into it, knowing that the word "elegy" appears in the title. The four heavy forms could be bunches of grapes, or fruits on a table, like a famous Japanese painting of persimmons (fig. 8). And one wonders if the elegiac feeling of the great *Spanish Elegies* is not in part a function of scale. The third study in this sequence (fig. 9) is elegant black sweeps of acrylic paint on canvasboard, and it is too lyrical to be elegiac; the figures could be dancing within the space of a stage. I make these critical observations to suggest that more than artful scribbling is involved in transforming an artful scribble into an elegy. One has to achieve that feeling, and it is here, doubtless, that the values Motherwell brought in under his letter D do their work in finding a visual equivalent to the feeling with which the artist wished to infuse his drawings. If we subtract from an *Elegy* an artful scribble, the remainder is filled with what makes the difference between art and great art, depending upon what

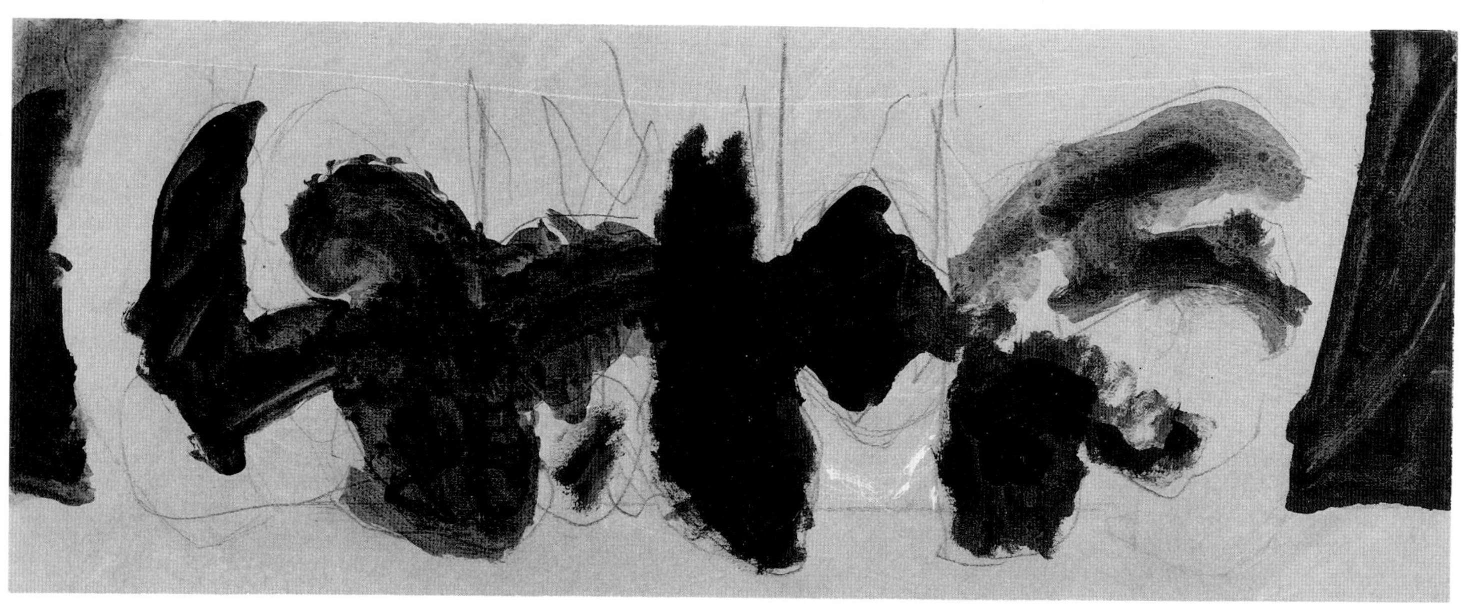

9. Robert Motherwell. *Elegy Study,* 1976. Acrylic and pencil on canvasboard, 10 x 25" (25.4 x 63.5 cm). Collection Dedalus Foundation, Inc. (Dedalus no. P76–1080)

Motherwell concedes are "the limitations of one's own beingness."[35]

In order to see what Motherwell refers to as "unadulterated automatism," one must turn to the *Lyric Suite* of 1965 (plates 14–37). These are unrevised paintings with watercolor brush on rice-paper sheets of a uniform size (11 by 9"). One is here especially conscious of the physical properties of the paper to absorb the ink, and of the ink to spread "like a spot of oil on a smooth surface."[36] The medium allowed no revision, really, and though the paintings differ one from another in terms of the original impulse each reveals, of blots and splatters, dashes and drips, the feeling is not particularly of something human *in* the space—no mourning figures, no architecture, no dance—but at most of something outside the human range altogether, like microscopic encounters and engulfments by minuscule creatures of one another, or of perturbations in a cloud chamber. The items in the *Lyric Suite* are cosmological notations, but what we are put in mind of is the action of making them rather than what they mean. They represent their own making, and are, I suppose, exemplifications of the theory that explains them. And they express a determination to be no more than that, as if Motherwell had decided once and for all to see how far automatism could take him. They enable *us* to see how crucial the factors Motherwell implies in D are: Nothing else, after all, is "unadulterated automatism." Automatism is necessary to the great art he achieved, but not, as philosophers say, altogether sufficient. He tells us he had finished about six hundred when the death of David Smith brought the series to an end. One cannot help but feel that death, friendship, loss reminded him that there was more to art than art.

Notes

1. Barbaralee Diamonstein, "An Interview with Robert Motherwell," in H. H. Arnason, *Robert Motherwell*, 2nd ed., new and revised (New York: Harry N. Abrams, 1982), esp. p. 228.
2. Preface to the Second Edition, *Immanuel Kant's Critique of Pure Reason*, trans. Norman Kemp Smith (London: Macmillan & Co., 1963), p. 11.
3. *Discours de la méthode pour bien conduire la raison et chercher la vérité dans les sciences* is the full title of Descartes's text of 1637, which was published together with *La Dioptrique, les météores, et la géometrie*, characterized by Descartes as "des essais de cette méthode."
4. Diamonstein, "An Interview with Robert Motherwell," p. 228. I find it endearing that Motherwell should have used the word *doodling* where a Surrealist would have sought out some immeasurably more portentous term. Doodles, after all, are in their nature ephemeral and rarely of any consequence, though they have a possible diagnostic value. In Frank Capra's film *Mr. Deeds Goes to Town* (1937), a witness in a trial scene uses the word *doodle*, which is not understood by the court. The implication is that it is part of the patois of the bumpkin community from which Mr. Deeds comes, and my inference is that it entered American English through that scene. The scene would not have been funny if the term were part of a viewer's language in 1937.
5. Kant, *Critique of Pure Reason*, p. 32.
6. Ibid., p. 33.
7. And possibly, or at times, he was also interested in the act of pure painting, which of course is a different matter.
8. Arnason, *Robert Motherwell*, pp. 80, 162, reprints the definitions of "open" from the *Random House Dictionary of the English Language*. It compasses eighty-one entries, plus (as number eighty-two) "the open." As to which of these Motherwell had in mind, he would answer, "I'm open."
9. I once heard Rudolph Arnheim deliver a lecture called, I believe, "The Toad and the Centipede," in which the toad, admiring the grace of the centipede in its dancing, asks merely what the centipede does with the thirty-seventh leg on the left side when it lifts the seventeenth leg on the right. As the centipede tries to find out, it loses the power of dance. Presumably, it learned to dance by learning to place its legs in prescribed positions, but the action became automatic in a sense of the term in which something can be at once automatic and inspired.

10. James M. Baldwin, ed., *Dictionary of Philosophy and Psychology* (New York: Macmillan, 1901), vol. 1, pp. 55–56.

11. As it was for his disciple, the painter Gordon Onslow-Ford, who wrote Breton from Mexico that "Whether I want it or not, the depths of my imagination are stronger than I am, and it's there that I live." Cited in Martica Sawin, *Surrealism in Exile and the Beginning of the New York School* (Cambridge, Mass., and London: MIT Press, 1995), p. 260.

12. André Breton, *Manifestoes of Surrealism*, trans. Richard Seaver and Helen R. Lane (Ann Arbor: University of Michigan Press, 1972).

13. Cited in Dore Ashton, *The New York School: A Cultural Reckoning* (New York: Viking Press, 1972), p. 128.

14. Or in the paintings of Gordon Onslow-Ford. "Onslow-Ford was still following a practice of keeping notebooks at his bedside and attempting to draw his dreams while in a semiawake state, so that in its genesis his work was spontaneous and automatist," Sawin writes. "Yet a large work like *The Luminous Land* was months in the making, its light-dark contrasts carefully worked out . . ." (*Surrealism in Exile*, p. 261).

15. Hal Foster, *Compulsive Beauty* (Cambridge, Mass., and London: MIT Press, 1993), pp. xii–xiii.

16. "Interview with Sidney Simon: Concerning the Beginnings of the New York School, 1939–1943," in *The Collected Writings of Robert Motherwell*, ed. Stephanie Terenzio (New York and Oxford: Oxford University Press, 1992), p. 160.

17. Letter to Edward Henning (18 October 1978), in *Collected Writings*, p. 230.

18. Ibid.

19. Diamonstein, "Interview with Robert Motherwell," p. 228.

20. Ibid.

21. Letter to Edward Henning (18 October 1978) in *Collected Writings*, p. 229.

22. Ibid. Motherwell's point, obviously enough, was that Americans do not need to do something in particular to be American artists. They in particular would not need to paint the American landscape, the folk, or to illustrate American songs. He certainly always thought of himself as American *von Haus aus*—as the Germans say. It is interesting that American English lacks a comparable expression. We have only similes like "As American as apple pie."

23. Ibid.

24. Arnason, *Robert Motherwell*, p. 172.

25. Diamonstein, "Interview with Robert Motherwell," p. 229.

26. Nancy K. Miller, *Matta: The First Decade* (Waltham, Mass.: Rose Art Museum, Brandeis University, 1982), p. 31.

27. Quoted in ibid., p. 13.

28. Ibid.

29. Ibid., p. 31.

30. Ibid.

31. It would be a marvelous topic for a Saul Steinberg drawing to have the Ghent Altarpiece take form beneath the doodler's pen.

32. Sidney Simon, "Concerning the Beginnings of the New York School, 1939–1940: An Interview with Peter Busa and Matta," *Art International* 11 (Summer 1967), p. 18.

33. Ibid., p. 19.

34. I have designated such events "basic actions," and have worked out in considerable detail the theory of such actions and the kinds of causation they involve, in my *Analytical Philosophy of Action* (Cambridge: Cambridge University Press, 1973).

35. Diamonstein, "Interview with Robert Motherwell," p. 230.

36. Quoted in Arnason, *Robert Motherwell*, p. 154.

Provisional Dualism: Robert Motherwell and Zen

Stephen Addiss

Robert Motherwell's abiding interest in East Asian art is confirmed by the marginal scoring in two books in his own library: *Chinese Calligraphers and Their Art* by Ch'en Chih-mai and *Zen Painting* by Yasuichi Awakawa. The passages he marked indicate just how fully he read as a visual artist, and how much he loved the medium of painting. He delighted in every aspect of his craft; for example, he noted three different passages about how ink was made in China from the soot of burned tree branches mixed with glue made from the horns of animals.[1] This interest is matched in Motherwell's own writings; he noted in 1950 that "The chemistry of the pigments is interesting: ivory black, like bone black, is made from charred bones or horns. . . . Sometimes I wonder, laying in a great black stripe on the canvas, what animal's bones (or horns) are making the furrows of my picture."[2]

In traditional China, it was known that the best way to get a master artist to begin a painting or a work of calligraphy was to offer him exceptionally fine paper. Upon receiving a gift of various Japanese handmade papers, Motherwell said with obvious anticipation, "They're ravishing. . . . All of these beg to be marked on."[3] "I infinitely prefer paper to any other medium," he confessed. "It's a struggle to get a canvas to have the beautiful surface that paper, by nature, already has. . . . Something that's very important, that I call viscosity, is the resistance of the material; it can drive me crazy, [but] some I find much more sympathetic—for example, ink on rice paper is music."

Motherwell's greatest excursion with Japanese rice paper was his *Lyric Suite* of 1965 (see plates 14–37). As a way of breaking free from a serious painting block, he bought one thousand sheets of *unryu* ("dragon cloud") paper; determined to paint without critical judgments or revisions, he set out during a hot New York summer to cover these sheets with American fountain-pen ink. "I didn't want to be involved in fake Oriental things . . . so I used English [brushes] for the *Lyric Suite* because the shape of the brush also partly determines the kind of mark you're going to make." The particular combination of materials led to a great deal of bleeding of the ink. He was delighted. "Like the first stages of a passionate affair. With paper!"[4] Some of them, he later recalled, "would spread so much . . . they would totally surprise me. I would watch them like baking bread as they browned and changed. . . . [They] self-increased at least fifty percent, and it was amazing to see them on the floor as it took half an hour to see them expanding."

Like an ancient potter working with constantly changing earth and fire, Motherwell had found a way to paint that allowed the nature of the materials to collaborate with him in the process of creating the artistic result. "Art is a form of action, a drama, a process. . . . Of course, everyone undergoes risks just by living. From one point of view, the artist's function is to give each risk its proper style."[5]

Finding the proper style for each risk involves finding the proper medium. One of the joys of working with paper is the variety it offers; the experience can be quite opposite to Motherwell's suffusing *unryu* with fountain-pen ink in hot and humid weather. But whatever the kind of paper, it promotes spontaneity of expression. Frequently, "the paper absorbs and dries almost instantly . . . and I think that unconsciously makes me [create] less considered works; they're more a throw of dice, you just do it and that's that. . . . [On canvas,] painting is just the opposite, a complex of possibilities, what Kierkegaard called 'the despair of the aesthetic.' . . . On paper, everything is fresh; I like painting that's fresh-looking. . . . Japanese calligraphy always makes my heart stand still because it's completely and totally fresh."

In traditional East Asian calligraphy, there is no way to correct a stroke, and so the ink lives on the paper, a direct expression of the character of the artist as expressed in an individual moment. It becomes, as John Cage used to offer as his definition of art, "a doing, leaving traces." For Motherwell, paper offered the potential for creative dialogue with the material, including the possibility of surprises. Discussing his collage series *Night Music*, he stated, "The subject matter *is* paper . . . [working on it] was an apparition to me; I hadn't the remotest idea of what was going to happen . . . and that was part of my fascination with it. . . . Each one was . . . the object revealing itself to me."

Self and Transcending Self

Of his various markings in the two East Asian art books, one phrase was triple underlined by Motherwell: "a kind of provisional dualism."[6] Awakawa in *Zen Painting* was here writing about balancing transcendent values with those of everyday life, and for Motherwell this can be seen in the specific context of his art.

The process of painting, for Motherwell, took place as a subtle and complex relationship between the artist and the medium. As he wrote in 1949, "A painter, in working a canvas, sensing it all over, watching it shift and change and slowly emerge from its flat void . . . may have the illusion that the picture is not being painted by him, but rather is painting him, that he who is supposed to be the subject has become the object, that the picture knows him better than he knows it."[7] Two years later, Motherwell described the work of his colleagues and himself: "Spontaneity and a lack of self-consciousness is emphasized; the pictures stare back as one stares at them; the process of painting them is conceived as an adventure, without preconceived ideas. . . . Fidelity to what occurs between oneself and the canvas, no matter how unexpected, becomes central."[8]

Every painter, poet, and composer knows this potentially dangerous dialogue with the medium and material, in which the fear of chaos may arouse great anxiety, while the need to control can stifle exploration. A certain number of creative people, for at least some of their works, intuitively understand the totality of the work and merely have to bring it forth; one imagines Mozart worked this way. Others, like Beethoven, struggled, as can be seen in his heavily reworked sketchbooks. Motherwell often worked quickly and spontaneously, as in the *Lyric Suite*, but he also continued to revise large paintings over long periods of time; some works in his studio when he died had been "in process" for years. That is one example of his provisional dualism.

Motherwell liked creating works on paper in part because "there's no way of correcting them; at times that's a great relief." But he also believed that "the real content of a painting is the rhythms and the proportions, just as a real person is his own rhythms and proportions, not what he happens to say to you when you meet him on the corner."[9] This can lead to endless changes, trying to get the rhythm right. Questioned about the inspiration for one of his works in an exhibition, Motherwell realized that the painting had "been painted over several times and radically changed in shape, in balance, in all kinds of things, in weight. At one time it was too black, at one time the rhythm of it was too regular, at one time there wasn't enough variation in the weights of the shapes."[10]

But how does one know when it *is* right? "It's a decision not only aesthetically—will this look more beautiful?—it's a decision that has to do with one's gut . . . to do with one's sense of sensuality . . . to do with one's sense of life. . . . If it took two months to paint, my basic character has to be involved. I mean on a single day or in a few hours, I might be in a very peculiar state, to make something much lighter, much heavier, much smaller, much bigger than I normally would. But when you steadily work at something, your whole being comes out."[11]

The sense of one's personal character determining art is parallel to the East Asian idea of brushwork coming from the inner nature of the artist. A passage from Ch'en Chih-mai's book on calligraphy that was scored by Motherwell states that "the artistic worth of a particular style is always determined by its purity, what Chou Hsing-lien called the 'face,' which alone belongs to the calligrapher, as personal to him as the timbre of his voice or the twinkle of his eyes."[12] Another marked passage in the same book is significant because it contains the word *automatism*, which was so important to Motherwell as a method of bringing forth the inner self: "a calligraphic piece is a type of automatism, a realization of the artistic concept through the application of sophisticated brushwork. When the calligrapher's art is mature, his work is a grand display of linear ecstasies."[13]

With Motherwell, however, the process of painting was quite different from the usual Chinese method of fully developing a mental image of the work before starting. In contrast, Motherwell searched for what he called "feeling" by exploring the unknown; in his larger paintings, this often involved making many changes, as he explained on a number of occasions:

The game is organizing states of feeling . . . [through] light, color, weights, solidity, airiness, lyricism.[14]

My pictures have lots of mistakes buried in them—an X-ray would disclose crimes—layers of consciousness, of willing. They are a succession of humiliations resulting from the realization that only in a state of quickened subjectivity—of freedom from conscious notions . . . —do I find the unknown, which nevertheless I recognize when I come upon it, for which I am always searching.[15]

No wonder the artist is constantly placing and displacing, relating and rupturing relationships; his task is to find a complex of qualities whose feeling is just right—veering toward the unknown and chaos, yet ordered and related in order to be apprehended.[16]

But look for yourselves. . . . If the *amounts* of black or white are right, they will have condensed into quality, into feeling.[17]

Transforming the materials of painting into feeling while searching for the unknown puts a great stress on the self, and the self-confidence, of the artist. In 1970, Motherwell told a group of high-school students:

The "nerve" is in not being afraid of what's in your gut, and most people, unless they've had to face their gut, are terrified of it. . . . It's very easy to make a good picture *if you're not trying to*. All of you. I could choose things from your rooms that would be much better than any of the pictures you're making *on purpose*. What would be very difficult would be to get one of you to sign and exhibit it; by doing that to say, "This is my identity." In that sense, there is as much risk in staying at home drawing one line, as there is in getting into a space capsule and going to the moon. But the risks are psychological and spiritual.[18]

These risks took a toll on many of the original Abstract Expressionists; Motherwell was an exception among them in that he reached a full lifespan and was creatively productive to the end. Artists of other eras and other cultures had not depended so fully on their inward sensibilities, being able to rely on more fully accepted visions of reality and value within their societies. But the Abstract Expressionists not only expressed their vision of the world, they also discovered it, through the process of painting. Motherwell commented in 1950, "It is only through the process of making that I really know—if you will excuse a sloppy idiom—what I feel about the world. The content of any art is just the world as felt."[19] And here another provisional dualism emerges: Is the content the world or the self? "Any work of art, even a 'bad' one, is a self-expression; its qualities depend on the qualities of the self who made it. An unbalanced, incomplete self makes an ill-proportioned, fragmentary work."[20]

But what for the artist may be balanced might not seem that way to a critic. For example, Michael Brenson wrote in the *New York Times* on October 29, 1983, that "Motherwell's painting is not always coherent. . . . In the 1970 'Elegy to the Spanish Republic,' for example . . . the artist was never able totally to take control. The rectangular and ovoid forms do not seem to know where they are going. They face out, they face in. The composition seems to stagger like a drunk tottering down the street. One reason why space in this and other paintings seems to reel is that Mr. Motherwell did not have a painter's touch."

How can we resolve this issue? Is it totally subjective to each viewer, or are there more universal values? Or might this question too create a provisional dualism? On the one hand, through his identification with his art, Motherwell was being attacked personally; on the other hand, he might not entirely have disagreed with the critic. For example, in interviews from his final years he stated:

> I've always been clumsy about making transitions between stronger areas. . . . I'm essentially self-taught, which obviously has great limitations, but I also think to myself that in another way it has the advantage that I can't betray myself with skill because I don't have any skill, and so I'd rather just remain a lumpen-artist.
>
> After 73 years, I can still make an awful picture; after 73 years, I'm just beginning to learn the rudiments of painting.[21]
>
> To put it very simply, I don't know how to paint on purpose. So, after days or weeks of suffering, finally I just pick up a tool and make marks, then the internal dialectic takes over, and I can truthfully say that quite often I'm more astonished than anybody else could be at what comes out. Yet, if it's any good, I recognize myself.[22]
>
> What I know how to do is make *the experience* of making a picture.
>
> The process of painting is constantly a self-criticism—is this the truth or not?[23]

This sense of truth was crucial. Early in his career, Motherwell had declared of the Abstract Expressionists, "We know what we believe by what we paint. Our criterion of when a canvas is finished is not how beautiful it is, but how true to our experience as felt."[24] Motherwell had here reached the point of equating feeling with truth, something that many might find surprising. However, he made it clear elsewhere that feeling is not the same as emotion:

> Commonly people use the two words interchangeably, e.g., someone's full of feeling . . . or he's too emotional, or conversely, he's too cold. By the word feeling, I mean something very specific. . . . I mean just the way things feel. For example, the California sun on a clear day makes the air aromatic, etc. In one sense feeling is the objective response to what externally actually is. For me emotion is something that originates in oneself. . . . In the 'Spanish Elegies' and several other things, I seem to have hit something which, though meant to arouse feeling, also arouses some deep emotion. In the Jungian sense of something archetypal. . . . Maybe there's something inside people that is more universal than one's immediate responses to the outside world.[25]

Here Motherwell is suggesting that feeling can be shared (all of us would sense the air in California) but emotions are usually more individual (to someone it might suggest a happy or an unhappy childhood). In this sense, feeling is a truth that extends to all of us, if momentarily, while emotion is more personally limited. But the deeper emotion (which Motherwell suggests may be archetypal) could represent another layer of truth. If an artist can reach and express it in his own being, then he has transcended the self through the self.

Zenga and Abstract Expressionism

The question of self and self-transcendence is also addressed in the field of Japanese Zen art. Since 1600, Zenga (Zen painting and calligraphy) has not been created by professional painters working for temples, but by enlightened Zen Masters themselves. After viewing some of their scrolls, one learns quickly to identify the works of major Zen Masters such as Hakuin, Sengai, Nantembo, and others, because their styles are so personal. This is hardly strange in view of traditional East Asian art theory, which holds that the marks of the brush cannot help but reveal the individual personality and character of the artist. Yet, since these Buddhist monks had presumably gone beyond personal ego, why should we find so clear a personal sense of touch in their "brush traces." Is this also a provisional duality?

Zen paintings and calligraphy are done as a Zen activity, and used primarily as teachings. The monk regarded as the most important Zen Master of the past five hundred years, Hakuin Ekaku (1685–1769) must have spent much of his final decades with the brush, since thousands of his works remain from his sixties, seventies, and early eighties; perhaps he believed that visual art could convey meanings that words could not. His paintings and calligraphy were usually done very simply, without regard for formal skill, and even today many lovers of Japanese art have no interest in them. Worse, they are offended; by deliberately avoiding "beauty" Zen art sometimes gives rise to disdain for much the same reasons that Abstract Expressionism created a furor in its own day.

Both arts represent the experience rather than the form, or, as a Chinese connoisseur might say, the bones and not the skin. Motherwell noted, "True originality is that which originates in one's own being."[26] A painting by Hakuin of Daruma (fig. 1), the first Zen patriarch, represents Hakuin's experience of meditation more than it does a portrait of Daruma. Hakuin has here ventured closer to abstraction than most artists of his time, but he and other Zen Masters sometimes went much further, rendering Daruma with only one or two brushstrokes (fig. 2).

Motherwell scored a page of Awakawa's book illustrating a similar image and noting that "It is typical of the Zenga that the founder of the whole sect should be disposed of in this way, with one swift motion of the brush."[27] This process was what Motherwell described in his own work as a kind of visual shorthand: "Abstraction adds emphasis, and emphasis vivifies life."[28] For Motherwell, "Authentic creativity puts us again in connection with what's alive and real. . . . You see, the whole problem is for one's experience to be authentic."[29] Similarly, for those who prefer Japanese paintings of Daruma done by Zen Masters to those done by more skilled (more "aesthetic") professional artists, the authenticity of the meditation experience is what counts the most.

Motherwell, however, marked several passages in Awakawa's book in which the author noted that it took some training and technical excellence to produce the finest Zen art: "Neither literature nor the visual arts can exist without the techniques necessary to self-expression. . . . The increasing popularity of the work of Hakuin and Sengai, those twin peaks of the art of Zenga, is due to the fact that they were not only, as goes without saying, profoundly experienced in the field of Zen, but were also exceptionally gifted as artists."[30]

Awakawa also wrote that Zen works are "both aesthetic objects and manifestations of universal principles."[31] So there are two provisional dualities at work here: the first between technique and experience, the second between beauty and meaning. Another sentence scored by Motherwell in *Zen Painting* attempted to resolve this latter question by means of the same conception of "truth" that Motherwell himself believed in: "Seen in this light—when a work of art is an expression of truth—the distinction between didactic art and 'art for art's sake' becomes blurred or disappears altogether; in the same

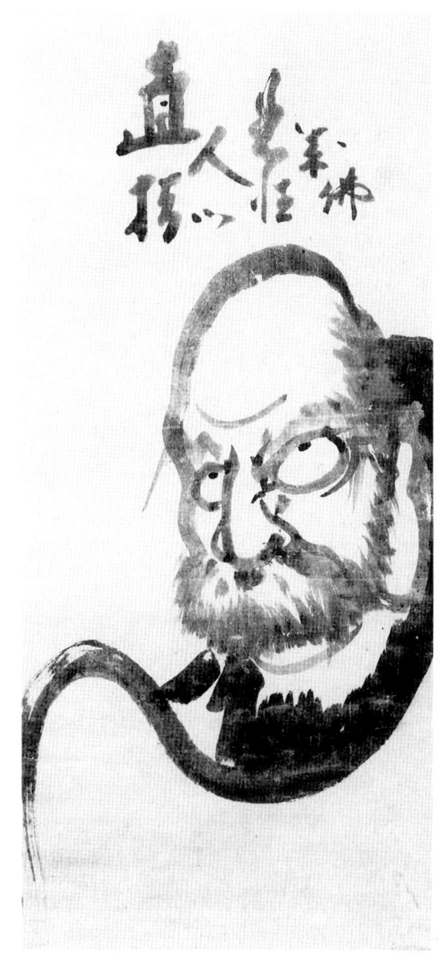

1. Hakuin Ekaku (1685–1768). *Daruma*. Ink on paper, 49½ x 21¾″ (125.7 x 55.2 cm). Formerly Yabumoto collection, Tokyo

2. Konoe Nobutada (1565–1614). *Single-Line Daruma*. Ink on paper, 13⅜ x 22¼″ (34 x 56.5 cm). Private collection

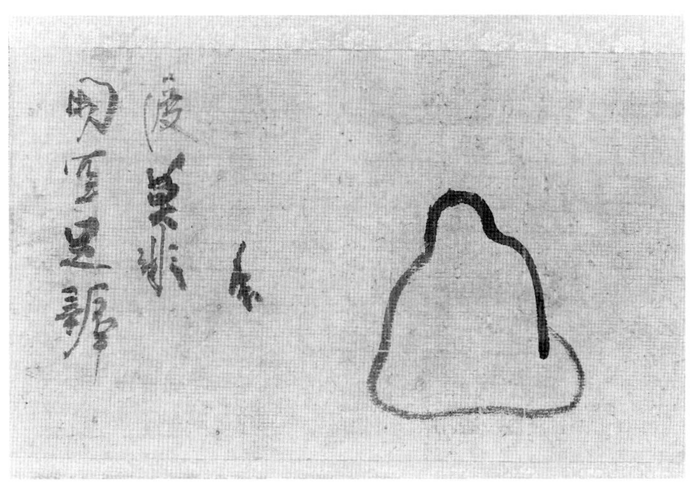

way, art 'for the sake of the self' and art 'for the sake of the ideal' fuse together and become art expressing the universal."[32]

Motherwell and Zen

Motherwell first became interested in East Asian art while still in San Francisco, and had read about Zen at least by the mid-1940s. Considering their similarities in approach, we may ask how much he learned from Zen painting and calligraphy. He scored this passage from Awakawa:

> A man who can paint Zenga need not be a Zen monk. If a painter is steeped in Zen, then his work will automatically have a Zen flavor. . . . "Contemplation" entails, of course, an act of selection in terms of a particular work of art—taking a particular scene or aspect of human life as it unfolds before one and emphasizing—knowing, understanding, feeling it as part of one's own experience. The Japanese word *kansho* translated here as "contemplation" means to "turn a Zen light on things," to become one with nature, and is part of personal development toward full insight. The important thing here is that the content, style, and subject matter of a painting are decided by the artist's own view of life.[33]

This is very close to Motherwell's own view. In 1973 he even called a group of charcoal sketches his "Zen series."[34]

Zen practice means discovering enlightenment, the Buddha, within oneself. To do this requires casting away illusions, and it is no accident that Zen paintings are made up of very clear, simple brushstrokes with ink on paper, not at all illusionistic. Similarly, Motherwell noted that "painting is flat space, and you can make it illusionary if you want to, but one of the main thrusts of modernism is to get rid of illusion . . . to get rid of the enchantment of illusion."[35]

As we shall see later, Motherwell occasionally found an East Asian calligraphic form of interest, but the only case I know of what may be a direct borrowing of Zen imagery comes from a famous scroll by Sengai Gibon (1750–1838), a Zen Master usually known for the warmth and wit of his paintings. The particular Sengai image that struck Motherwell, however, is a painting (illustrated in a full double-page spread in Awakawa's book) called *Circle, Triangle, Square* (fig. 3). Motherwell created several similar images, including a print in the *Hollow Men Suite* (plate 101). I asked Motherwell if he had had Sengai's work specifically in mind when he created his image, and he replied that he hadn't seen or directly thought about it for perhaps twenty years, but that the image must have been lodged in his subconscious.

Comparing the two images is instructive. Sengai's work is a painting with his signature in a line of calligraphy to the left; Motherwell's is a smaller and unsigned print. Sengai painted (as East Asians write) from right to left, while Motherwell seems to have begun in the center. Both put the square (actually a rectangle) on the left (although the reversal in printing Motherwell's etching must be acknowledged), but Sengai placed the triangle in the center as the linking form; Motherwell had the circle hold the center. Motherwell inverted his triangle and completely broke its form. Overlapping the shapes, both created active "negative" spaces within them. Both artists utilized "flying white" (the white of the paper showing through the dry brushstroke) in the square. Although Sengai varied the tone of ink for each shape and Motherwell did not, both saved their heaviest ink for the circle, the most primal of the three basic forms, which was executed first in each image. Finally, although neither adhered to pure geometry, the speed of Motherwell's gesture has significantly overcome the regularity implicit in the iconography itself.

What does this tell us? If one encountered these two works knowing nothing about the respective artists, which image would suggest that its author lived a more turbulent life during unsettled times? Which artist lived within a tradition, which one created a new tradition? Is one image more emotional? More

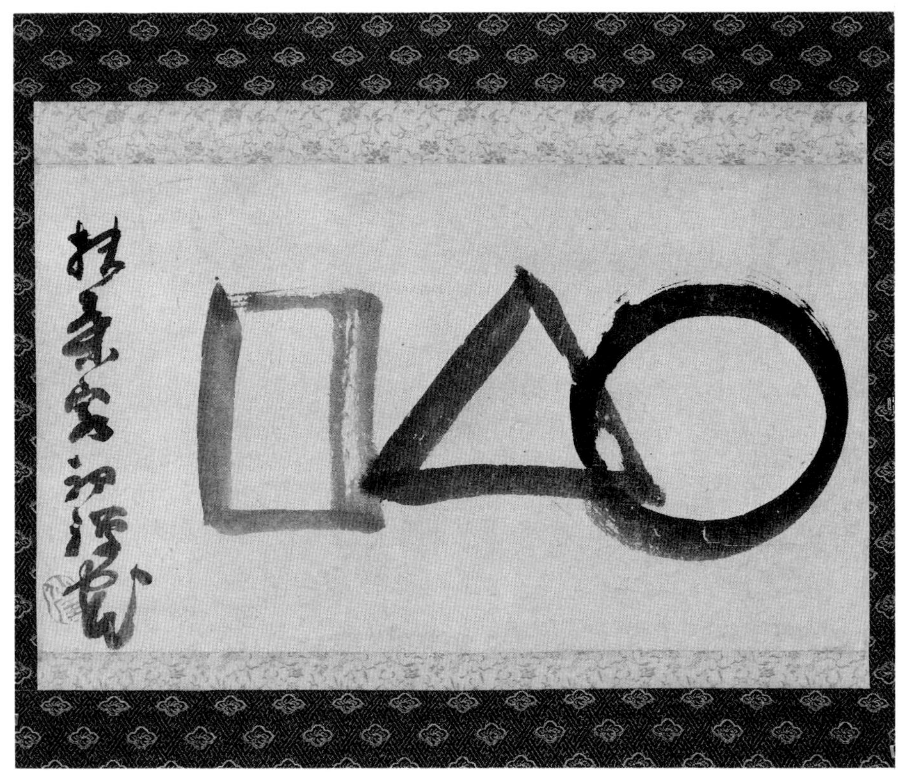

3. Sengai Gibon (1750–1838). *Circle, Triangle, Square.* Ink on paper, 11⅛ x 19" (28.3 x 48.3 cm). Idemitsu Museum of Arts, Tokyo

Eastern or Western? More modern? More conducive to meditation?

Historians of East Asian art are sometimes satisfied to find the model or predecessor for a work of art, but we should inquire further. Why did Motherwell retain and eventually re-create this image among all others? I suspect it was because of the primal nature of the forms. His comments on children's art are pertinent here: "Modern art is more closely rooted in children's art than is generally understood. . . . All children start with scribbling . . . with drawing around and around with circles. There's a whole sequential development with them that is universal . . . the same images at the same moment in human development. . . . That's one of the reasons I think art is really profoundly basic or generic to the human being."[36]

The circle, triangle, and square are among the most basic of forms that children draw and adults doodle. As well as admiring children's art, Motherwell had the deepest respect for doodling as the prelude to personal expression. It is perhaps for this reason that the image remained in his mind—and by no coincidence, Sengai's painting has been extremely popular in both Japan and the West, judging from the frequency of its reproduction in books and posters. In Japan, Sengai's simple image has given rise to many explanations of the "meaning" of its components, ranging from heaven, man, and earth to three forms of Buddhism, but the image transcends specific symbols. Sengai's image resonates with a deep, generic level of human development, and it is significant that by connecting the forms while leaving them imperfect, both Sengai and Motherwell

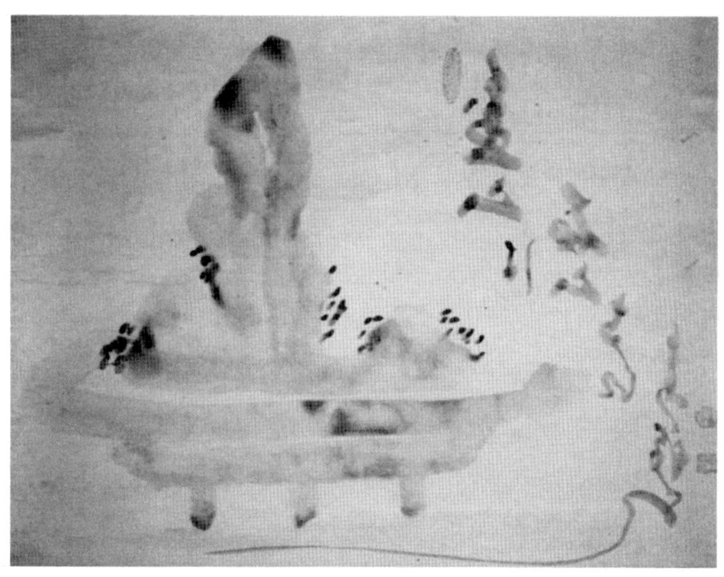

4. Hakuin Ekaku (1685–1768). *Bonseki (Tray Landscape)*. Ink on paper, dimensions unavailable. Tanaka collection

gave vitality and meaning to what might otherwise have been sterile, mechanical shapes.

Other works by Motherwell echo the sensibility of Zenga without reflecting its images. It is his use of primal forms that gives the strength to his *Elegies*, works that can be read from left to right, in Western style; from right to left, in East Asian style; or as a whole, in a Whitmanesque "barbaric yawp." More directly akin to Zen painting, however, are such works as those he called, significantly, *Samurai* (plates 80, 81, 83, 84, 86) and the boldly stroked horizontal form of the untitled lithograph of 1972 (plate 82). The former, in which vertical energies ascend from a horizontal foundation, slightly (and surely coincidentally) resemble Hakuin's paintings of tray landscapes called *bonseki* (fig. 4). The latter resembles the Chinese character for "one," a single horizontal brushstroke. When writing this "one" in formal script, East Asian masters sometimes curl the brush around at the beginning and end of the stroke to produce a more rounded form; one way of reading Motherwell's powerful image is as a bending, moving, thoroughly alive "oneness." Among the most cherished objects in his own collection was a Zen scroll of the character for "one" (fig. 5), testimony to his deep interest in this single, basic, horizontal stroke.[37]

Similarly, *Brushstroke*, a lithograph of 1979–80 (fig. 6), seems to rotate the basic gesture of the scroll to the vertical. Although thicker and shorter, with an odd little tail breaking up the almost oppressive solidity of the image, *Brushstroke* also has some affinity with Zen paintings of monks' staffs, which were sometimes used to whack recalcitrant disciples, giving them the shock that might lead to enlightenment. Zen artists of the modern era such as Nantembo (1839–1925) painted staffs frequently; in fact, the name Nantembo means literally "Nandina Staff." The particular monk-artist often began his compositions, whether of the staff or of other subjects, with a great splashing stroke (fig. 7), the kind of gesture central to Motherwell's images like *Black on Black* (fig. 8). Motherwell took such splashing effect to its ultimate conclusion in the series *Beside the Sea* (plates 53–55)—where he was (rather

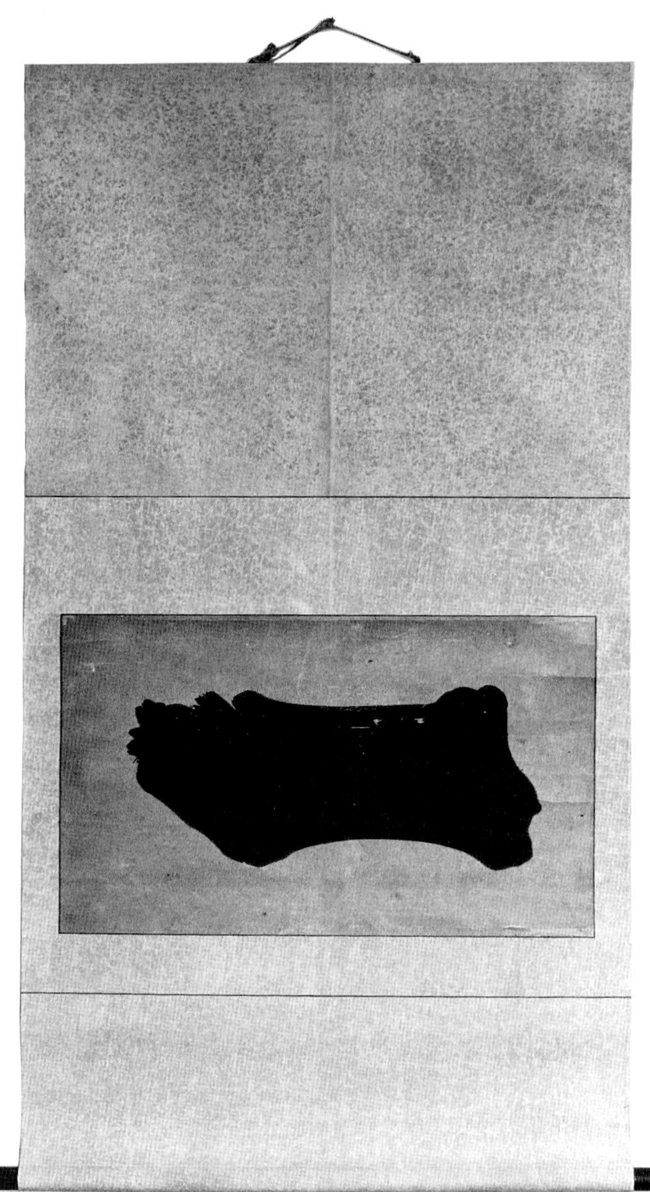

5. Japanese, 17th century. *Ichi (One)*. Ink on paper, 13¼ x 22" (33.7 x 55.9 cm). Collection Renate Ponsold Motherwell, Greenwich, Connecticut

OPPOSITE:

6. Robert Motherwell. *Brushstroke*, 1979–80. Lithograph; image: 15¾ x 11" (40 x 28 cm); paper: 31½ x 16" (80 x 40.6 cm). Collection Dedalus Foundation, Inc. (Belknap no. 218)

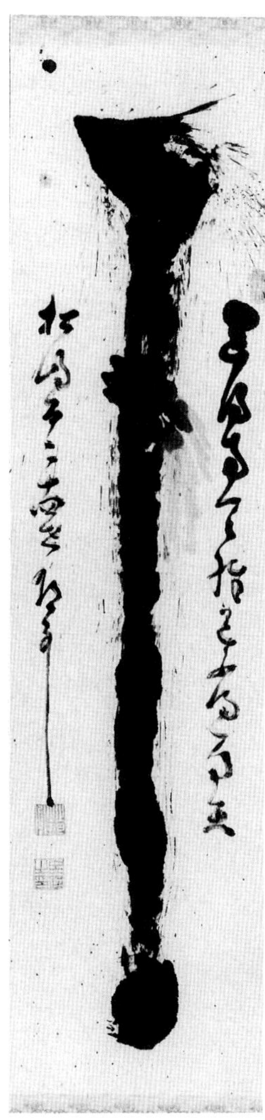

7. Nantembo Toju (1839–1925). *Staff*. Ink on paper, dimensions unavailable. Private collection

OPPOSITE:
8. Robert Motherwell. *Black on Black*, 1978. Lithograph from one aluminum plate, Chine collé; image (collé sheet): 21¾ x 16" (55.4 x 40.8 cm); paper: 27¾ x 22¼" (70.5 x 56.5 cm). Collection Dedalus Foundation, Inc. (Belknap no. 191)

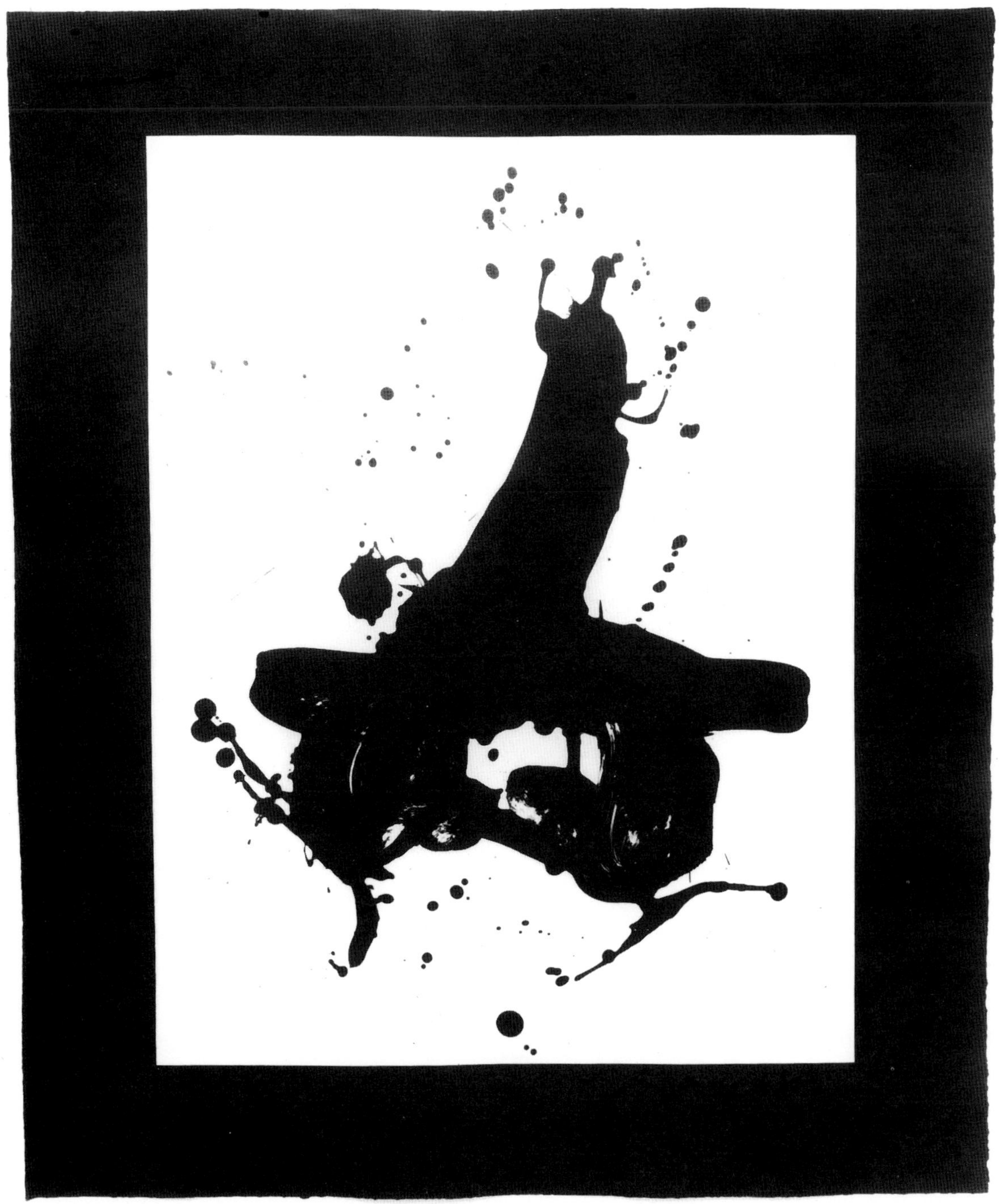

unusually) inspired by the natural phenomenon of sea spray—and its graphic recapitulation, *A Throw of the Dice* (plates 56–62).

Despite such similarities, however, Motherwell's art is more like Zenga in spirit than in appearance. He was surely impressed by Zen art. For the dust jacket of my book *The Art of Zen*, he wrote: "For a sensibility grounded in high Modernism of the twentieth century, there is perhaps no foreign culture in time and space that strikes me so forcibly as the Japanese art of Zen." He then went on to note Zen's "subtlety, contradictions, paradoxes, and almost untranslatable spirit."[38]

This is a powerful statement, one that deserves closer examination. Motherwell defines his own sensibility as that of "high Modernism," to which Zen art is a "foreign culture." And what is it about Zen that strikes him? First, "subtlety." Here, Motherwell is looking beyond the force of the tradition and its images to note the less overt aspects of Zen culture and art. Next, "contradictions" and "paradoxes." Again we can see why Motherwell gave a triple underline to the term "provisional dualism" in Awakawa's book. Finally, "almost untranslatable spirit." This is the clearest indication that Motherwell was not attempting to translate that spirit directly into his own works. And yet for an artist who did not practice Zen or attempt Zen painting, there are still some remarkable correspondences of both purpose and process.

Looking beyond individual works, we can trace further connections between Motherwell and Zenga. In Japan, contemplation is not merely a passive act but is, rather, an active experience. As Awakawa stated and Motherwell scored, it is "taking a particular scene or aspect of human life as it unfolds before one and empathizing—knowing, understanding, and feeling it as part of one's own experience. . . . When an artist produces a work, his awareness expands in every direction and is amplified."[39] The artist can only create what is in him. "Only a man in harmony with the world can produce a harmonious picture."[40] Is this an East Asian pronouncement or one by Motherwell? "In the end, art is self-revelation."[41] Again, who wrote this? One more: "An artist's 'art' is just his consciousness, developed slowly and painstakingly with many mistakes en route."[42] The words are Motherwell's, who also said that "a picture should represent all one's internality, one's internal world of sensitivity, of anger, of rhythm . . . and that, people do not choose, everybody already has it."[43]

Motherwell's idea that "everybody has it" is central to Zen, in which enlightenment does not come from outside, but is within us all along if we can only see it. In Motherwell's words, "Everybody—artist or not—wears a costume so as not to be revealed. The real trick is to get the self to come out against tremendous odds."[44] Art is one way to reach that goal. Motherwell's "interest in the language of art is quite simply an interest in the tool that can lead one to being honest, [but] which used without great care leads one inevitably to the lie, the cliché, the standardized, and to all one thinks one thinks and feels rather than to what one actually does."[45]

This is an extraordinary statement from someone who is not a follower of Zen, but there is more: "Perhaps—I say perhaps because I do not know how to reflect, except by opening my mind like a glass-bottomed boat so that I can watch what is swimming below—painting becomes Sublime when the artist transcends his personal anguish, when he projects in the midst of a shrieking world an expression of living and its end that is silent and ordered."[46] Motherwell's image of opening the mind describes an effective form of meditation, and his goal of silence and order could be a motto in a monastery.

How does an artist render quiet and order? One way that does not invite boredom is through space. Motherwell scored several passages in Ch'en Chih-mai's book on calligraphy relating to the use of space; for example: "A character which is out of balance cannot be considered a character at all. An improperly placed dot is like a beautiful maiden with a blind eye. A badly done hook is like a warrior with only one art."[47] Ch'en also quotes Laurence Binyon as writing "of the formal elements of design, this gift of spacing is China's greatest contribution to the world's art."[48] As for Motherwell himself, he wrote in 1983: "Any painter knows that empty space is his most powerful artistic weapon, *if* he can adequately animate it. The void need not be terrifying. It can indeed vivify, when contrasted as an image with the fragility of human life—as centuries of Oriental painting and calligraphic poetry, not to mention our own century's essays in modernism, reveal."[49]

The Literati Spirit

Zen culture in China and Japan has many affinities with the literati world, the culture of poet-painter-calligraphers in the scholarly tradition. Both Zen and the literati masters believed that if art is a form of self-expression, the best way to improve one's art is to improve oneself. This tended not to be done primarily through struggles with morality, but rather with developing one's personal and artistic spirit. Therefore, composing and chanting poetry, walking through nature, playing quiet music, and reading history, literature, and philosophy were all ways to develop one's individual character.

We in the West, despite lip service to the ideal of "the Renaissance man," seem to prefer that each creative artist be known for, and stick to, a single medium of expression. For example, we seem to have little interest in e. e. cummings's claims to be a painter, and perhaps only William Blake has achieved equal consideration as both poet and artist. For Motherwell, his intellectual activities became a source of suspicion, and some critics still seem to feel that being so articulate in words made him less of a painter. In reply, Motherwell quoted Charles Baudelaire: "The arts aspire, if not to complement each other, at least to lend one another new energies."[50]

Drawing support from the literati tradition, Motherwell wrote in 1949: "I resent the invidious implication of the word [intellectual] in American society, the belief that an artist must be a feeling imbecile or probably is not an artist. . . . I do not regret my innocence in supposing that an artist might be something of a scholar and a gentleman. The Chinese have thought it necessary."[51] He noted a passage in Ch'en's book that begins by quoting the scholar-artist Chu Ho-keng: "Calligraphy is a craft, and its first essential is the personal integrity of the calligrapher. To the Chinese, an artist is a noble person. . . . Most calligraphers were retired scholars . . . [who] took themselves out of the mundane world to lead a life of calm contemplation."[52] Inspired by the example of French modernism and its aesthetic camaraderie between poets and painters, Motherwell declared in 1944: "The function of the artist is to express reality *as felt*. In saying this, we must realize that ideas modify feelings. The anti-intellectualism of English and American artists has led them into the error of not perceiving the connection between the feeling of modern forms and modern ideas. By feeling is meant the response of the 'body-and-mind' *as a whole* to the events of reality. It is the whole man who feels in artistic experience."[53] Some four decades later he insisted, "I never met an outstanding artist not interested in ideas, as well as in sensuality."[54]

Motherwell, however, made a clear distinction between symbolic thought expressed in words and in painting:

> It is not possible to think without symbols. But the symbolic thought is *in* the work, and not *about* it. . . . I have never had a thought about painting while painting, but only afterwards. In this sense one can only think in painting while holding a brush before a canvas, and this symbolization I trust much more than the thinking I do *about* painting all day. And I think that most artists tend to trust the canvas much more than the words about it.[55]

What then is the role of the intellect for the artist?

> Part of the artistic task is to find identity in differences, metaphors. Metaphors of painting and of poetry and of workshops and of women and of men that are in turn metaphors for reality itself. Indescribable as it is (whatever it is), directly.[56]
>
> I think part of what art is consists of finding correspondences that are unexpected to the ordinary eye.[57]
>
> I have always assumed that the essential nature of intelligence's functioning is the grasp of relations. Many of these relations are nonverbal. Indeed, one of the worst things that a painter can say about a painting is that it is a "literary" painting.[58]

Here again is a subtle point.

For Motherwell, perhaps the clearest statement on the joining of the arts and the intellect was written by his friend William Seitz. The artist admiringly quoted the following passage of this statement in his foreword to Seitz's *Abstract Expressionist Painting in America*:

> . . . the more [the artist] can broaden and intensify his knowledge, sympathy, and cognizance of the world and himself, the richer is the raw material which gives meaning to his paintings. I cannot believe that the humanist scholar and artist must, by definition, be separate. The barrier which has arisen between their twin approaches toward the truth of existence is one of the sad phenomena of modern life. Intellect, emotion, and sense need not be separated.[59]

Before leaving the subject of the literati world, we should consider an image created by Motherwell that might seem to have been directly based on a Chinese character. The English word is *mountain*. Of relevance here is not the current version of the character, but rather its ancient pictographic shape of two lesser peaks on either side of a major peak. Motherwell seems to have reinvented the form in, for example, a lithograph like *Black Mountain* (fig. 9). A number of ancient Chinese "seal-script" forms of the character are recorded in figure 10. A scroll by Fukushima Keido, the current Zen Master and Chief Abbot of the Kyoto temple Tofuku-ji, which says simply "Mountain is Mountain," represents a recent calligraphy creating new variations on an ancient character (fig. 11). As in the comparison with Sengai, Motherwell has broken the form more freely, giving it a secure but less obvious structure, and the added three dots lend the image a distinctly physiognomic expression, like eyes staring back at us.

How did Motherwell conceive this "mountain" character? Did he possibly come to the same shape by coincidence? With his knowledge of East Asian calligraphy, this is doubtful. Once again, it would seem that the primal nature of the shape, a simple pictograph of mountains that becomes almost pure form, is what interested him. He himself, in his choice of titles and in his own comment on the possibilities of meaning in his M strokes, acknowledged the ancient meaning of "mountain."[60] Through the natural translation of his own gesture, he was able to instill in an ancient symbol new life and vitality.

Differences

We have seen similarities. What then are the differences between Motherwell and traditional East Asian brushwork? There are many, of course, led by the fact that Asian art was never purely abstract—although calligraphy may seem that way to Westerners unable to read it. Fully cursive calligraphy, it is true, is unreadable by anyone but a few genuine specialists, so the gestural marks of the brush make works in this script visually semiabstract even to most East Asian viewers. However, it is important to keep in mind that it is never the words of calligraphy that carry the visual meaning, but rather the dance of line and shape in space, and in this way the appreciation is indeed much like that of abstract art.

A second issue is the respect for tradition in China and Japan as opposed to the revolutionary aesthetics of modernism. Motherwell marked a passage in Ch'en's book, quoting the

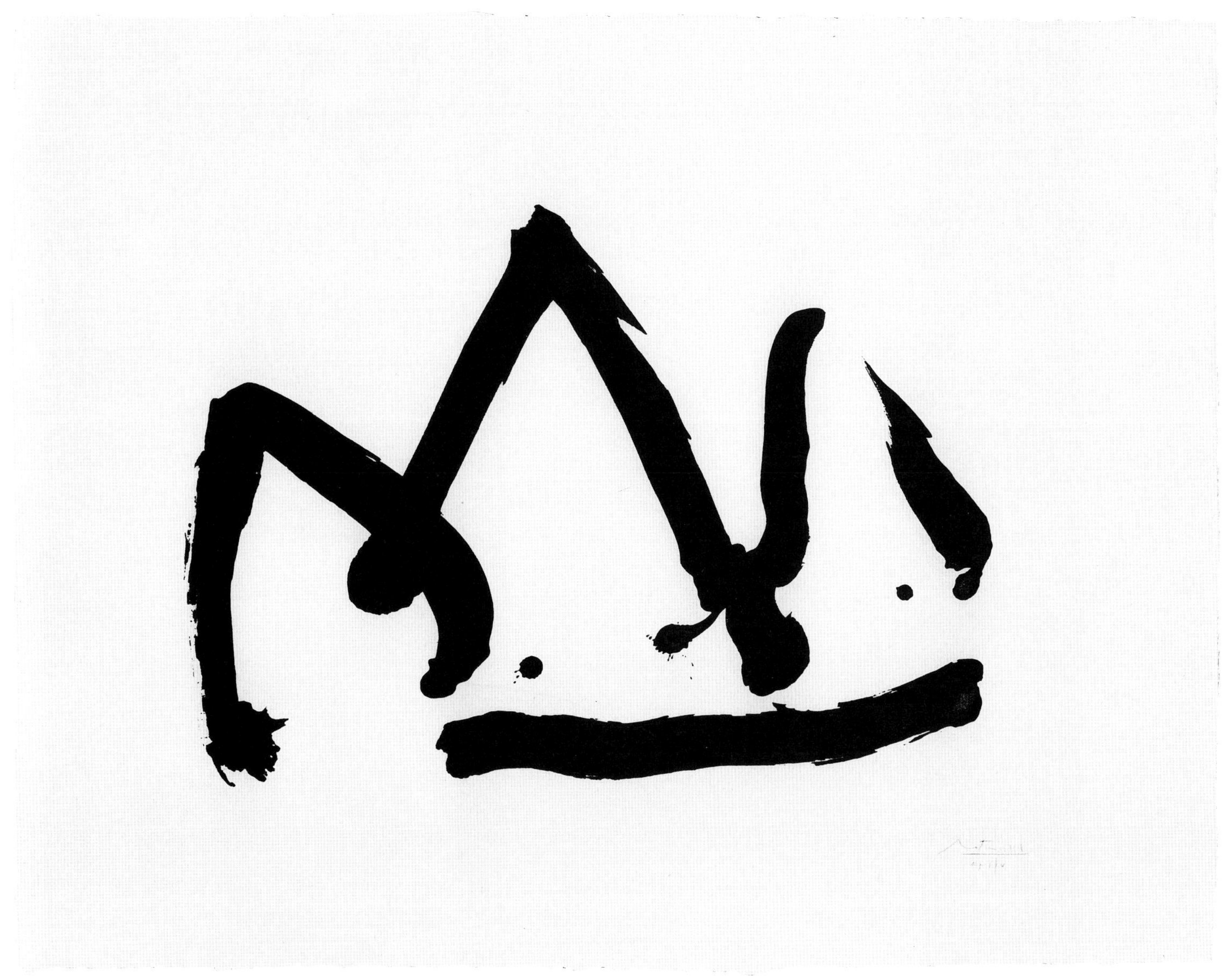

9. Robert Motherwell. *Black Mountain (State I)*, 1980–83. Lift-ground etching and aquatint from one copper plate, plate: 17¾ x 23½" (45.1 x 59.8 cm); paper: 24¼ x 31" (61.7 x 78.8 cm). Collection Dedalus Foundation, Inc. (Belknap no. 266)

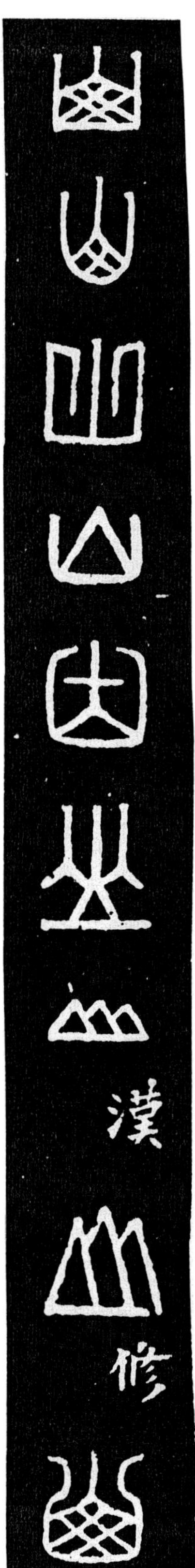

10. After *Shodo Daijiten*.
Seal-script forms of the word "Mountain"

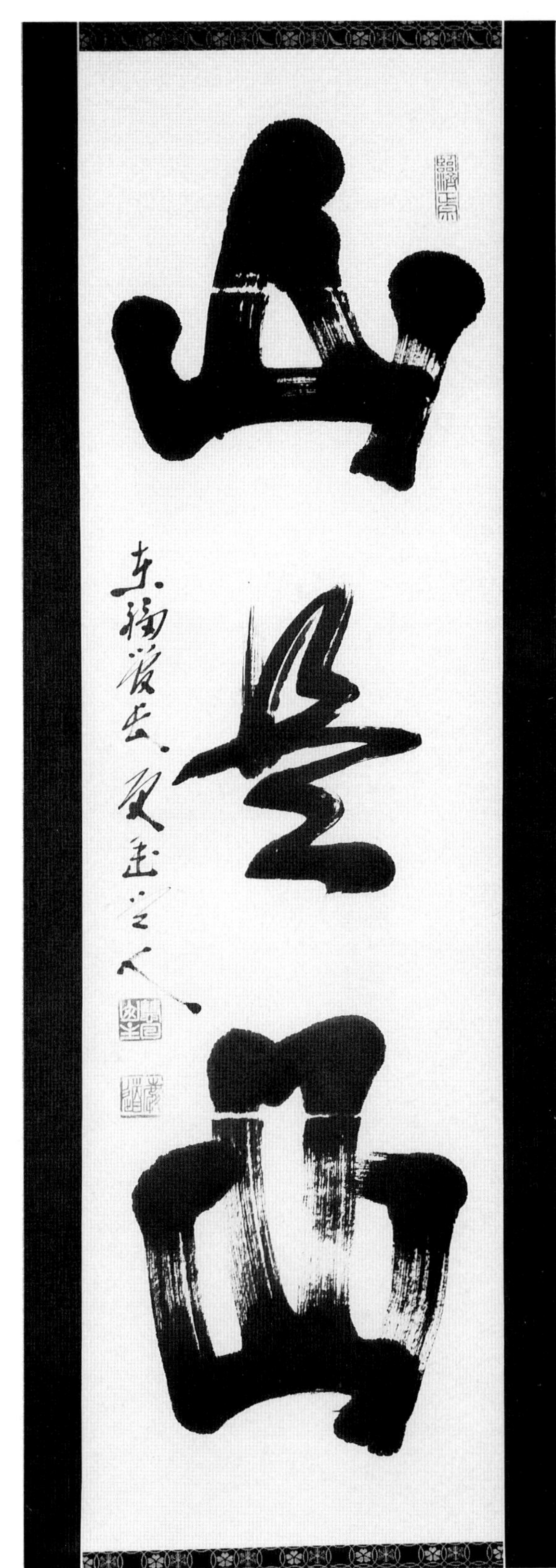

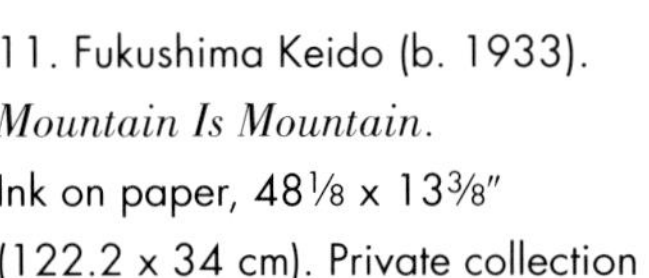

11. Fukushima Keido (b. 1933).
Mountain Is Mountain.
Ink on paper, 48⅛ x 13⅜"
(122.2 x 34 cm). Private collection

major thirteenth-century artist Chao Meng-fu: "The most desirable quality in a painting is the air of antiquity enveloping it. If it is not there, the work is not worth much, however skillfully done it may be."[61] This would seem very far from Motherwell's own view, but he once noted that "The ancient Chinese painters, who did all the writing about art in China and almost gave the word to the wordless, used to say that no truth is true that is not subtle."[62] Regarding the past, he said in his final television interview, "Part of any person's search, artist or not . . . is a search for ancestors."[63] However, this search must fit current experience. He wrote that his "students know that their work has so 'modern' an aspect in part at least because it has so broad a background of traditional culture, that past can be recovered only through the needs of the present. . . . Otherwise it remains a series of alien monuments to be forgotten as soon as they walk out into the street. . . . In this sense, modern art is universalizing and humanizing."[64]

A third apparent difference between Motherwell and East Asian Zen and literati artists is in the creating of series. Much of Motherwell's work falls into this category. However, once again, some of the difference may be more apparent than real. In an interview for French television in 1988, Motherwell commented:

> In relation to series, I think there are two main issues. One is—one's *never* satisfied. . . . One's working with an imagery that's meaningful to oneself, and tries again and again to get the perfect one, which one never does. It's just an endless search that one's never satisfied with, and often spoils pictures in trying to make them more "right." . . . And also, one picks up a certain rhythm, so that if in drawings and watercolors one makes a lot, very quickly, they begin to develop a certain degree in a way that painting doesn't . . . you're much more free.[65]

Comparing East and West, we should here distinguish between literati artists and Zen Masters. The latter are not searching for the perfect work when creating painting and calligraphy, but neither are they concerned about repeating the same compositions in the same way. As a result, there are many paintings of Daruma by Hakuin that are very similar, and we may well see them in retrospect as a series, since each is similar but each also is unique.

Consider Motherwell's ten lithographs of the *Madrid Suite* (plates 39–48): ten variations of a figure that might remind us of an umbrella or a mushroom with two circles within its triangle, all contained within a rectangle that is usually partially or almost completely darkened. These recapitulate the effect of drawings made in Madrid several years earlier (see figs. 7 and 8 on pages 28, 29) and developed before that in the *Je t'aime* paintings. Working with the basic shapes of circle, triangle, and square that interested him in the scroll by Sengai, he changes size and weight and relationship from print to print. No one is picked as the best or as the culmination, the closest to perfection; all are allowed to exist singly and in relation to each other. The central triangle recalls earlier efforts, when it was accompanied by inscribed phrases in French: "Je t'aime" and "ce dessin me plait" (plate 38), a design that would in turn be revived as a lithograph over twenty years later (plate 49). The words themselves are a major part of the composition, a series of linear accents that reinforce the rounded, angular, vertical, and horizontal lines of the more abstract forms. The uniting of image and word, of painting and calligraphy, is a hallmark of Motherwell's work—as it has been a feature of Japanese Zen art of the past four hundred years.

Literati artists, unlike their Zen colleagues, tend not to repeat their images quite so often, but they too are essentially deepening their expression rather than seeking new subjects for it. A Chinese landscape painter, for example, might well spend most of a lifetime reworking six or seven of the major traditions created by masters of the past, and many scrolls are inscribed as "Following the style of Ni Tsan" or "After the brush idea of

Chao Meng-fu." Similarly, calligraphers copy the works of respected artists of the past, sometimes blending two styles together. There is little of Western concern for originality, because, as mentioned earlier, it is believed that brushwork cannot help but show one's inner character. In literati art the series is implied; it might be said to begin with the work of an earlier master, and is then carried forth over the years and decades by later artists.

Like Motherwell, East Asian masters were aware that sometimes the work seemed to come out better, more fully responsive to one's inner core, more free, more creatively alive. Some works would be destroyed by the artist, some given or traded away, some kept, a few treasured. How to distinguish? Motherwell wrote: "My effort is to get to the absolute essence; to make the painting look like it happened totally spontaneously, at that magical moment when for one second your wrist, your arm, your shoulder, your heart, are totally at one with each other. . . . The effort is almost to reach what an Oriental would call the moment of enlightenment."[66] Or, as in a passage that Motherwell scored in Awakawa's book, "The divine principle of painting is to be in a constant state of enlightenment."[67]

For Motherwell, art was an aesthetic, ethical, and ultimately spiritual force. He wrote in 1944:

> The social condition of the modern world which gives every experience its form is the spiritual breakdown which followed the collapse of religion. The condition led to the isolation of the artist from the rest of society. The modern artist's social history is that of a spiritual being in a property-loving world. . . . It is true that each artist has his own religion. It is true that artists are constantly excommunicating each other. It is true that artists are not always pure, that sometimes they are concerned with their public standing or their material circumstances. Yet for all that it is the artists who guard the spiritual in the modern world.[68]

Ceding to a poet he admired, he asked, "What better expression of modern art is there than Mallarmé's '. . . the expression of the mysterious meaning of aspects of experience . . . [that] endows our sojourn with authenticity, and constitutes the only spiritual task.' "[69]

This view of life at once urged Motherwell to his expression of basic forms, while at the same time making him aware that humanity, and therefore art, had not really made true progress, spiritual progress, through prehistory and history. During our interview in 1991, he confessed:

> Painting has not advanced since Lascaux. I'd rather be a cave-painter, the whole thing is so organic. . . . What I like about all primitive art is that it's not meant as art, but meant to evoke and invoke the essence of their beingness in an unsophisticated way that's just a direct way of communicating their preoccupations. . . . Most art, "civilized" art, is filled with trivia and seduction and all kinds of things, as civilized life is filled with trivia and expensive goods and God knows what all, and to get back to something basic. . . . It's all fundamentals . . . [that and] modern man with all his solitariness and lack of any connections. . . . These two extremes move me, and all the rest is soap opera.

Cave dwellers or the solitary man: these are Motherwell's avatars and subjects; both, in Zen terms, face the void. Painting was his own personal attempt to find an answer: "Abstract art is an effort to close the void that modern men feel."[70] "Only love—for painting, in this instance—is able to cover the fearful void."[71] But how can this love for painting develop? Here Motherwell had an idea that he expressed in a true outburst in 1963:

> . . . an artistic medium is the only thing in human existence that has precisely the same range of sensed feeling as people themselves do. . . . Now, if a creative person in the arts is a person with an extraordinary capacity for love, who for whatever reason—say

because of his early experience with his mother—as an example—cannot direct his love toward another person in full strength, but who nonetheless *must* love—he therefore directs his love toward the other thing in human existence as rich, sensitive, supple, and complicated as human beings themselves. . . . The artist's medium is his conscience and his collaborator.[72]

Motherwell told us in the interview not long before he died that "I work with an other, a dialectic. . . . I could paint 'je t'aime'; I could never paint 'I love you.' . . . In the same way, it's very hard for me to say 'I love you' in English. It's not that the sentiment cannot be there, but that it sounds like a cliché." This dialectic, this interest in an "other," this provisional dualism, was the creative tension that led him to fifty years of creating art. As he said, "It's the long haul that counts, and in that sense, all these pictures to me—everybody talks of them as individuals, and they *are* in some sense—they're all sentences, or paragraphs, or slices from a continuum that has gone on my whole life, and will till the day I die."[73]

The ultimate rule of East Asian brushwork was formulated in the late fifth century. It consists of four words, *ch'i yun sheng tung*, that can be translated as "spirit resonance, rhythmic vitality." The rules that followed went on to deal with technical and representational issues, but the first and foremost rule was, simply, life. If a painting lacked this vitality, this sense of breath and spirit, it was dead, and no technical merit could save it. I leave the final word to Motherwell. During our interview of June 23, 1991, we were discussing his series *Drunk with Turpentine* (plates 91–94):

It has a deeper meaning. At some time during the day I get drunk on painting, almost every day, and sometimes it's miserable, and let's say I've drunk too much and it becomes incoherent or I've no judgment. At other times there's an inspired twenty minutes. And then there are lots of efforts that are abortive in the sense that there's something there but it's not a satisfying, complete expression—and I struggle sometimes for months or years with one of these things, so it is unsystematic . . . because I think . . . I've never thought of it till this moment. . . . In a way I've tried to suppress my learning and my intellectualism, and have almost deliberately gone out of my way *not* to do things rationally. It's the fore-ordained end that bothers me. . . . There's always got to be an opening for life to creep in. . . .

Notes

1. In Ch'en Chih-mai, *Chinese Calligraphers and Their Art* (London and New York: Cambridge University Press, 1966), p. 224.
2. "Black or White," preface to the catalogue of an exhibition at the Kootz Gallery (1950), in *The Collected Writings of Robert Motherwell*, edited by Stephanie Terenzio (New York and Oxford: Oxford University Press, 1992), p. 72.
3. This was during a visit to his Greenwich, Connecticut, studio on June 23, 1991, shortly before his death. Unless otherwise credited, all quotations are from this interview.
4. "Addenda to The Museum of Modern Art *Lyric Suite* Questionnaire—from Memory . . . with Possible Chronological Slips" (Fall 1969), in *Collected Writings*, p. 172.
5. "A Personal Expression" (19 March 1949), in *Collected Writings*, p. 62.
6. Yasuichi Awakawa, *Zen Painting*, trans. John Bester (Tokyo and New York: Kodansha International, 1970), p. 28.
7. "Reflections on Painting Now" (11 August 1949), in *Collected Writings*, p. 66.
8. Preface ["The New York School"] to *Seventeen Modern American Painters* (1951), in *Collected Writings*, p. 83.
9. Robert Motherwell, "The Rise and Continuity of Abstract Art" (1951), as quoted in Robert Saltonstall Mattison, *Robert Motherwell: The Formative Years* (Ann Arbor and London: UMI Research Press, 1987), p. 201.
10. "A Conversation with Students" (6 April 1979), in *Collected Writings*, p. 227.
11. Ibid., pp. 227–28.
12. Ch'en Chih-mai, *Chinese Calligraphers and Their Art*, p. 204.
13. Ibid., p. 222.

14. Quoted from the Public Television program "Robert Motherwell and the New York School" (1991).
15. Statement in *Motherwell*, exhibition at the Kootz Gallery (1947), in *Collected Writings*, p. 43.
16. "Beyond the Aesthetic" (April 1946), in *Collected Writings*, p. 37.
17. "Black or White" (1950), in *Collected Writings*, p. 72.
18. "On the Humanism of Abstraction" (6 February 1970), in *Collected Writings*, pp. 175, 180.
19. "The New York School" (27 October 1950), in *Collected Writings*, p. 79.
20. "Reflections on Painting Now" (11 August 1949), in *Collected Writings*, p. 67.
21. The Public Television program "Robert Motherwell and the New York School" (1991). One recalls Hokusai's famous comment about just beginning to know how to paint only in his seventies—indeed, at the age of seventy-three—and hoping to continue making progress until, at one hundred, "I shall become truly marvelous, and at one hundred and ten, each dot, each line shall surely possess a life of its own."
22. Interview with David Hayman (12 and 13 July 1988), in *Collected Writings*, p. 288.
23. The Public Television program "Robert Motherwell and the New York School" (1991).
24. "The New York School" (27 October 1950), in *Collected Writings*, p. 79.
25. Interview with Robert Wagener (14 June 1974), in *Collected Writings*, p. 215.
26. "Remarks" on the 150th anniversary of the Yale University Art Gallery (30 October 1982), in *Collected Writings*, p. 262.
27. Awakawa, *Zen Painting*, p. 109.
28. "What Abstract Art Means to Me" (5 February 1951), in *Collected Writings*, p. 86.
29. Interview with Richard Wagener (14 June 1974), in *Collected Writings*, p. 216.
30. Awakawa, *Zen Painting*, p. 31.
31. Ibid.
32. Ibid., pp. 30–31.
33. Ibid., pp. 39, 30.
34. Robert C. Hobbs, "Robert Motherwell's Open Series," in *Robert Motherwell* (Düsseldorf: Städtische Kunsthalle, 1976), p. 54.
35. Quoted from the French television interview of 1988, "L'Atelier de Robert Motherwell."
36. From an interview of 1979, in Stephanie Terenzio, *Robert Motherwell and Black* (Storrs, Conn.: The William Benton Museum of Art, University of Connecticut, 1980), p. 134.
37. The scroll was acquired from Ulfert Wilke, director of the University of Iowa Museum of Art, in exchange for several pictures. See Ulfert Wilke, *An Artist Collects: Selections from Five Continents* (Iowa City: University of Iowa Museum of Art, 1975), p. 66.
38. Stephen Addiss, *The Art of Zen: Paintings and Calligraphy by Japanese Monks, 1600–1925* (New York: Harry N. Abrams, 1989).
39. Awakawa, *Zen Painting*, p. 30.
40. "Expressionism" (c. 1950), in *Collected Writings*, p. 128.
41. Quoted in Terenzio, *Robert Motherwell and Black*, p. 126 (1979).
42. "A Painting Must Make Human Contact" (1955), in *Collected Writings*, p. 108.
43. From "L'Atelier de Robert Motherwell" (1988).
44. Quoted in Terenzio, *Motherwell and Black*, p. 126 (1979).
45. "The New York School" (27 October 1950), in *Collected Writings*, p. 79.
46. "A Tour of the Sublime" (15 December 1948), in *Collected Writings*, p. 53.
47. Ch'en Chih-mai, *Chinese Calligraphers and Their Art*, p. 202.
48. Ibid., p. 218.
49. "Kafka's Visual Recoil: A Note" (19 March 1983), in *Collected Writings*, p. 266.
50. Preliminary Notice to Marcel Raymond, *From Baudelaire to Surrealism* (1949); in *Collected Writings*, p. 69.
51. "A Personal Expression" (19 March 1949), in *Collected Writings*, p. 62.
52. Ch'en Chih-mai, *Chinese Calligraphers and Their Art*, pp. 203–4.
53. "The Modern Painter's World" (10 August 1944), in *Collected Writings*, p. 28.
54. Quoted in Jack Flam, "With Robert Motherwell," in *Robert Motherwell*, exhibition catalogue for the Albright-Knox Art Gallery (New York: Abbeville Press, 1983), p. 26.
55. "Symbolism" (24 February 1954), in *Collected Writings*, p. 98.
56. "The Book's Beginnings" (1972), in *Collected Writings*, p. 214.

57. Interview with Richard Wagener (14 June 1974), in *Collected Writings*, p. 216.
58. "Symbolism" (24 February 1954), in *Collected Writings*, p. 99.
59. Foreword to William C. Seitz, *Abstract Expressionist Painting in America* (Cambridge, Mass., and London: Harvard University Press, 1983), p. xiv; in *Collected Writings*, p. 258.
60. In 1950, Motherwell taught at Black Mountain College in North Carolina. For his observations on the meanings of M—an "imagery full of ambiguities, mountains, massive blacks against pure white paper, rhythms of my arm-mind . . ."—see David Rosand's essay, "'My I': Toward an Iconography of the Self," in the present volume.
61. Ch'en Chih-mai, *Chinese Calligraphers and Their Art*, p. 208.
62. "Symbolism" (24 February 1954), in *Collected Writings*, p. 100.
63. "Robert Motherwell and the New York School" (1991).
64. "The Rise and Continuity of Abstract Art" (12 April 1951), in *Collected Writings*, p. 89.
65. "L'Atelier de Robert Motherwell" (1988).
66. Interview with Richard Wagener (14 June 1974), in *Collected Writings*, p. 219.
67. Awakawa, *Zen Painting*, p. 39.
68. "The Modern Painter's World" (10 August 1944), in *Collected Writings*, pp. 29–31.
69. "Letter from Robert Motherwell to Frank O'Hara" (18 August 1965), in *Collected Writings*, p. 154.
70. "What Abstract Art Means to Me" (5 February 1951), in *Collected Writings*, p. 86.
71. "Black or White" (1950), in *Collected Writings*, p. 72.
72. "A Process of Painting" (5 October 1963), in *Collected Writings*, pp. 139–41.
73. "A Conversation with Students" (6 April 1979), in *Collected Writings*, p. 228.

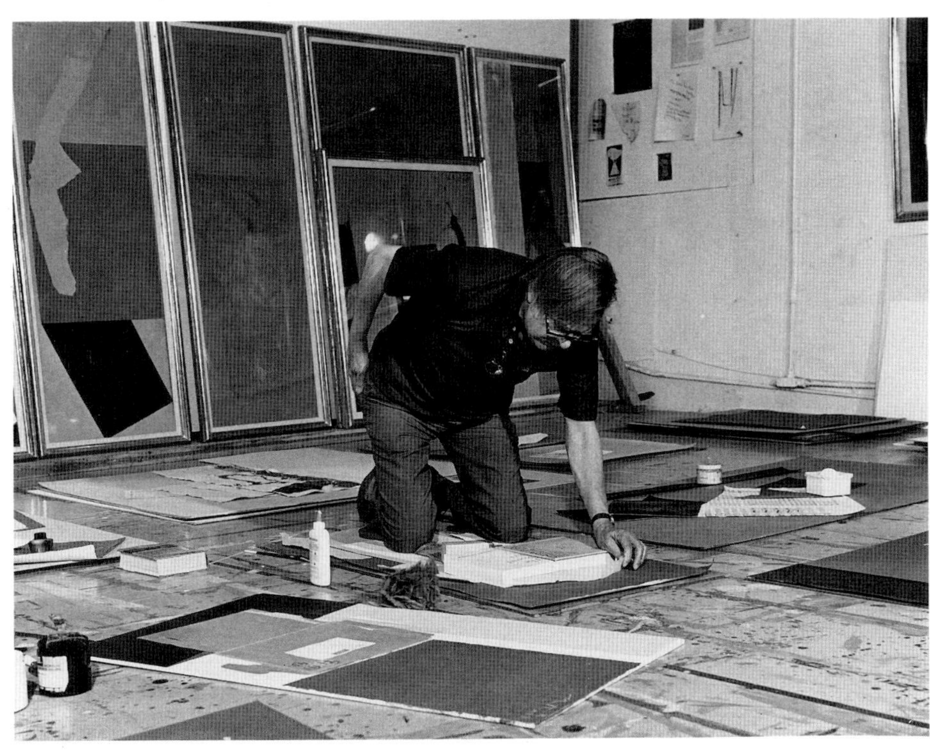

Robert Motherwell: Working Through the Night

Mary Ann Caws

What sort of way leads through a series? What kind of narration does a series call for or forth? How will it all end? Robert Motherwell used to say of all his serial paintings that he never resolved any of them, and so continued challenged.[1] This challenge is part of his legacy to his viewers, and of the fascination of his great series: the *Opens*, the *Elegies*, the *Lyric Suite*, and the others—but in particular, of his *Night Music* series of 1989 (plates 129–135).

I remember confronting this series for the first time, in Robert Motherwell's studio in 1989 (see plate 135). Later, remembering it, I thought of a black horizontal strip—the binding of a sheaf of wheat, as it seemed to me then—reaching straight across the vertical rectangles as if to hold their colors, standing up against the night. The word *courage* came to mind.

That word comes often to mind with Motherwell.

It seemed no accident that the binding was black. It participates in what it holds against.

What also comes to mind is hope. These collages nourish the mind and senses with full sheaves, and they hold firm. They hold against despair. You may think something impossible, and such images will prove the contrary.

André Breton used to say, with Matisse, that art had to hold its own against a wheat field; then he said later, more urgently, that it must hold even against famine. In trying to say why Motherwell's work strikes me as having a moral force, what I am speaking about, among other things, is that "holding."[2] And, indeed, that is a sufficient reason for speaking.

•

But it is in fact a central black rectangle that holds here in these images, anchoring the paper forms even when they are textured hard as stones, even splayed apart, as in *Night Music Opus No. 14* (plate 129); or divergent and scattered, like *Night Music Opus No. 24* (plate 132), where the black rectangle is echoed by a smaller eggshell rectangle to its upper right, as if to strengthen the hold. It is in the mind that the central rectangle stretches to a binding strip.

That binding strip, that dark holding, feels strong in its blackness. Look back at Motherwell's *Metaphor and Movement* from 1974 (fig. 1), strong to the point of fierceness, where the horizontal black rectangle is set against an earth-toned background, a white bit of torn paper, yet moves toward the left, toward a smaller beige rectangle, attached by bands of an ochre hue. What Paul Feeley said to Motherwell in the 1960s rings true here: "You have made it impossible for anyone else to use ochre."[3]

The ochre of earth, crumbly, rich. In the prehistoric caves such as Lascaux and Les Eyzies, the conjunction of ochre and red and black with white persuades us how some works of art meet across centuries and lands, to make a statement both fundamental and essential. Not with words but earth. Look at the height of such images as *Opus No. 25* (plate 133), where the large blue-gray form—on the left straight as a column and protruding into the right-hand blackness—coincides with the top and bottom edges; and *Opus No. 17* (plate 131), where the sober verticality of the forms stands with such dignity sheer against the walls of their cave, like *In Plato's Cave*, the series Motherwell associated with Delmore Schwartz's poem of the same name.

Impossible not to connect these images of movement and transfer—metaphor in its strict sense—to Motherwell's *Voyage* of 1949 and his epic *Golden Fleece* painting of 1961, both

1. Robert Motherwell. *Metaphor and Movement*, 1974. Paper and acrylic on Upsom board, 48 x 36" (121.9 x 91.4 cm). Albright-Knox Art Gallery, Buffalo. George B. and Jenny R. Mathews Fund, 1977

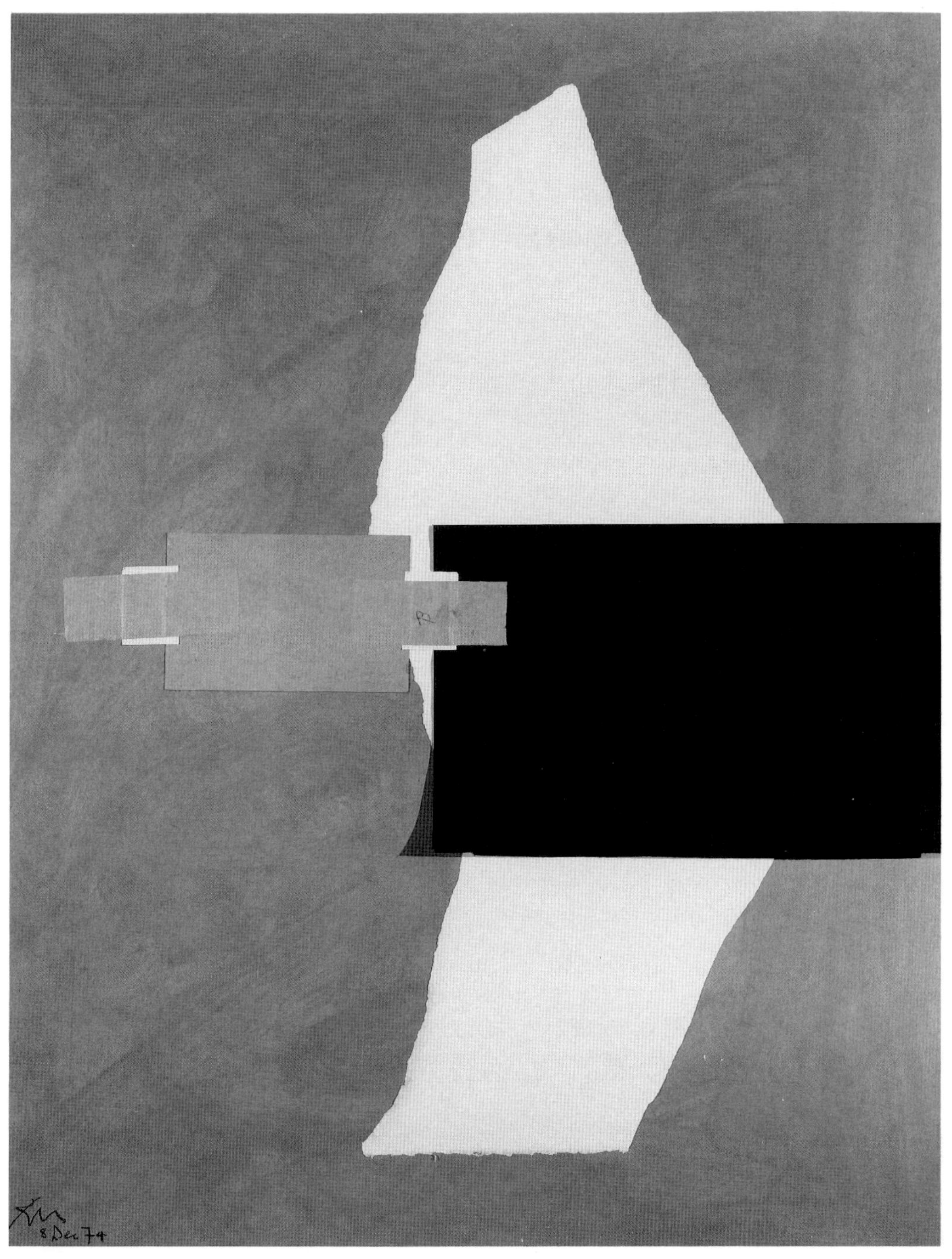

stretching out at arm's length. *The Voyage* presents the identical colors of battle as the *Night Music* series: white, black, and shades of ochre; *The Golden Fleece*, the same vertical and intrusive forms running across them, struggling against each other, with the same heart-stopping authenticity.

Take *The Voyage Ten Years After* of 1968, that rereading by the artist of his own distance covered, his own space traversed. Look how it is marked, with its great cloud, borrowed from *The Golden Fleece*, drifting across the dark rectangle at the right. By such means, monumentality teaches patience.

•

The metaphor placed in motion in the 1974 collage represents relation itself, as it deals with holding and keeping and moving, all at once. Some great force moves toward simultaneity in Motherwell's creation, so that everything is able to transpire conjointly.

To return mentally to that metaphor of motion is to prepare a voyage through a painterly, gestural, monumental work. Robert Motherwell's work is about a moral depth sensed through luminosity and grave statement: this is visible from the beginning. It is not something we have to be told about his work; this we all know, and do not have to learn. It was always clear.

Clearly, too, that metaphor helps us read *Night Music*, as it does with the voyage. "Vehement and compassionate," says Gabriella Drudi of Motherwell's work.[4] Vehement: how right the word sounds here. Somehow it goes with the intensity of the color ochre. As for what the ochre plays against, that black stagedrop, it is necessary, we might think without having to say it, for the soul. And for the temperament, the spirit deepest in us: Motherwell's painting is full of that music, that unending, abyssal truth-telling.

But there is more to be heard in this particular and strange *Night Music*. Some of it relates to a symbolic writing, as of stars white against the dark sky. Motherwell's *Mallarmé's Swan* of 1944 is black and reflected red, is red and reflected black; his swan is Baroque, combining in itself and in its backdrop the implicit white and the explicit red and black of Baroque coloring, setting this work high and tragic-colored within the bounds of the poetry of the Baroque, beneath the sail shape at the top of the composition. That sail suggests an urge toward departure, toward the flight of the swan.[5] In one of the remarkable recalls that this great opus is able to summon in the observer's mind, the large bird-shaped translucent form at the back of *Opus No. 16* (plate 130) takes its own flight toward the upper left, its head soaring past the color of night, while the central black rectangle rocks like a toy ship on a wave, above a folded triangle of paper like a child's airplane. Childhood and age, liberty and death, meet here in the play of a form anchored and yet supremely free in the imagination of an artist or a poet.

For that swan, the one shared by Motherwell with Mallarmé, is stuck perhaps only for the moment in the blank space of a page or a canvas. It will someday release itself into its own soaring power. "This work," Motherwell says of it, "was first titled *Mallarmé's Dream*. Joseph Cornell, with whom I shared in those days a lonely preoccupation among American painters with French Symbolism, misremembered the title as *Mallarmé's Swan*, which along with white or blankness was the symbol for Mallarmé of purity. I preferred Cornell's misremembrance, and the picture has been so named ever since."[6] Here Motherwell displays a generosity typical of his own openness: he lets others name. Even what matters most—his dreams, his swans, and those of the poets to whom he is close.

Now the lake of ice, the prison of the page or the canvas in which the great poet's bird was forever self-condemned, is rectangular here, but resounding with a potential that is formal as well as metaphoric. In a sense, that rectangular canvas will travel through its own silent *Voyage*, its origins retrieved from the past, and its will going on to recognize its own possibilities. Openness on the moral plane as on the aesthetic is the point here.

They are always taking their chances, these pictures. Motherwell makes it painfully clear, referring—again, implicitly—to Mallarmé's epic salute to modernism, "Un coup de dés jamais n'abolira le hasard" ("A throw of the dice never will abolish chance"):

> It is not commonly understood that the linear so-called "window" shapes of the *Open* series are as much a one-shot throw of the dice, in execution, as my more gestural works. . . . In short, the lines in the *Opens* are not measured or mathematically proportioned but purely intuitional and immediate.[7]

The *Open* series came about from one canvas leaning on another, larger one, its outline lifted then up from the floor, where it seemed a door, toward the top of the canvas, like a window. Such formal uplift has sufficient power to avoid the sentimental.

A Positive Misremembering

Now I have gone back again to hear the *Night Music*. And, to my surprise, the holding is of a different sort than I remember. No less powerful, but different.

I had remembered a sheaf upstanding, in *Night Music Opus No. 7*: such is the force of the metaphoric imagination, not to its shame, but bearing witness to its sway. It is now seen to be two ochre strips, into the right one of which the thickish black strip seems to be penetrating. It is indeed held against the whitish form, but to its left, the other ochre form, partly hidden, is partly free. Behind the black, the white, the ochre, part of a red-orange rectangular shape appears, against the black background. The black strips, then, both touch and leave open. What had seemed a simple holding is more complex by far.

These black strips recall that strong red strip stretching across three of the yellow and white bars at the upper left of *The Little Spanish Prison* of 1941–44. It stops mid-bar as if to show us it is outside, unimplicated, unimprisoned. It is not held in, and does not restrain. The moral lesson takes on more layers: Mallarmé's swan will fly free of prison as of lake and page.

Compare the way the black stripe in *Voluptuousness with Bar Sinister* of 1976 plays against the vast red expanse, with the equal-sized white bar of cloth below it. The play stretches out three-colored like a great Romantic-Baroque expanse of *Liebestod*, the fatal black playing against the passionate red, death against life and love, a voluptuous struggle to the end. The stripes and bars of the pictures work like the bars of musical scores to set the harmonies of life and art resounding in the mind.

In all the works of this great opus, the black bar calls on the night behind, echoes, holds, yet does not restrain. It can take the form of a simple square, a patch, or a memory. It has an impact equal to that of the celebrated little patch of yellow wall in Jan Vermeer's *View of Delft*, which Proust's character Bergotte rises from his bed to see once more, and before which he will die.

In *Opus No. 13*, the upright white form holds against a luminous ochre background; the black patch of a strip is echoed below by a bar, whose black color is dripping into the ochre. We are reminded again of *In Plato's Cave* of 1972 and its liquid black, which had to be held and "cradled"[8] in its dripping by the painter, thus nourished at the beginning of a birth-death cycle. We remember best what we hold unto death.

I had forgotten, too, in the force of my initial encounter and its remembrance, how deeply the gesture of tearing is still felt, as in the torn forms of *Opus No. 26* (plate 134), with its wisps of gray translucent against the dark and its anguished flailing out on all sides; and in *The Tearingness of Collaging* of 1957.

Violence is inscribed into the membrane of the work, so that the collage always feels like a conquest of something—of inertia at the very least:

> The sensation of physically operating on the world is very strong in the medium of the papier collé or collage, in which various kinds of paper are pasted to the canvas. One cuts and chooses and shifts and pastes, and sometimes tears off and begins again. In any case, shaping and arranging such a relational structure obliterates the need, and often the awareness, of representation. Without reference to likenesses, it possesses feeling because all the decisions in regard to it are ultimately made on the grounds of feeling.[9]

Had I been reading as a monolithic gesture one constituted of parts? Had I imposed my own rhythm upon the reading of another's statement? Such a personal response risks such misunderstanding. Yet I would not want to lose the voicing of what spoke so loudly to me; passionate reading is also passionate listening, and then passionate voicing, in return. It is a generous risk, in response to a generous work: I believe it is required.

How can you speak of what you would most prefer not to betray? Is it not better to say nothing, betraying nothing? Of course you have to speak of works only as you are confronting them. Of course the memory betrays. Yet the art of response has to include that of remembrance, even if it is—as in the Cornell case—a misremembrance. The reading may speak of something else. Suggestion may unfold as widely as real matter. Mallarmé knew it, Motherwell knew it, and we may tend to forget it, in our own attempts to remember *correctly*. Exactly "the flower absent from all the bouquets," as the poet put it, is what matters, about matter. It is what is most profoundly held, and held out. It is what requires an answer.

•

In *Opus No. 12*, the black strip speaks again of insertion and of superimposition, and less of holding than I remember. Against the greenish beige and slate gray vertical rice-paper forms, the black bar of this section of *Night Music* reads still as a response to the black background, yet also in horizontal correspondence with the pink-gray paper, with whose bottom edge its own almost coincides. I had eliminated in my memory the other horizontal form, so strong was my desire for the holding, against the night.

In the complexities of *Opus No. 3*, where the layers of paper are clearest, the black astride the cream-colored translucent strip steps tall over the next two layers, the darker earth tones of the bottom one showing slightly through, as the next layer itself in its turn shows through the next in a system of echoes and overlappings. Again, the slightly curved bottom edge of the black strip echoes the bottom form in its own slight curve of lower edge: I had read at first only the echoes of the night, and not of the other forms.

For night always seems stronger than we are. It prevails over light, in these statements about, say, personal fate. About death, but also about what holds against this death; the painter's, ours, everyone's. These collages record a secular pilgrim's progress, if you like. They are about Everyman.

About Time

> I want that height and prospect such as music
> Brings one to—music or memory,
> When memory gains ground drowned-out
> By years. I want the voyage of recovery . . .
>
> —Charles Tomlinson, "Movements"[10]

Metaphor and Movement (fig. 1), the originary collage for the *Night Music* series, was already doubly in movement. Since metaphor signifies both transport and change, the cornerstone of this series of collages, so simple in appearance and so meaningful in connotation, was marked by its willingness toward motion and away from the static and the repetitive. Put this way, however, the original dynamic appears to contradict the overall impression of the series. For, as the bands of the few colors—black, ochre, eggshell or écru, and white—cross each other, the first impression of reading any one of the series is that of an angular, layered, relatively unmoving work. How *Night Music* develops—like any series, perhaps, but with a specific difference, given its topic—is part of the reading.

Yet it is far from static. In the pull between its few basic elements and its—can I say life force?—against the death that night would seem to connote, lies part of its fascination on a second reading. These works on paper make a monumental statement about motion, development, and the holding impulse of great art.[11] But their statement and their implication can be seen to be in struggle: what is said and what is implied do not always coincide. In the space of this noncoincidence you can just hear the "strains" of the kind of night music this is: I am thinking of that tension between the musical and the figural in Wallace Stevens's remarkable poem "Peter Quince at the Clavier," based on Tintoretto's two great paintings *Susanna and the Elders*, where the violence (the "viol" and "scraping") of the instrument violates the quiet of the garden and the solitary bathing, becoming the emblem of other basic tensions: between youth and age, between seeing and hearing, between privacy and what spies upon it. These strains—however troubling to the late-coming viewer who sees the spying, in particular the feminist viewer—can, in their tension, nourish an oppositional reading. As in much of Motherwell's work, struggle deepens sight.

For art work which would seem to be so abstract, the sheer representativity of the forms in *Night Music* is impressive, inescapable. The abstract is what is said; but what is represented here—night, death, what can be held as endurance against it—is not said, except in the title and in the observing mind. That is the music of this art.

So the strains of the *Night Music* series, itself also torn between the auditory and the visual, are other than they might seem. Based on the simplest of forms, some cut straight, some torn unevenly in the many variations on the theme, this series appears to be about continuity and buildup, triumphing over the tearing of form that would ally itself with the music of night. Inevitability, to be sure. But also, the individual, human strength of the individual art object, holding out on its own score and with its own variety and its own continuity against what must be the common end.

We know what end is in sight for all of us, after any play of a series however long in its elements, parts, variations. We know, of course, that the night Motherwell consecrated this specific music to and our own end are identical. But his long struggle against closure, to which this essay is dedicated, should not be simply swallowed up in the category label of any particular series. Even one so marked by its inevitability.

So I have written against that night, for the artist of this series, his last and perhaps his least known. There was not—could there ever be?—time.

Not to Resolve

Different things, it is true, come back—or then come forward—to haunt you at different moments. As I think now of Robert Motherwell's *Night Music* series, I cannot shake off the impression that what he once said to me about the unresolved nature of all of his series in general applies with a particular relevance to this one. Let me say at once how different his knowing *un*resolution is from any trace of *ir*resolution. The very dynamism of his gesture, the intense resolve with which it is made, gives his recognizable touch to the work. What is lacking—so wonderfully lacking—is a closing gesture. It is quite as if the keystone were there, but not the seal that would finish, or finish off, the series. It is as if this artist so known for his series of *Opens* were in fact to have left, by temperament and by philosophical outlook, all of his series in a state of openness. He hadn't finished. And so, it seems to me, we haven't finished either, in our looking and wondering about him or his work.

To Leave Things Open

Now this unresolvedness, this unresolution, is particularly appropriate for the *Open* series. But it is, you may say, less appropriate for the *Night Music* series, with its formal black bars, like the tar—the pitch—of death. We hear Gerard Manley Hopkins: "Pitched past pitch of grief . . ." We know how things end, after all. Whether it is in the mode of bang or the mode of whimper, it is, all the same, definitive. Whether it is (deceptively) entitled as something slight, like Mozart's *Eine kleine Nachtmusik*, or then as something grave, music of the night would seem closed by its nature.

But, taken from another angle, Motherwell's *Night Music* series is openly referential, and in any case leaves itself open, like his major works. There is room for whatever the reader/observer brings to the viewing, not only the memory of Mozart, but of the way, at the beginning of Bach's *Musical Offering*, which Motherwell loved, there is a dark slide downward from a diminished seventh interval to a descending chromatic sequence.[12] Or consider Lewis Thomas's *Late Night Thoughts*, or the great French poet René Char's *Talismanic Night*, with its aphorisms and small paintings on stone done in a time of insomnia, like so many candles lighting the way to something inside.

This is not just a way of conceiving and constructing, but of thinking and, above all, of being. A being stretched toward what is profound, grave, and—necessarily—obscure.

To Redo the Gesture

Why does a repeated gesture affect us so strongly? Something primitive speaks therein, something about ritual. Or better, about necessity, about urgency. Kierkegaard's *Repetition*, an essay and experiment in the impossible recapturing of a first time, is as ancient as it is modern.

It was not that Motherwell, repeating his *Night Music* gesture, thought he hadn't gotten it right the first time. It was rather that an incantatory spirit was felt here, more and more strongly. You had only to see all the gestures of this series lined up on his studio wall to understand something about death-in-life. Something also about the will, in fact the desire, of a monumentalizing artist to make, through the medium of collage—with *this* translation of night into music—this startlingly simple thing of such startling complexity.

The intense effect of layering, the way one level leads down deeper to another, makes a statement as philosophical as aesthetic. So the ochre penetrates the black, so the color of eggshell—with all its sense of fragility, with its slight translucence—mediates between the other colors. These shifting interconnections and this tenuousness, this depth and this fragility: I find them nowhere else in Motherwell's work to such an extent.

The work is about being as well as looking. Here, patience is to be learned, depth is to be recorded. In the matter of night, nothing should be lost.

Thinking About Being

From this the poem springs: that we live in a place
That is not our own and, much more, not ourselves
And hard it is in spite of blazoned days.

—Wallace Stevens, "Notes Toward a Supreme Fiction"[13]

Let me start afresh. The *Night Music* series is about exile also. From a world of sunny outlines, sharp representations, certain beliefs. The artist, the thinker, the reader: these persons we are do not live where art and thinking and reading are valued. The upstandingness of this sheaf of wheat/paper/color that occupies the center of the works of this series bears witness to a determination—as the predominance of black marks its tragic end.

As the shapes intermingle and are seen each through the other, so the temporary actualizations of form play out the ephemeral realizations of thought. More than any other series in Motherwell's canon, I find *these* shapes in *this* series to be the infinitely touching statements of something avowed as impossible: the lastingness of anything we might build.

These are haunted works, as haunted as Stevens's early poems in the vein of "Domination of Black," for example, in which the circling of the blackness encompasses both the background and foreground of the poem, as the two shift into each other, with all the appalling strength of remembering and foreseeing:

I saw how the night came,
Came striding like the color of the heavy hemlocks
I felt afraid.
And I remembered the cry of the peacocks.[14]

Like the separate works of the *Night Music* series, each line picks up the blackness, never mentioned except in the title, but all the heavier in the hemlocks and the great birds' cry.

Bareness and Splendor

No, this is not the Motherwell of the *NRF* collages, or of *The French Line*. These colors of earth and day and death are not those reds and those greens of the *Je t'aime* series, not the bright colors of Matisse's *Bonheur de vivre* or Motherwell's *Joy of Living*. These are not the splashes and exuberance of the *Lyric Suite* (plates 14–37). This series says something different, something more intimate, less public. These are testimonies to private pain, the silent traces of an artist of whom I sensed this part as well as the other.

The artist, some of whose last traces we are seeing here, was not this time making a public statement. Yet he was perhaps remembering those great *Elegies* and the poem "Llanto por Ignacio Sánchez Mejías" by Federico García Lorca that accompanies them, that lament for the death of a bullfighter, and for the death of liberty. Celebrating "El Negro Motherwell" ("Motherwell's Black"), Rafael Alberti had composed a poem that he recited for the artist, in a reverse illustration of how color can, upon occasion, inspire verbal expression, instead of the contrary.

The feeling in the Lorca and Alberti references is Baroque in the positive sense, that sense that Motherwell appreciated when I would apply it to his painting, to the reds and blacks and whites. Fact: a bullfighter dies. Form: a poet writes an epic lament for and celebration of that bullfighter. Response form: an artist paints a lament, an elegy, for that bullfighter figure and for his country. And finally a second poet, inspired by that lament, laments in his turn both the death and the idea of death, rising to chant his homage to the artist who had known how to capture the only black which would do to lament the whole thing, the tradition, the figure, the death of that figure, and our own. But which would, at the same time, celebrate the human celebration of courage, our common and singular courage against our fate and our night.

It makes a great story, and deep art.

Motherwell's Black

For years the artist and the color had kept grave company. The kind of depth that black can give to other colors had occupied Motherwell's mind as a kind of miracle. But a miracle traditional to art, and so bringing with it a gravity that would outweigh any particular tragedy or talent. Look at the background of Goya's last great still lifes, those four remarkable heaps of fish with their glint of silver, of game with its textured rich color piled up on a plate against that space of gleaming black behind them.[15] We contemplate richness and tragedy; life consumed and ongoing and ended; what there is to be said and to be silenced.

Motherwell's blacks say all this too. In particular, for those who know the rest of his work, they say: Look! This is not, now, that artist you knew. Not the one who celebrated love in its *jouissance*, as in his *Beside the Sea* (plates 53–55), with its splash and brush against the wall and paper. Not the one who might have been speaking, as he often did, of painting in its many guises of studio and statement, private and public works. Not the one who would involve himself here with the communications and sendings of such transatlantic nature as the Gauloise packets and the drawing paper or wrapping paper bore witness to in the *NRF* series; or the work *Gift*, which calls attention to its own function.[16] No, the artist of the *Night Music* series was none of those.

That last great series is unlike any other, nearest perhaps to the *Elegies*, but different. Not lamenting for another, or for a country, but, this time, for ourselves, in our own night. This remembrance series is close also to the simple and immensely deep series of *Stones*, to the blacks and greens and blues of those simple rectangular witnesses to the act of printing itself—those stones with an irregular corner biting into the background.

Here is where I want to place the classically simple constructions and collages of *Night Music*, among these *Stones*, among these *Elegies*, yet in their own very particular place. They have, just as authentically, their own tone and something remarkably nourishing, as if the analogy with sheaves of wheat were to sustain.

When, as in *Opus No. 13*, the black streams downward, the ribbons seem to take the form of blood dripping. The effect is all the stronger when you compare this streaming image with that of *In Plato's Cave*, which is like an immense eye weeping, paler into darker, white into black. Here, black into white. Opposite poles, yet unforgettable, precisely because so rare, are the drips to be "cradled" in Motherwell. Spurts, blobs, doodles, if you like, and frequent—but the drips have another message, that, I think, of death and its cyclical other, the cradling gesture of the painter who must arrest the paint by holding the paper or the canvas horizontal once the drip has taken its place.

"You see," Motherwell said to me one day, commenting on the drips of *In Plato's Cave*, "here I cradled the image. See, here."

"Yes," I said, "I see."

Here, the black is weeping against the night. As the band gathers up the sheaves, like a fistful of nourishment let fall, a surplus of liquid drips against the white background, signaling plenteousness. So the same signs can be read as weeping and dying, or as life.

"Ah," says a painter friend in awe before this image in a simple photograph, having chosen it from among all the others; "How he has looked at Matisse and Braque! The work," he continues, "is so strong that the picture of it takes your breath away." Just so. That is, I think, what happens when you see.

To Rhyme with Black

Seen from another angle, the parts of such a series can be considered, as time goes on, like so many members of a poetic phrase, building up the emotion to its height; for example,

a las cinco de la tarde
(at five in the afternoon)

repeated, like the tolling of a death bell, in Lorca's famous

"Llanto," the verbal accompaniment for Motherwell's equally famous *Elegies*, to which I have paid earlier homage. Or, to take another example from the Spanish-speaking world, the repetition throughout *Chronicle of a Death Foretold*, by Gabriel García Márquez, of the death sentence:

On the day they were going to kill him . . .
. . . the men who were going to kill him . . .
. . . waiting in order to kill him . . .
. . . the men were waiting . . . to kill him . . .
. . . already knew that they were going to kill him . . .
. . . they're going to kill her son . . .
There had never been a death more foretold.[17]

The buildup is part of the death sentence, but also the sentence constructed the length of the story by the chronicler, to take hold of the point, reinforce it, drive it in. This is the way, of course, that many monumentalizing poems work, like T. S. Eliot's "Ash-Wednesday," weaving its repetitions and variations in a moving simplicity, like a litany and a prayer, never finished:

Because I do not hope to turn again
Because I do not hope
Because I do not hope to turn . . .

The very repetitiveness gives the drama of the poem its accumulated store of emotion, leading up to the repeat:

Although I do not hope to turn again
Although I do not hope
Although I do not hope to turn . . .[18]

But in the normal expectation of narrative, as in *Chronicle of a Death Foretold*, there is a resolution, and the buildup is perceived as linear; whereas, in poetry and—I will claim—in such series as those of the *Night Music* construction, the perception may be offered from all sides at the same time, with slight variations. To such perception, there is no necessary resolution, only a continuity with its own complexities. It is, nevertheless, the case that the reader/observer's grasp of the presentation is in all likelihood deepened by the repeated viewing. So, I would claim, seeing *Night Music Opus No. 1* before, say, *Night Music Opus No. 10*, may appear to make visible a development in thought and vision; yet this is more a celebration of increasing profundity than a necessary step in appreciation.

Colors of Earth

There is, in the *Night Music* series, the ochre and the black of ancient cave paintings, charred by fire, darkened by age; and there are earth colors, of clay and soil. And there are the lighter, fragile eggshell colors of day. These are all offered up, in the bands and layers of their forms, whether perfect in their angles, or incomplete, ragged. Both the sense of the inevitable and the sense of the daily are ours to read as much as Motherwell's to picture. His night is ours, and his daylight.

All we can add is patience. This is the reading of our lives on their way to something else. Motherwell's work on paper with its rectangular forms recalls his own work with stones, in a sense his most metapoetic work. Prints about the art of prints and, literally, of the lithographic stone, those stones are chipped, their corners imperfect and peculiarly moving. And so, these other rectangular forms, themselves imperfect, as if worn away, are also keepsakes of his anguish as they are sources for his art.

Lasting Power

We will not last. Motherwell's gesture repeats that certainty, every time with a slight difference. Here, the layers, like so many geological testimonies, build against each other and toward the end.

So the Magdalen contemplates the skull in Georges de La Tour's most famous *memento mori* of them all. Such is the *vanitas* tradition. This public yet private meditation on death is for all of us to know about—but it takes knowing so much else to be able to know this. We have to have heard many other strains to hear these, in their full tones, not altogether despairing.

For this is not a series of despair. As in *Black Refracts Heat* (plate 128), where the firm, solid rectangular forms atop each other hold easily against the dark gray ground, so do the members of the *Night Music* series refract a kind of warmth, holding on to the courage of gesture itself, through all the strains it occasions, remembers, embodies. To read in this series is to read, now, a life and not just the death that resolved it and its contradictions, necessary to art.

Motherwell wanted all of his series to be left open. Especially this one, his own more private and collaged, layered statement about what the *Elegies* lament in a more obvious form. Here, where layers read and are to be read through each other, we read those *Elegies* once more through these fragile shapes, papery and torn—but they have the texture of stone, and they will hold. I do not read *Night Music* as an elegy or an ending, public or private. I read it as I read great poetry, its statement ongoing. I read it above all as emblematic of the whole idea of series itself, as the sentence read against us and that we read, never closing it, never bowing to it, simply and superbly using it, too, as a matter of art, thought, and life.

Notes

1. In conversations with the author, 1990–91.
2. A few pages of this essay are based on my *Robert Motherwell: What Art Holds* (New York: Columbia University Press, 1996).
3. Robert Motherwell, commenting on his paintings in yellow ochre, cited "my colors, throughout my career, in order of frequency: chalky white, black, yellow ochre, blue, vermilion." He then quoted Paul Feely's remark. See H. H. Arnason, *Robert Motherwell*, 2nd ed., new and revised (New York: Harry N. Abrams, 1982), p. 182.
4. Gabriella Drudi, *Robert Motherwell: Notes romaines*, trans. Philippe de Montebello (Paris: Editions de la Différence, 1980), p. 50.
5. The reference is to Mallarmé's sonnet of the swan, "Le vierge, le vivace et le bel aujourd'hui . . ." ("The virgin, the lively and lovely today . . ."), where the swan is—like the poet—paralyzed in the frozen lake of the white page, uncertain as to the possibility of freeing himself.
6. Motherwell's commentary in Arnason, *Robert Motherwell*, p. 112. In my picking up of the term *misremembrance* I am remembering also Harold Bloom's famous misreadings, but intending it in a slightly different sense.
7. In Arnason, *Robert Motherwell*, p. 171.
8. In conversation with the author.
9. From "Beyond the Aesthetic" (April 1946), in *The Collected Writings of Robert Motherwell*, ed. Stephanie Terenzio (New York and Oxford: Oxford University Press, 1992), p. 37.
10. Charles Tomlinson, *Written on Water* (Oxford: Oxford University Press, 1972), p. 50.
11. On the topic of holding, see my *Robert Motherwell: What Art Holds*.
12. When we were discussing this, at some length, Motherwell said, with his familiar enthusiasm, that his assistant Mel Paskell had just been showing him a diminished seventh in a jazz piece.
13. In Wallace Stevens, *Collected Poems* (New York: Alfred A. Knopf, 1954), p. 383.
14. "Domination of Black," in Wallace Stevens, *The Palm at the End of the Mind* (New York: Vintage Press, 1965), p. 9.
15. Seen in the "Spanish Still Life" exhibition at the National Gallery, London, in the spring of 1995.
16. I have discussed at some length the idea of the works called *Gift* and those in relation to communication in my *Robert Motherwell: What Art Holds*.
17. Gabriel García Márquez, *Chronicle of a Death Foretold*, trans. Gregory Rabassa (New York: Ballantine Books, 1982), pp. 1, 11, 13, 16, 57.
18. In T. S. Eliot, *Selected Poems* (New York and London: Harcourt Brace Jovanovich, 1964), pp. 83, 92.

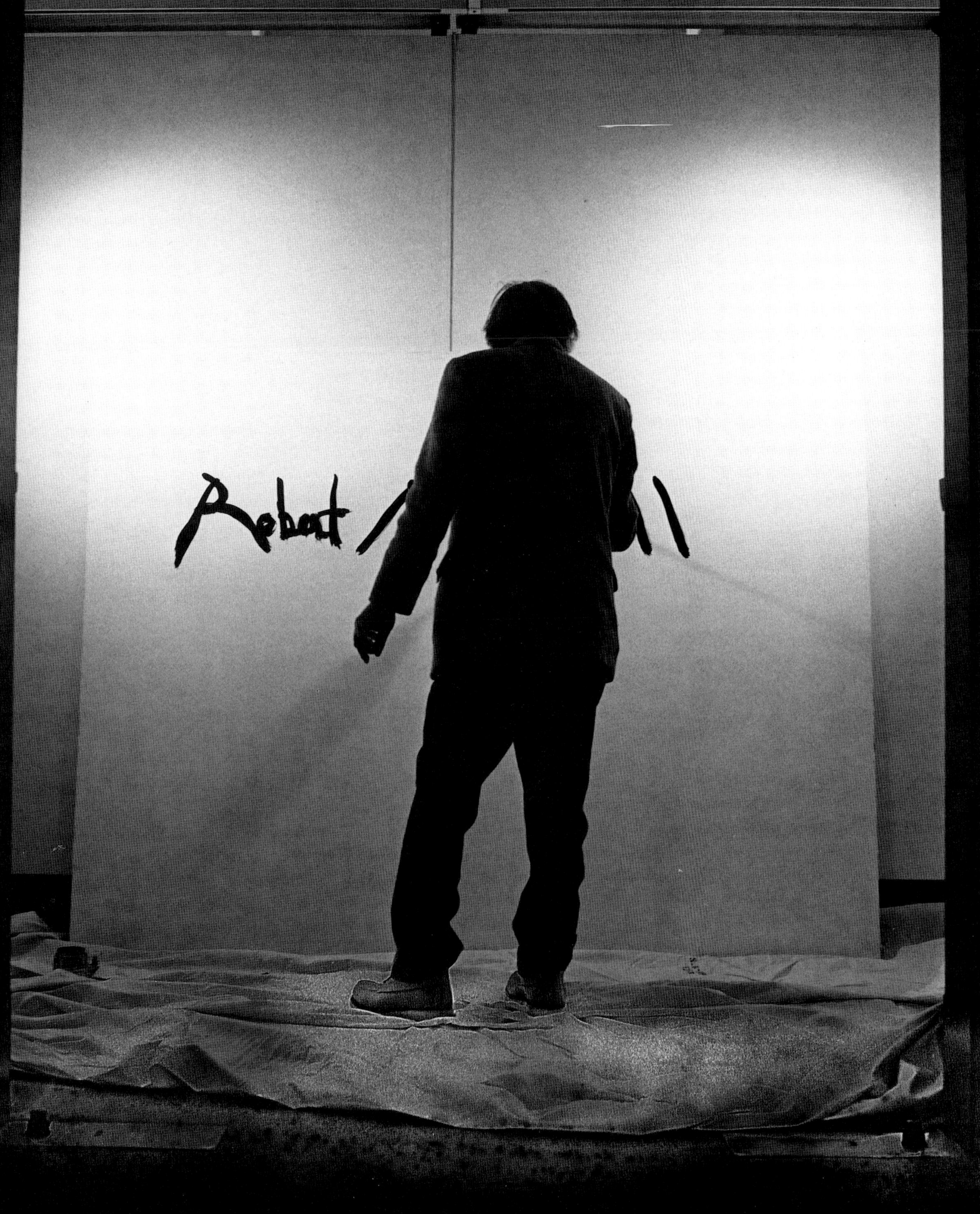
Robert

Plates

Unless otherwise noted, all works are from the collection of the Dedalus Foundation, Inc.

I. *Elegies to the Spanish Republic*

1. *At Five in the Afternoon*, 1949. Casein on paperboard, 15 x 20″ (38.1 x 50.8 cm).
Collection Helen Frankenthaler, New York. Cat. no. I.2

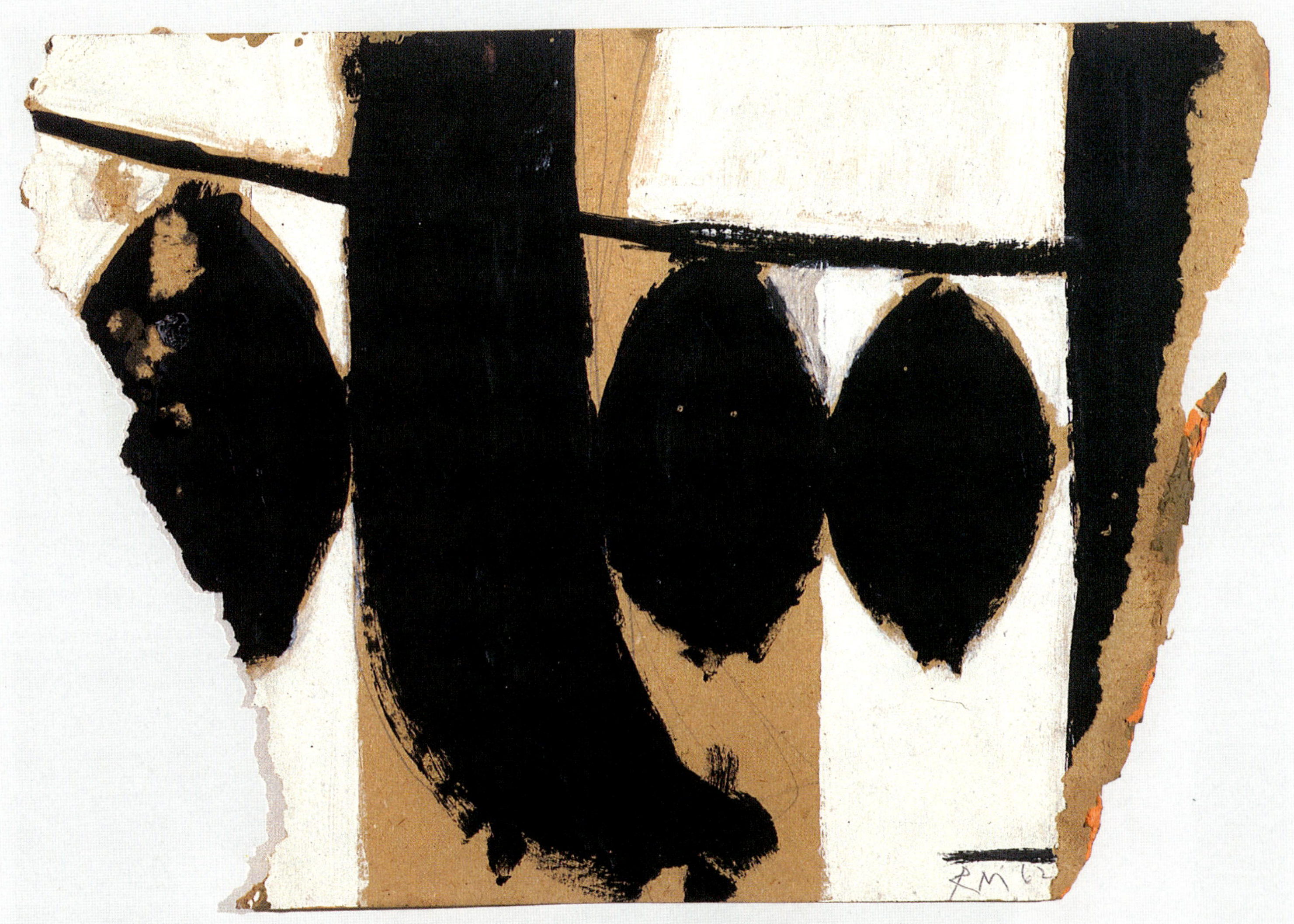

2. *Torn Elegy*, 1962. Acrylic on cardboard fragment, 10⅝ x 15″ (27 x 38.1 cm).
Collection Renate Ponsold Motherwell, Greenwich, Connecticut. Cat. no. I.3

OPPOSITE:
3. *Alberti Elegy*, 1981–82. Lithograph, Chine appliqué; image (appliqué sheet): 10 x 12¼″ (25.4 x 31.2 cm);
paper: 14 x 15″ (35.6 x 38.2 cm). Cat. no. I.5

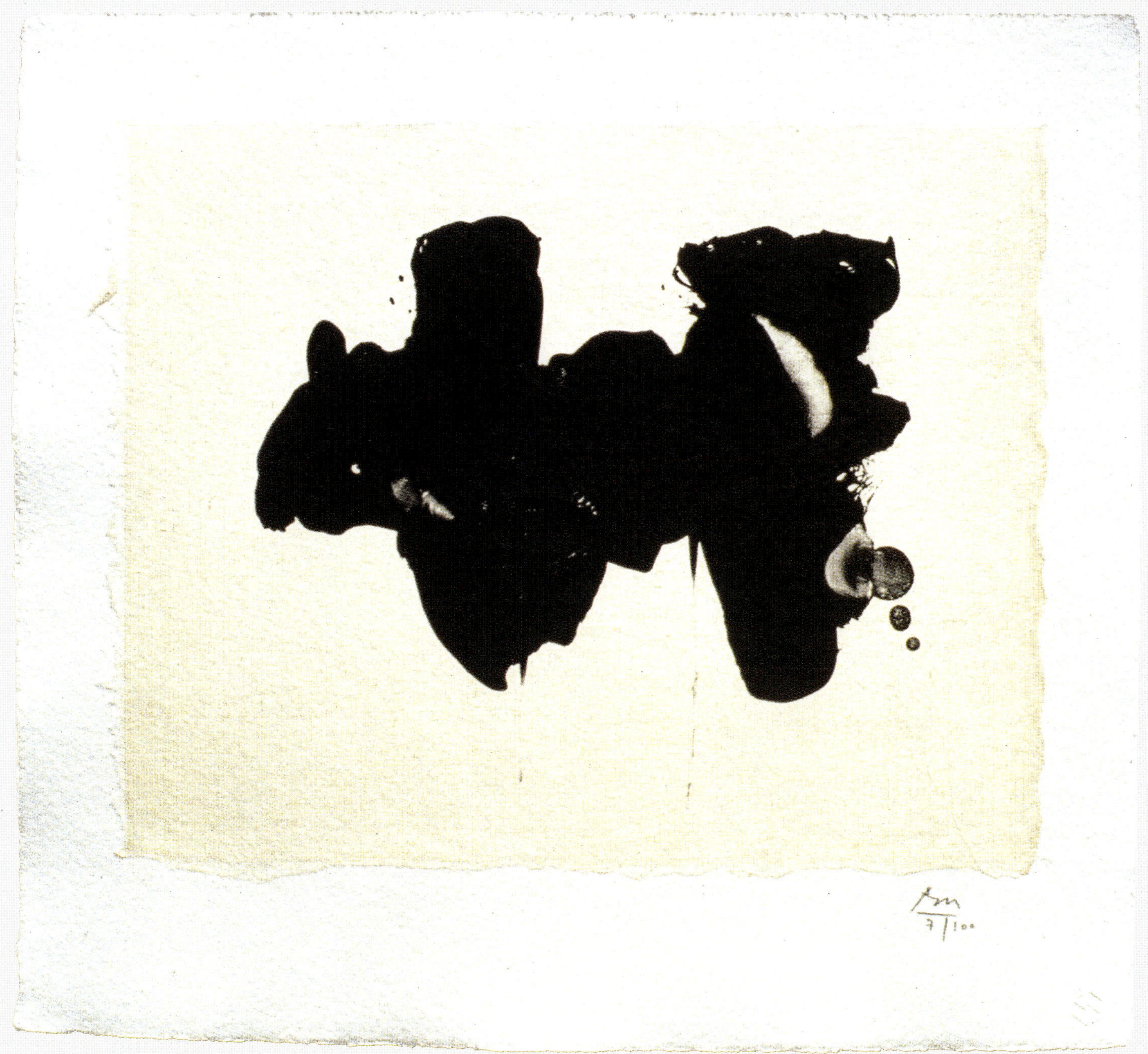

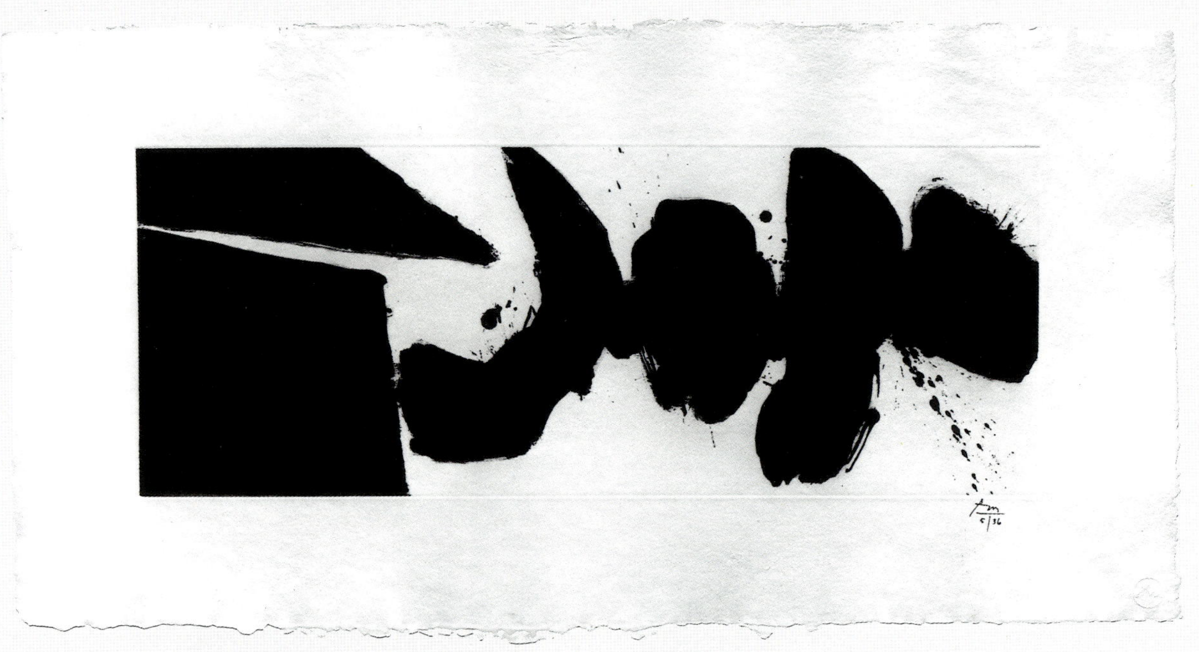

4. *The Black Wall*, 1980–81. Lift-ground etching and aquatint; plate: 10⅝ x 27″ (27.1 x 68.6 cm); paper: 18½ x 35¾″ (47.1 x 90.9 cm). Cat. no. I.4

5. *Running Elegy II, Red State*, 1983. Lift-ground etching and aquatint (black), soft ground etching (red); plate: 11⅝ x 29⅜″ (29 x 74.7 cm); paper: 18⅜ x 35½″ (46.6 x 90.1 cm). Cat. no. I.6

6. *Running Elegy II, Blue State*, 1983. Lift-ground etching and aquatint (black), soft ground etching (blue); plate: 11⅝ x 29⅜" (29 x 74.7 cm); paper: 18⅜ x 35½" (46.6 x 90.1 cm). Cat. no. I.7

7. *Running Elegy II, Yellow State*, 1983. Lift-ground etching and aquatint (black), soft ground etching (yellow); plate: 11⅝ x 29⅜" (29 x 74.7 cm); paper: 18⅜ x 35½" (46.6 x 90.1 cm). Cat. no. I.8

II. Automatism

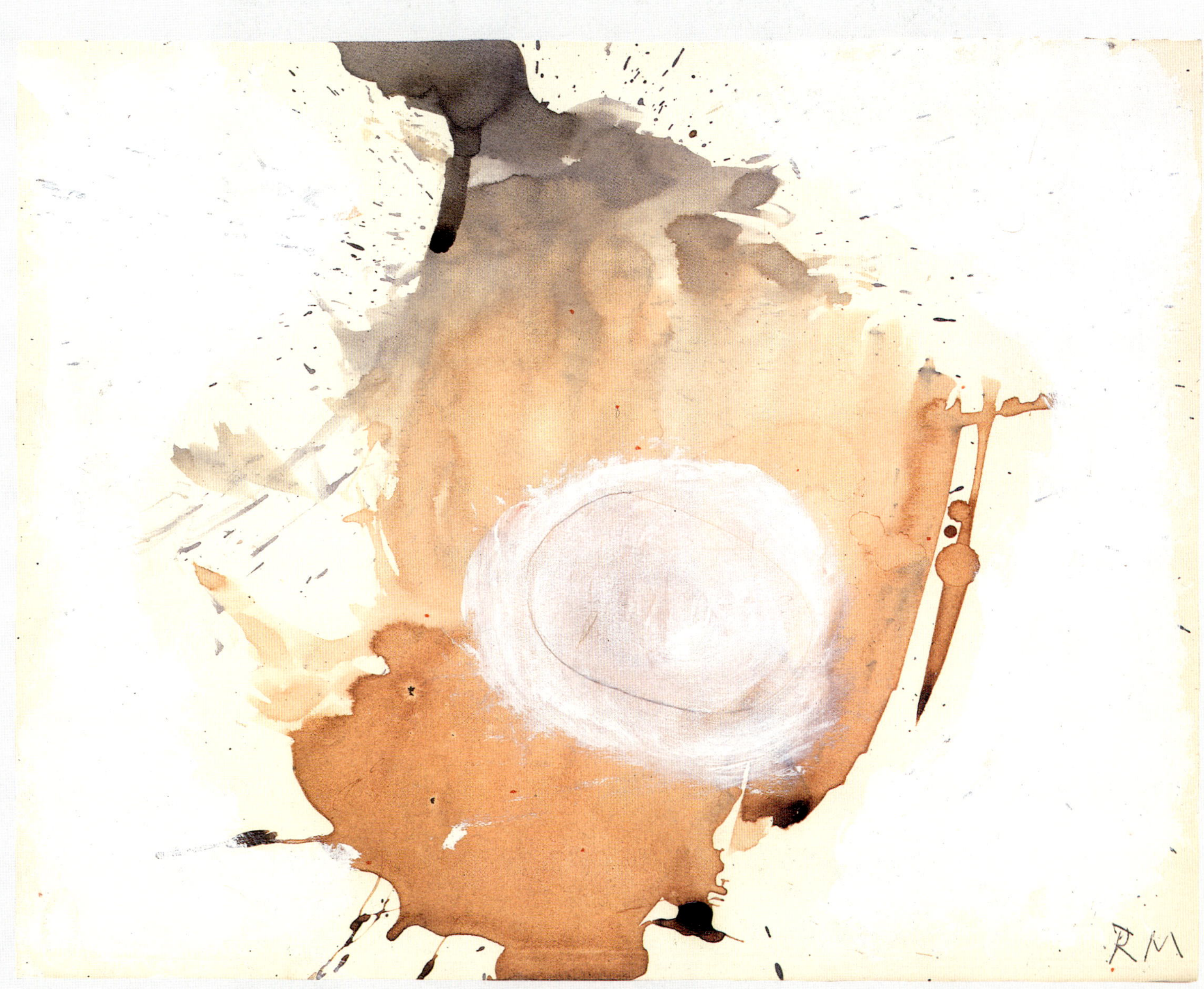

8. *Untitled*, 1957. Ink and oil on paper, 11⅝ x 14¼" (29.5 x 36.2 cm). Cat. no. II.1

9. *In Sepia Ink (Automatism Series)*, 1958. Ink on paper, 14½ x 11½" (36.8 x 29.2 cm). Cat. no. II.2

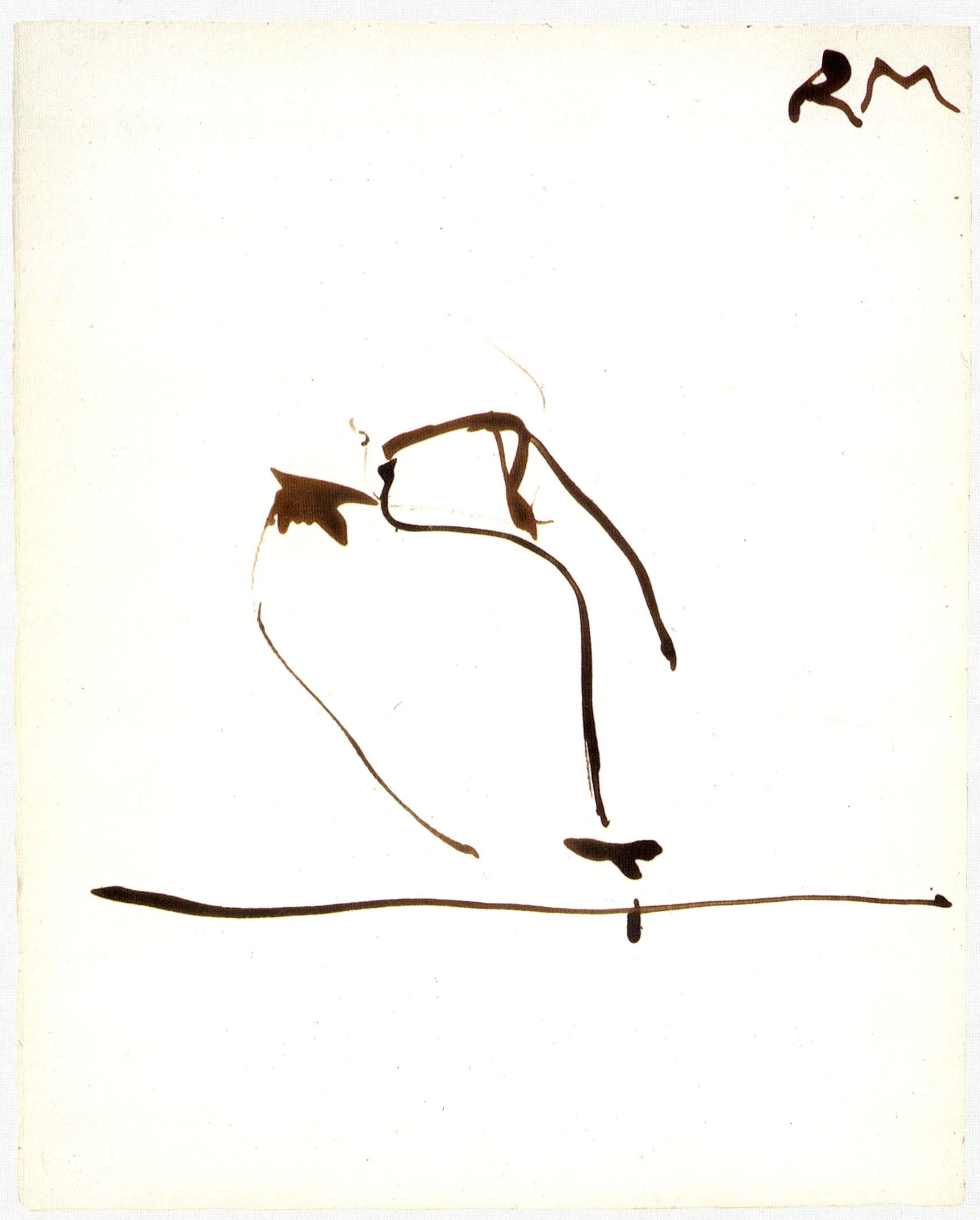

10. *Sepia Automatism*, 1958. Ink on paper, 14½ x 11½" (36.8 x 29.2 cm). Cat. no. II.3

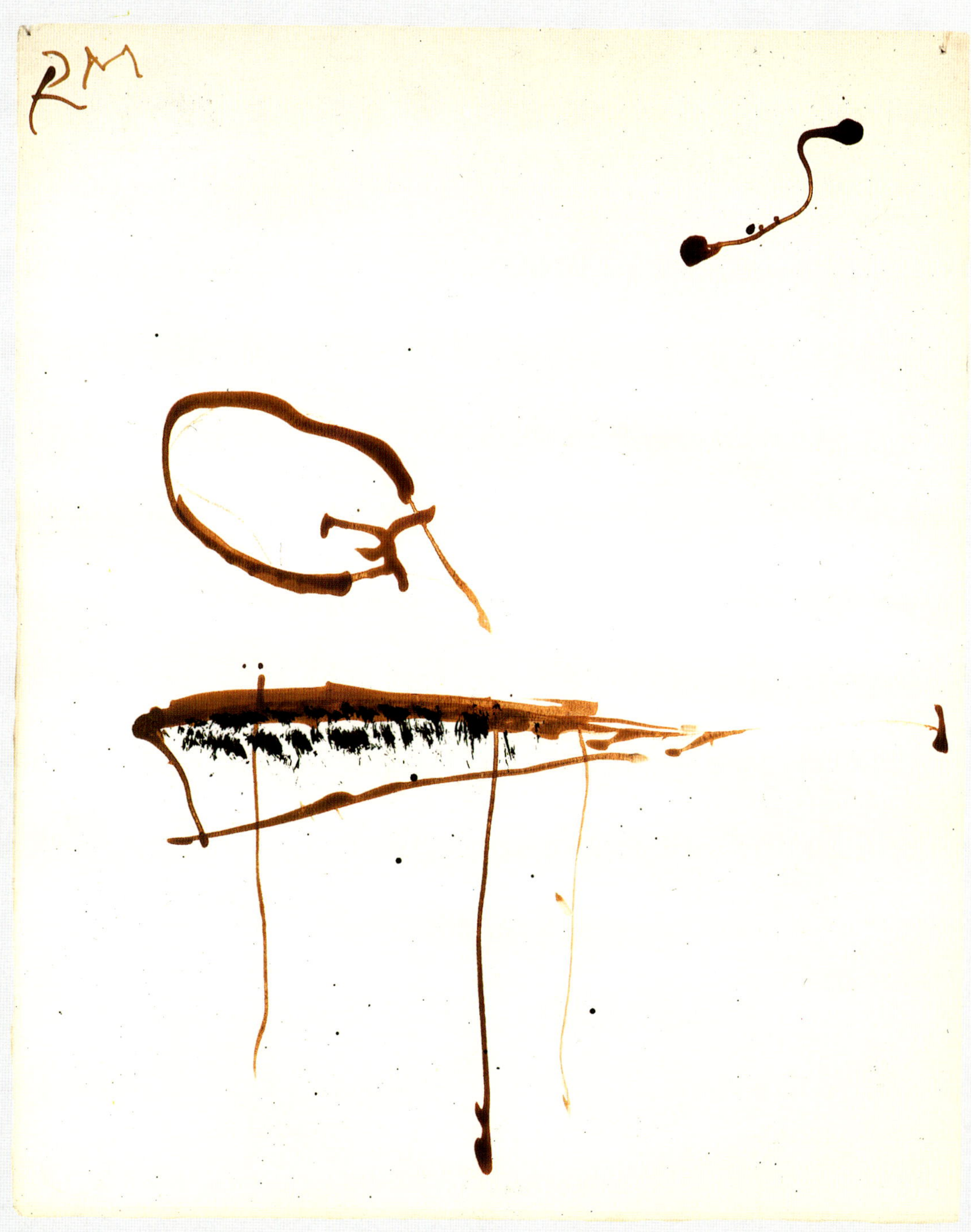

11. *Sepia Automatism*, 1958. Ink on paper, 14½ x 11½" (36.8 x 29.2 cm). Cat. no. II.4

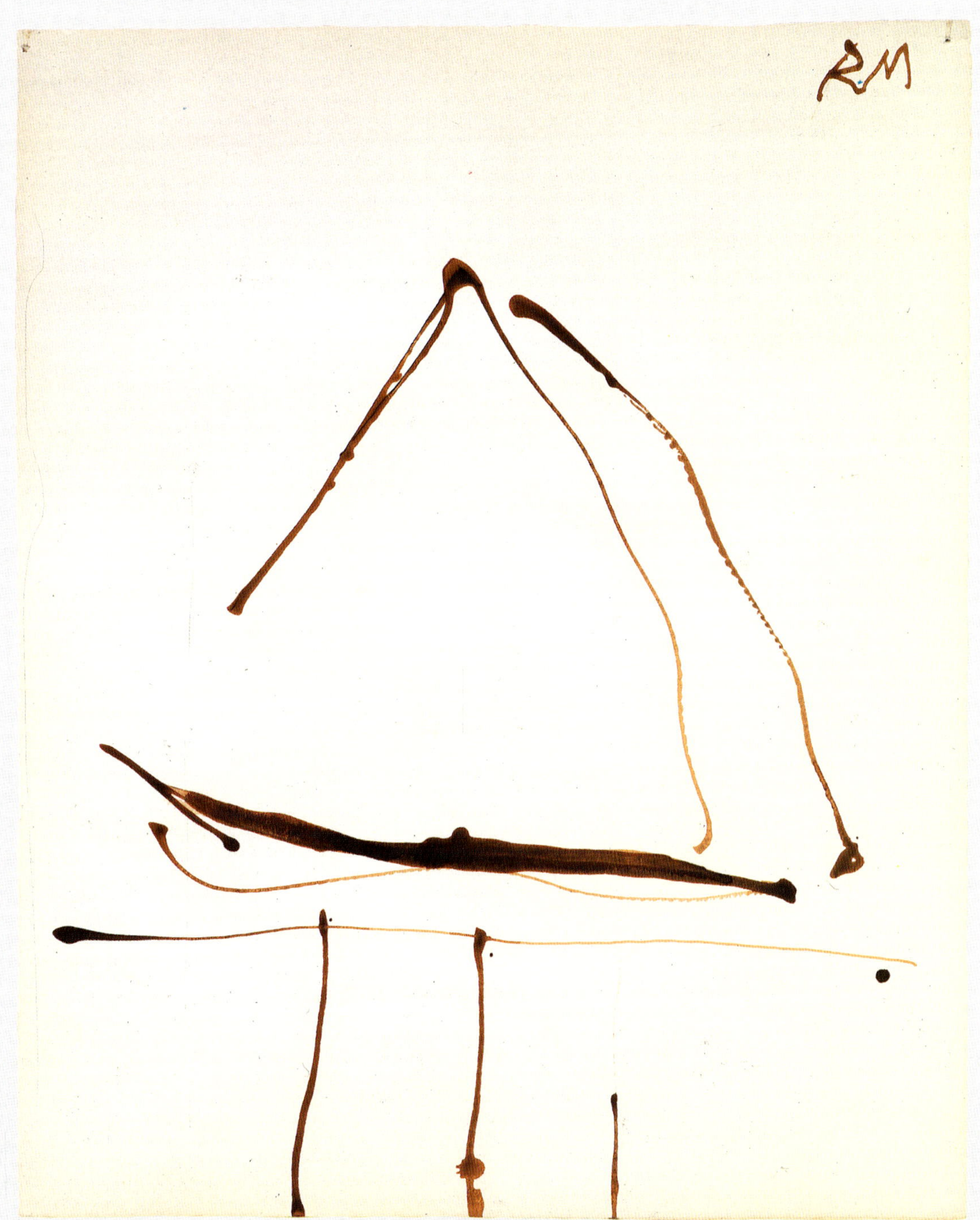

12. *Sepia Automatism*, 1958. Ink on paper, 14½ x 11″ (36.8 x 27.9 cm). Cat. no. II.5

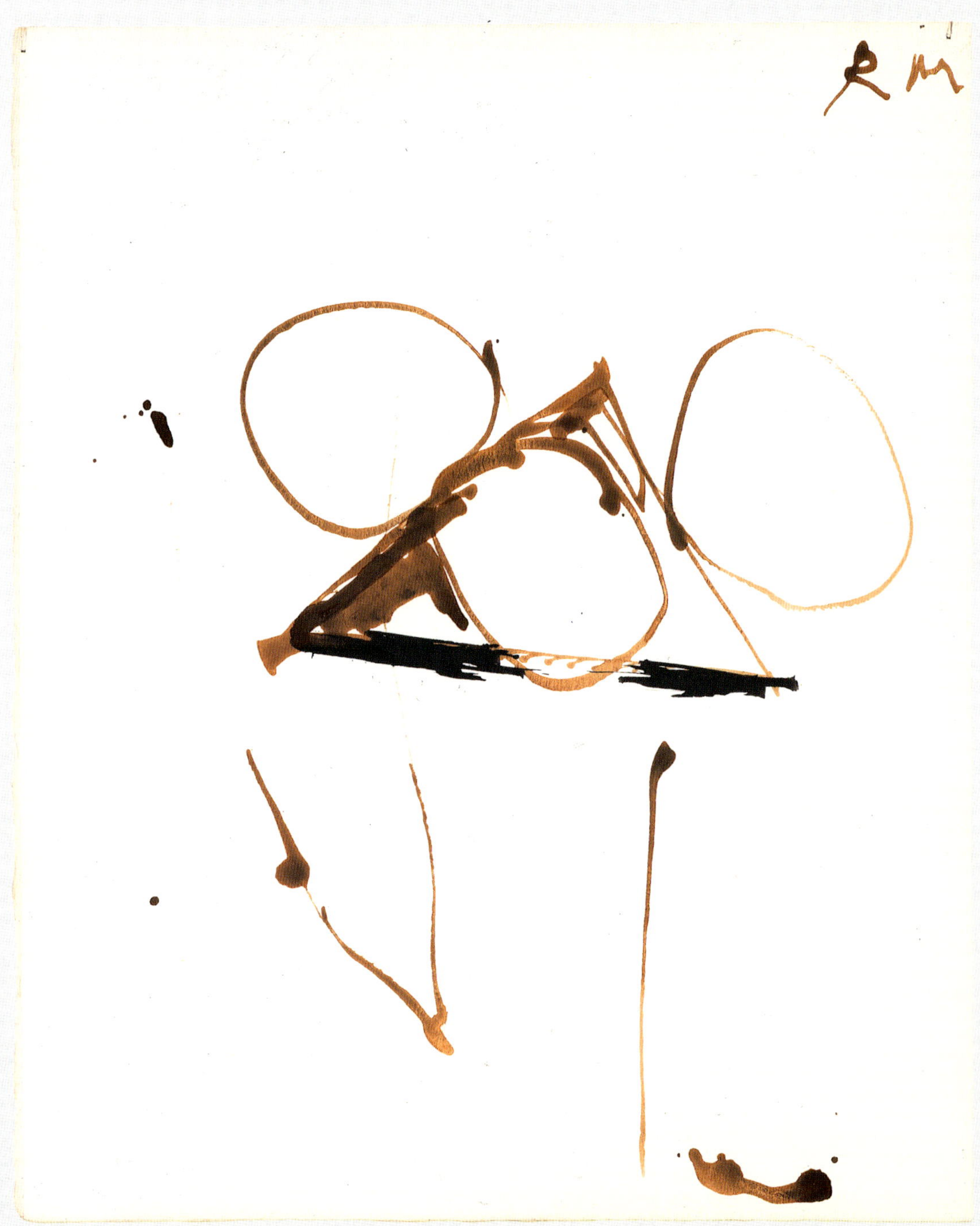

13. *Calligraphy*, 1965–66. Lithograph; image: 15 x 22″ (38.1 x 55.8 cm); paper: 19¼ x 26″ (48.9 x 66 cm). Cat. no. II.6

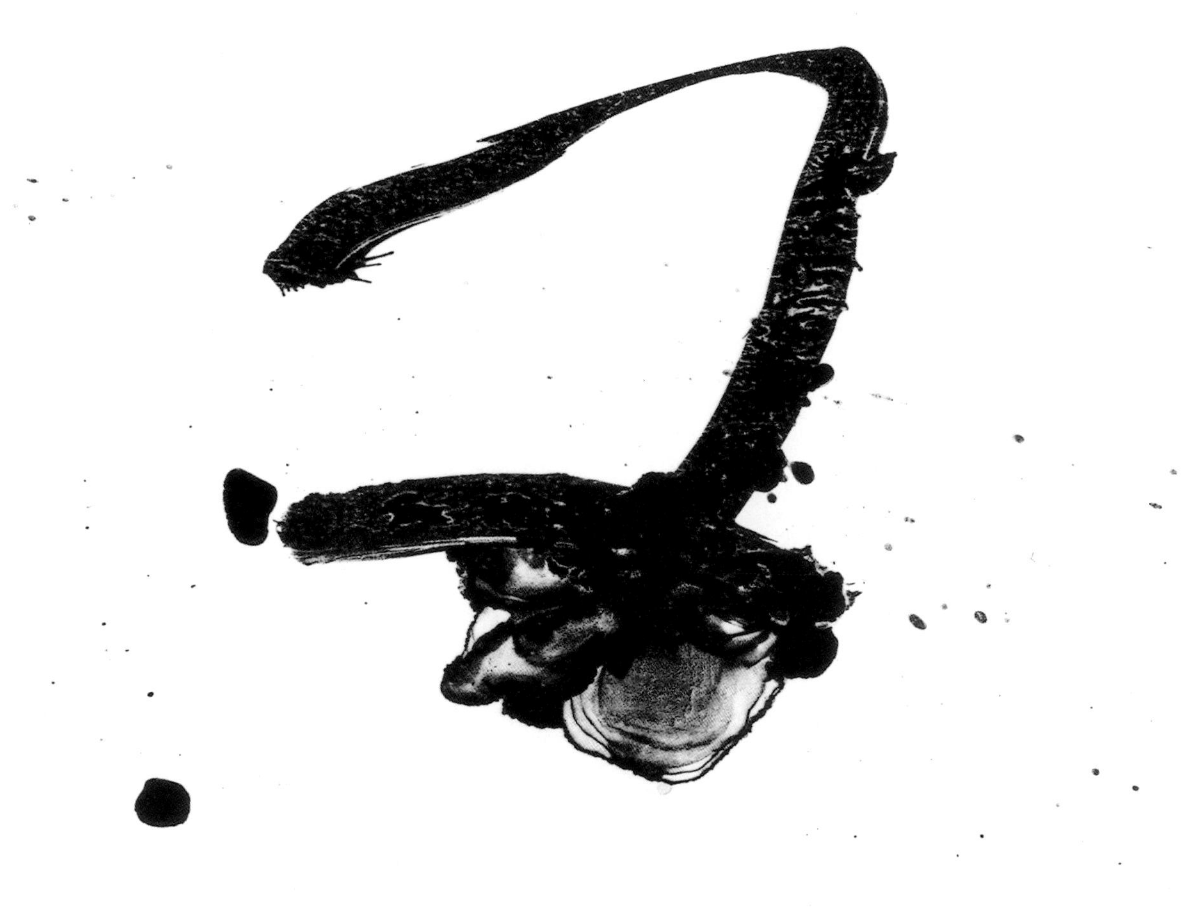

III. From *Lyric Suite*

14. *Lyric Suite*, 1965. Ink on rice paper, 11 x 9" (27.9 x 22.9 cm). Cat. no. III.1

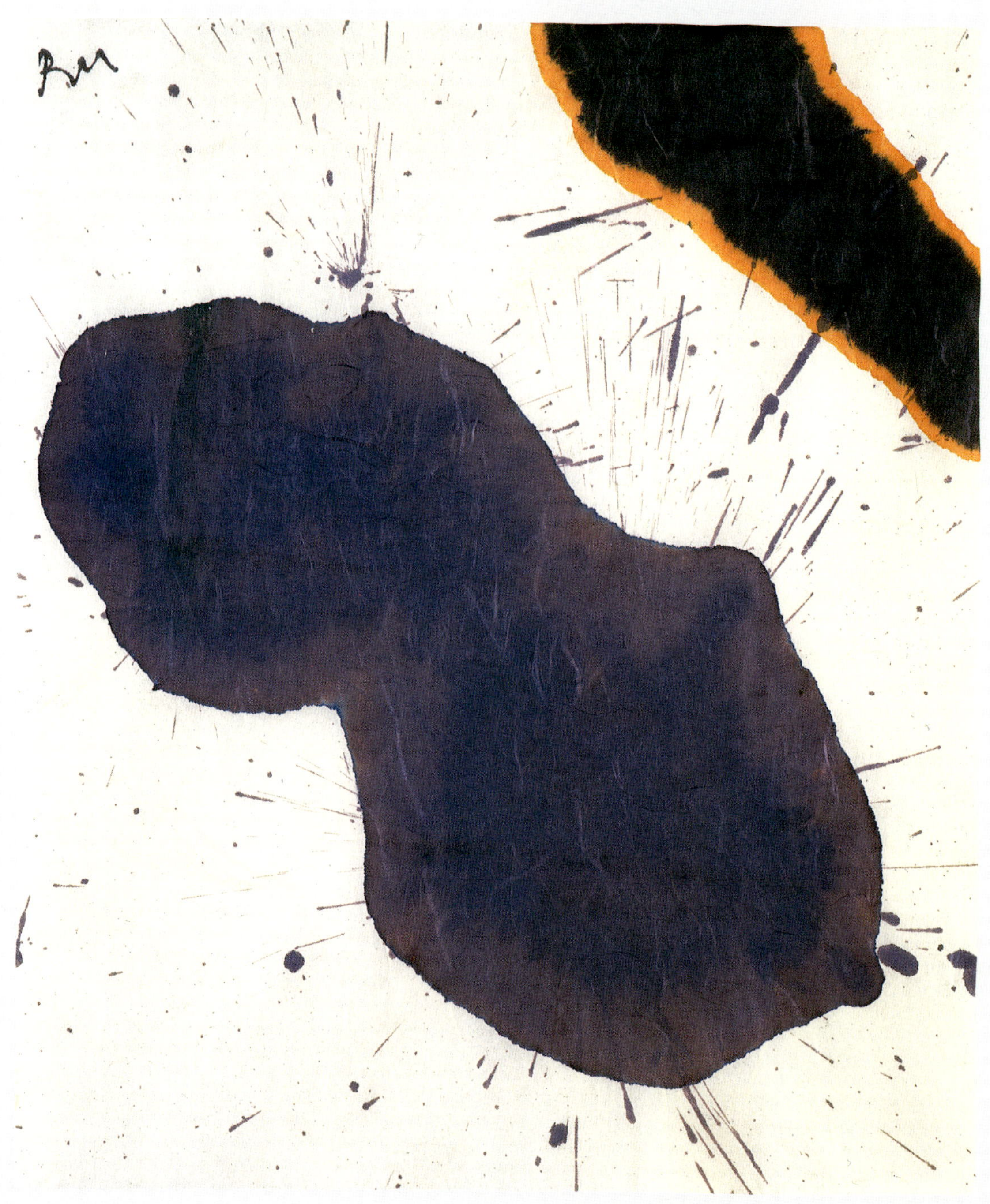

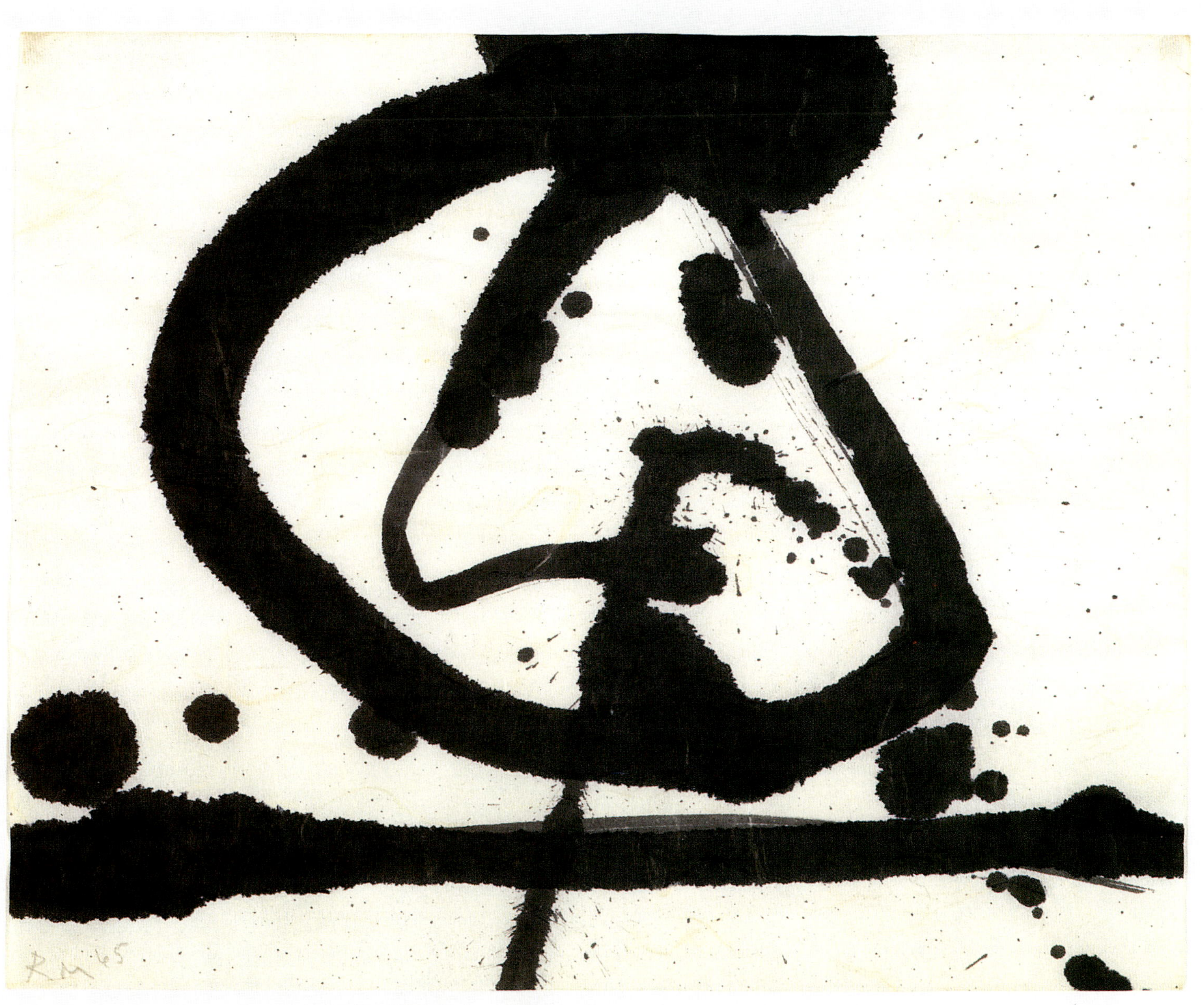

15. *Lyric Suite*, 1965. Ink on rice paper, 9 x 11" (22.9 x 27.9 cm). Cat. no. III.2

16. *Lyric Suite*, 1965. Ink on rice paper, 9 x 11″ (22.9 x 27.9 cm). Cat. no. III.3

17. *Lyric Suite*, 1965. Ink on rice paper, 11 x 9″ (27.9 x 22.9 cm). Cat. no. III.4

18. *Lyric Suite*, 1965. Ink on rice paper, 11 x 9″ (27.9 x 22.9 cm). Cat. no. III.5

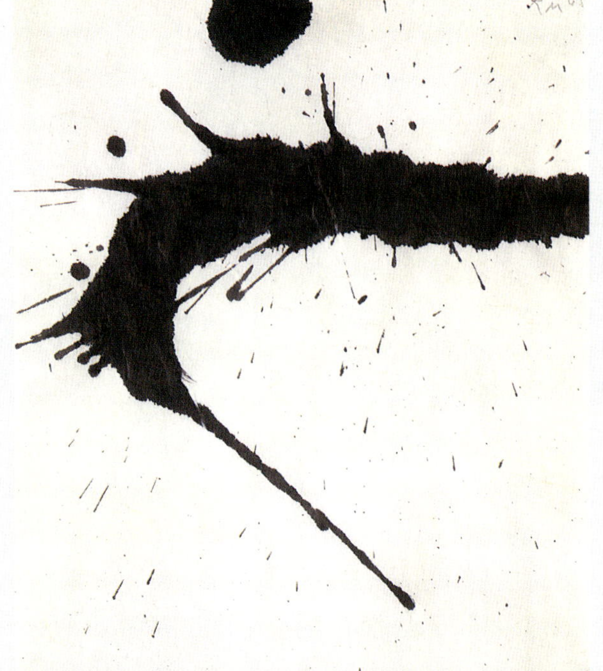

19. *Lyric Suite*, 1965. Ink on rice paper, 9 x 11″ (22.9 x 27.9 cm). Cat. no. III.6

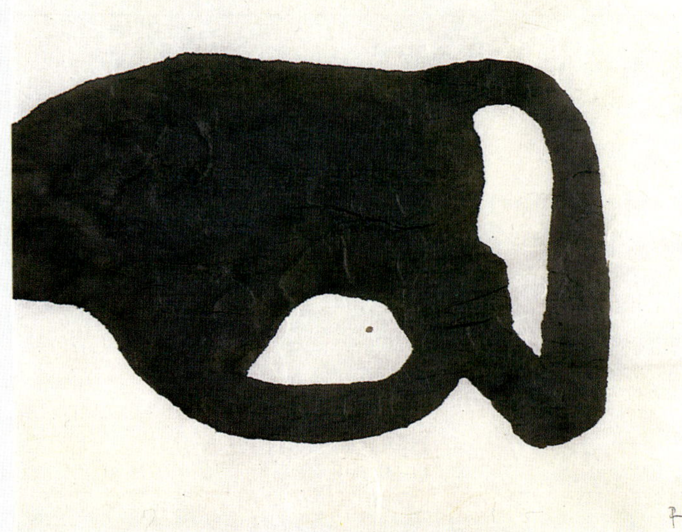

20. *Lyric Suite*, 1965. Ink on rice paper, 9 x 11″ (22.9 x 27.9 cm). Cat. no. III.7

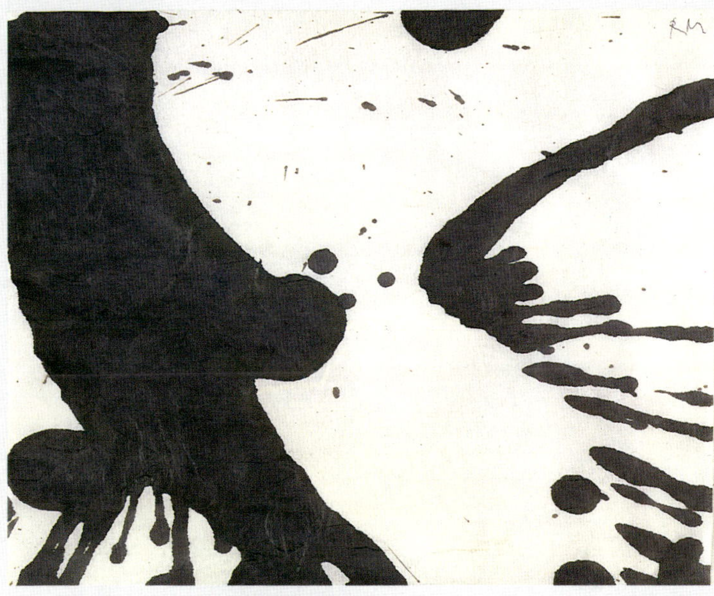

21. *Lyric Suite*, 1965. Ink on rice paper, 9 x 11″ (22.9 x 27.9 cm). Cat. no. III.8

22. *Lyric Suite*, 1965. Ink on rice paper, 11 x 9″ (27.9 x 22.9 cm). Cat. no. III.9

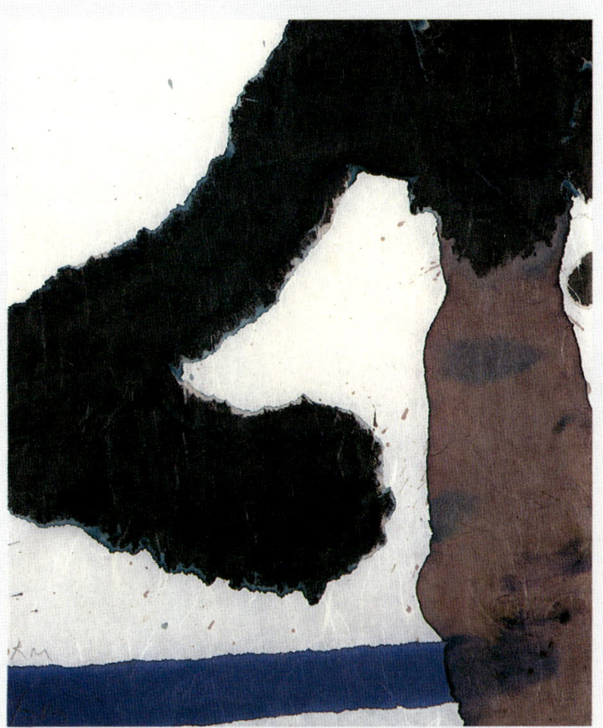

23. *Lyric Suite*, 1965. Ink on rice paper, 11 x 9″ (27.9 x 22.9 cm). Cat. no. III.10

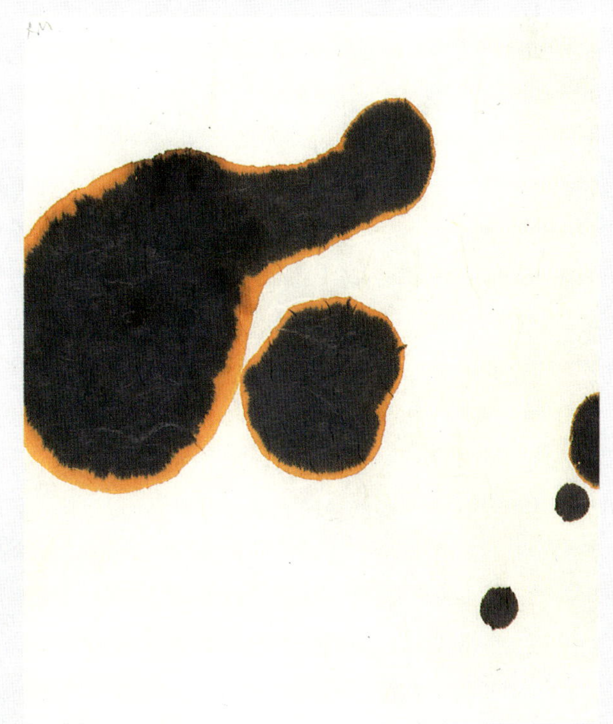

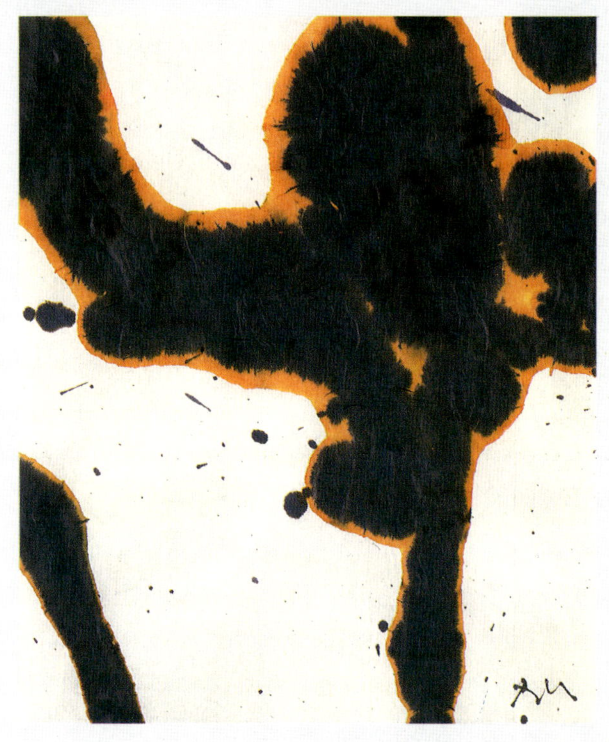

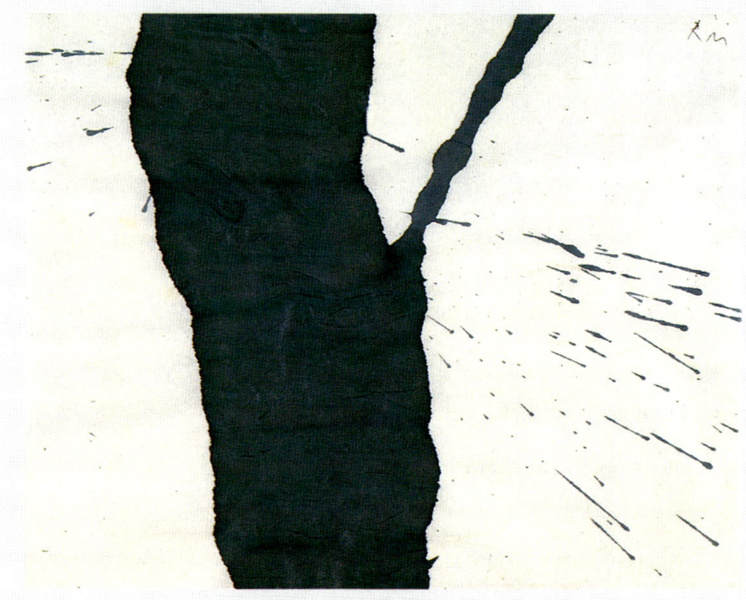

24. *Lyric Suite*, 1965. Ink on rice paper, 11 x 9″ (27.9 x 22.9 cm). Cat. no. III.11

25. *Lyric Suite*, 1965. Ink on rice paper, 9 x 11″ (22.9 x 27.9 cm). Cat. no. III.12

26. *Lyric Suite*, 1965. Ink on rice paper, 9 x 11″ (22.9 x 27.9 cm). Cat. no. III.13

27. *Lyric Suite*, 1965. Ink on rice paper, 9 x 11″ (22.9 x 27.9 cm). Cat. no. III.14

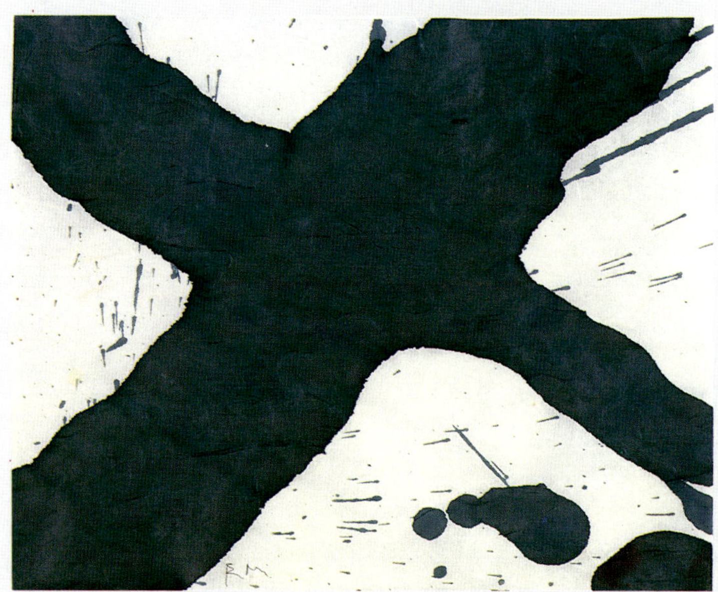

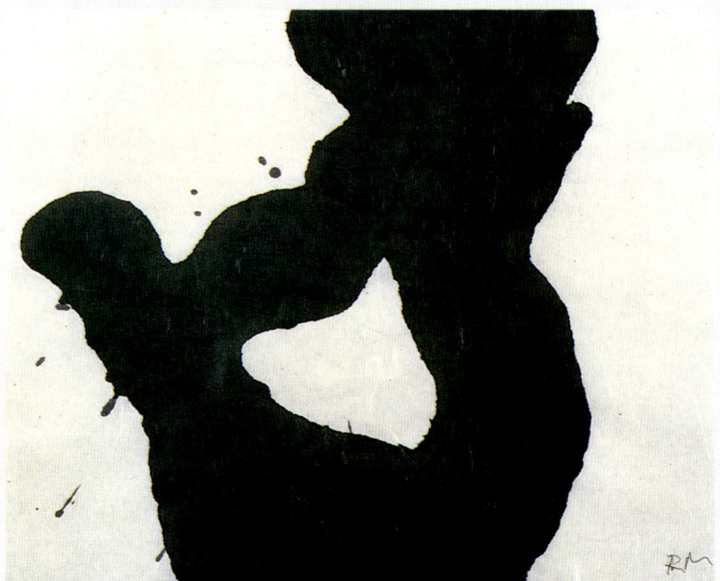

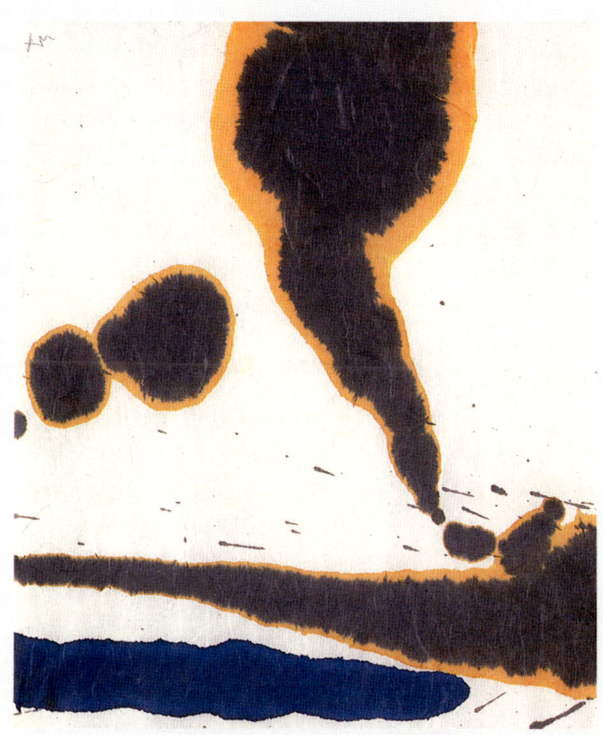

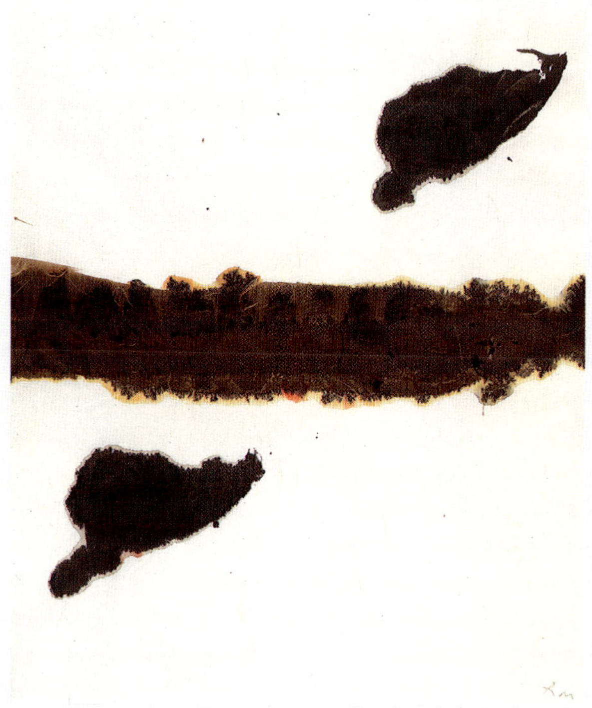

28. *Lyric Suite*, 1965. Ink on rice paper, 11 x 9″ (27.9 x 22.9 cm). Cat. no. III.15

29. *Lyric Suite*, 1965. Ink on rice paper, 11 x 9″ (27.9 x 22.9 cm). Cat. no. III.16

30. *Lyric Suite*, 1965. Ink on rice paper, 11 x 9″ (27.9 x 22.9 cm). Cat. no. III.17

31. *Lyric Suite*, 1965. Ink on rice paper, 9 x 11″ (22.9 x 27.9 cm). Cat. no. III.18

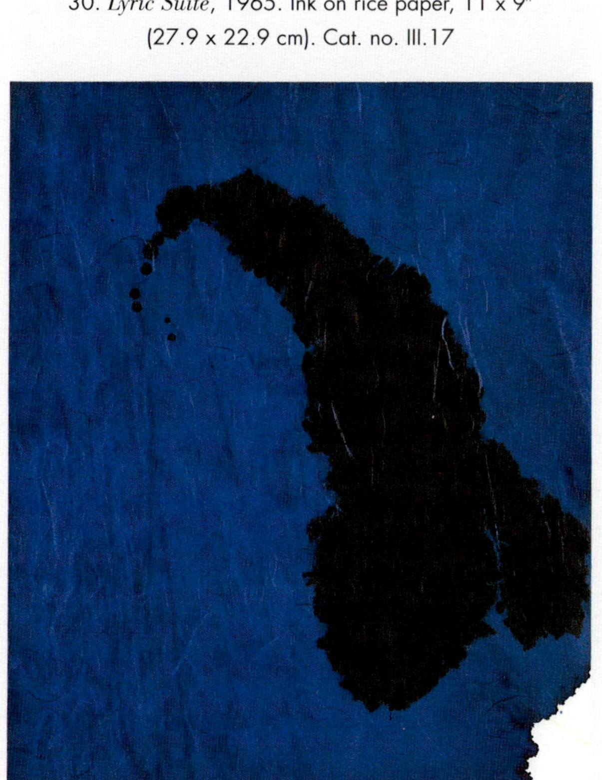

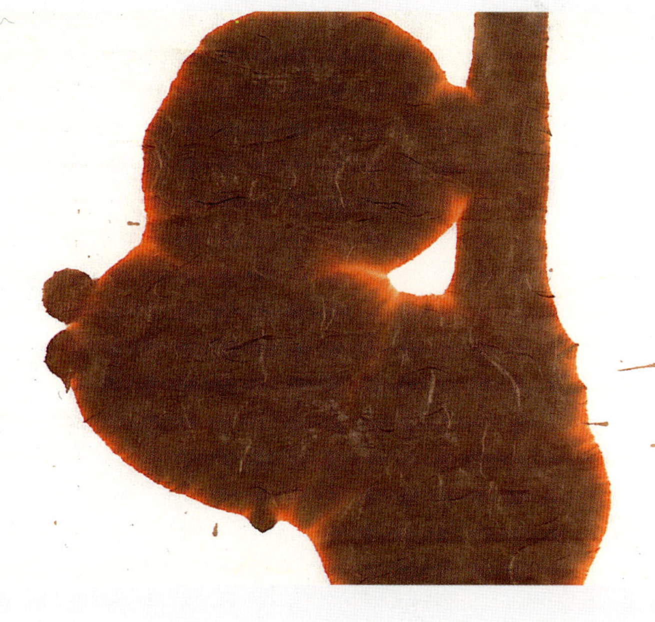

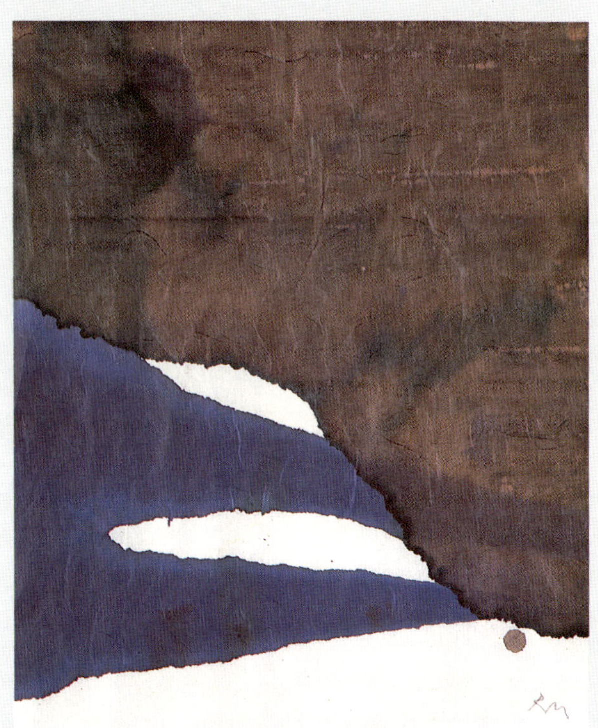

32. *Lyric Suite*, 1965. Ink on rice paper, 11 x 9″ (27.9 x 22.9 cm). Cat. no. III.19

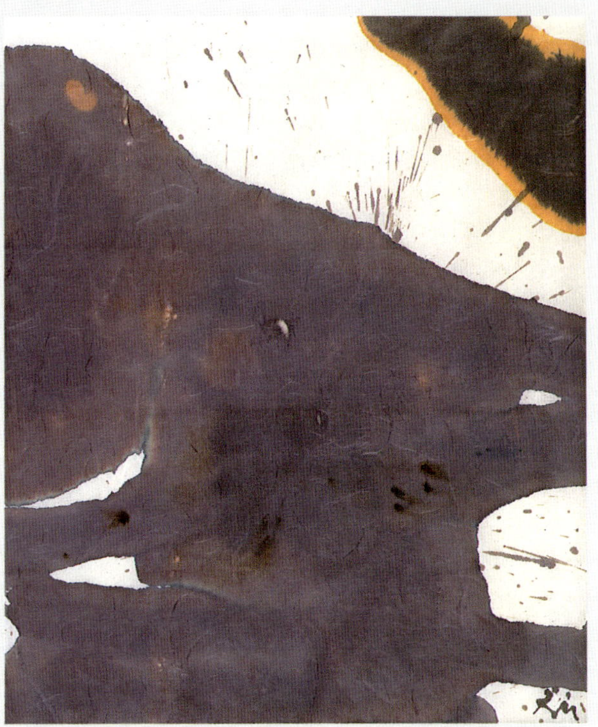

33. *Lyric Suite*, 1965. Ink on rice paper, 11 x 9″ (27.9 x 22.9 cm). Cat. no. III.20

34. *Lyric Suite*, 1965. Ink on rice paper, 11 x 9″ (27.9 x 22.9 cm). Cat. no. III.21

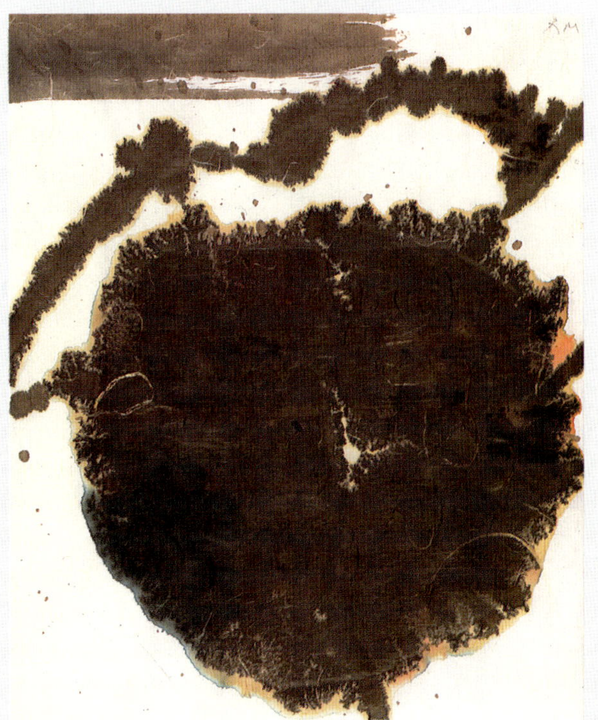

35. *Lyric Suite*, 1965. Ink on rice paper, 11 x 9″ (27.9 x 22.9 cm). Cat. no. III.22

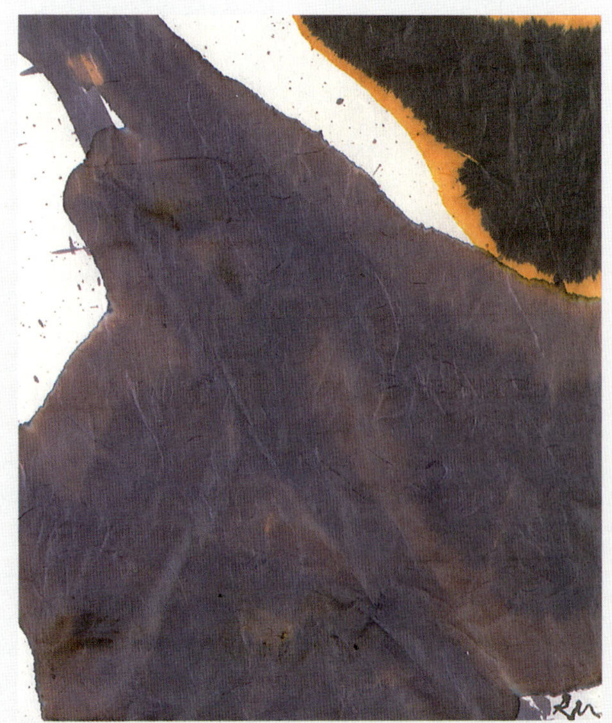

36. *Lyric Suite*, 1965. Ink on rice paper, 11 x 9" (27.9 x 22.9 cm). Cat. no. III.23

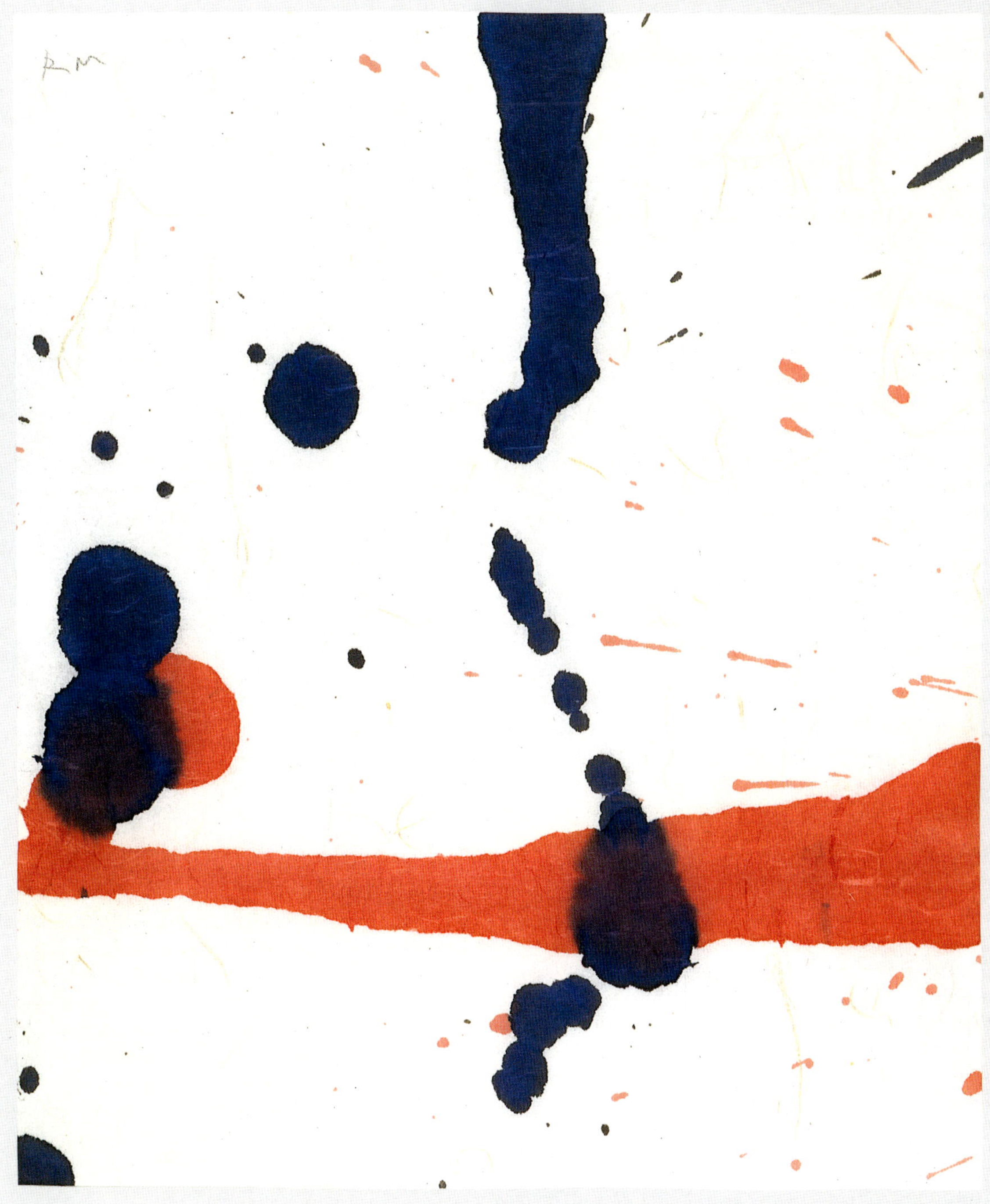

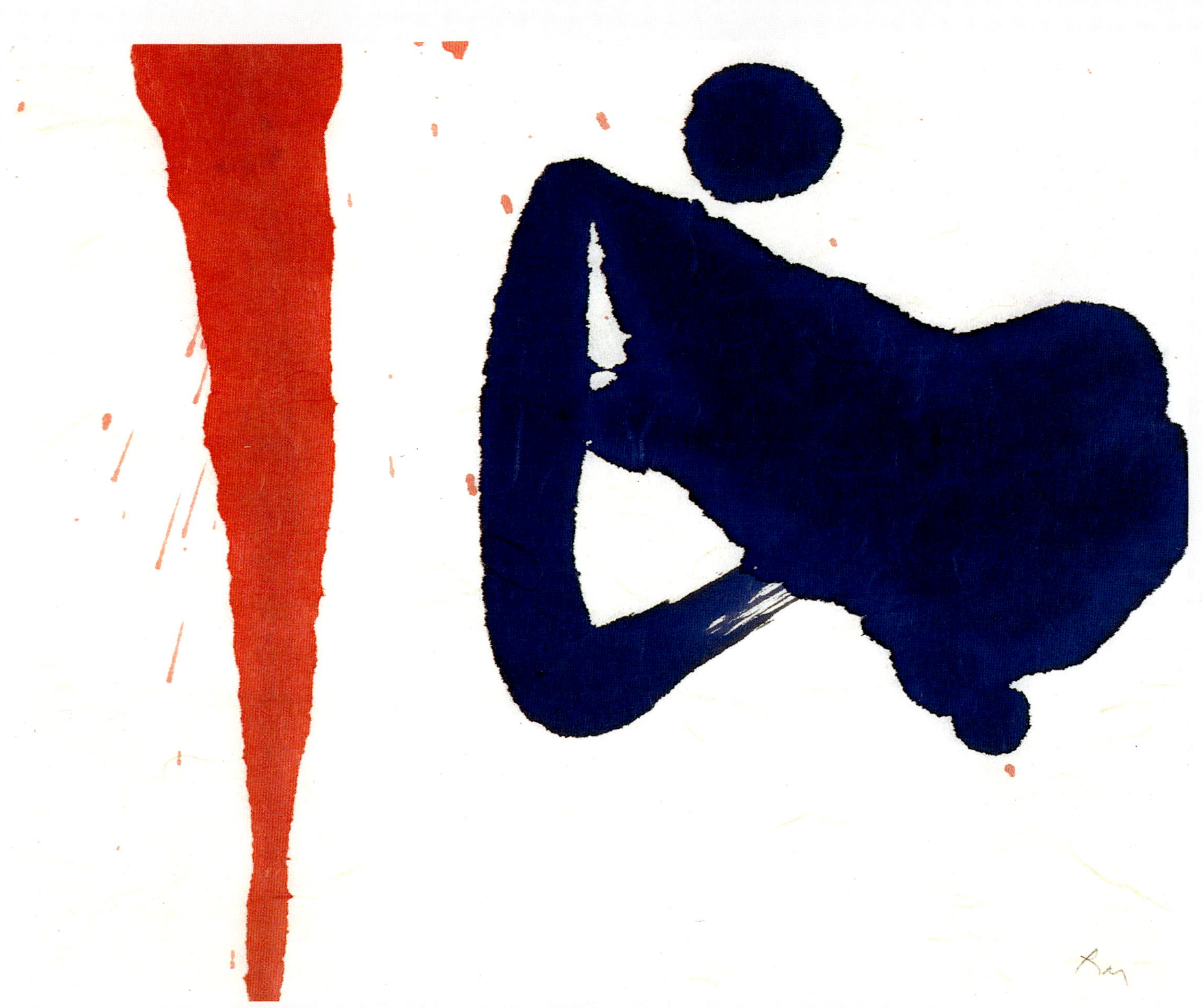

37. *Lyric Suite*, 1965. Ink on rice paper, 9 x 11″ (22.9 x 27.9 cm). Cat. no. III.24

IV. *Je t'aime*

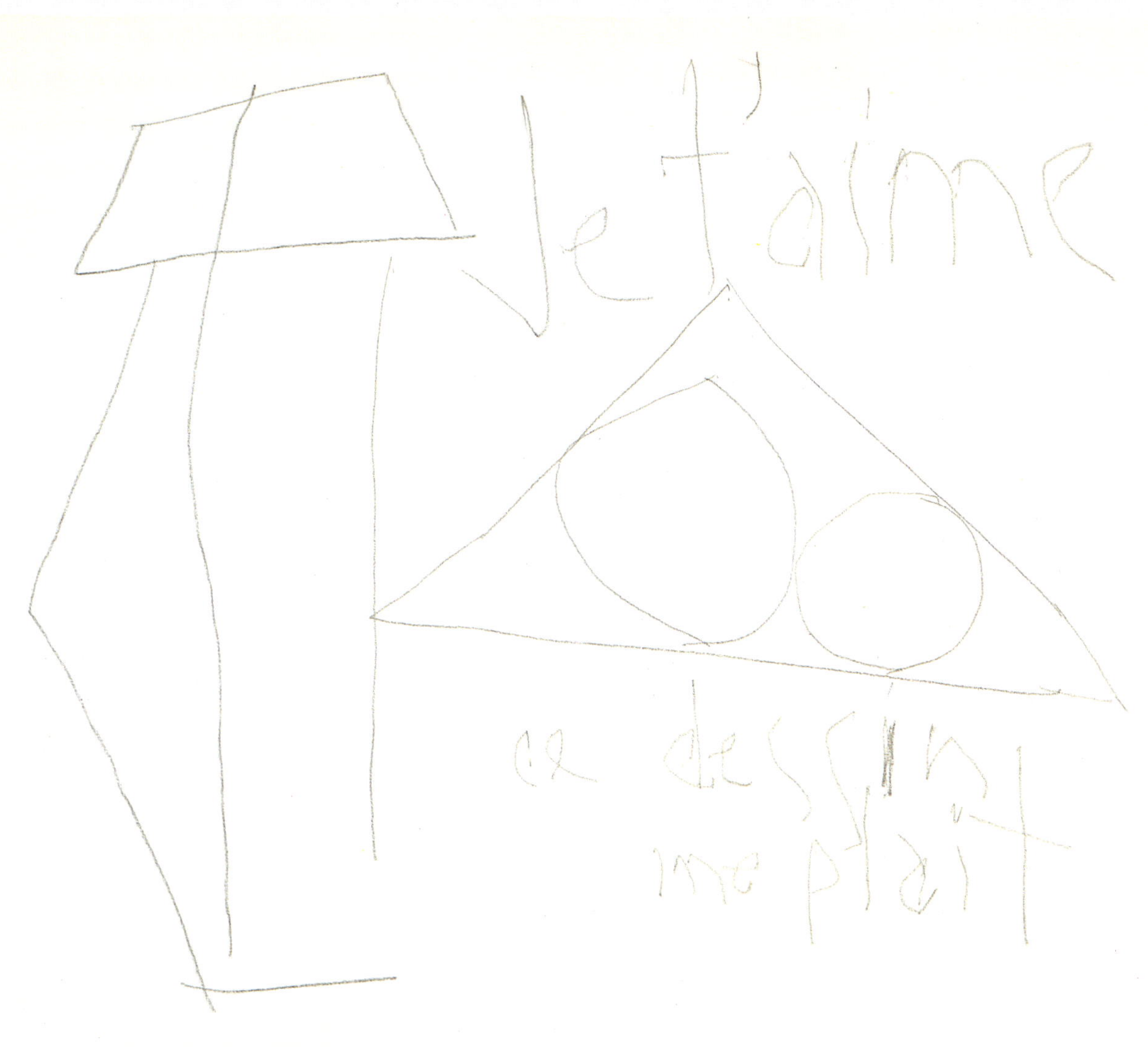

38. *Je t'aime (ce dessin me plait)*, 1956. Pencil on Strathmore paper, 23 x 29" (58.4 x 73.7 cm). Cat. no. IV.1

PAGES 118–122:
39–48. *Madrid Suite*, 1965–66. Suite of ten lithographs; image: 19¾ x 25" (50.4 x 63.5 cm) varies; paper: 22 x 30" (55.9 x 76.2 cm)

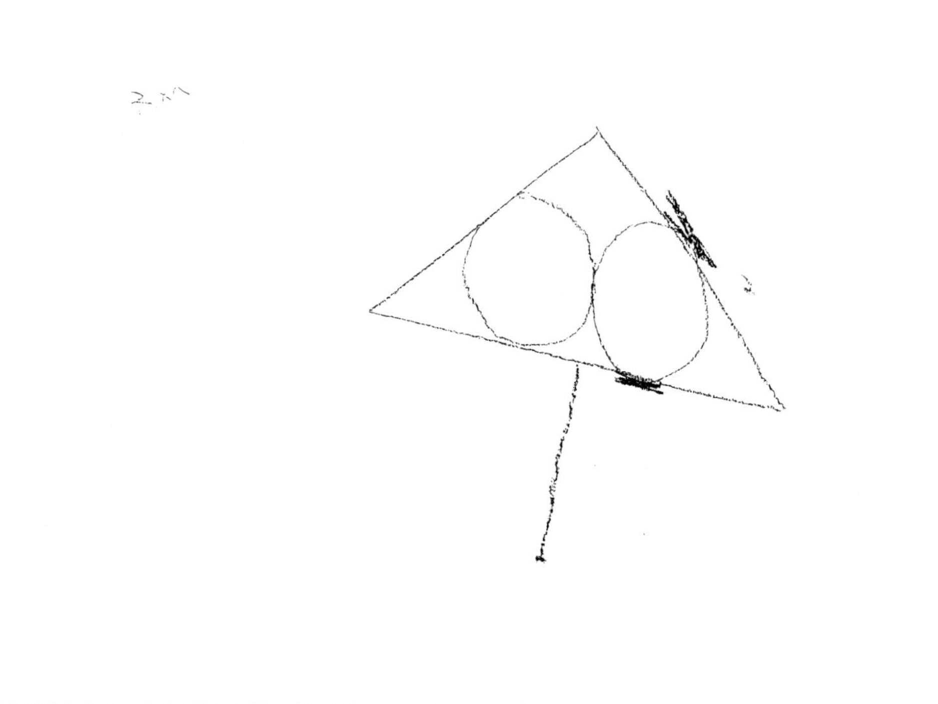

39. From the *Madrid Suite*. Cat. no. IV.2

40. From the *Madrid Suite*. Cat. no. IV.3

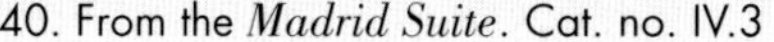

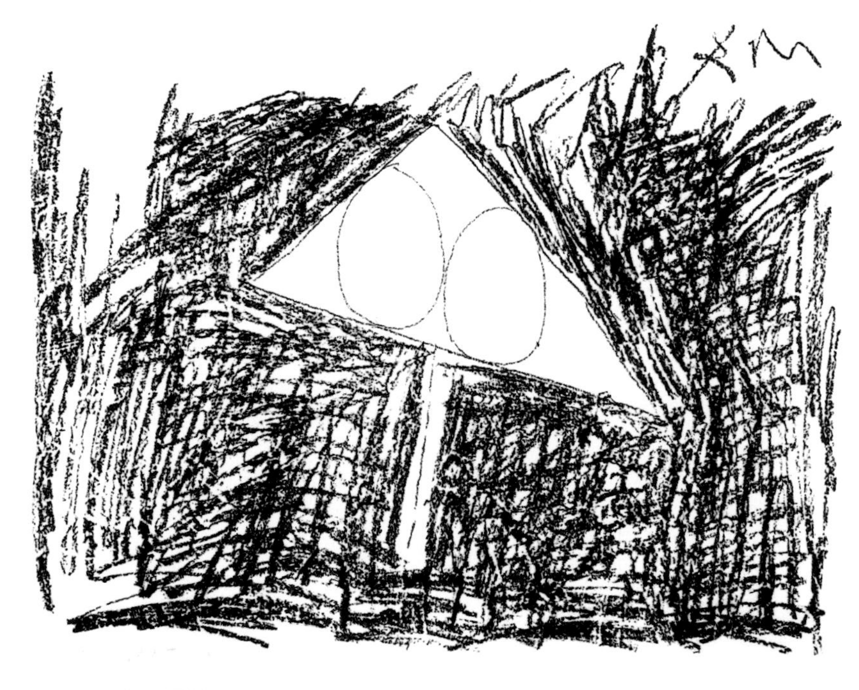

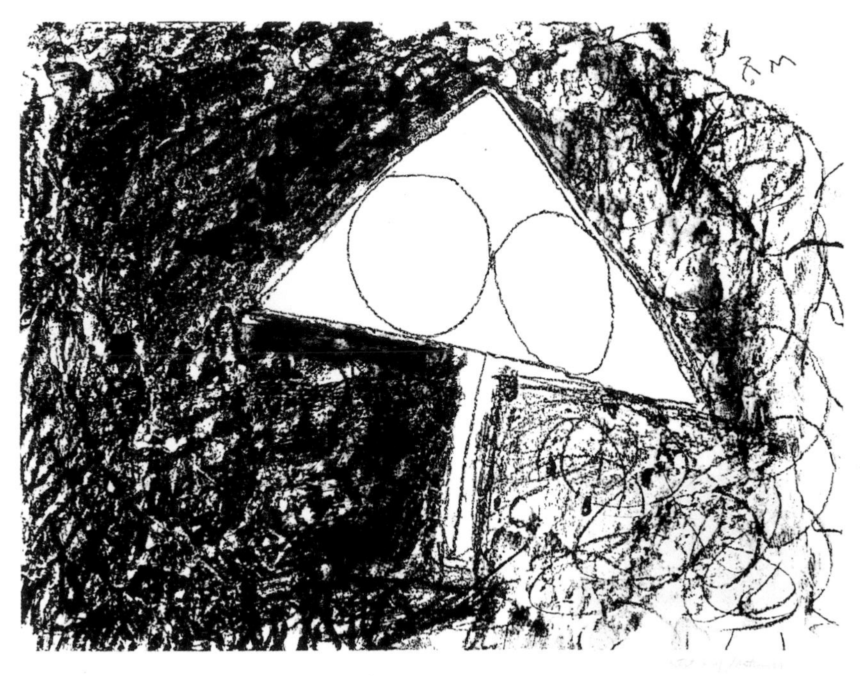

41. From the *Madrid Suite*. Cat. no. IV.4

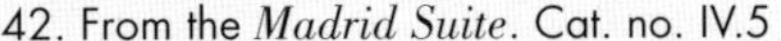

42. From the *Madrid Suite*. Cat. no. IV.5

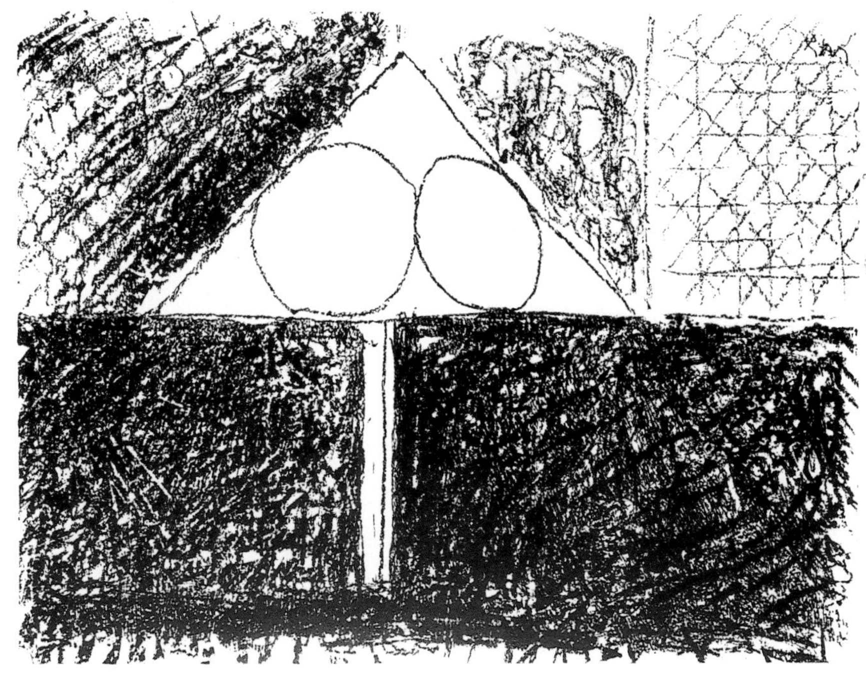

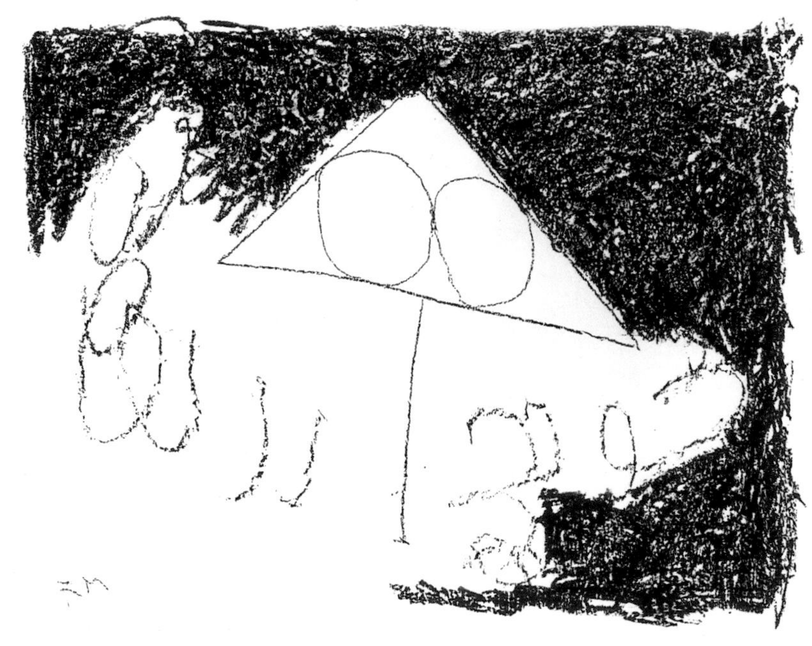

43. From the *Madrid Suite*. Cat. no. IV.6

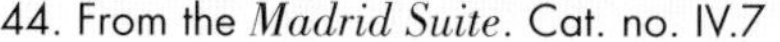

44. From the *Madrid Suite*. Cat. no. IV.7

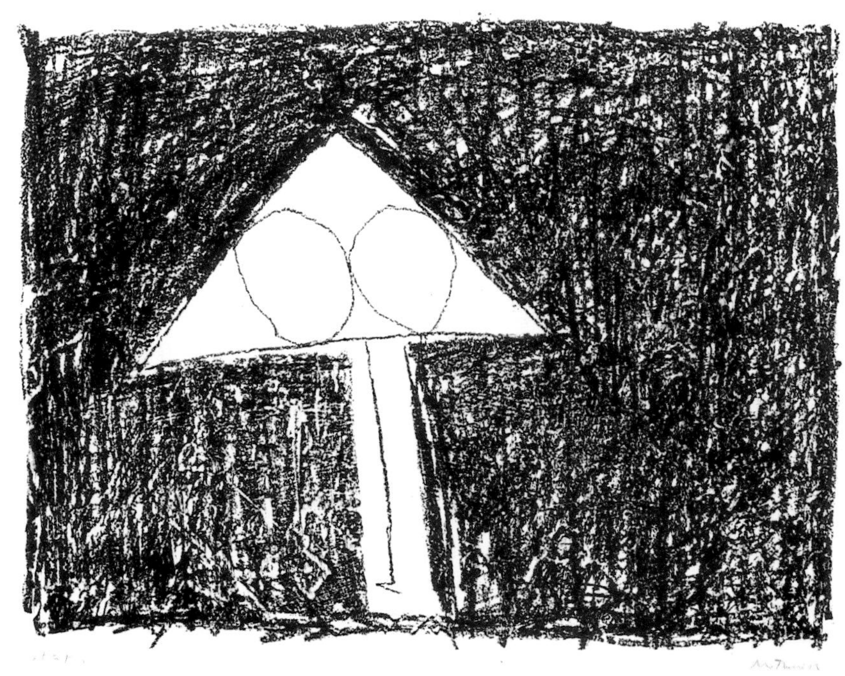

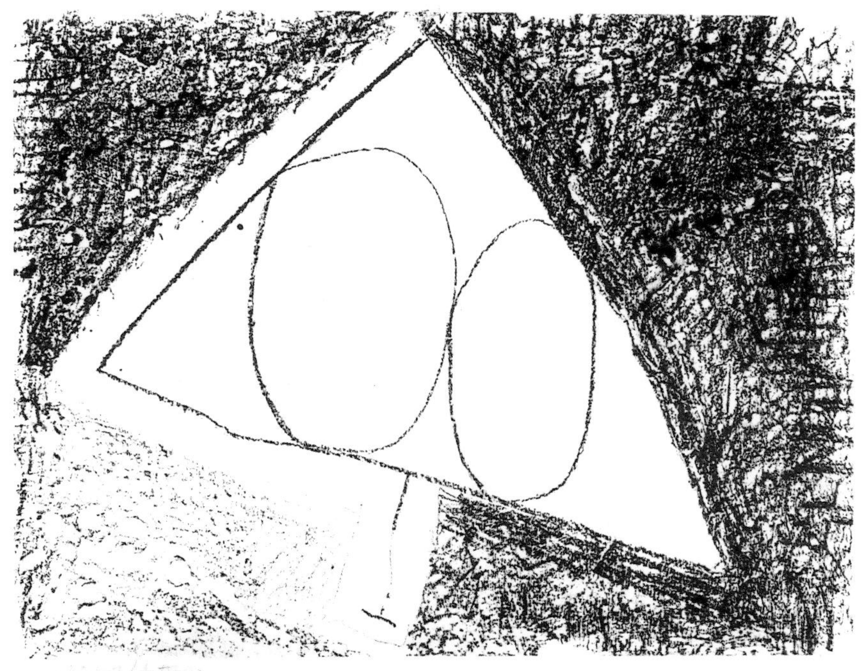

45. From the *Madrid Suite*. Cat. no. IV.8

46. From the *Madrid Suite*. Cat. no. IV.9

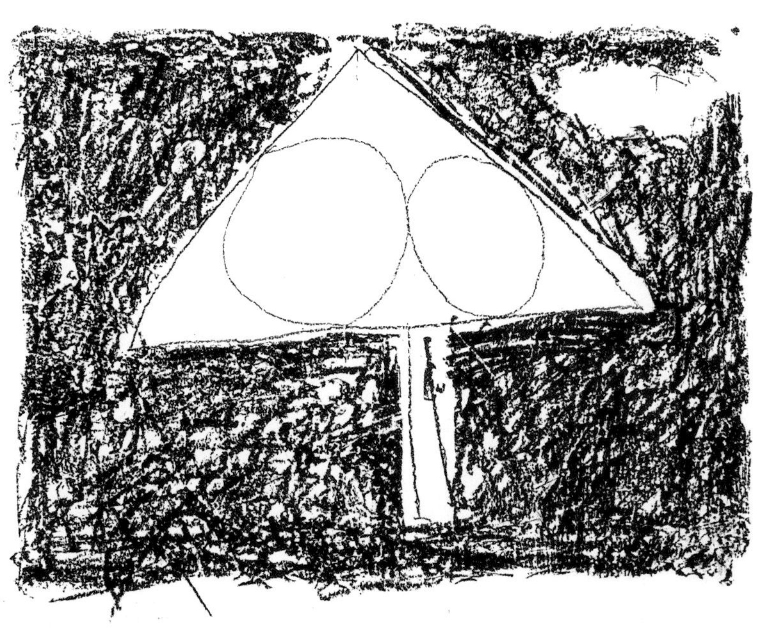

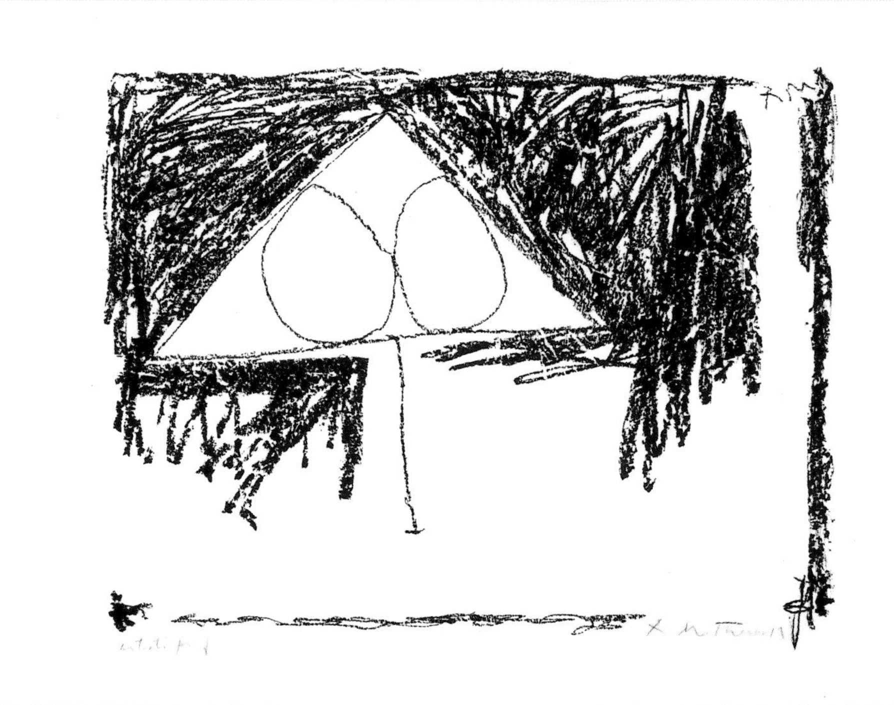

47. From the *Madrid Suite*. Cat. no. IV.10

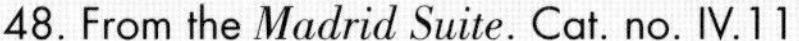

48. From the *Madrid Suite*. Cat. no. IV.11

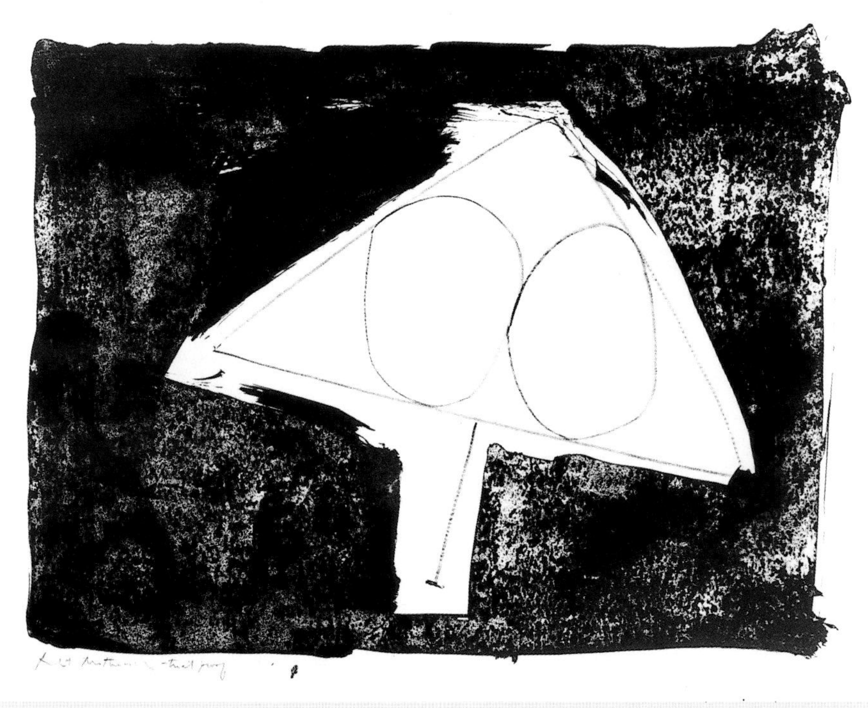

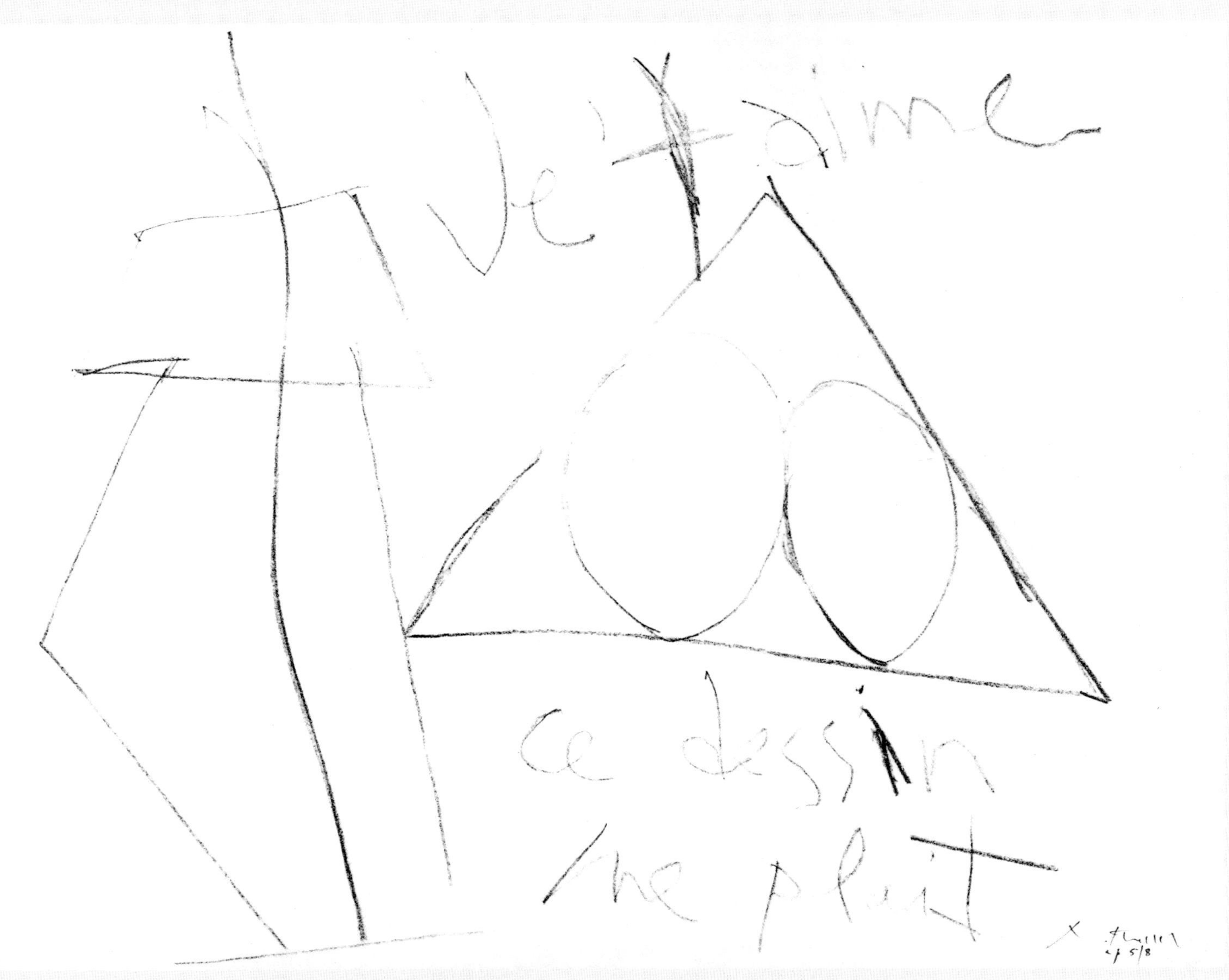

49. *Je t'aime*, 1977. Lithograph; image and paper: 18 x 23" (45.8 x 58.5 cm). Cat. no. IV.12

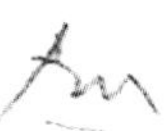

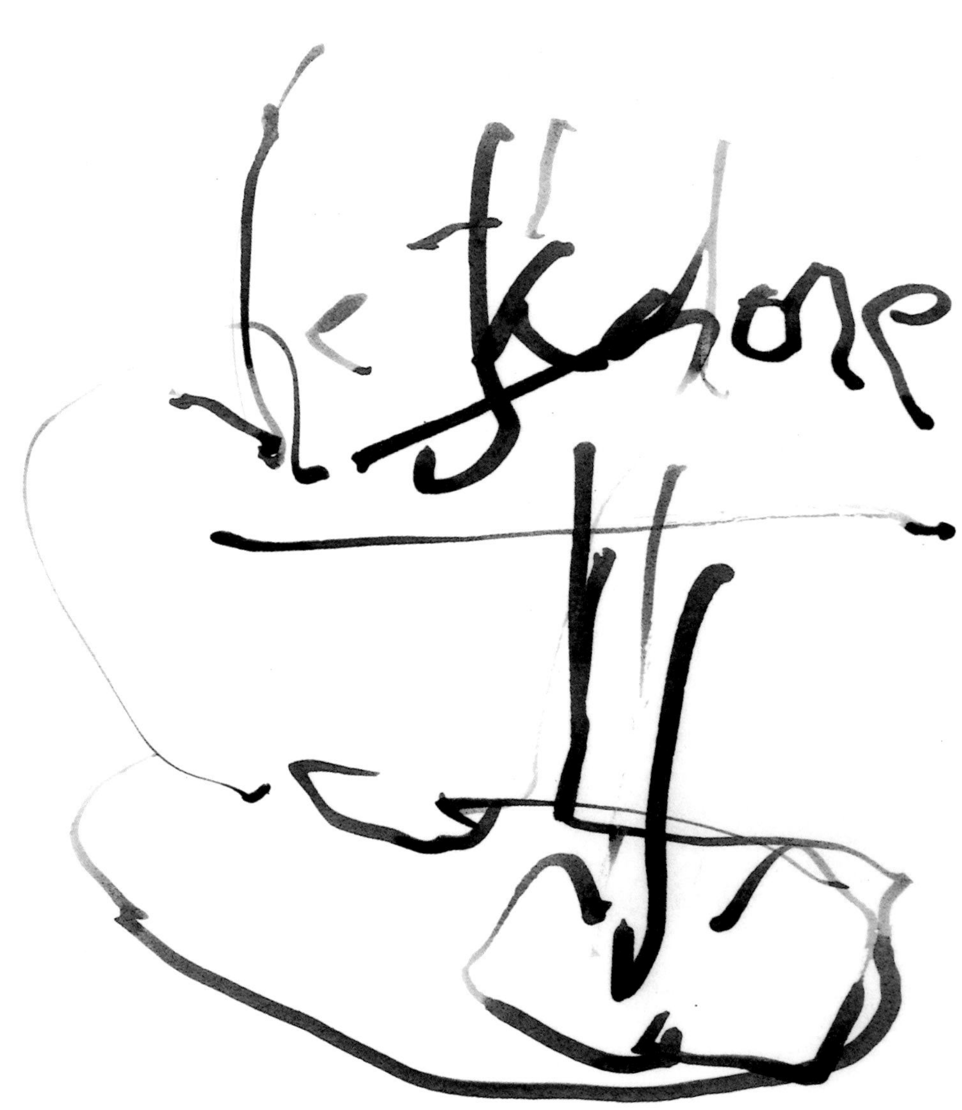

50. *Je t'adore*, 1982. Ink on paper, 8 x 9¾" (20.3 x 24.8 cm). Cat. no. IV.13

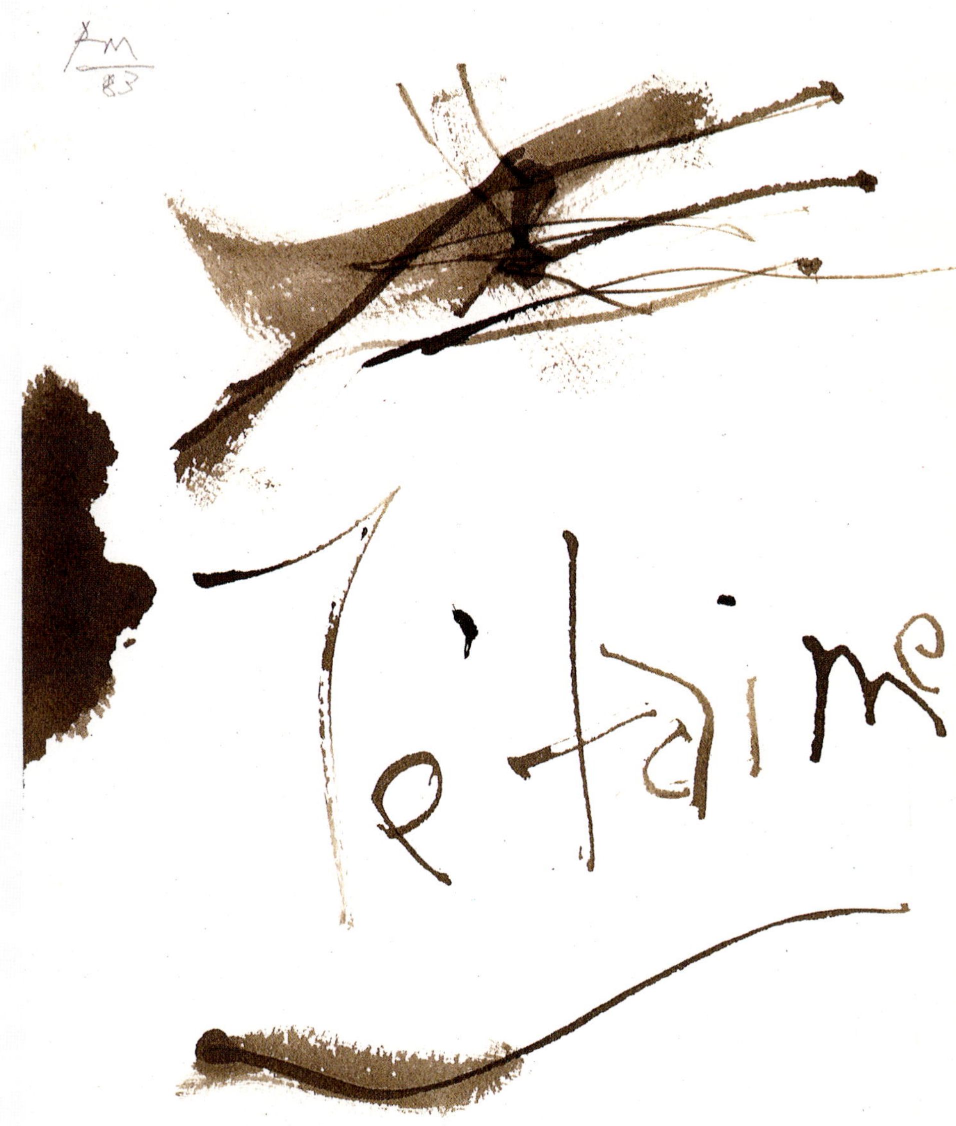

51. *Je t'aime*, 1983. Ink on paper, 10⅛ x 7" (25.8 x 17.8 cm). Cat. no. IV.14

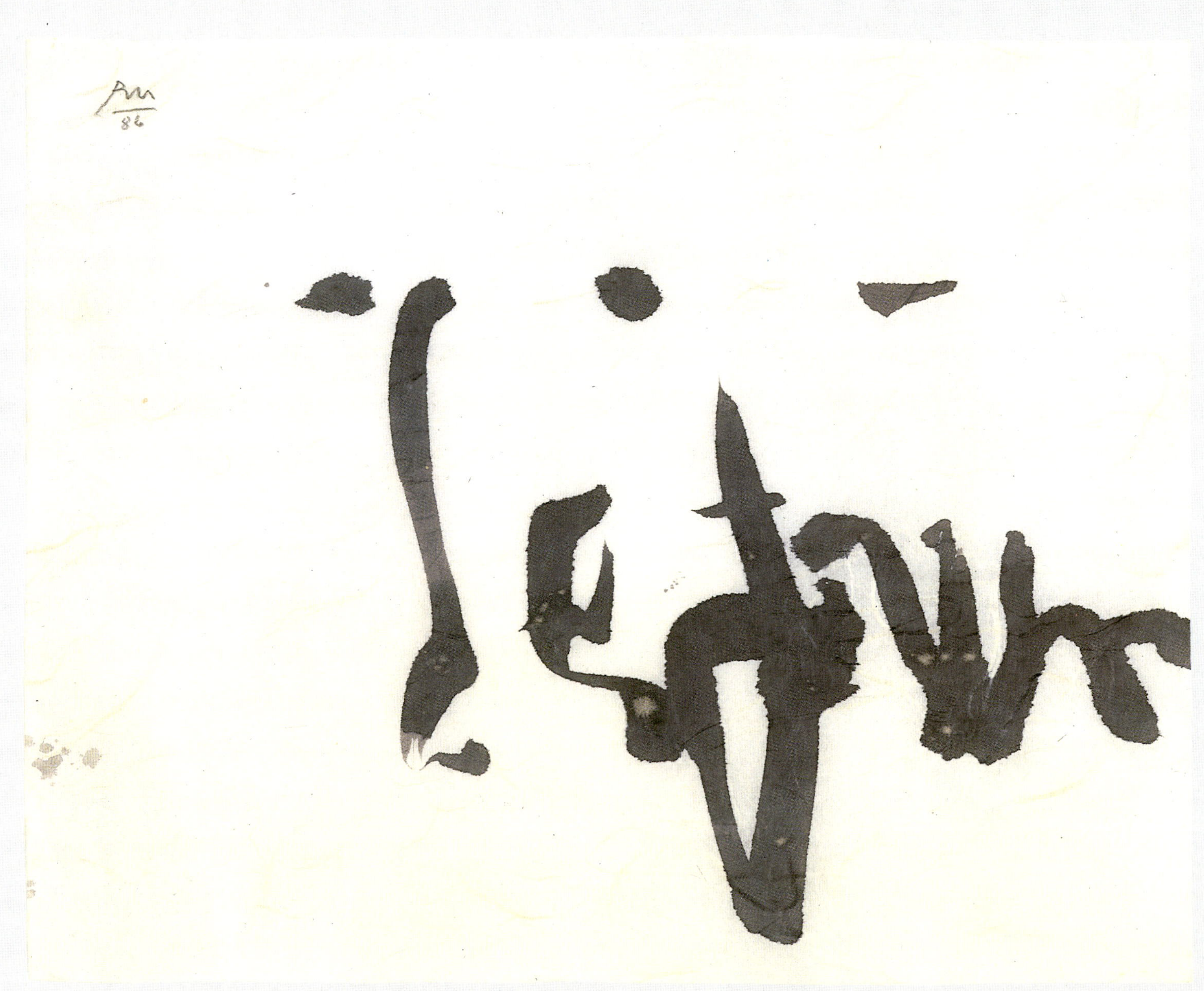

52. *Untitled*, 1986. Ink on rice paper, 9 x 11" (22.9 x 27.9 cm). Cat. no. IV.15

V. *Beside the Sea*

53. *Beside the Sea No. 5*, 1962. Oil on Strathmore paper, 29 x 23" (73.7 x 58.4 cm).
Smith College Museum of Art, Northampton, Massachusetts. Cat. no. V.1

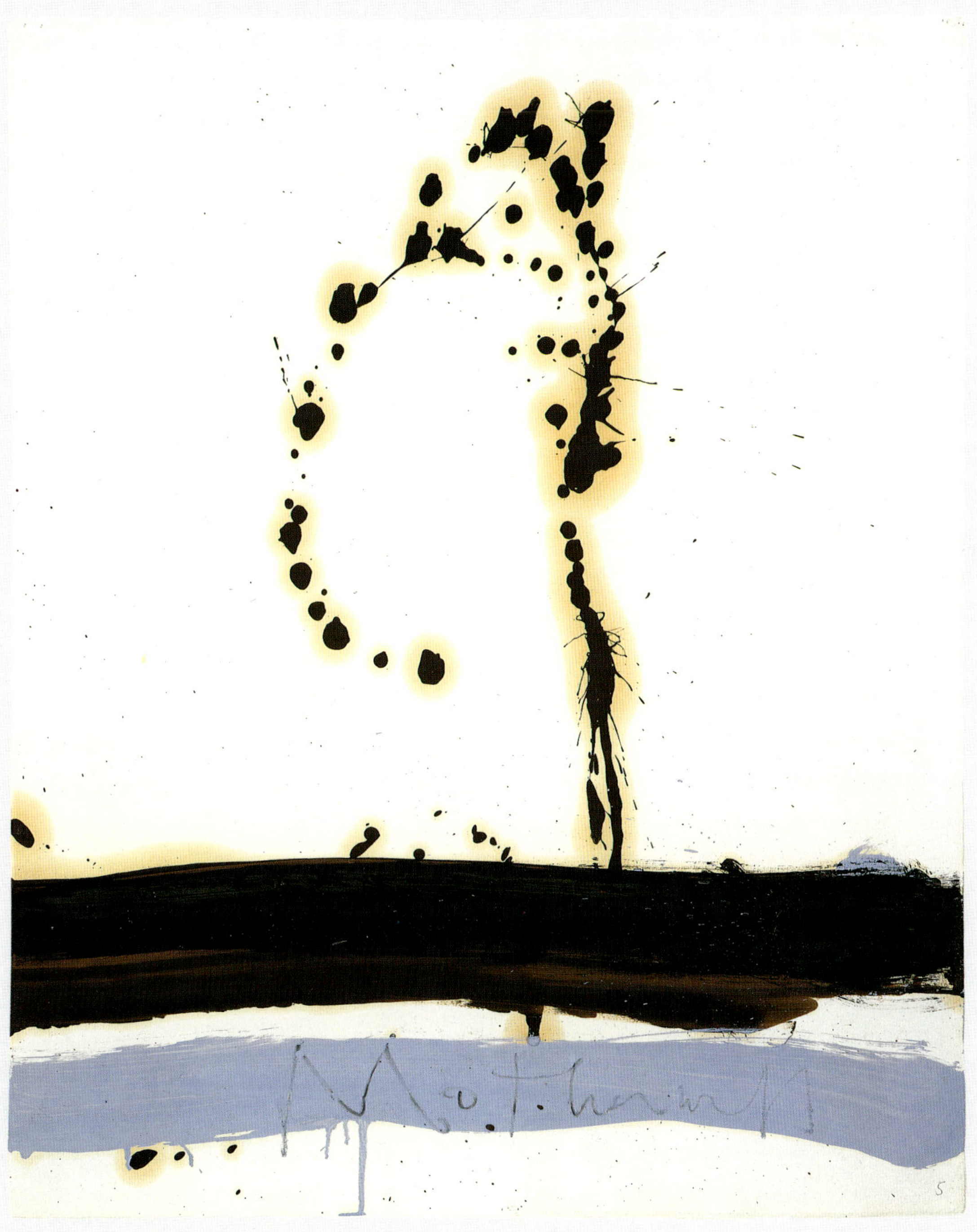

54. *Beside the Sea No. 22*, 1962. Oil on Strathmore paper, 29 x 23″ (73.7 x 58.4 cm). Cat. no. V.2

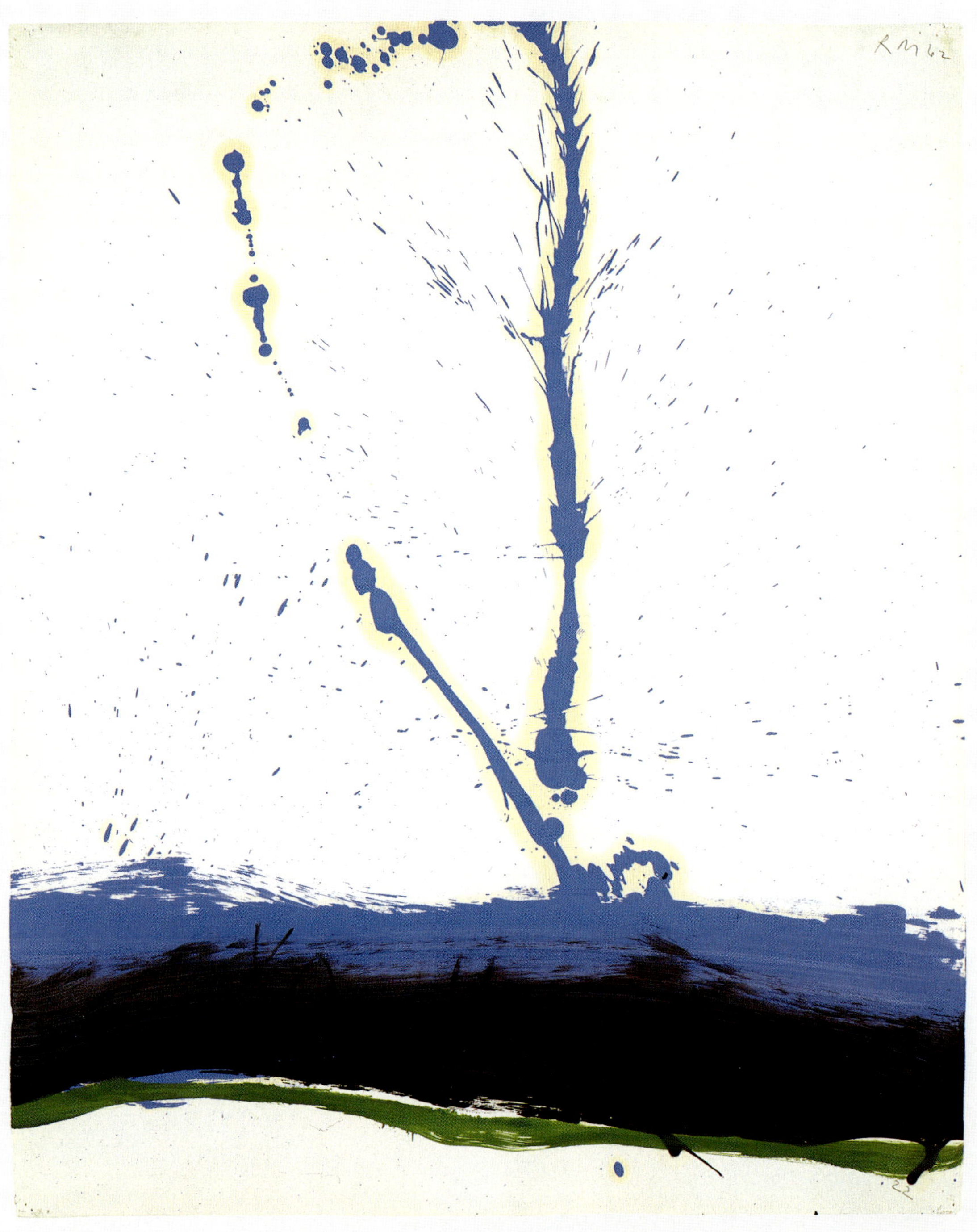

55. *Beside the Sea No. 30*, 1962. Oil on Strathmore paper, 29 x 23" (73.7 x 58.4 cm), Cat. no. V.3

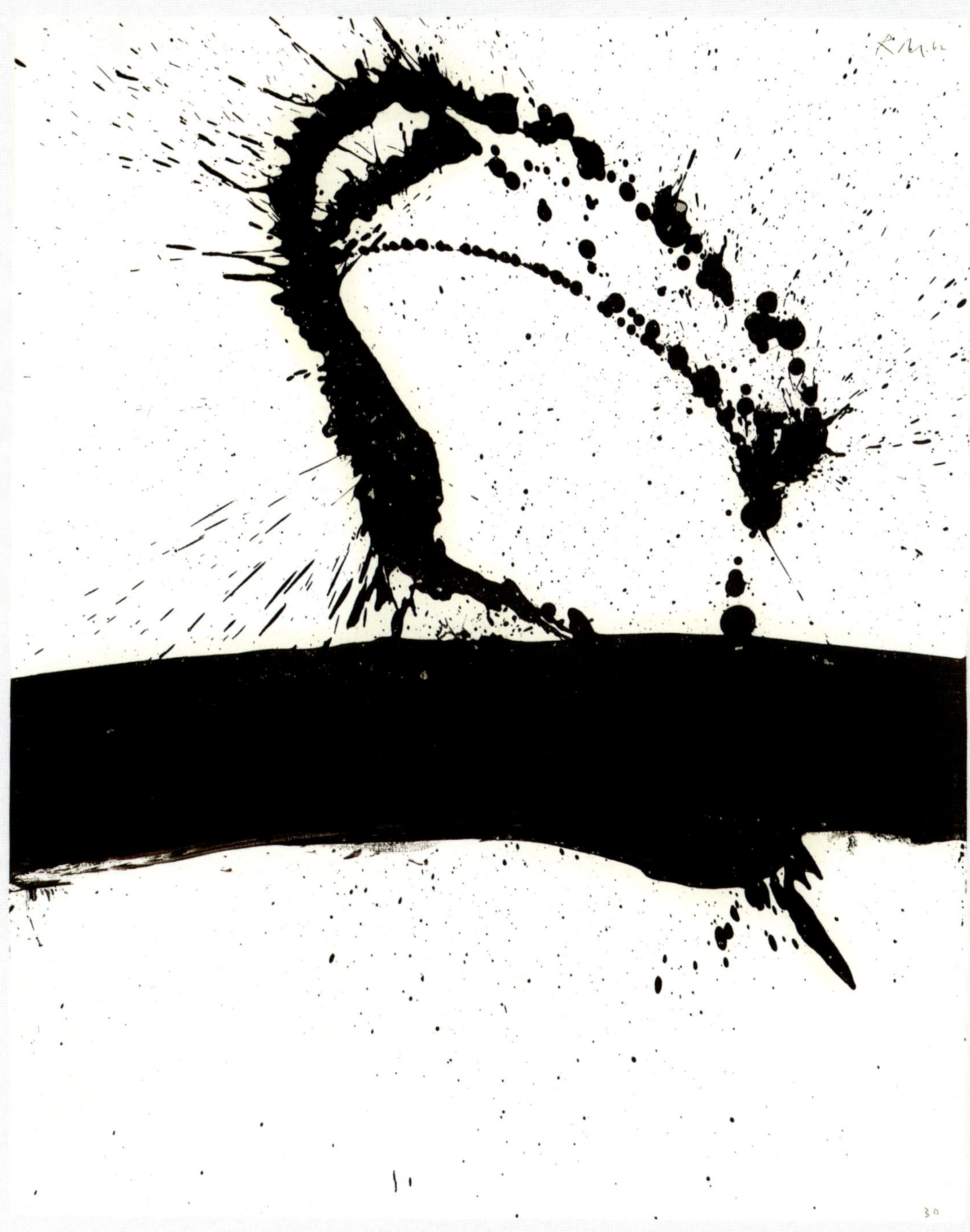

PAGES 130–133:

56–62. *A Throw of the Dice*, 1962–63. Suite of seven lithographs; image: 18 x 14″ (45.8 x 35.5 cm); paper: 30 x 22″ (76.2 x 56 cm)

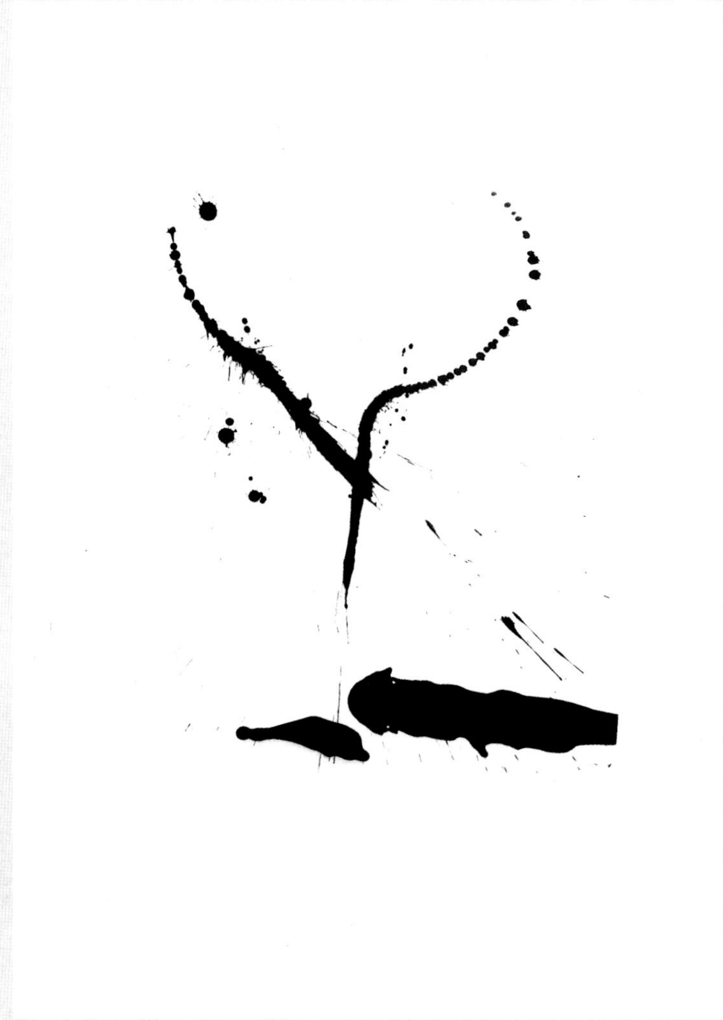

56. From *A Throw of the Dice*. Cat. no. V.4

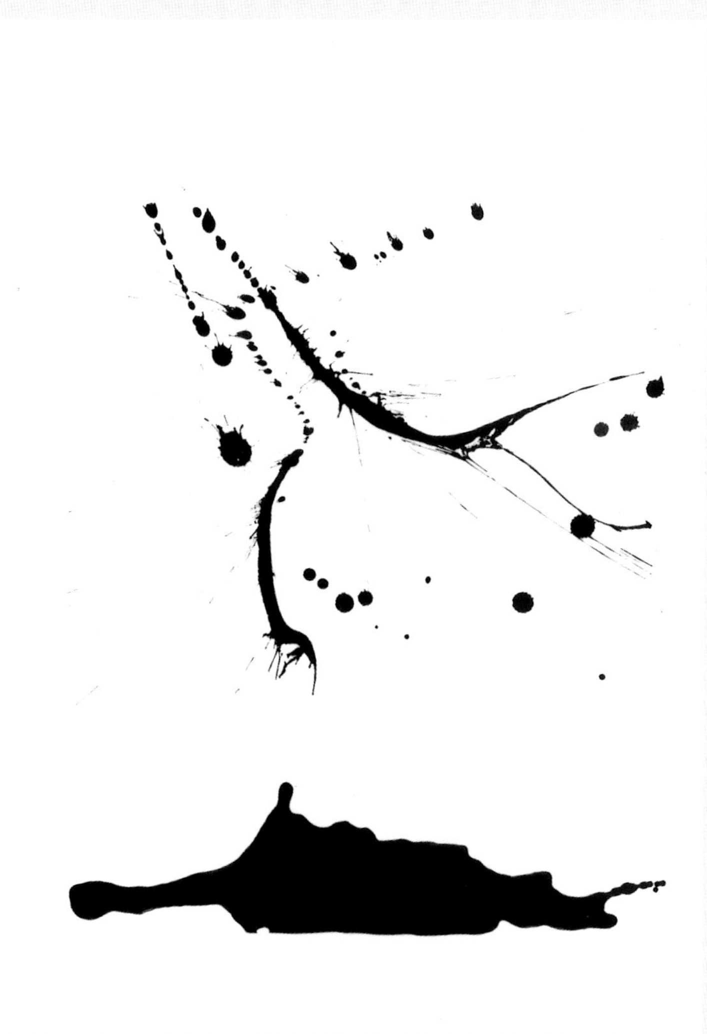

57. From *A Throw of the Dice*. Cat. no. V.5

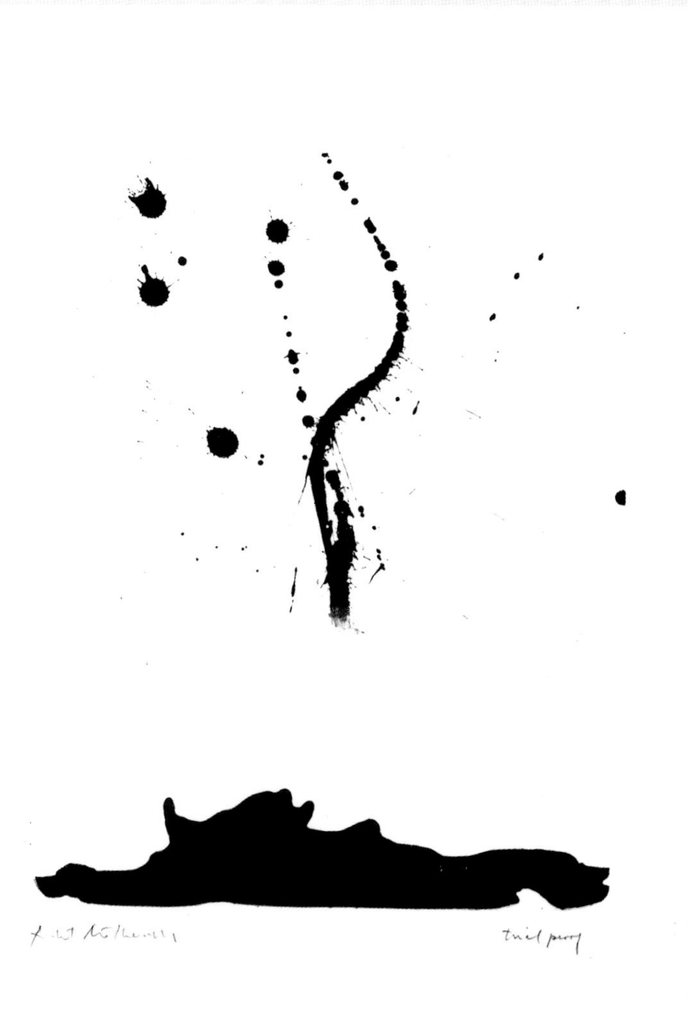

58. From *A Throw of the Dice*. Cat. no. V.6

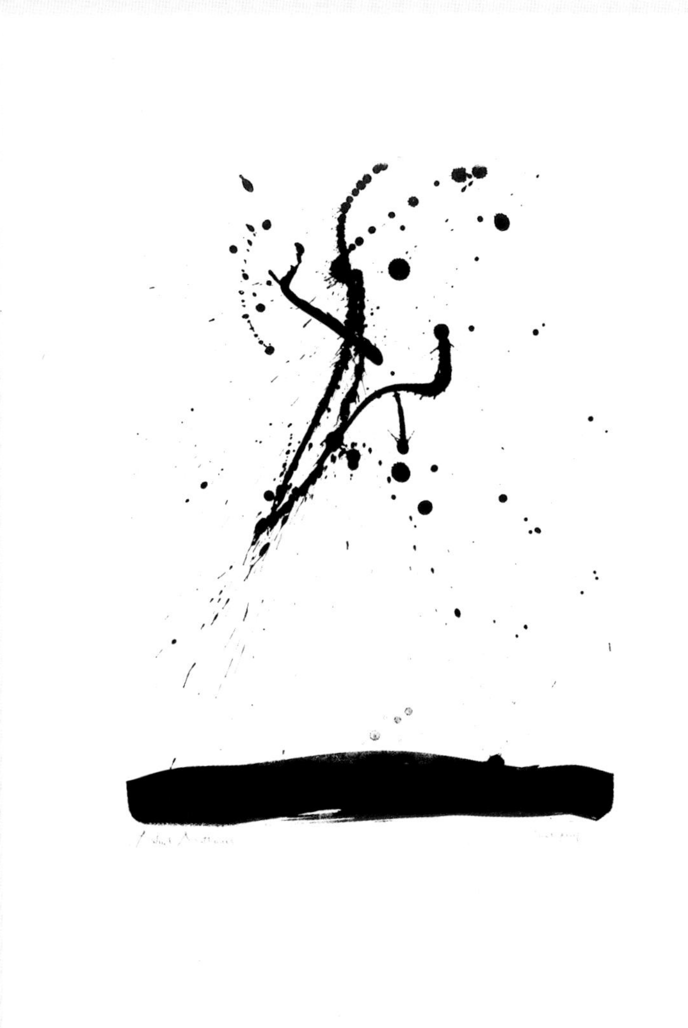

59. From *A Throw of the Dice*. Cat. no. V.7

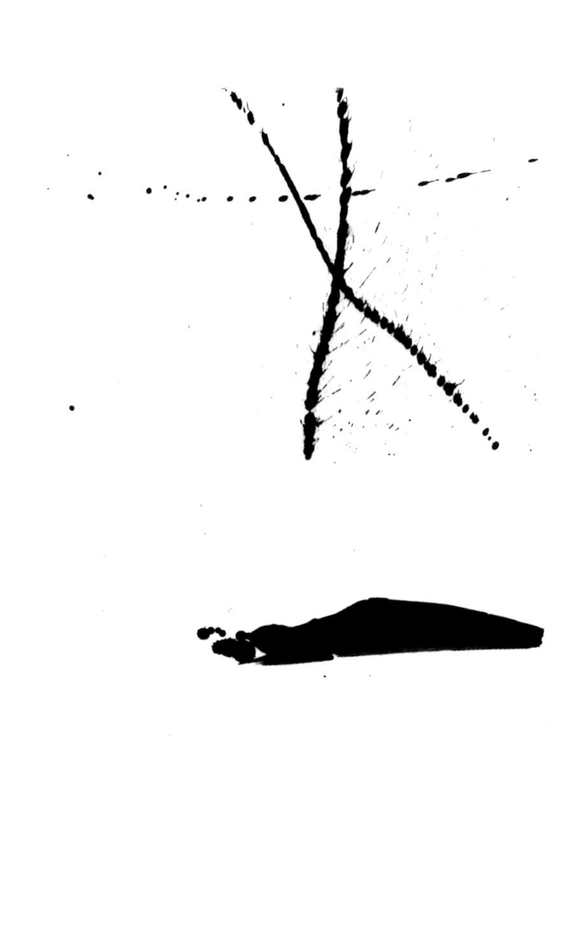

60. From *A Throw of the Dice*. Cat. no. V.8

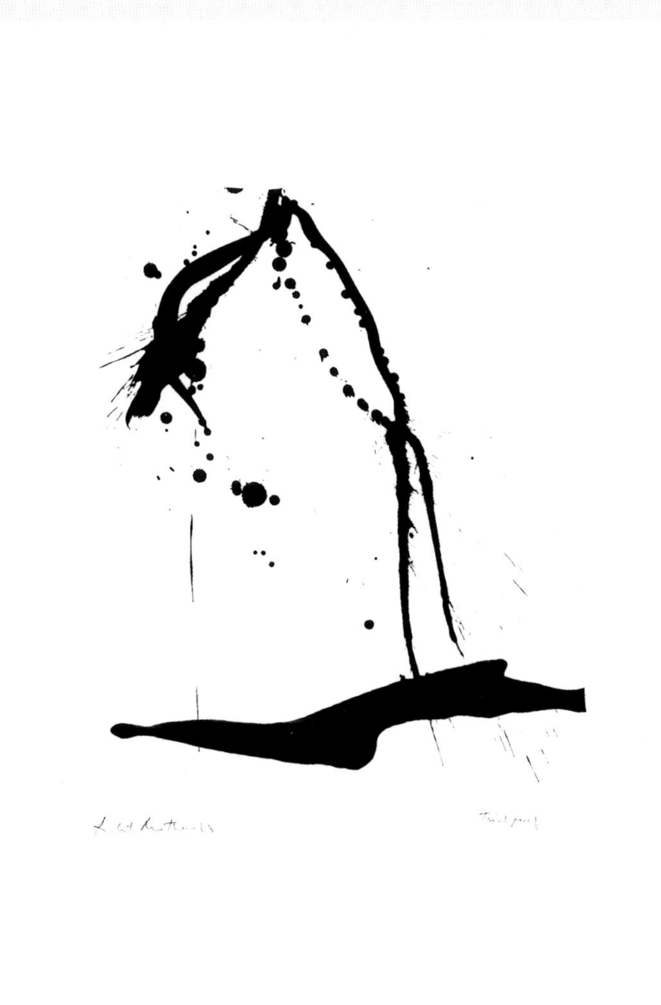

61. From *A Throw of the Dice*. Cat. no. V.9

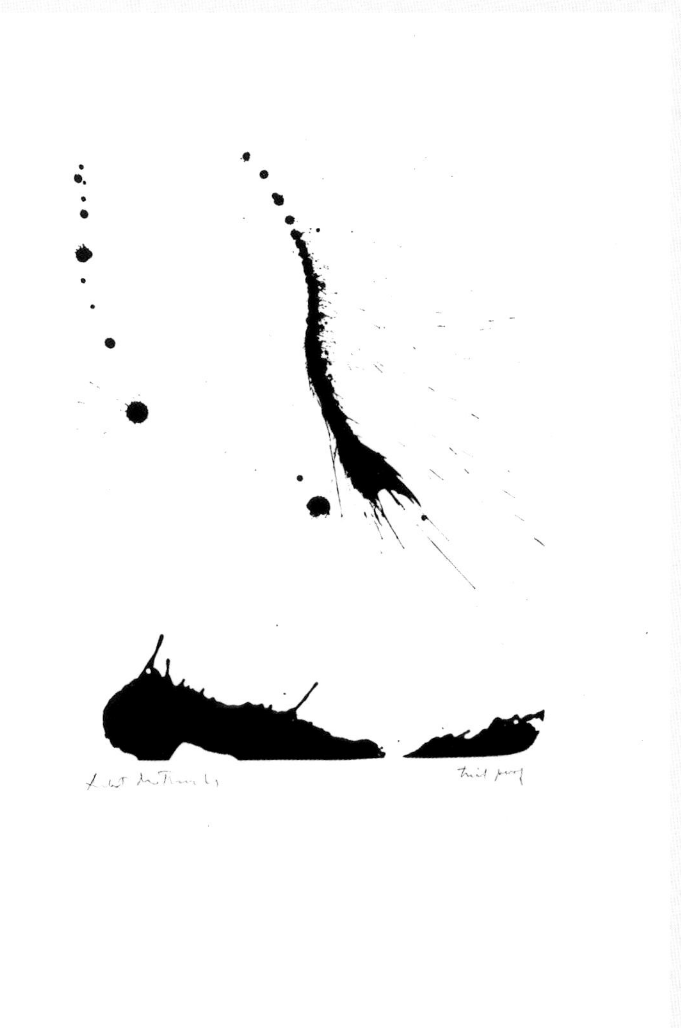

62. From *A Throw of the Dice*. Cat. no. V.10

VI. *Open* Studies and Beyond

63. *Black on White No. 6*, 1968. Acrylic and pencil on paper, 6 x 8″ (15.2 x 20.3 cm). Cat. no. VI.1

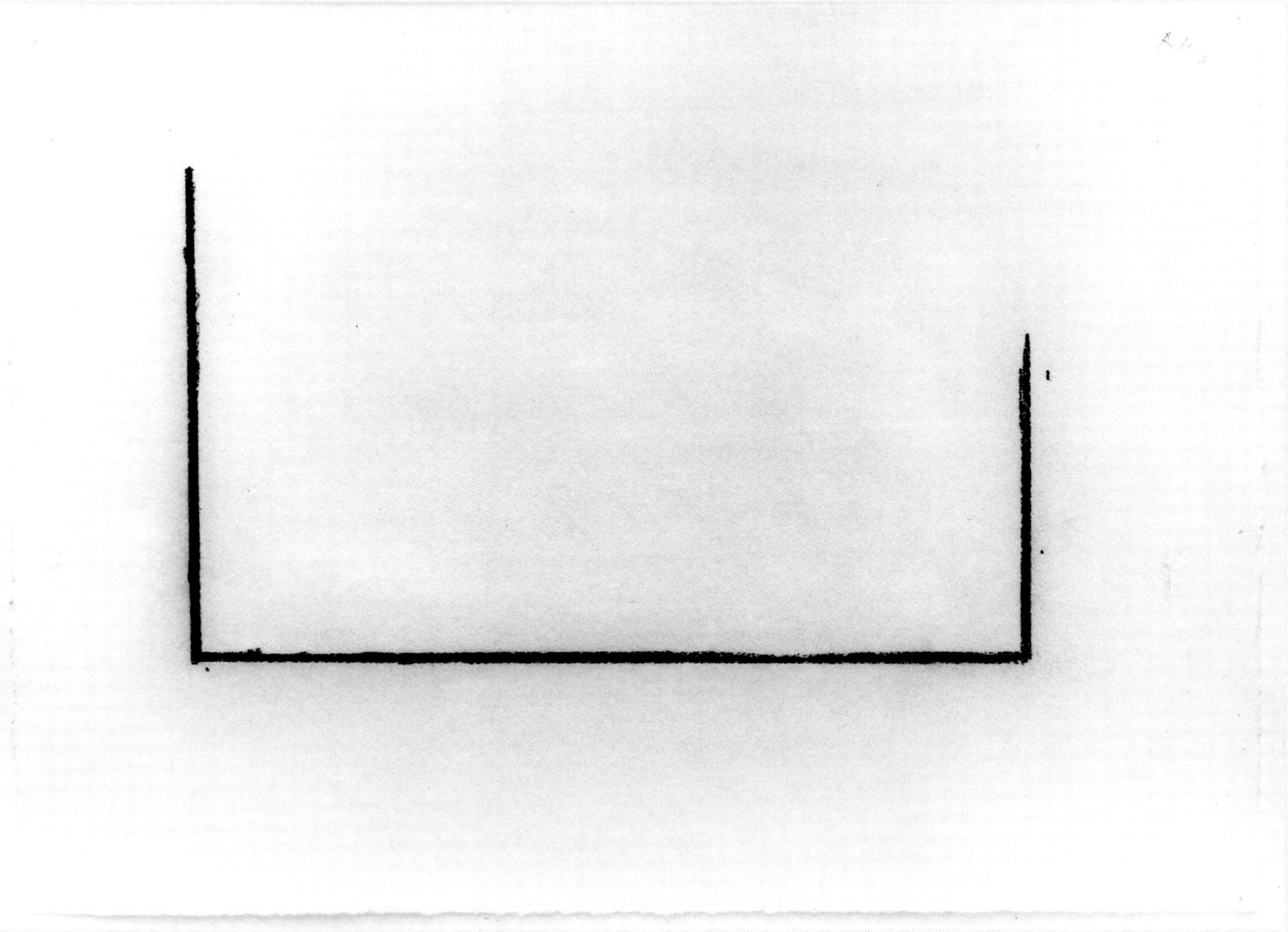

64. *Open Study No. 4*, 1968. Charcoal on paper, 22 x 30½" (55.9 x 77.5 cm). Cat. no. VI.2

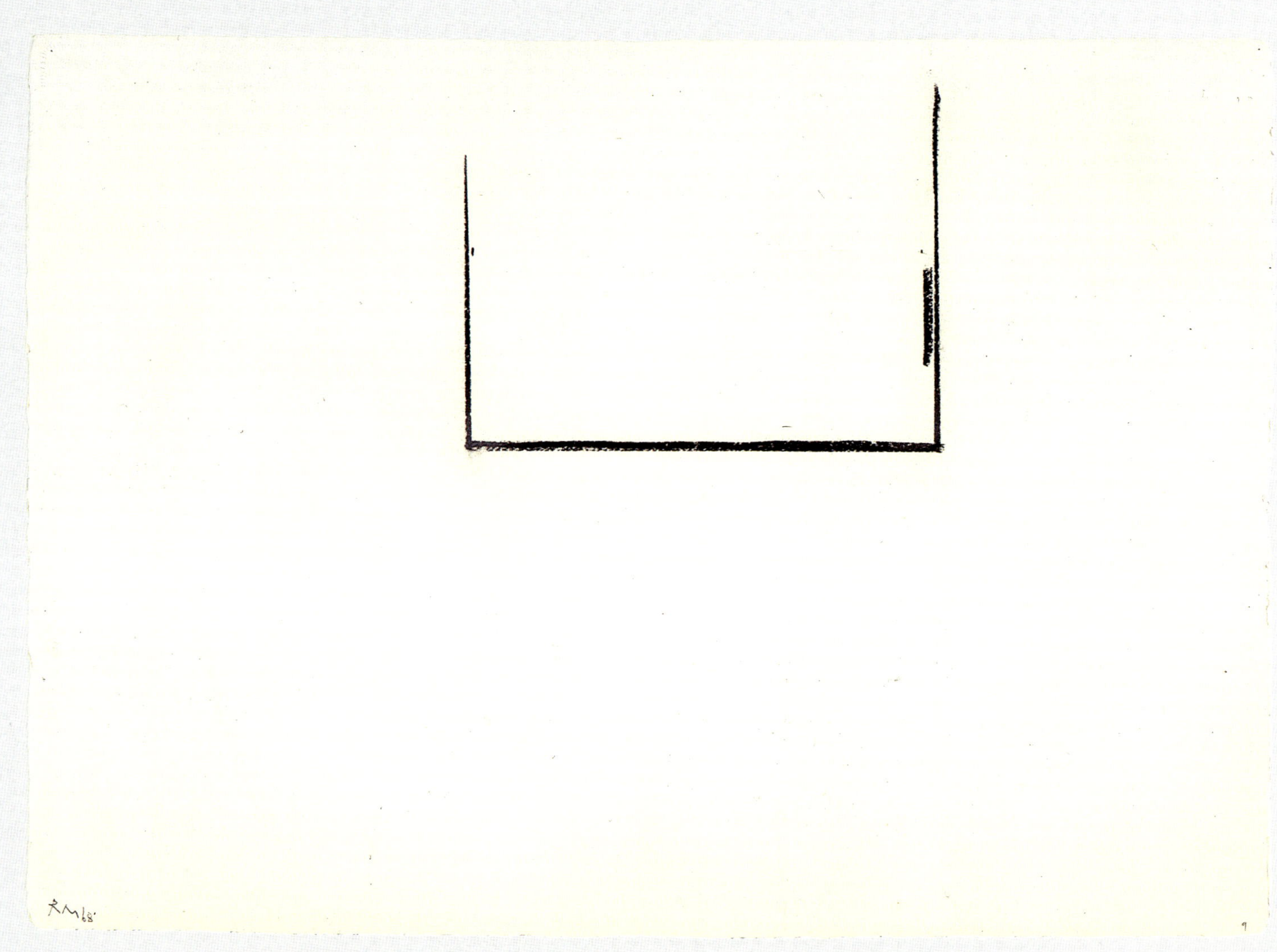

65. *Open Study No. 9*, 1968. Charcoal on paper, 22 x 30½" (55.9 x 77.5 cm). Cat. no. VI.3

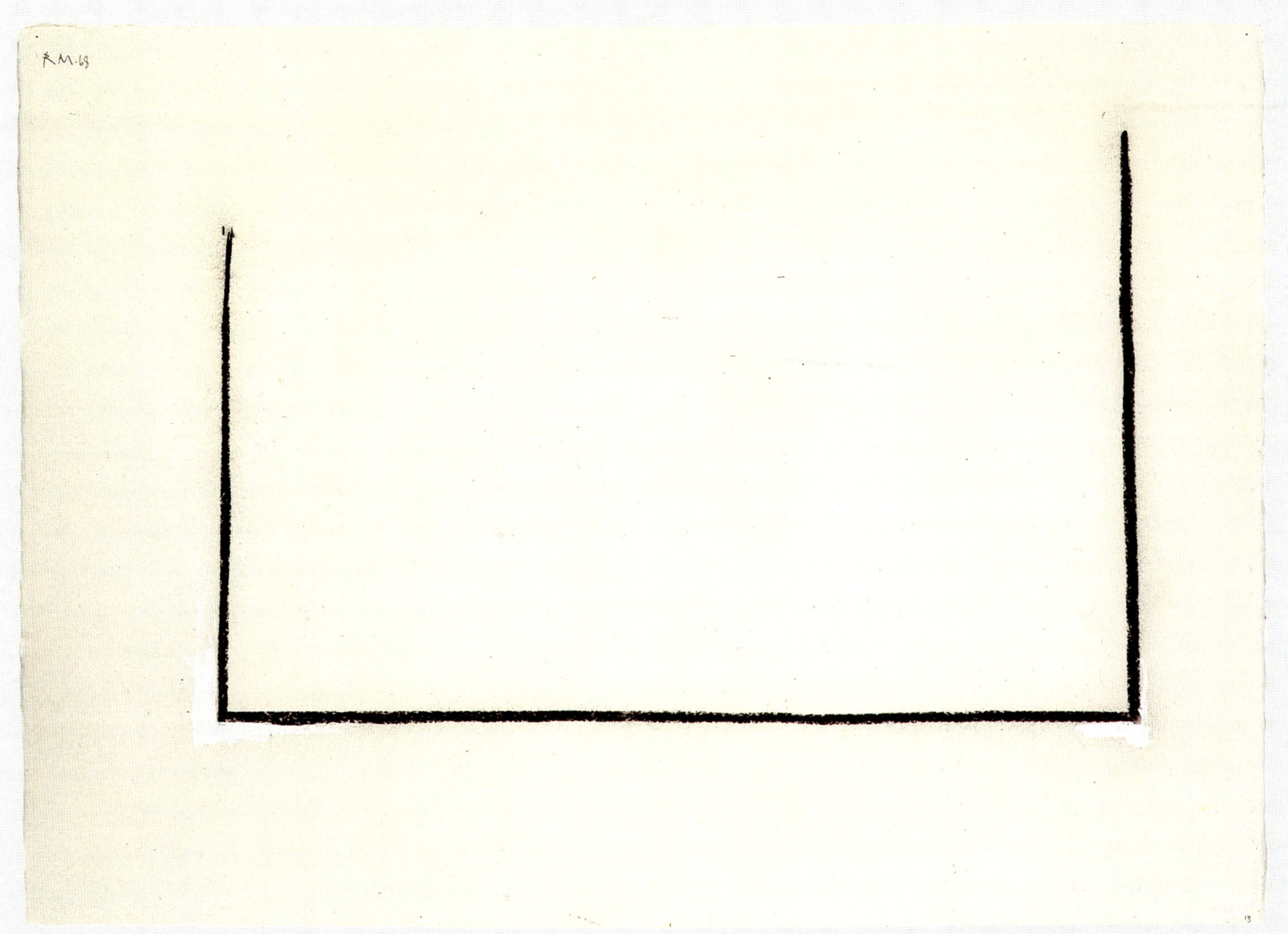

66. *Untitled (Open)*, 1968. Charcoal and acrylic on paper, 22 x 30¼" (55.9 x 76.8 cm). Cat. no. VI.4

67. *Study for "Shem the Penman," No. 9*, 1972. Acrylic and charcoal on Upson board, 8½ x 11½" (21.6 x 29.2 cm). Cat. no. VI.5

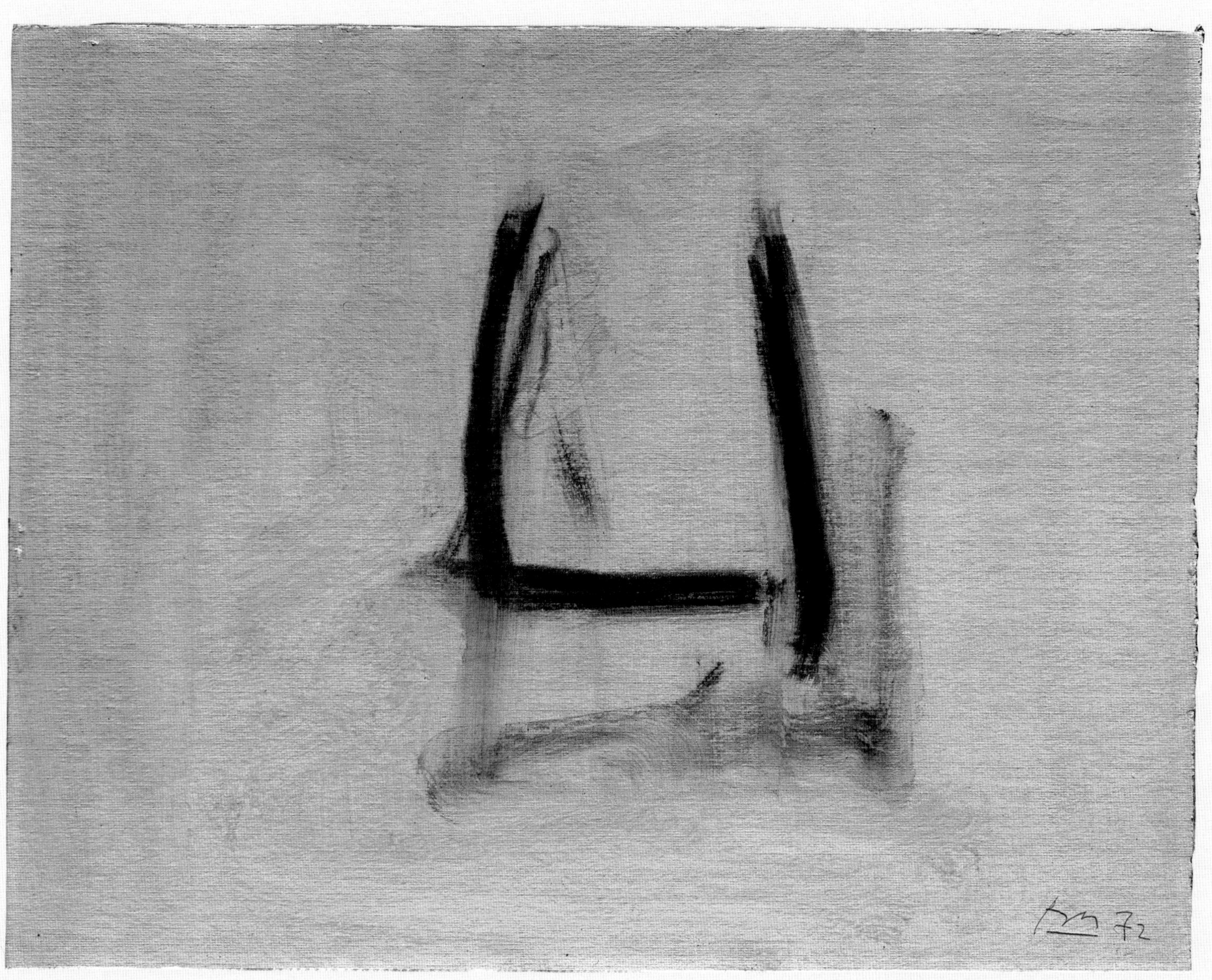

68. *Study for "Shem the Penman," No. 11*, 1972. Charcoal on tan paper, 8½ x 11½" (21.6 x 29.2 cm). Cat. no. VI.6

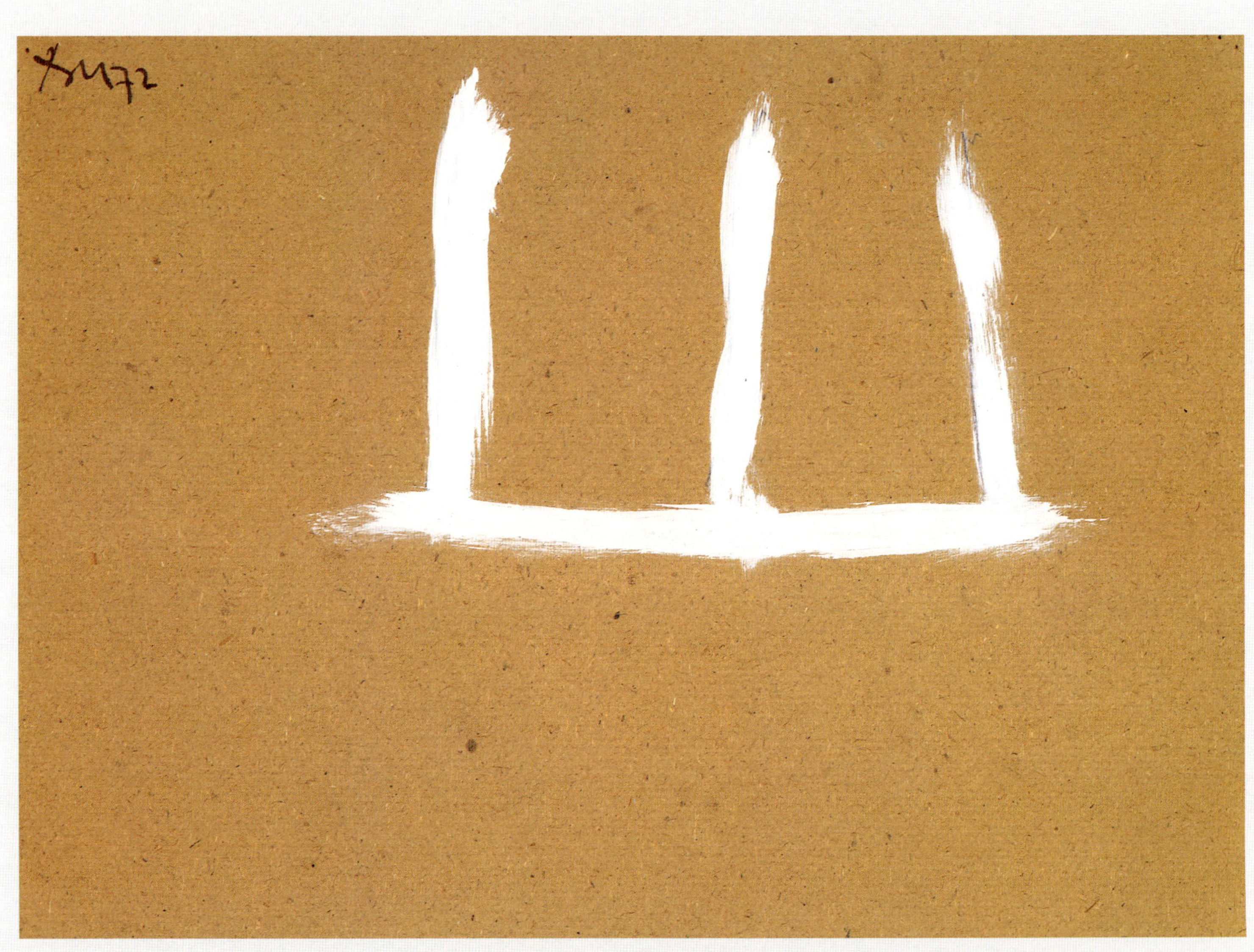

69. *Study for "Shem the Penman,"* 1972. Acrylic on board, 8¼ x 11″ (21 x 27.9 cm). Cat. no. VI.7

70. *Untitled (Open Study)*, 1974.
Charcoal on tan paper, 15 x 7¾" (38.1 x 19.7 cm). Cat. no. VI.8

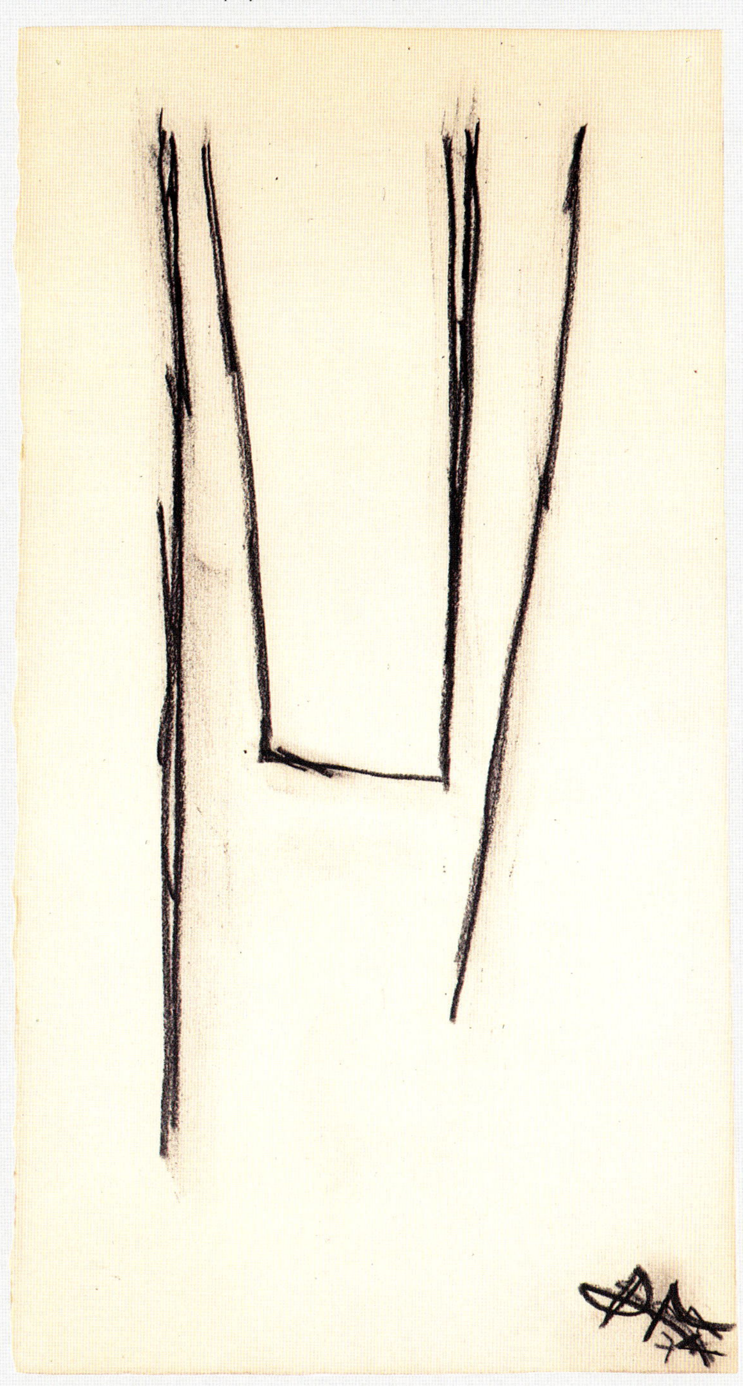

VII. Choreographics of *M*

71. *Calligraphic Study I*, 1976. Lift-ground etching and aquatint; plate: 6 x 8" (15.3 x 23 cm); paper: 23 x 18" (58.5 x 45.8 cm). Cat. no. VII.1

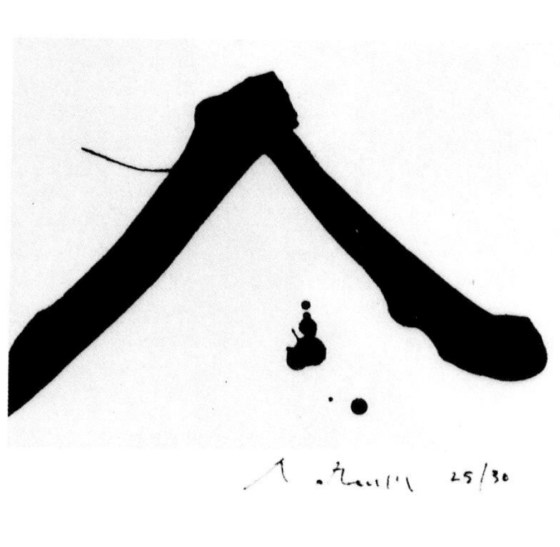

72. *Calligraphic Study II*, 1976. Lift-ground etching and aquatint; plate: 6 x 8″ (15.3 x 23 cm); paper: 23 x 18″ (58.5 x 45.8 cm). Cat. no. VII.2

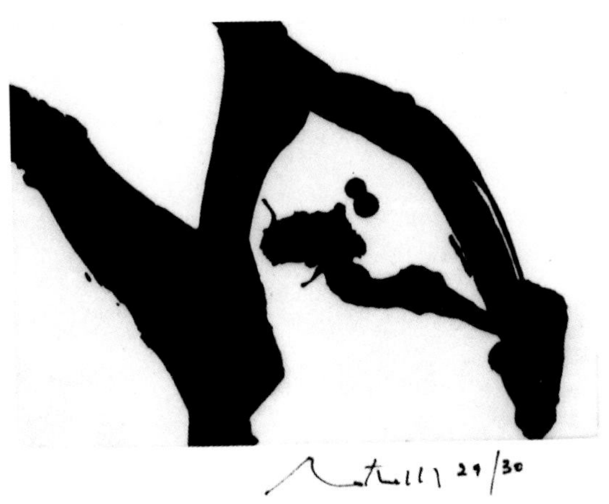

73. *Calligraphic Study III*, 1976. Lift-ground etching and aquatint; plate: 9 x 12″ (22.9 x 30.5 cm); paper: 23 x 18″ (58.5 x 45.8 cm). Cat. no. VII.3

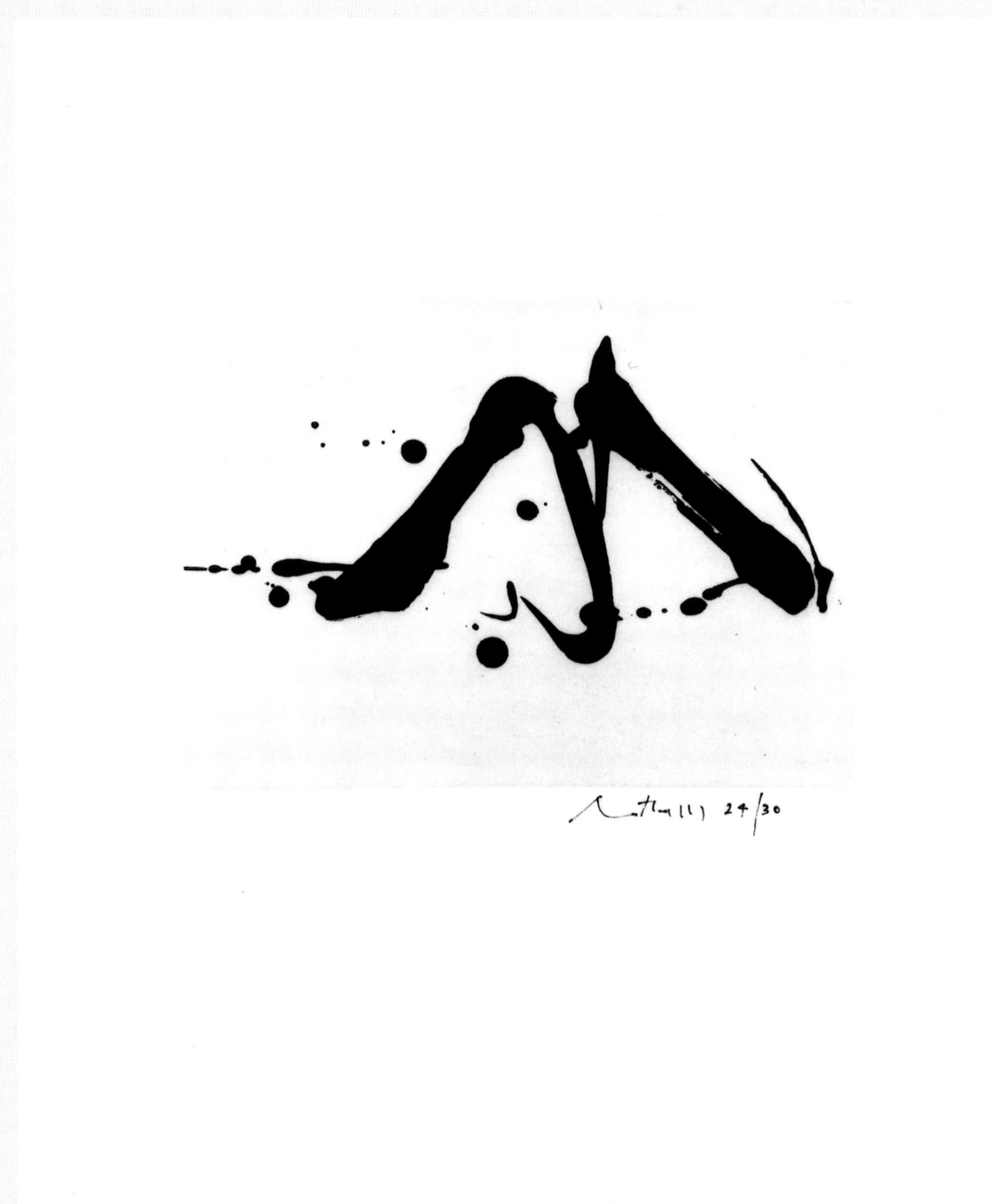

74. *Calligraphic Study IV*, 1976. Lift-ground etching and aquatint; plate: 9 x 12″ (22.9 x 30.5 cm); paper: 23 x 18″ (58.5 x 45.8 cm). Cat. no. VII.4

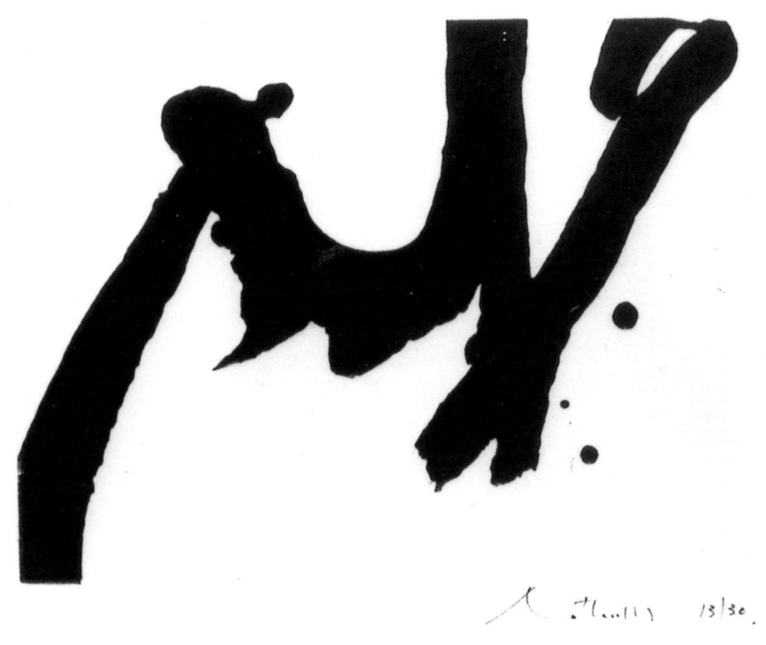

75. *Calligraphic Study V*, 1976. Lift-ground etching and aquatint; plate: 9 x 12″ (22.9 x 30.5 cm); paper: 23 x 18″ (58.5 x 45.8 cm). Cat. no. VII.5

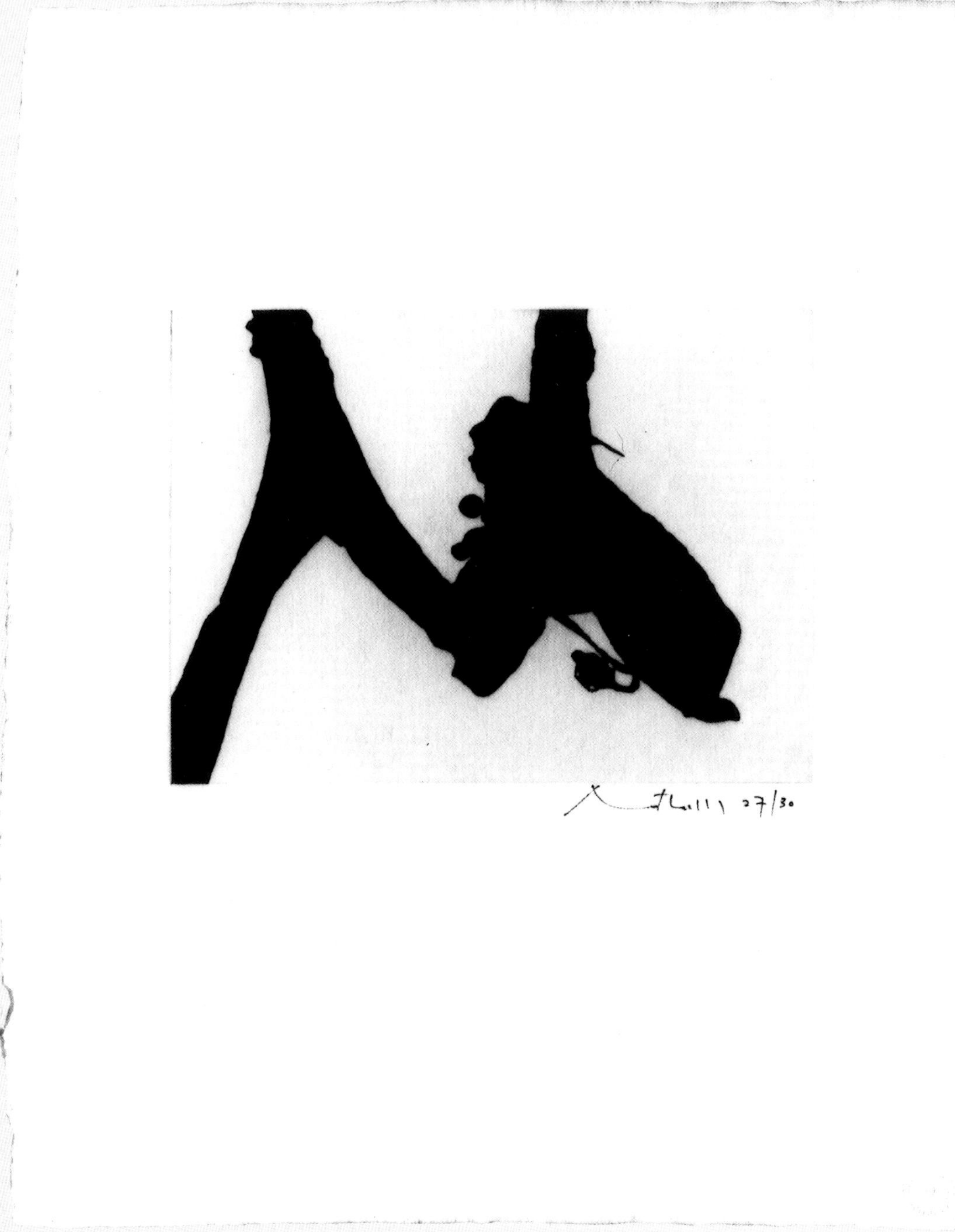

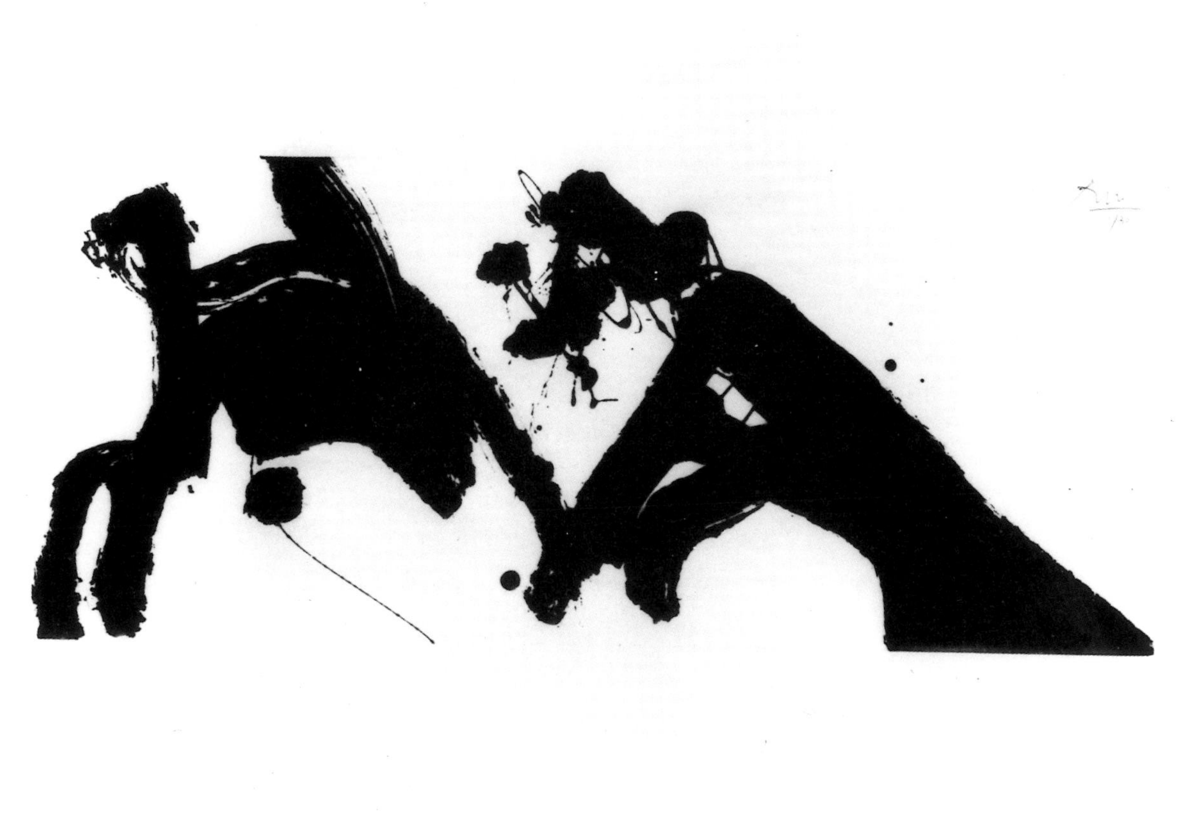

76. *Dance I*, 1978. Lift-ground etching and aquatint; plate: 10 x 24" (25.5 x 61 cm); paper: 19½ x 30½" (49.5 x 77.5 cm). Cat. no. VII.6

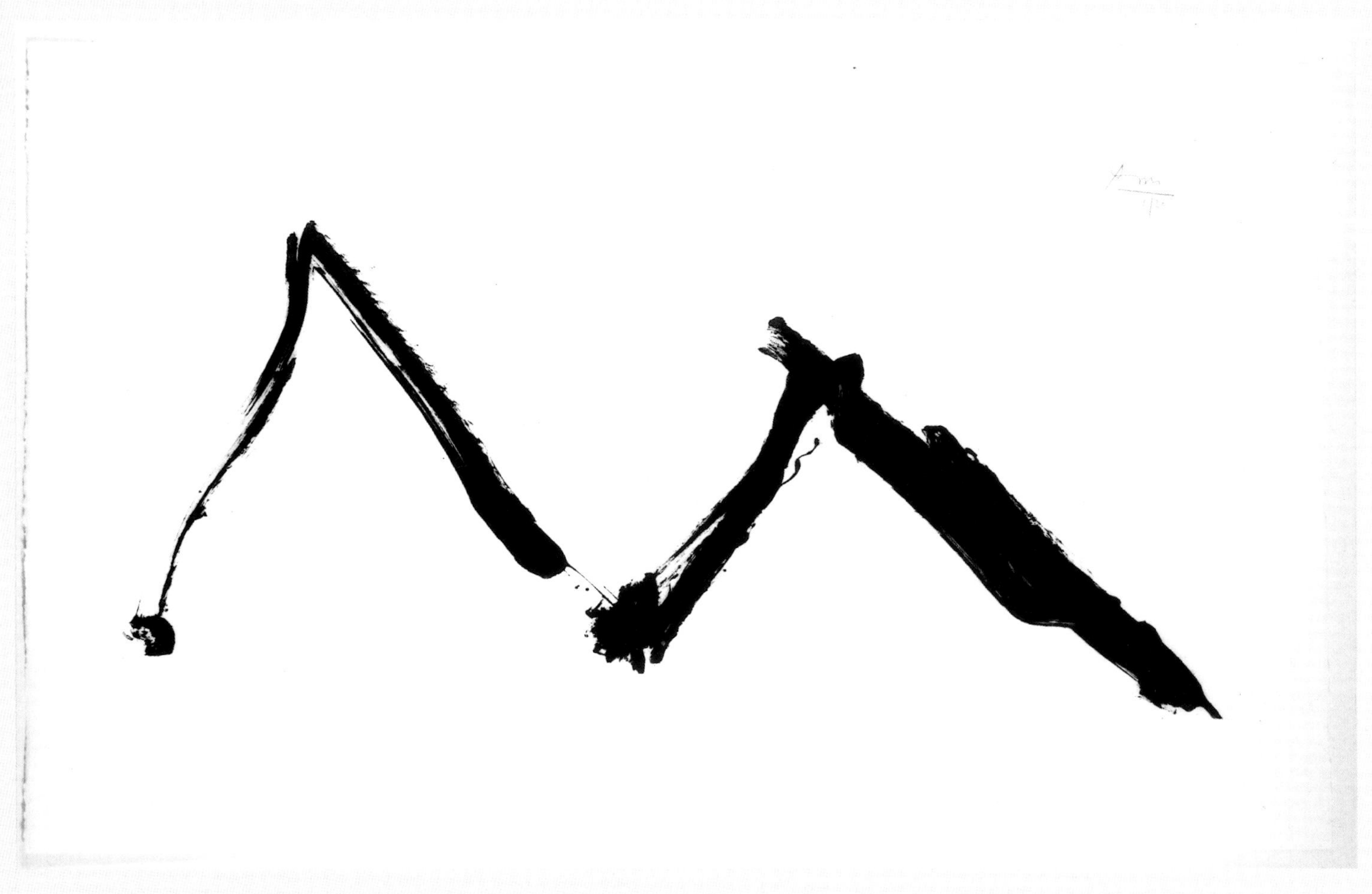

77. *Dance II*, 1978. Lift-ground etching and aquatint; plate: 18 x 36″ (45.8 x 91.5 cm); paper: 25½ x 41″ (64.8 x 104.1 cm). Cat. no. VII.7

78. *Dance III*, 1978. Lift-ground etching and aquatint; plate: 20 x 24″ (50.4 x 61 cm); paper: 27½ x 30½″ (69.9 x 77.5 cm). Cat. no. VII.8

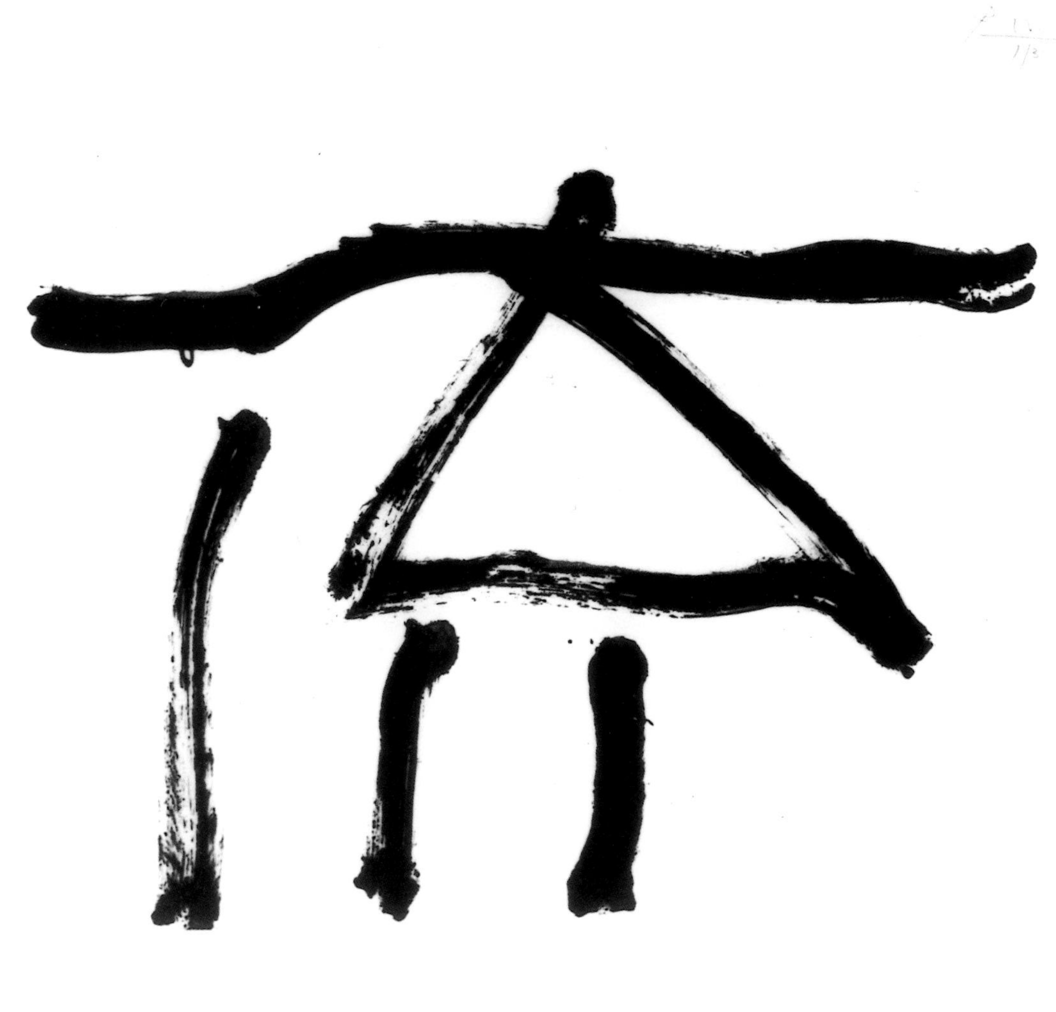

VIII. *Samurai*

79. *Totemic Emblem*, 1967. Acrylic on board, 20 x 16″ (50.8 x 40.6 cm). Cat. no. VIII.1

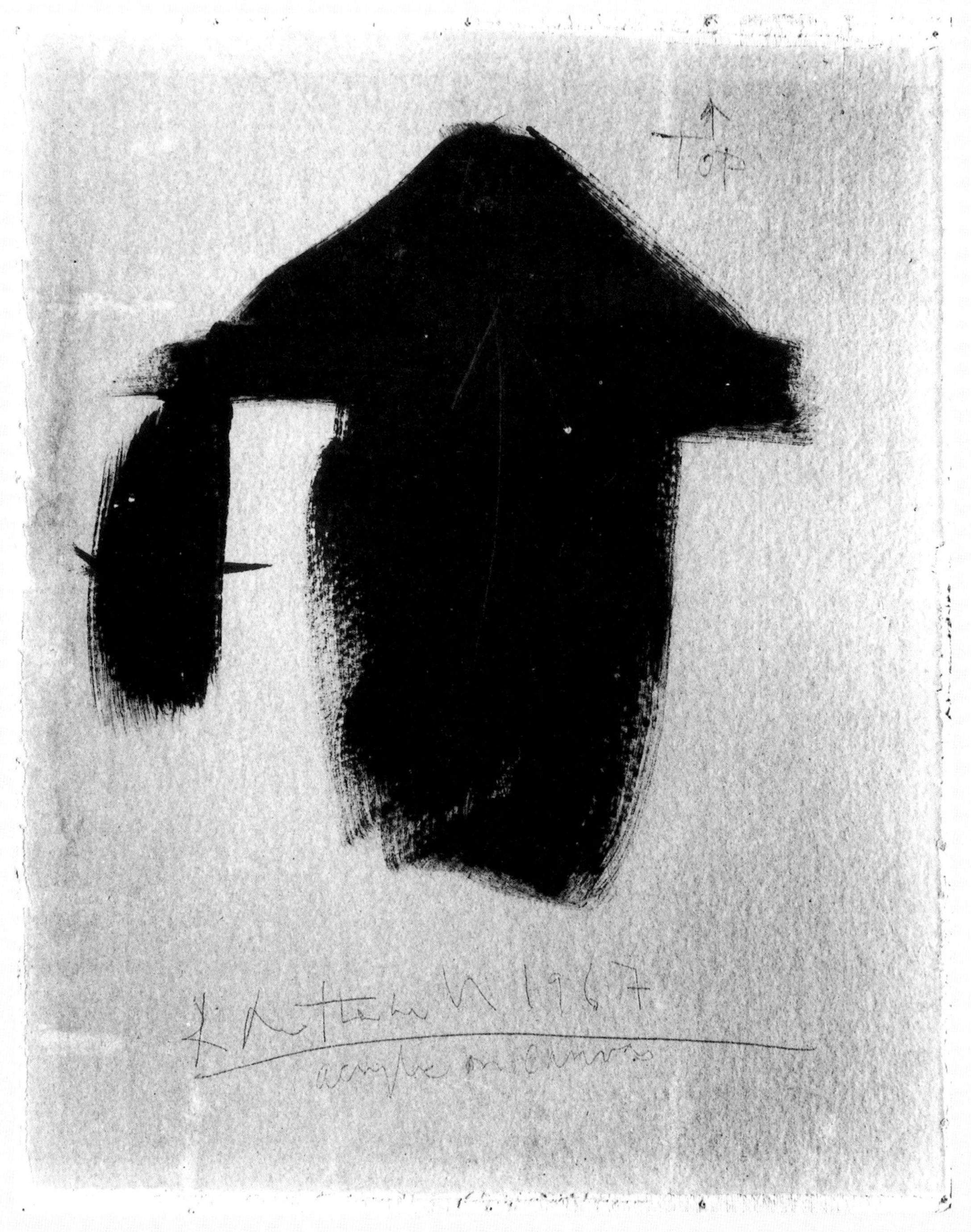

80. *Samurai*, 1971. Lithograph; image: 42 x 35½" (106.6 x 90.2 cm); paper: 73½ x 37" (186 x 94 cm). Cat. no. VIII.2

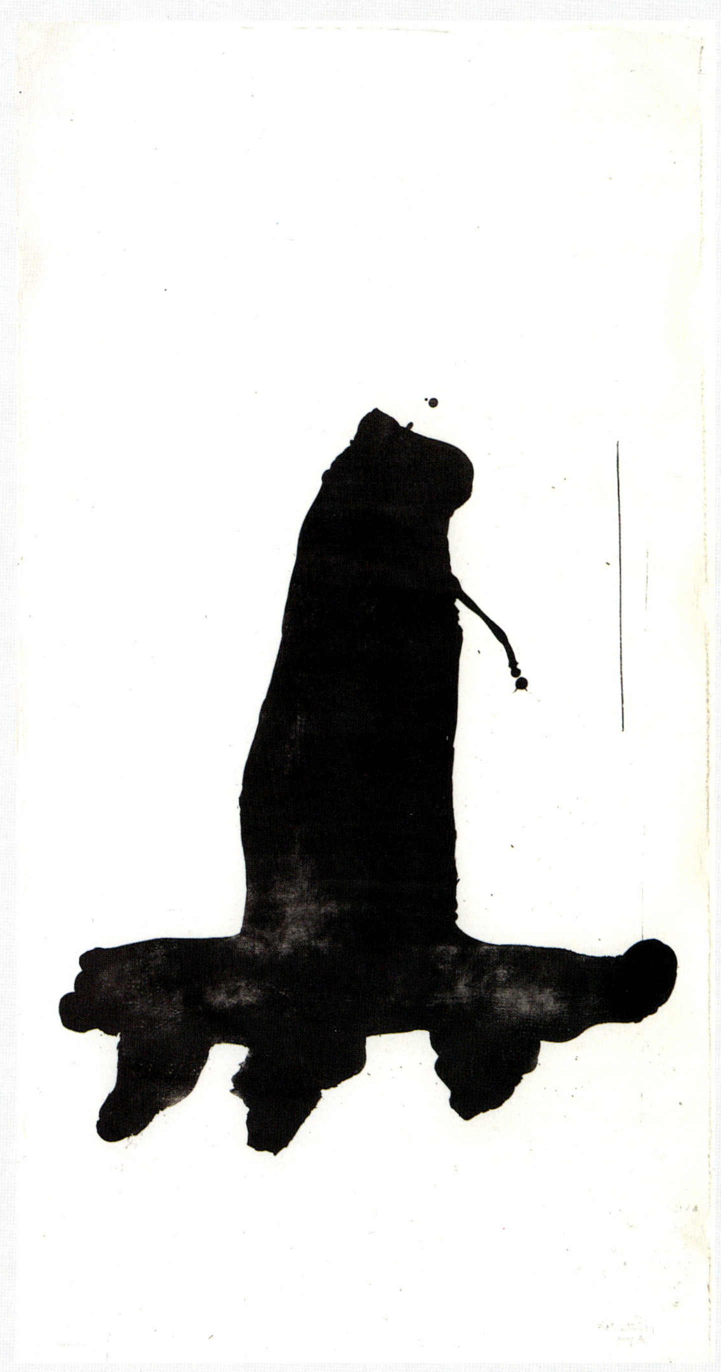

81. *Untitled (Samurai)*, 1972. Acrylic on paper, 22 x 11¾″ (55.9 x 28.9 cm). Cat. no. VIII.3

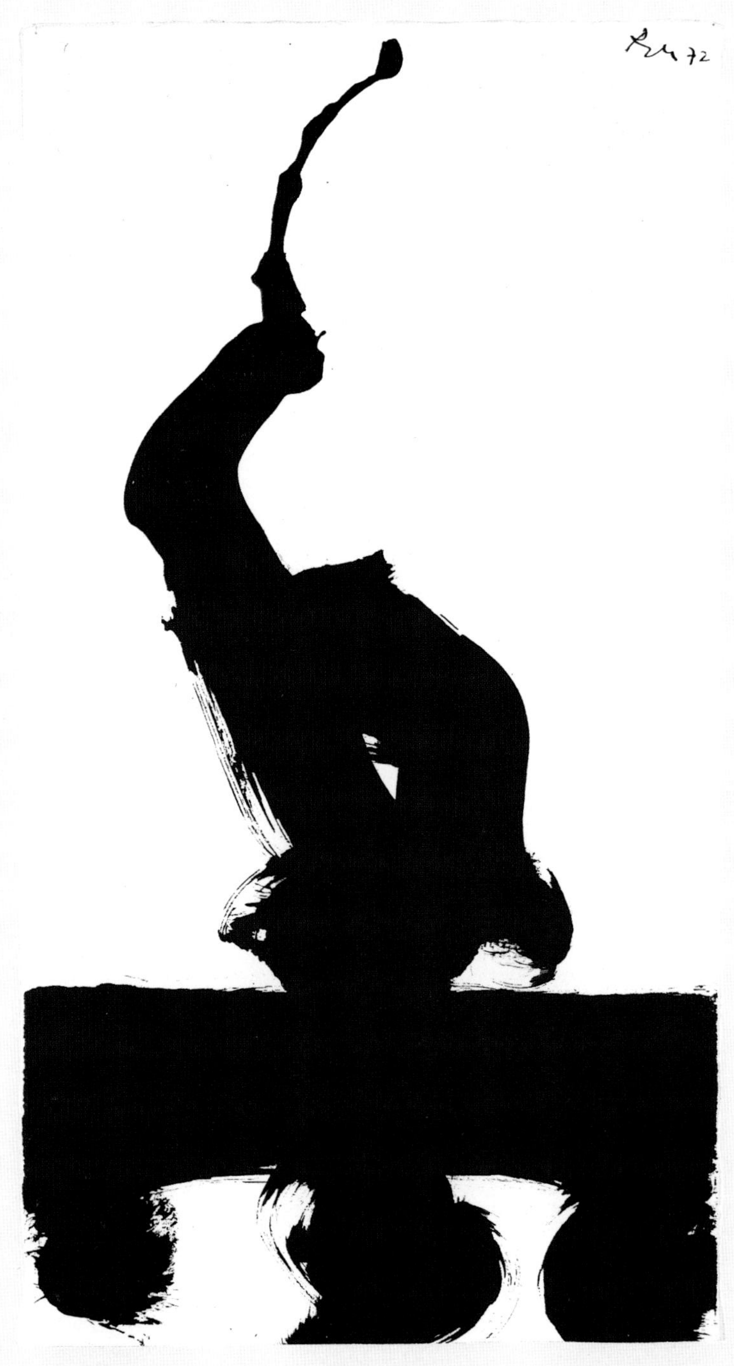

82. *Untitled*, 1972. Lithograph; image: 7 x 14" (17.8 x 35 cm); paper: 24 x 18" (61 x 45.7 cm). Cat. no. VIII.4

83. *Samurai No. 5*, 1974. Acrylic on Upson board, 48 x 36" (121.9 x 91.4 cm). Cat. no. VIII.5

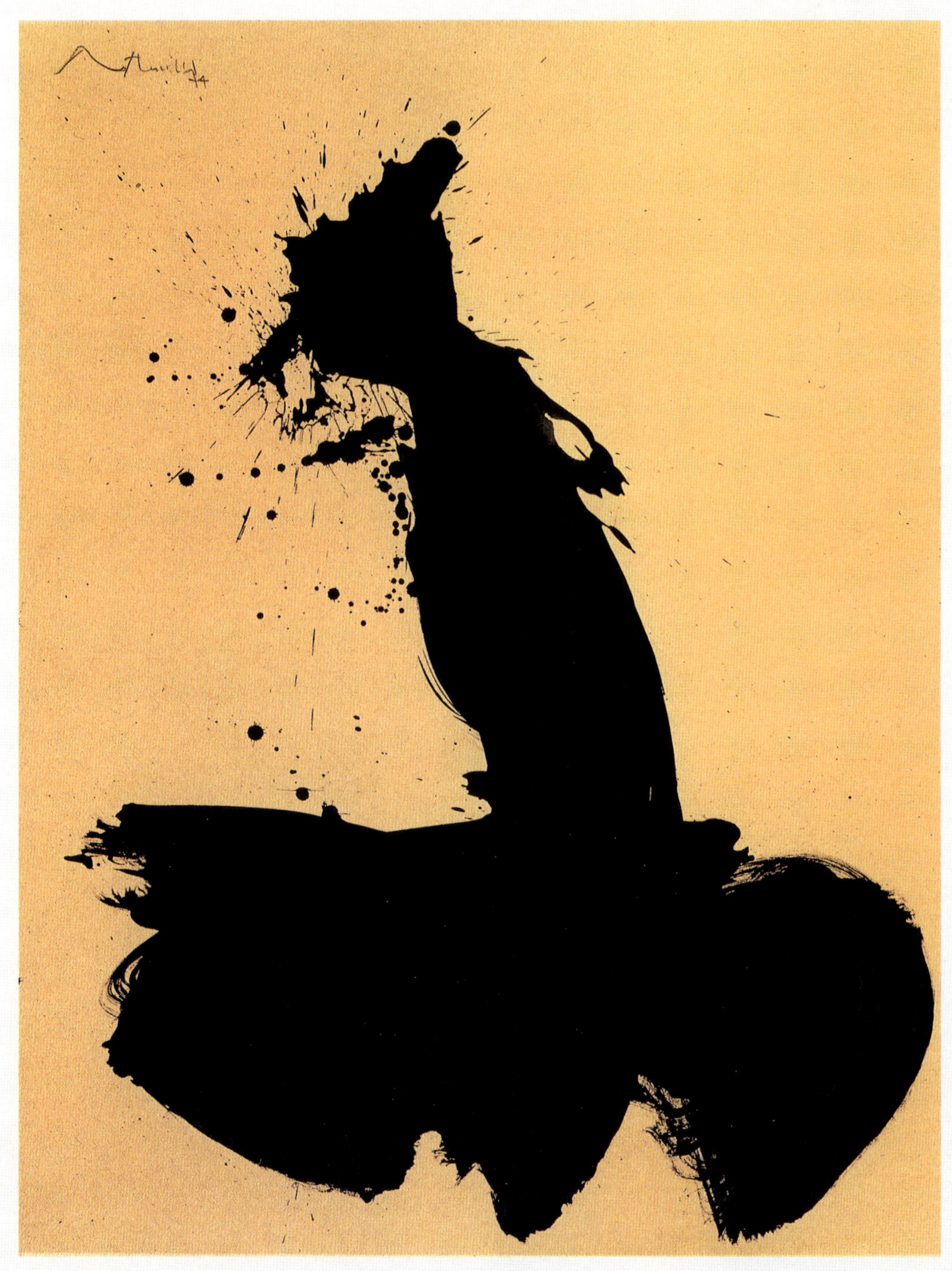

84. *Samurai No. 6*, 1974. Acrylic on board, 48 x 36″ (121.9 x 91.4 cm). Cat. no. VIII.6

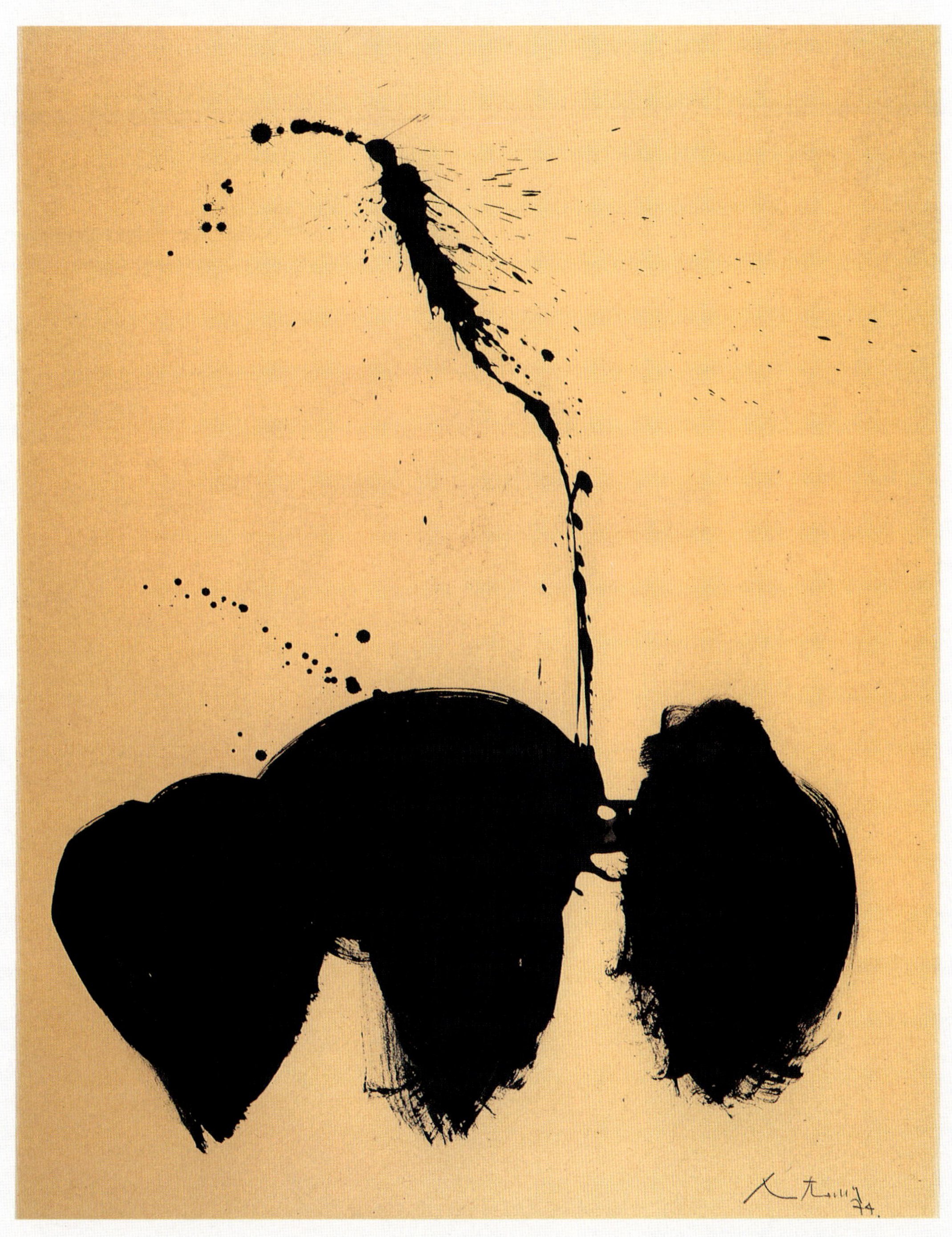

85. *Untitled*, 1978. Lithograph, Chine collé; image (collé sheet): 19 x 15¼" (48.3 x 38.8 cm); paper: 30 x 22¼" (76.2 x 56.5 cm). Cat. no. VIII.7

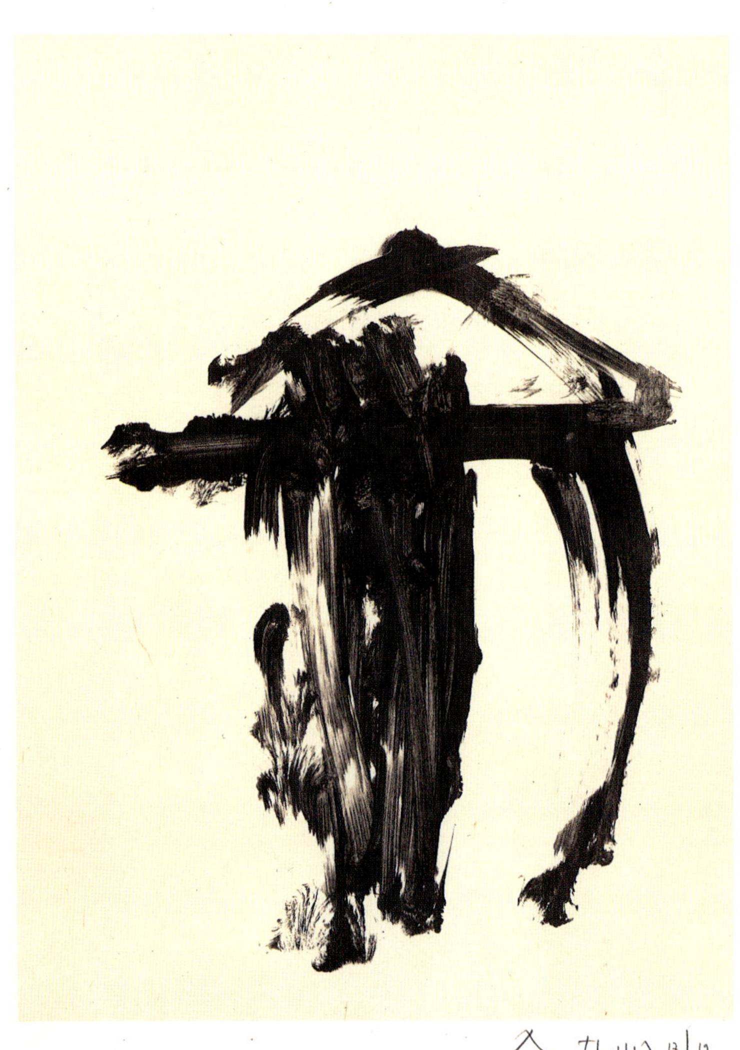

86. *Samurai II*, 1979–80. Lithograph, Chine appliqué; image (appliqué sheet): 39 x 24½" (99 x 62.2 cm); paper: 57 x 24½" (144.7 x 62.2 cm). Cat. no. VIII.8

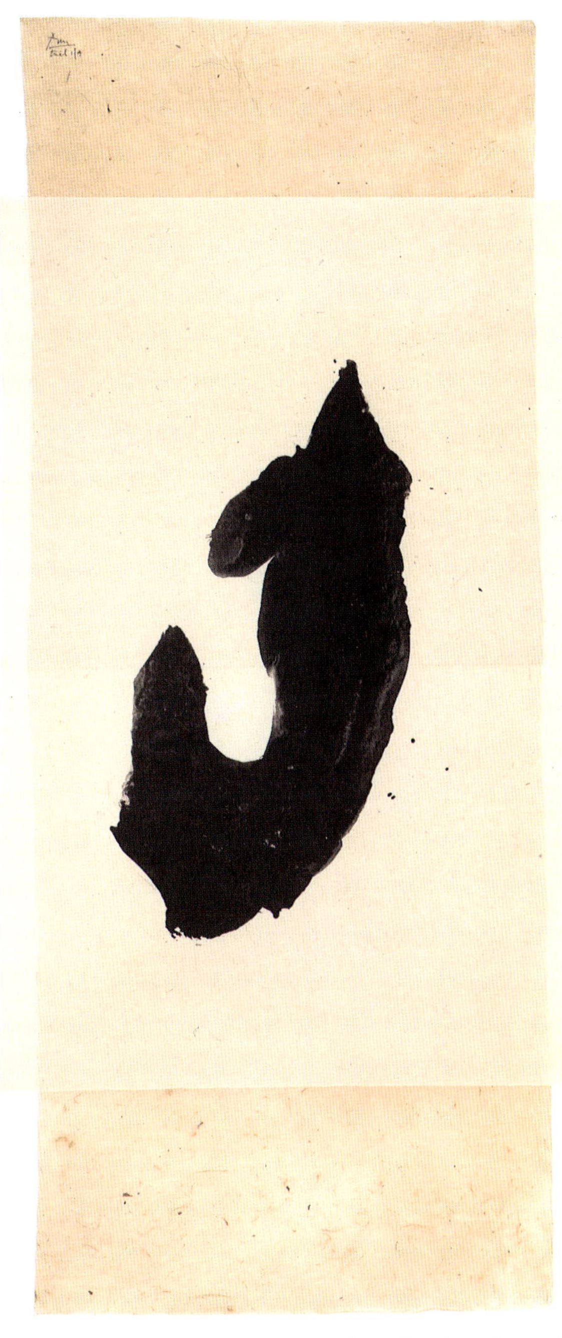

87. *Primal Sign I*, 1979–80. Aquatint (brown), lift-ground etching and aquatint (black); plates: 23½ x 18″ (59.7 x 45.2 cm) (black) and 23½ x 8″ (59.7 x 20.3 cm) (brown); paper: 28½ x 21½″ (71.9 x 54.6 cm). Cat. no. VIII.9

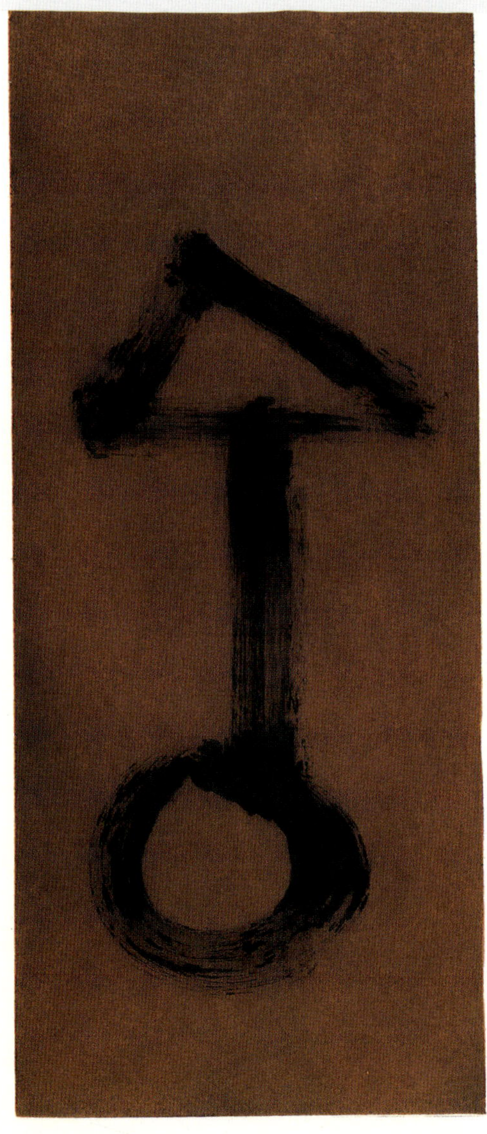

88. *Primal Sign II*, 1979–80. Aquatint (brown), lift-ground etching and aquatint (black); plates: 23 x 10″ (58.5 x 25.4 cm); paper: 30 x 21″ (76.2 x 53.4 cm). Cat. no. VIII.10

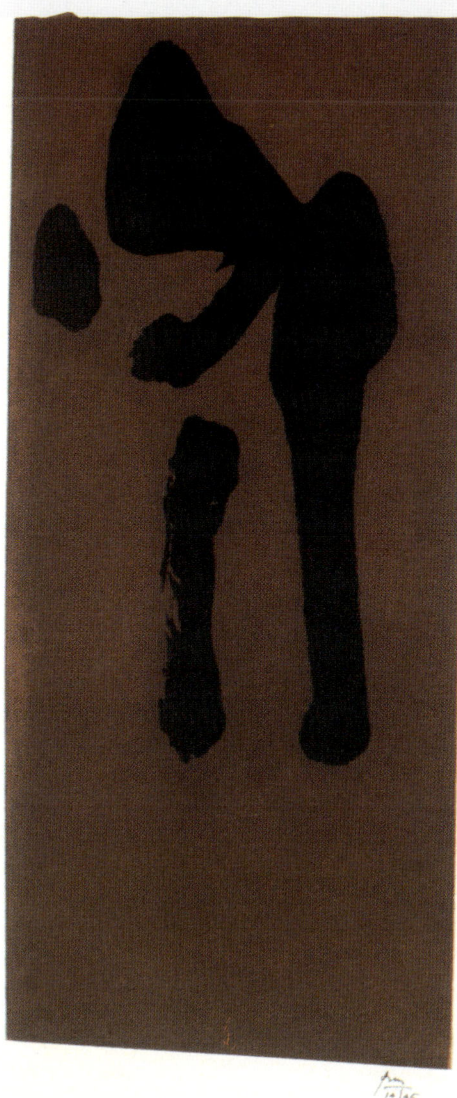

89. *Primal Sign III*, 1979–80. Aquatint (brown), lift-ground etching and aquatint (black); plates: 23 x 10″ (58.5 x 25.4 cm); paper: 28¾ x 20¾″ (73.1 x 52.9 cm). Cat. no. VIII.11

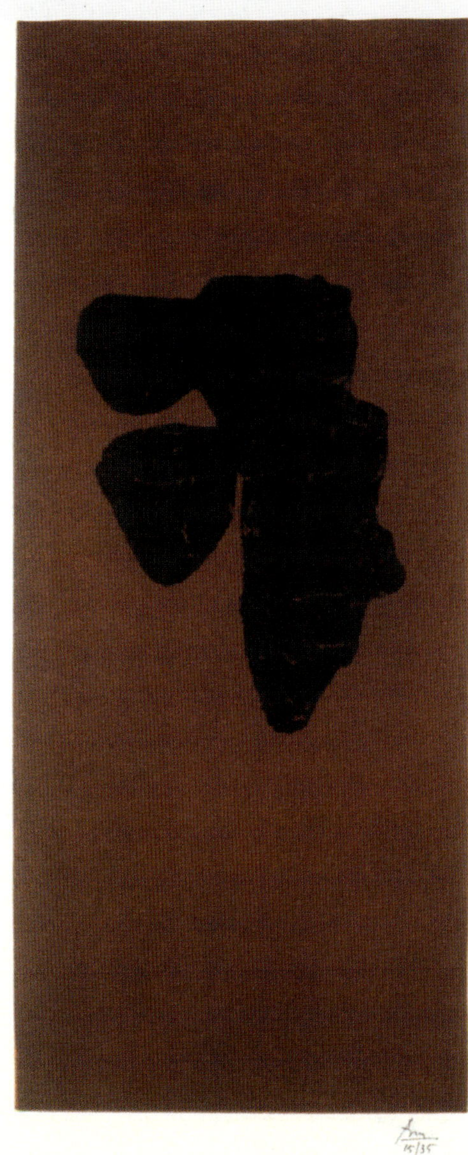

90. *Primal Sign IV*, 1979–80. Aquatint (brown), lift-ground etching and aquatint (black); plates: 23 x 11⅝" (58.5 x 29.6 cm); paper: 30 x 21" (76.2 x 53.4 cm). Cat. no. VIII.12

IX. *Drunk with Turpentine*

91. *Drunk with Turpentine Series*, 1979. Oil on paper, 29 x 23" (73.7 x 58.4 cm). Cat. no. IX.1

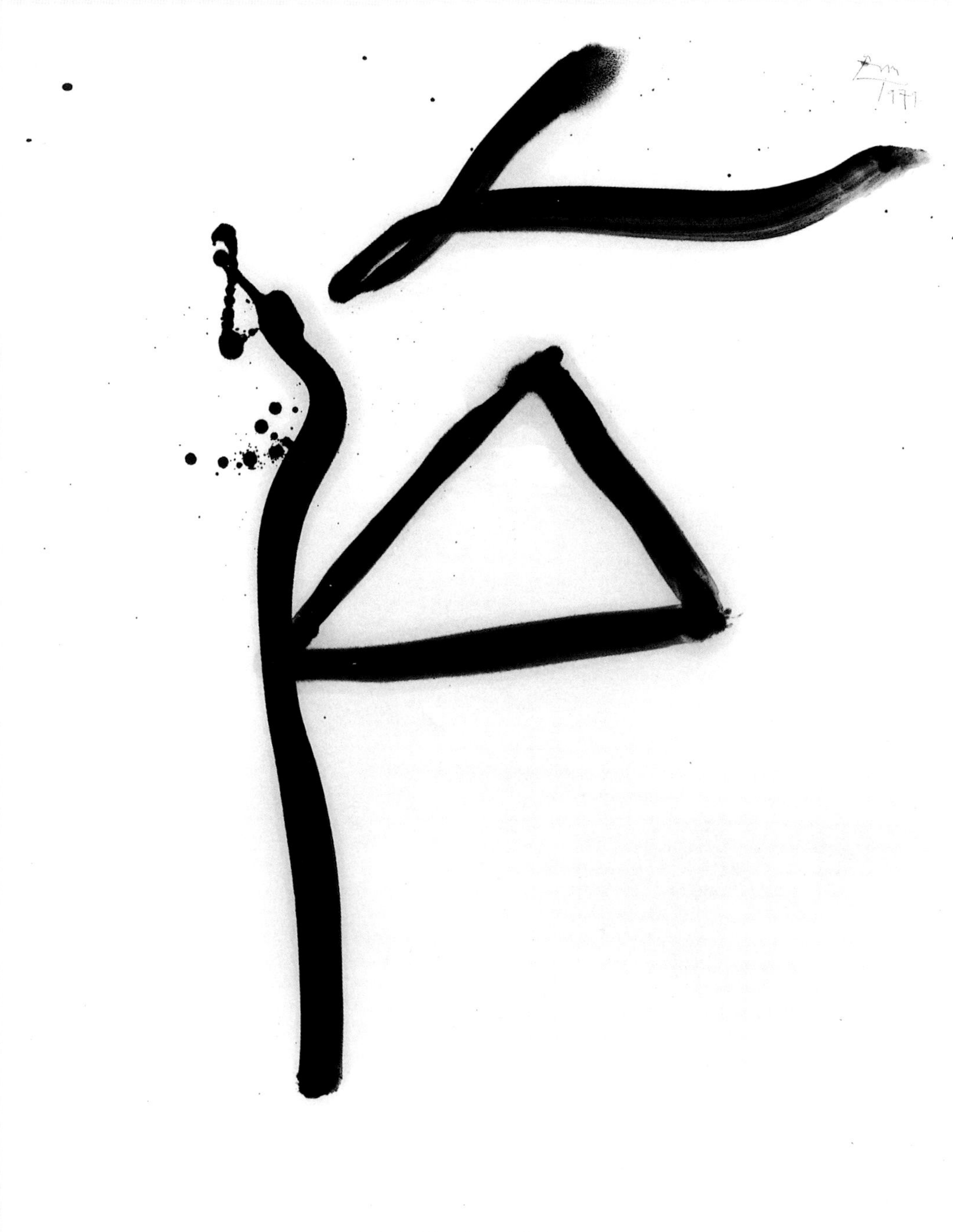

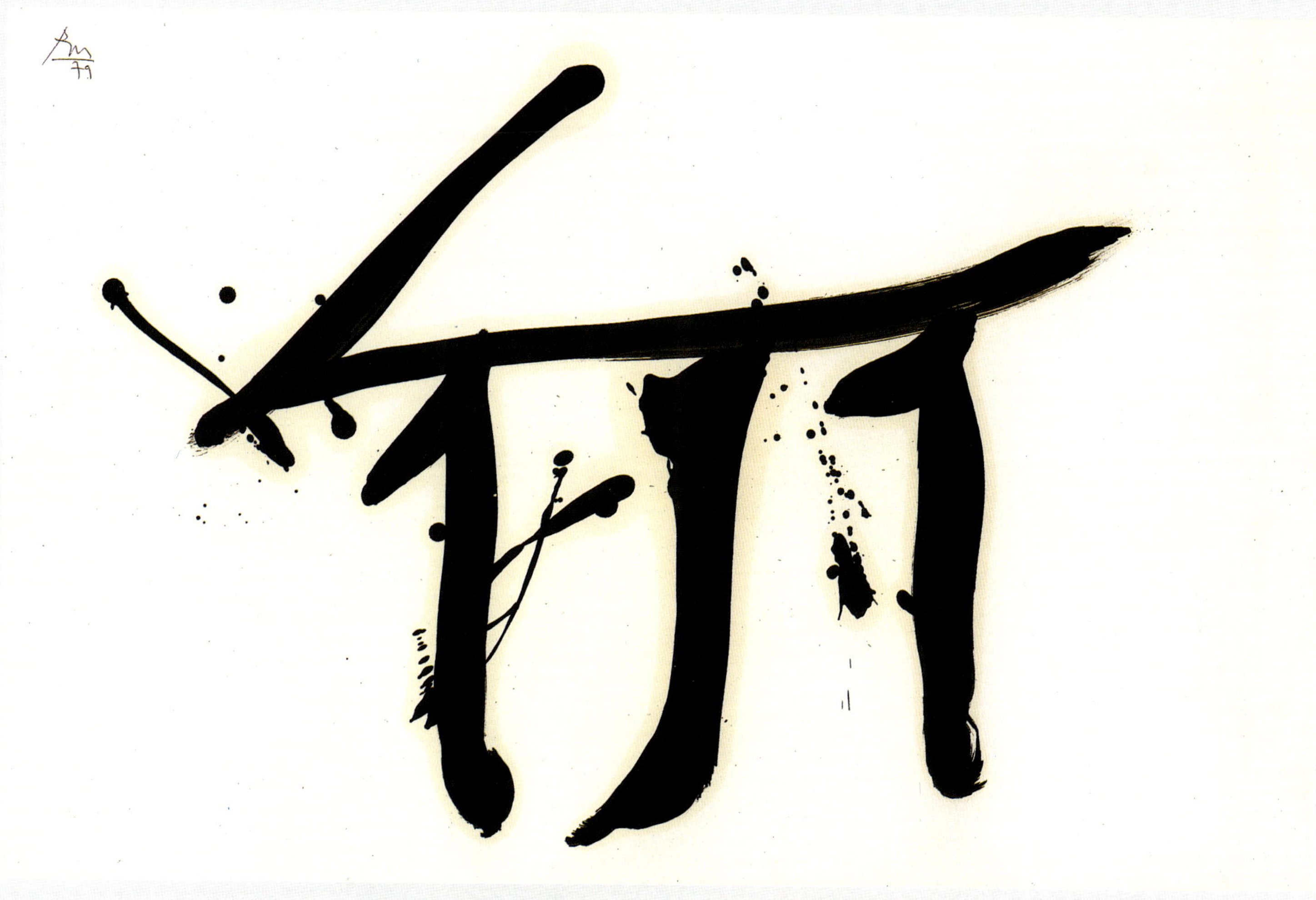

92. *Drunk with Turpentine No. 47*, 1979. Oil on rag board, 20 x 30″ (50.8 x 76.2 cm). Cat. no. IX.2

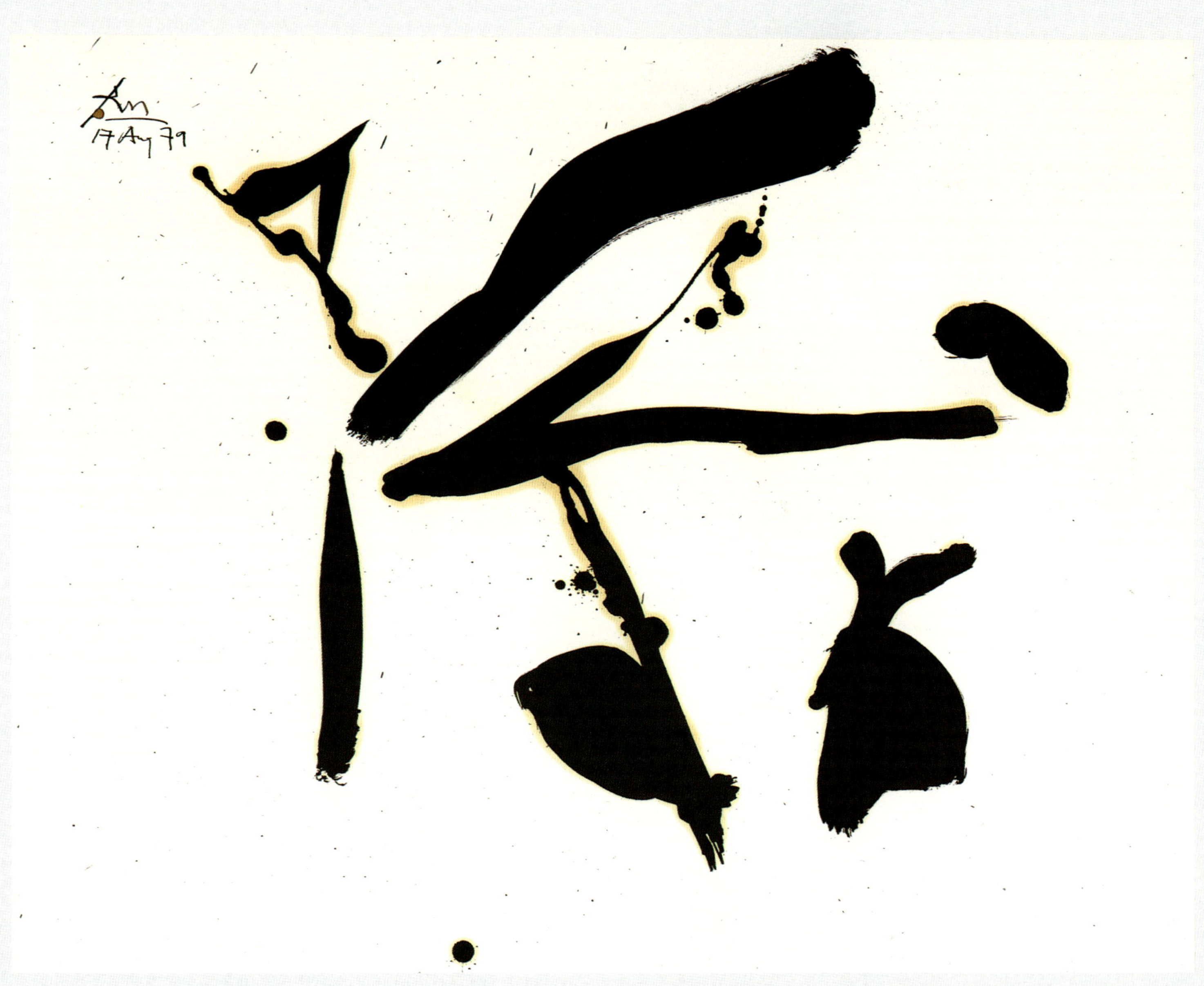

93. *Drunk with Turpentine No. 51*, 1979. Oil on rag paper, 23 x 29" (58.4 x 73.7 cm). Cat. no. IX.3

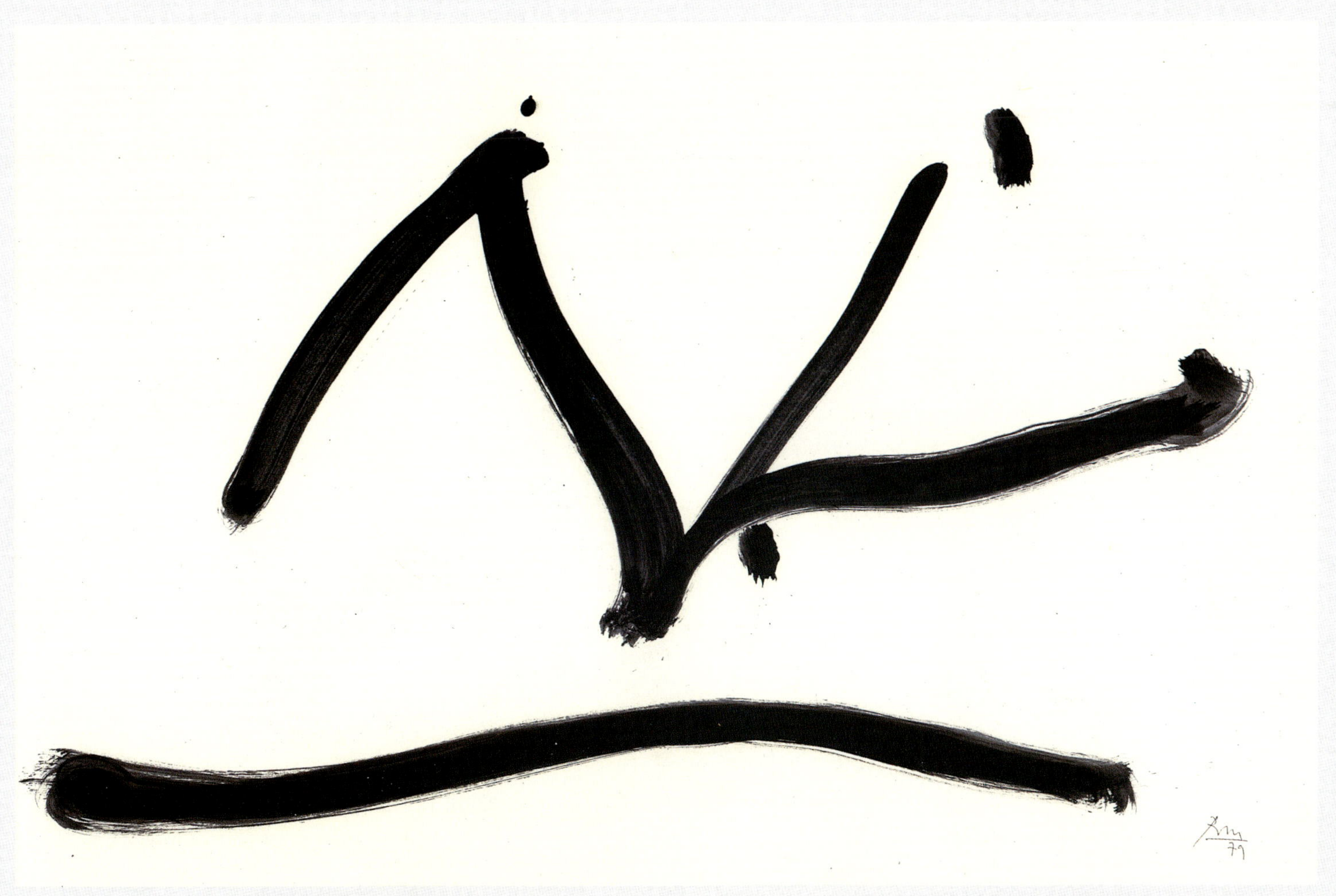

94. *Drunk with Turpentine Series*, 1979. Oil on rag paper, 20 x 30″ (50.8 x 76.2 cm). Cat. no. IX.4

X. Literary Figures

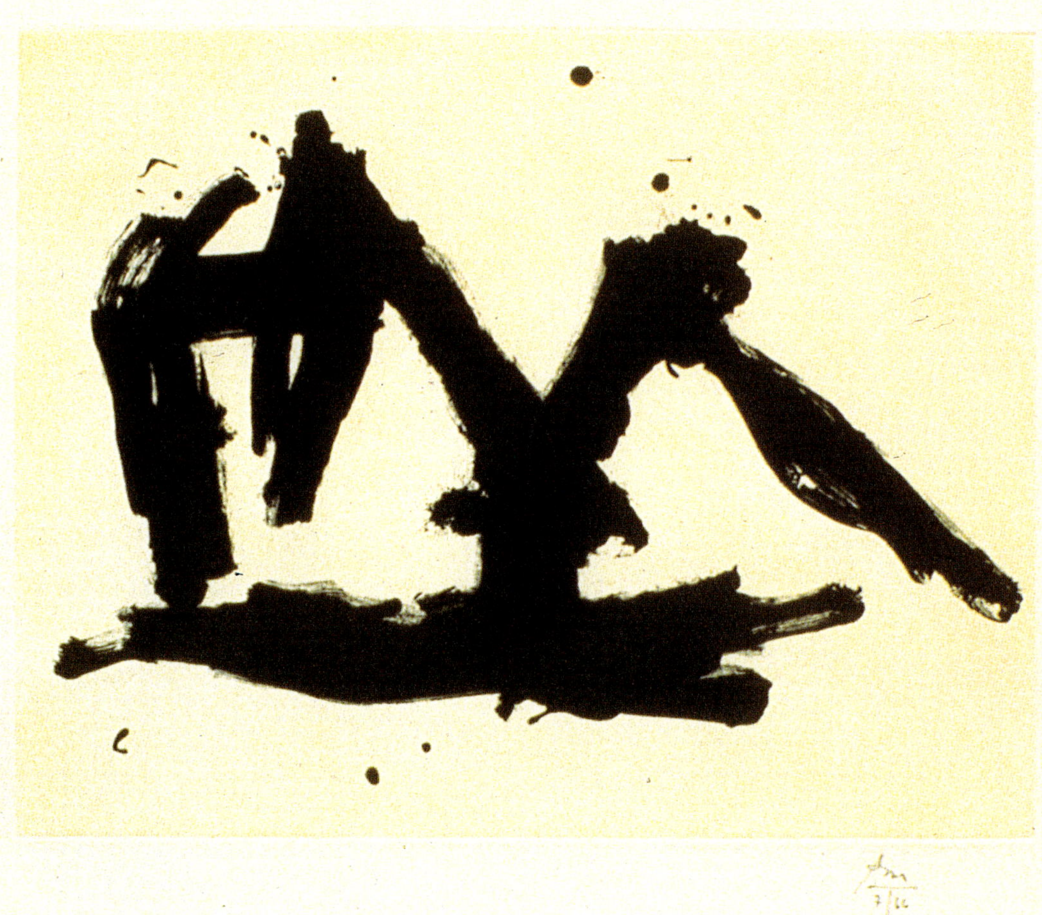

95. *Stephen's Iron Crown Etched*, 1981–82. Aquatint (cream); lift-ground etching and aquatint (black); plates: 15¾ x 19¾″ (40.1 x 50.3 cm); paper: 25 x 28″ (63.5 x 71.2 cm). Cat. no. X.1

96. *Mulligan's Tower*, 1982–83. Etching; plate: 9¾ x 6⅞" (24.8 x 17.5 cm); paper: 17 x 13" (43.2 x 33.1 cm). Cat. no. X.2

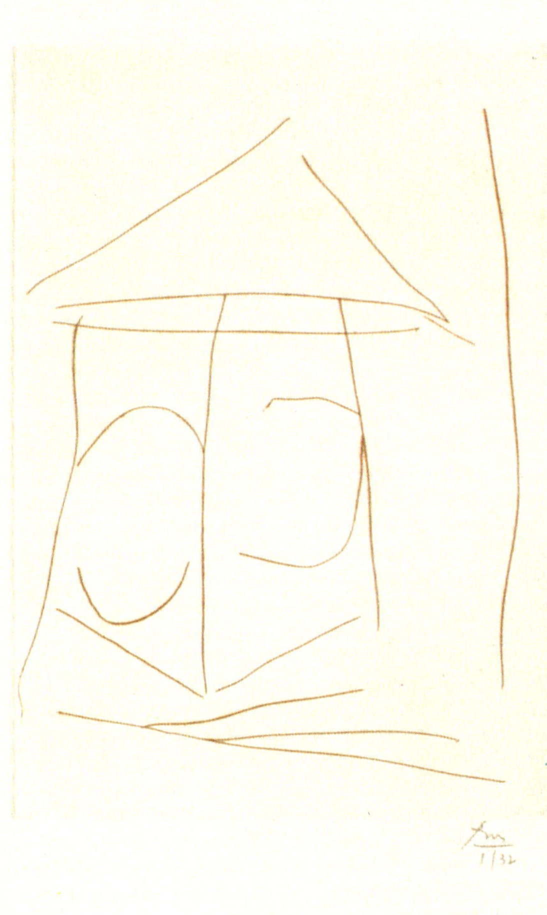

97. *Athena*, 1982–83. Lift-ground etching and aquatint; plate: 7¾ x 9¾" (19.7 x 24.8 cm); paper: 19⅞ x 17¾" (50.6 x 45.1 cm). Cat. no. X.3

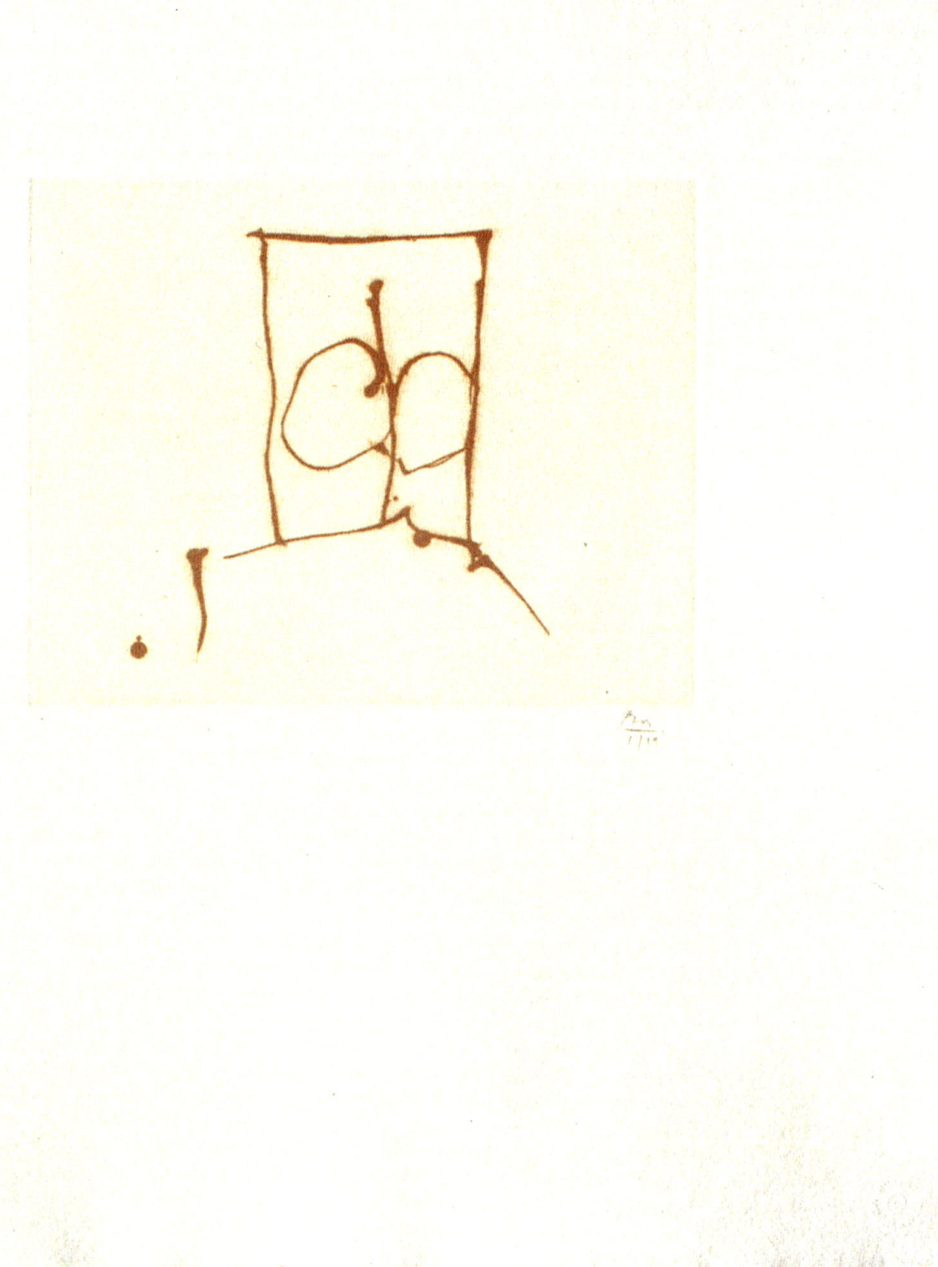

98. *Wind*, 1982–83. Lift-ground etching and aquatint; plate: 7⅞ x 9¾" (20.1 x 24.8 cm); paper: 20 x 17½" (50.9 x 44.5 cm). Cat. no. X.4

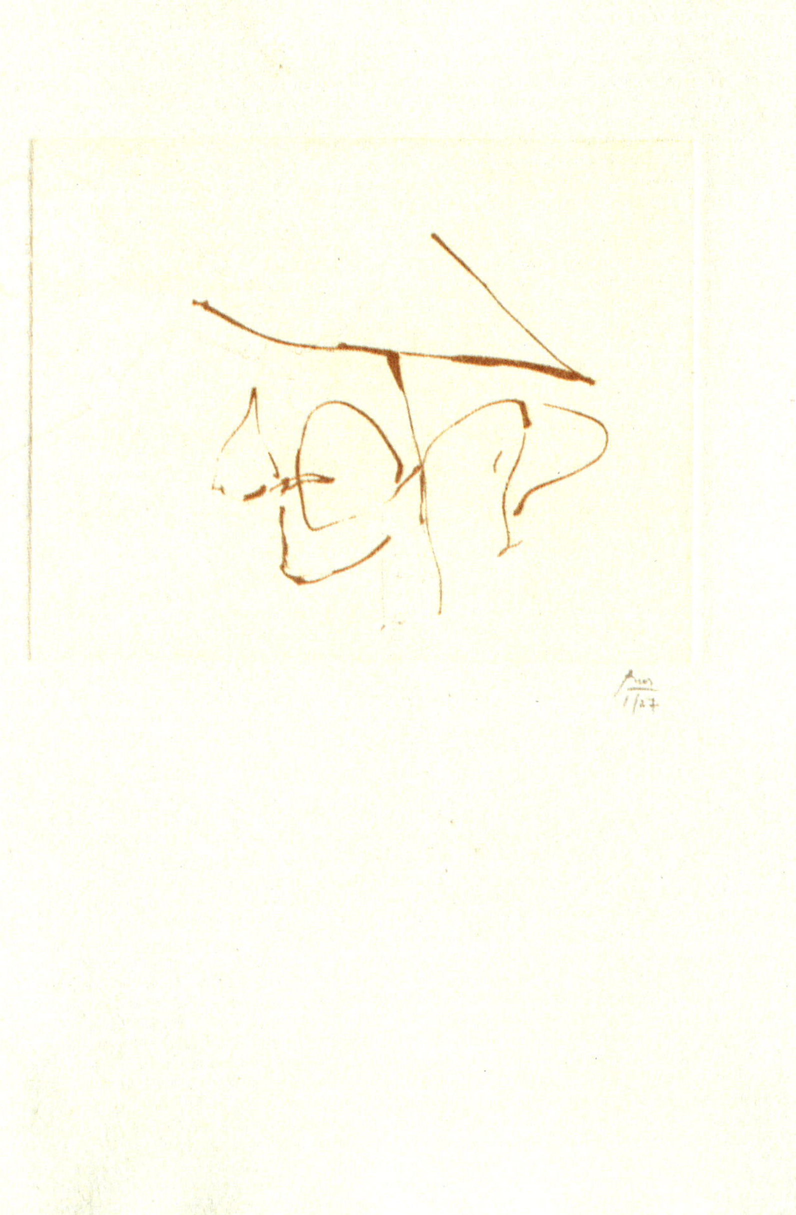

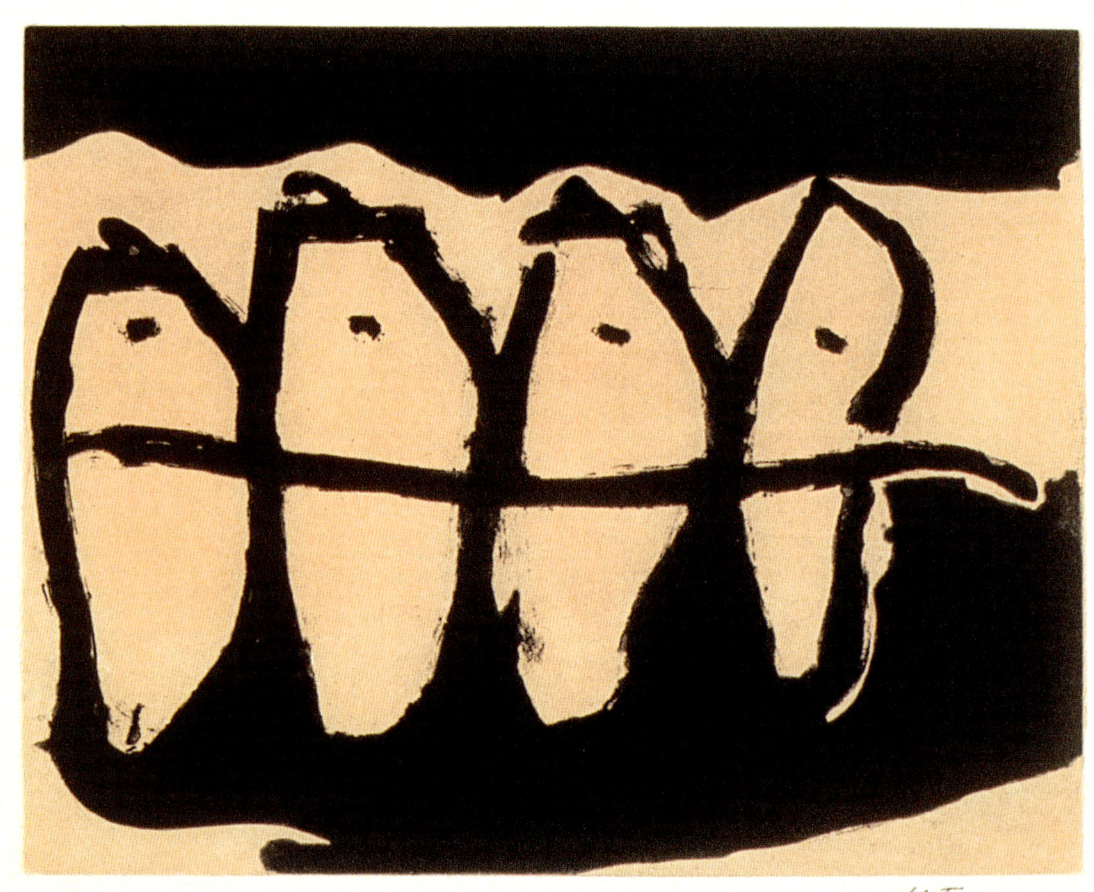

99. *Wanderers*, 1985. Aquatint (light salmon), lift-ground etching and aquatint (black); plates: 15¾ x 19⅝" (40.1 x 50 cm); paper: 23¼ x 27" (59.1 x 68.6 cm). Cat. no. X.5

PAGES 171–177:

100–106. *Hollow Men Suite*, 1985–86. Suite of seven lift-ground etchings with aquatint, Chine collé; paper: 11¼ x 12″ (28.7 x 30.5 cm)

100. From the *Hollow Men*. Plate (collé sheet): 4½ x 5⅞″ (11.5 x 15 cm). Cat. no. X.6

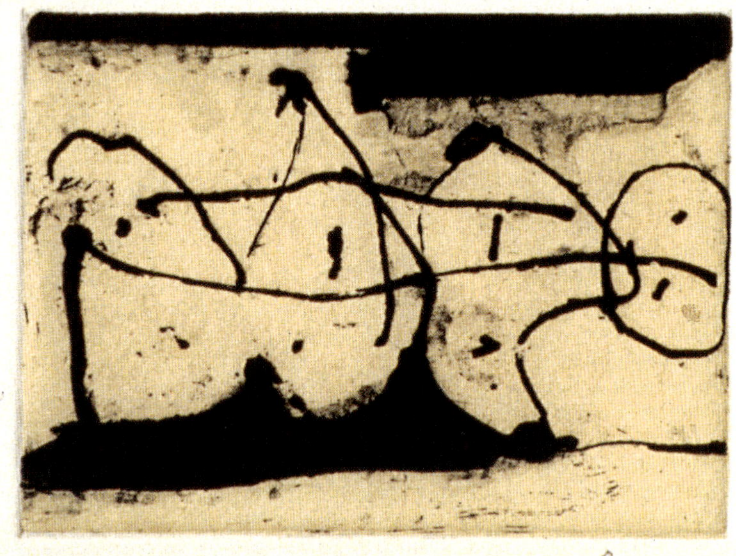

101. From the *Hollow Men*. Plate (collé sheet): 4 x 5⅞" (10.2 x 15 cm). Cat. no. X.7

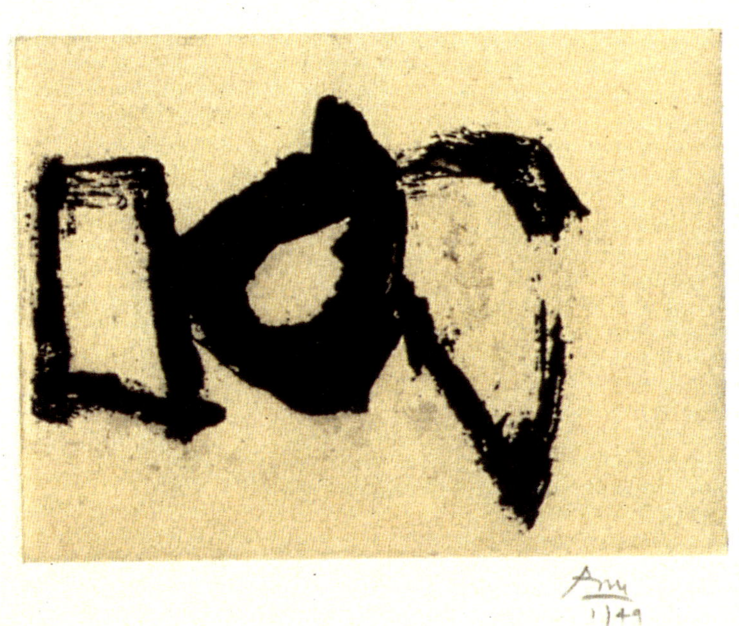

102. From the *Hollow Men*. Plate (collé sheet): 3¾ x 4⅞" (9.6 x 12.5 cm). Cat. no. X.8

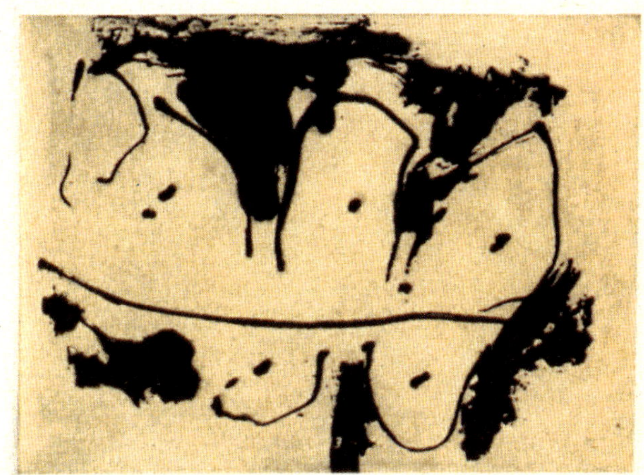

103. From the *Hollow Men*. Plate (collé sheet): 3⅝ x 4⅞" (9.3 x 12.5 cm). Cat. no. X.9

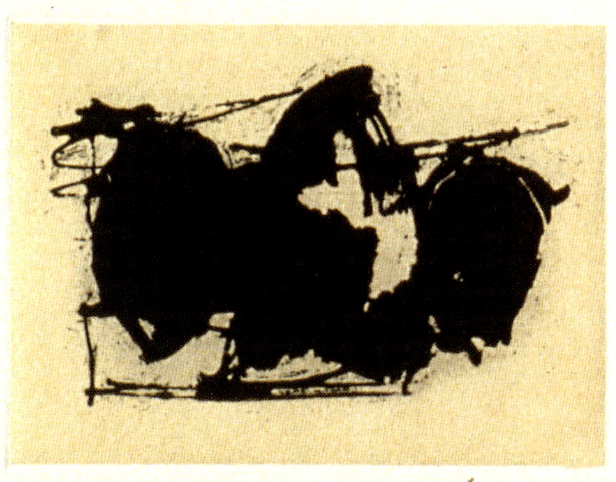

104. From the *Hollow Men*. Plate (collé sheet): 4 x 5⅞″ (10.2 x 15 cm). Cat. no. X.10

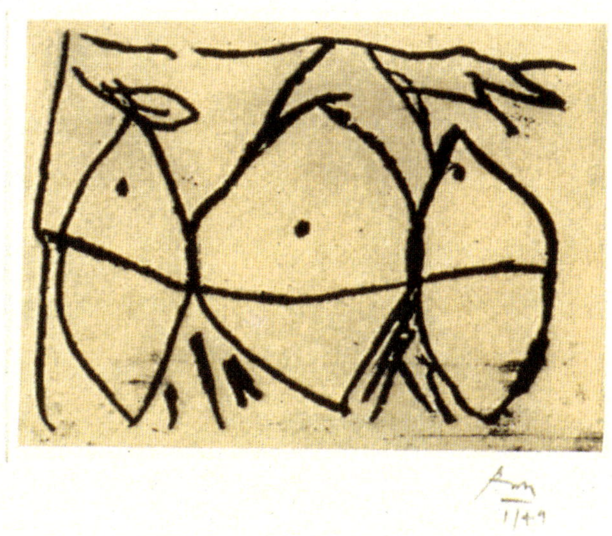

105. From the *Hollow Men*. Plate (collé sheet): 3⅝ x 4⅞″ (9.3 x 12.5 cm). Cat. no. X.11

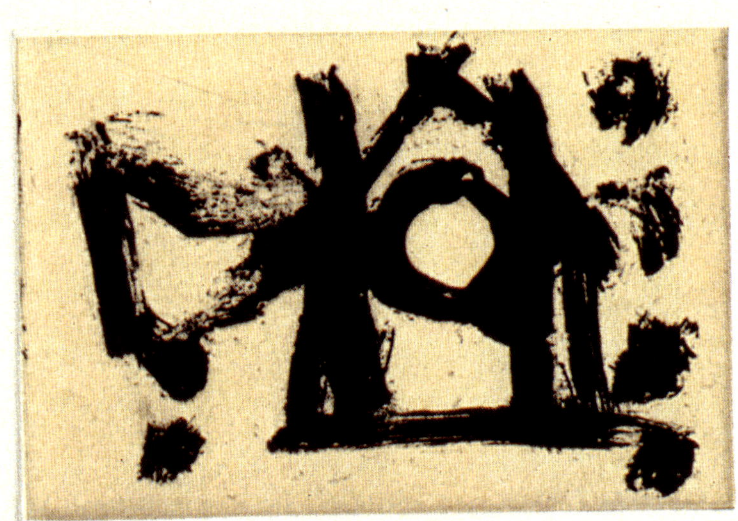

106. From the *Hollow Men*. Plate (collé sheet): 5 x 6⅞" (12.8 x 17.7 cm). Cat. no. X.12

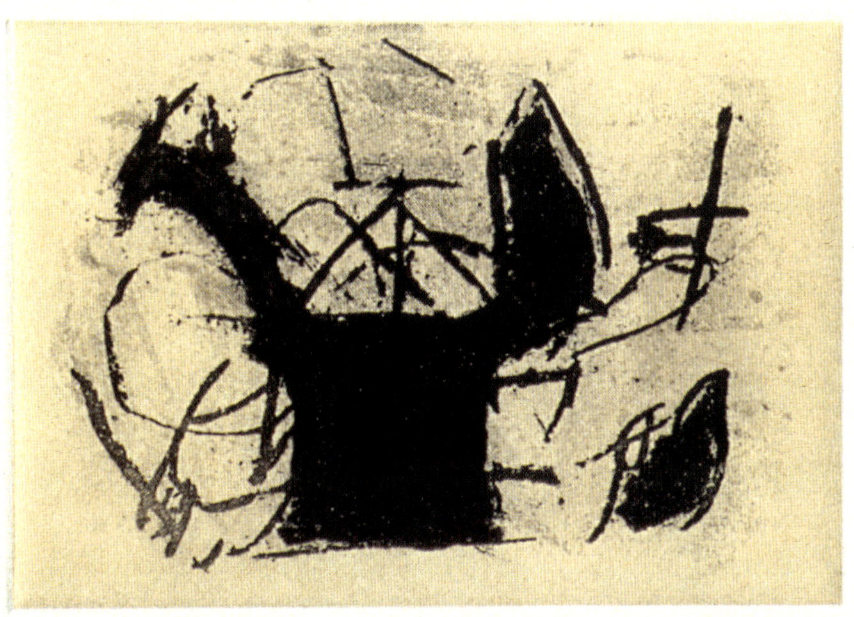

PAGES 178–184:
107–127. From the *Joyce Sketchbook*

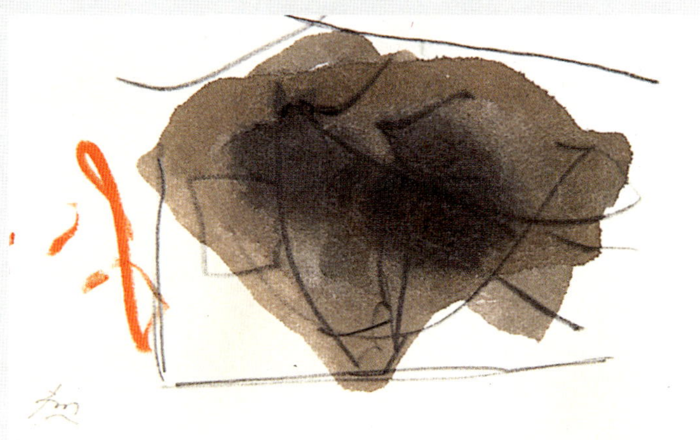

107. *Ulysses Drawing*, 1986. Pencil, China marker, and ink wash on paper, 3 x 5″ (7.6 x 12.7 cm). Cat. no. X.13

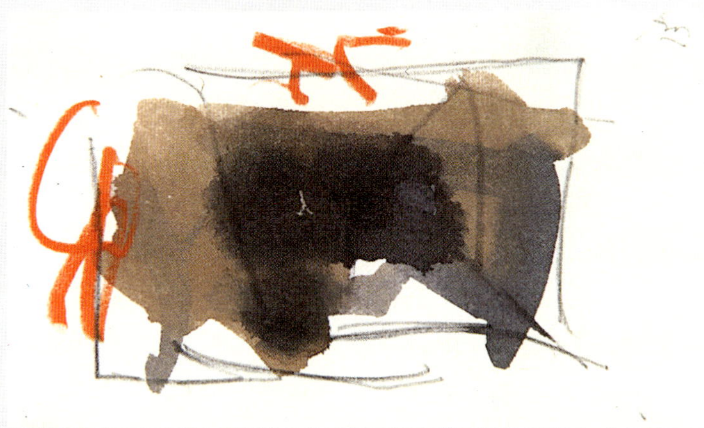

108. *Ulysses Drawing*, 1985. Pencil, ink, and China marker an paper, 3 x 5″ (7.6 x 12.7 cm). Cat. no. X.14

109. *Joyce Sketchbook II*, 1985. Pencil and ink on paper, 3 x 5″ (7.6 x 12.7 cm). Cat. no. X.15

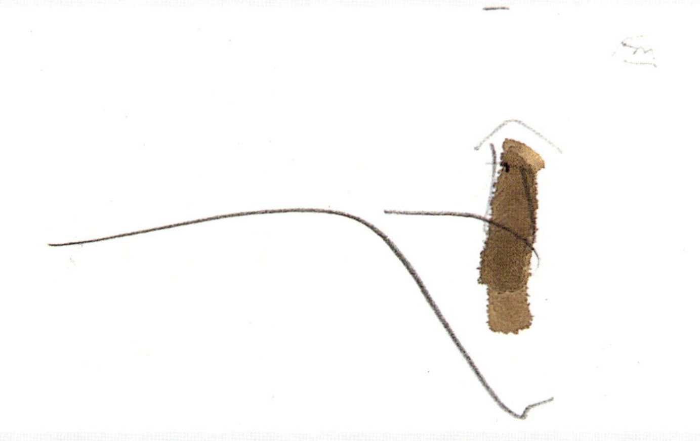

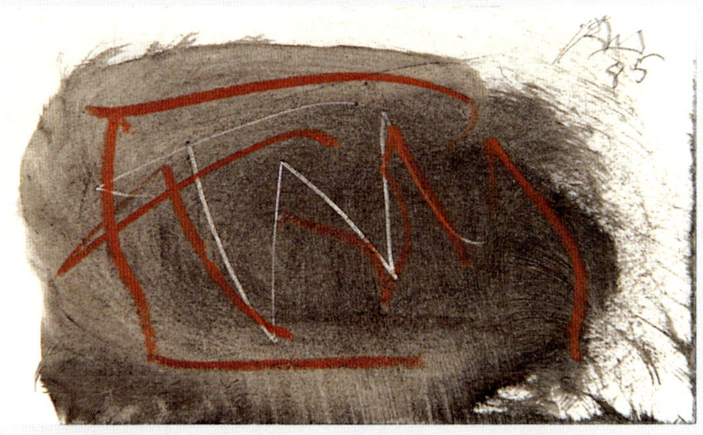

110. *Joyce Sketchbook II*, 1985. Ink wash and China marker on paper, 3 x 5" (7.6 x 12.7 cm). Cat. no. X.16

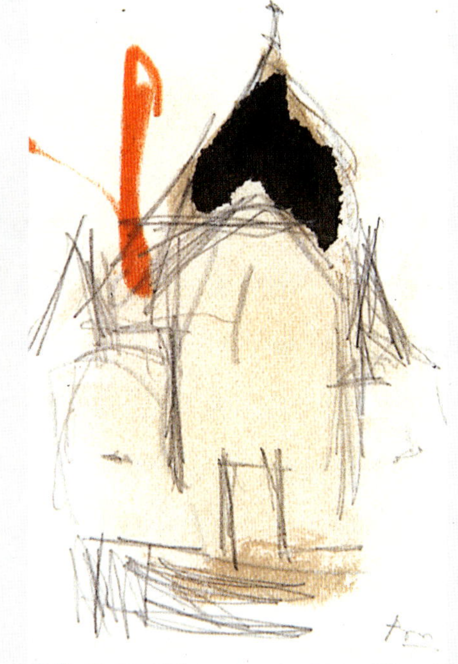

RIGHT:
111. *Joyce Sketchbook II*, 1985. Pencil, ink wash, and China marker on paper, 5 x 3" (12.7 x 7.6 cm). Cat. no. X.17

112. *Untitled*, 1985. Ink and China marker on paper, 3 x 5" (7.6 x 12.7 cm). Cat. no. X.18

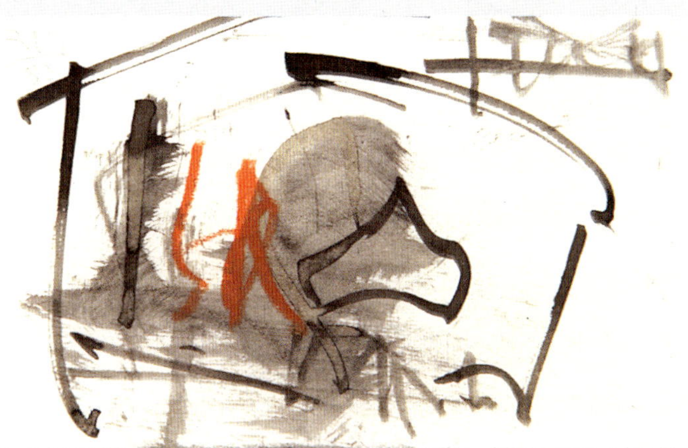

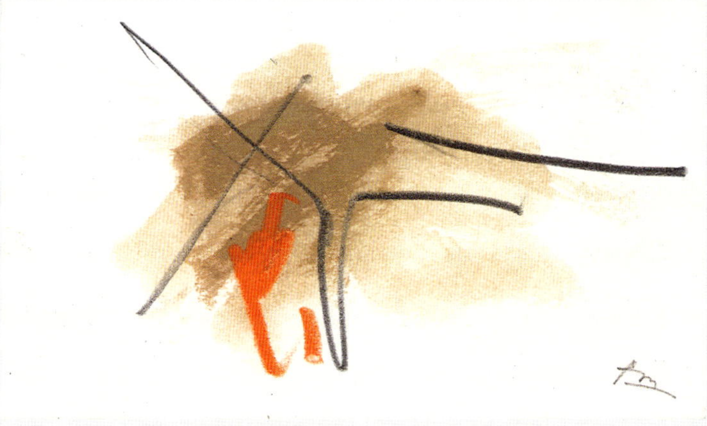

113. *Untitled*, 1985. Ink, pencil, and China marker on paper, 3 x 5″ (7.6 x 12.7 cm). Cat. no. X.19

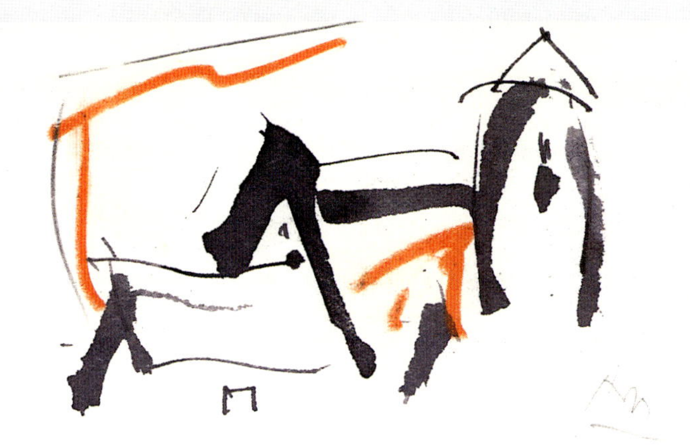

114. *Church*, 1985. Ink, pencil, and China marker on paper, 3 x 5″ (7.6 x 12.7 cm). Cat. no. X.20

115. *Untitled (Elegy Study)*, 1985. Pencil on paper, 3 x 5″ (7.6 x 12.7 cm). Cat. no. X.21

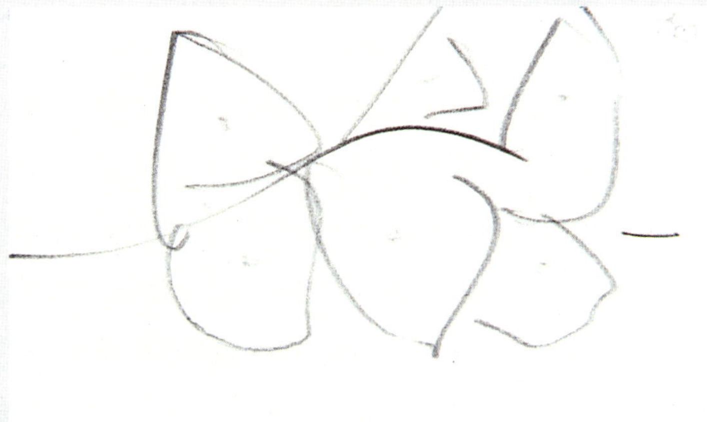

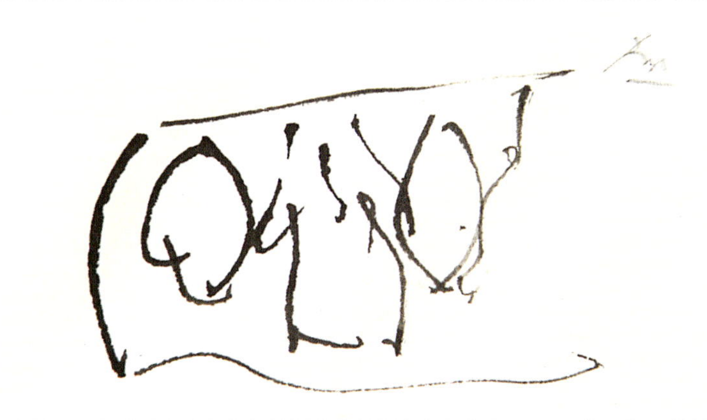

116. *Untitled (Open Forms)*, 1985. Ink on paper, 3 x 5″ (7.6 x 12.7 cm). Cat. no. X.22

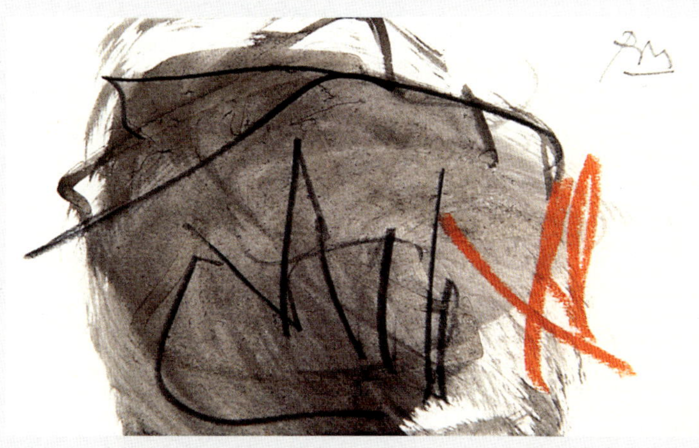

117. *Untitled*, 1985. Pencil, ink, and wash on paper, 3 x 5″ (7.6 x 12.7 cm). Cat. no. X.23

118. *Untitled*, 1985. Ink and China marker on paper, 3 x 5″ (7.6 x 12.7 cm). Cat. no. X.24

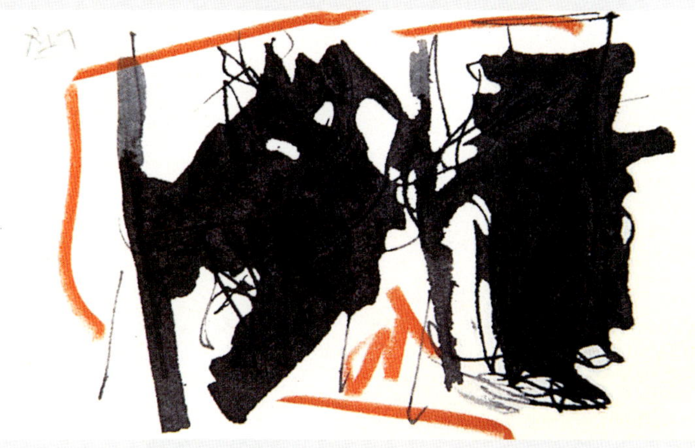

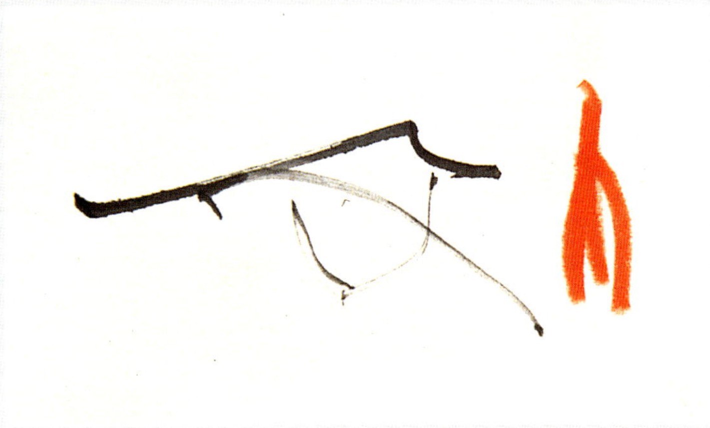

119. *Untitled*, 1985. Ink and China marker on paper, 3 x 5" (7.6 x 12.7 cm). Cat. no. X.25

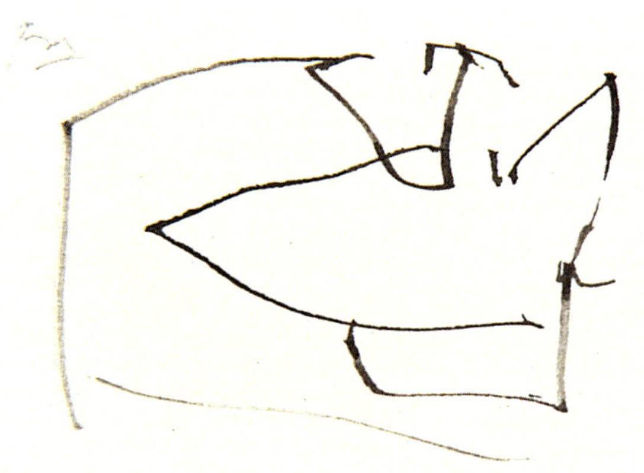

120. *Untitled*, 1985. Ink on paper, 3 x 5" (7.6 x 12.7 cm). Cat. no. X.26

121. *Untitled (Elegy Forms)*, 1985. Brown ink on paper, 3 x 5" (7.6 x 12.7 cm). Cat. no. X.27

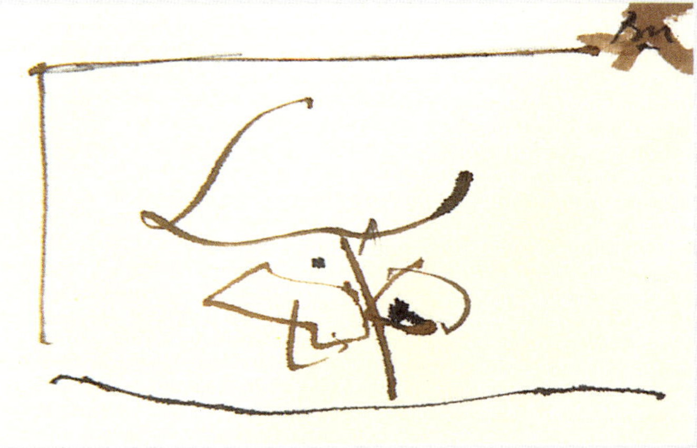

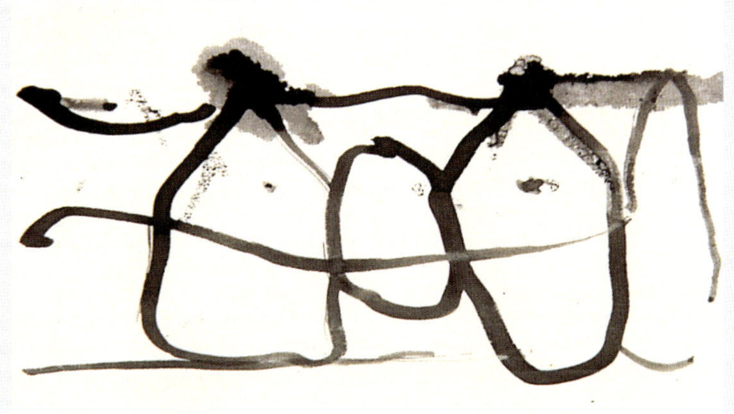

122. *Untitled*, 1985. Ink on paper, 3 x 5″ (7.6 x 12.7 cm). Cat. no. X.28

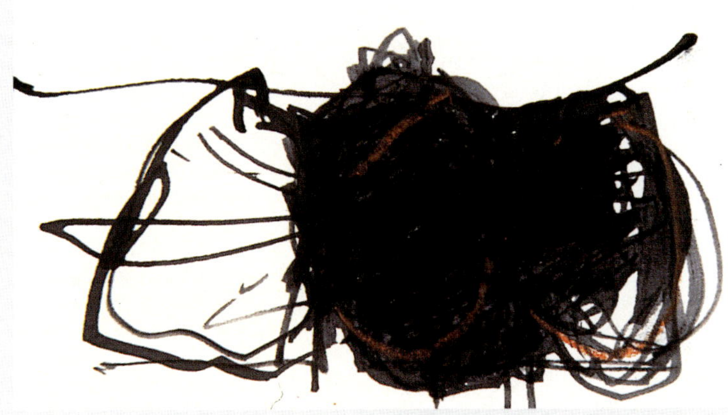

123. *Untitled*, 1985. Ink and China marker on paper, 3 x 5″ (7.6 x 12.7 cm). Cat. no. X.29

124. *Untitled*, 1985. Ink on paper, 3 x 5″ (7.6 x 12.7 cm). Cat. no. X.30

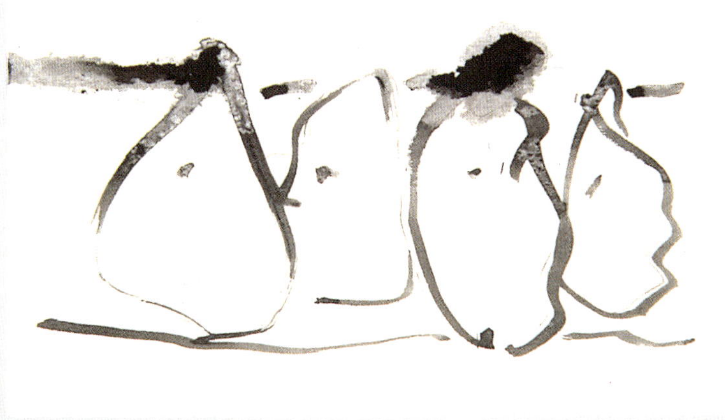

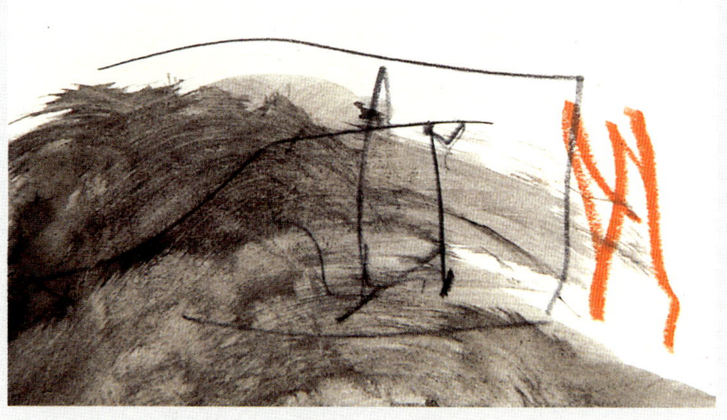

125. *Ulysses Drawing*, 1985. Ink, wash, pencil, and China marker on paper, 3 x 5" (7.6 x 12.7 cm). Cat. no. X.31

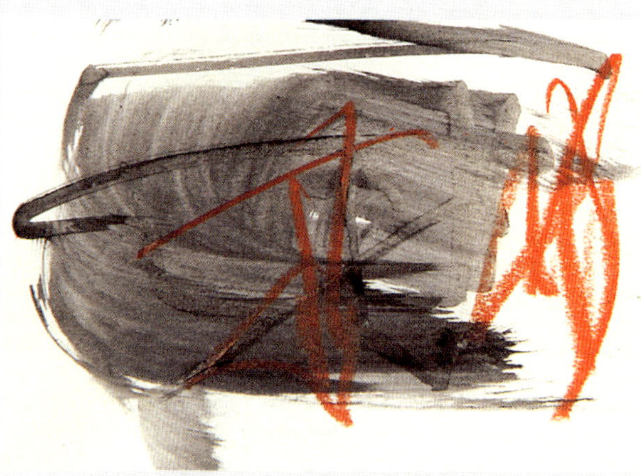

126. *Ulysses Drawing*, 1985. Ink, wash, and China marker on paper, 3 x 5" (7.6 x 12.7 cm). Cat. no. X.32

127. *Untitled*, 1985. Ink, wash, pencil, and China marker on paper, 3 x 5" (7.6 x 12.7 cm). Cat. no. X.33

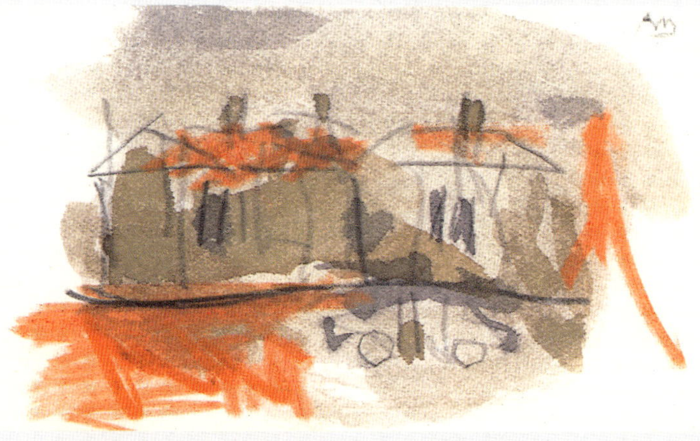

XI. *Night Music*

128. *Black Refracts Heat*, 1974. Collage and acrylic on Upson board, 48 x 36″ (121.9 x 91.4 cm). Walker Art Center, Minneapolis. Cat. no. XI.1

129. *Night Music Opus No. 14*, 1989. Collage of rice paper and acrylic on canvas panel, 33¼ x 25" (84.5 x 63.5 cm). Cat. no. XI.2

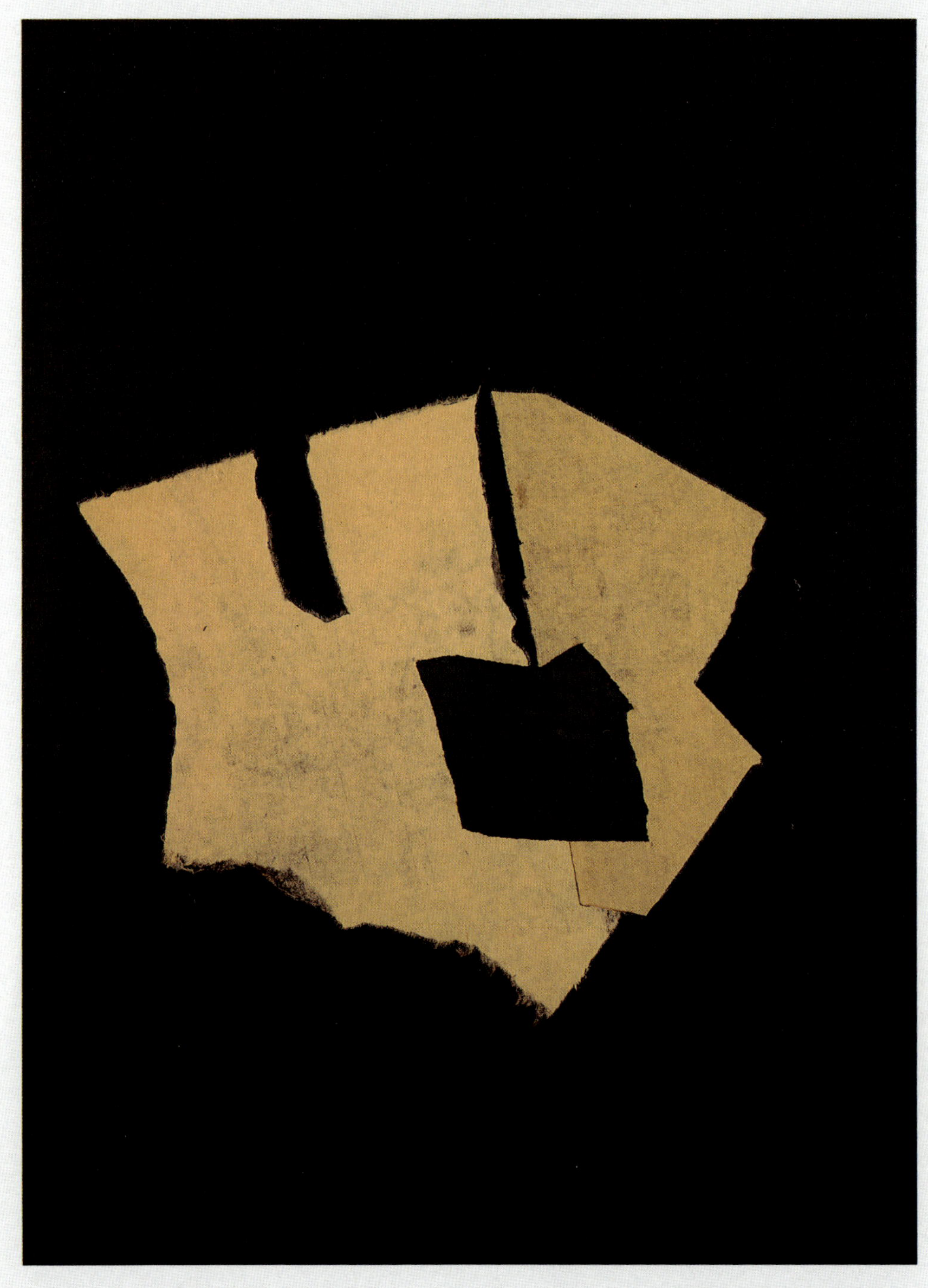

130. *Night Music Opus No. 16*, 1989. Collage of rice paper and acrylic on canvas panel, 32½ x 25¼" (82.6 x 64.1 cm). Cat. no. XI.3

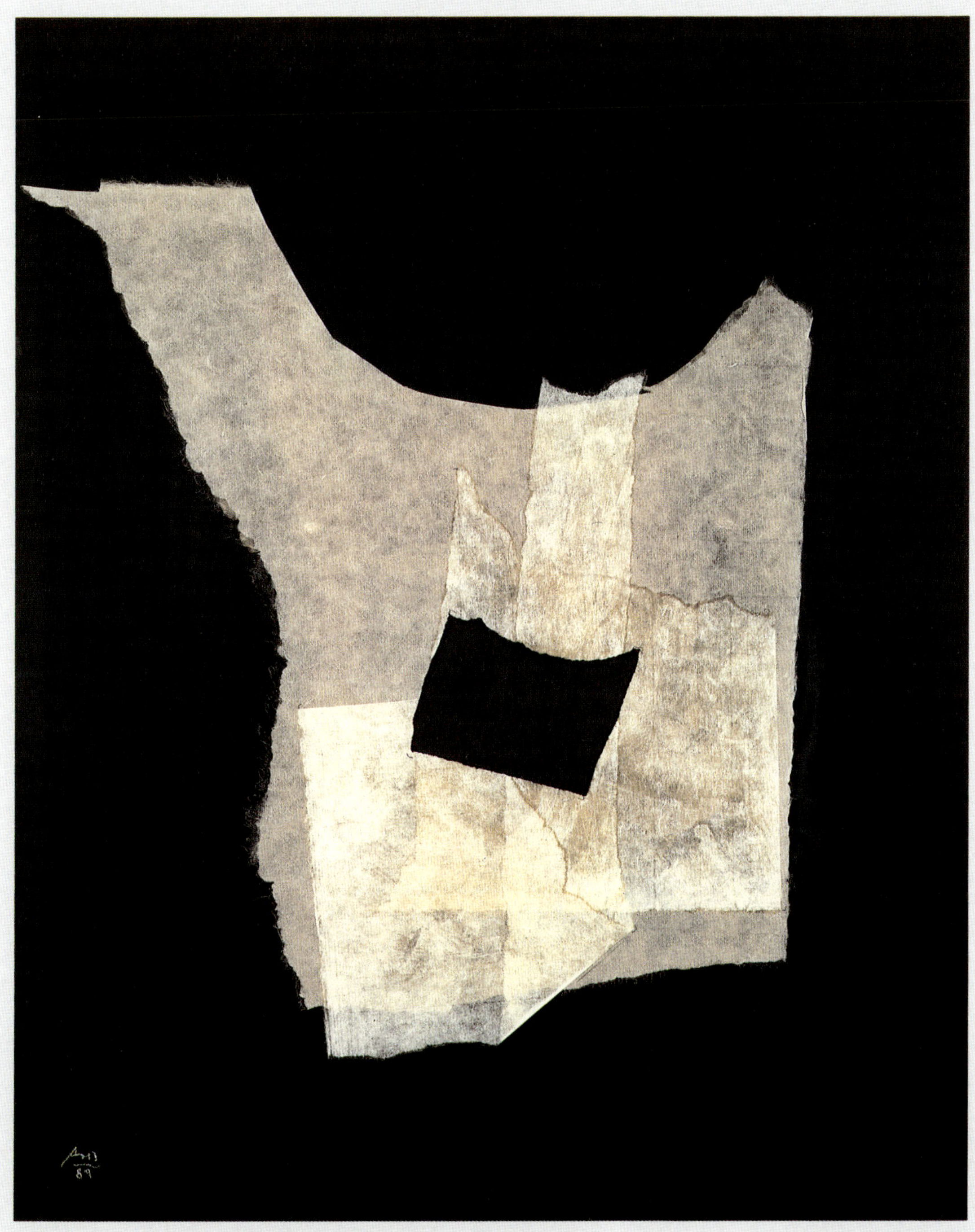

131. *Night Music Opus No. 17*, 1989. Collage of rice paper and acrylic on canvas panel, 32¼ x 25½" (81.9 x 64.8 cm). Cat. no. XI.4

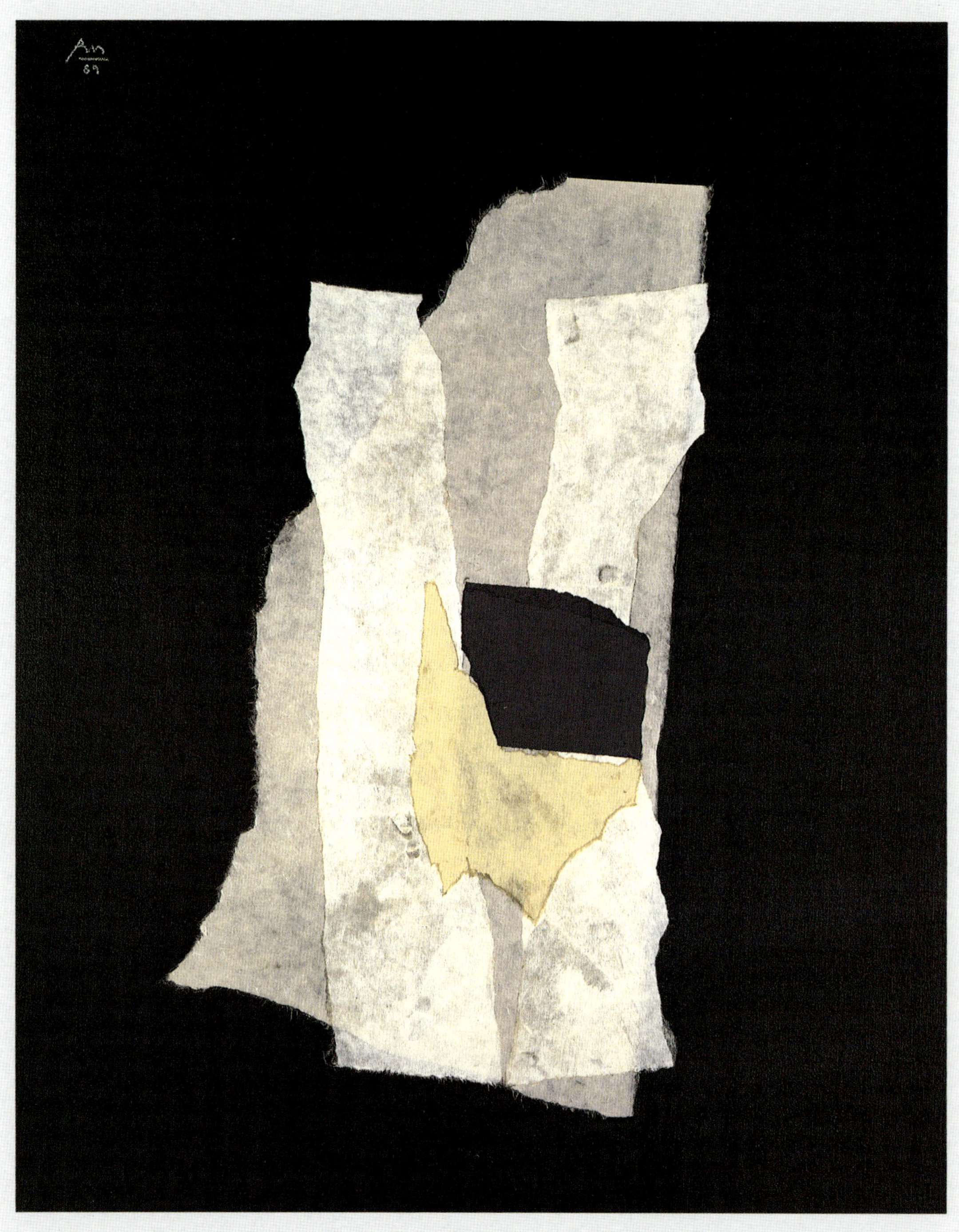

132. *Night Music Opus No. 24*, 1989. Collage and acrylic on canvas panel, 32½ x 25½" (82.6 x 64.8 cm). Cat. no. XI.5

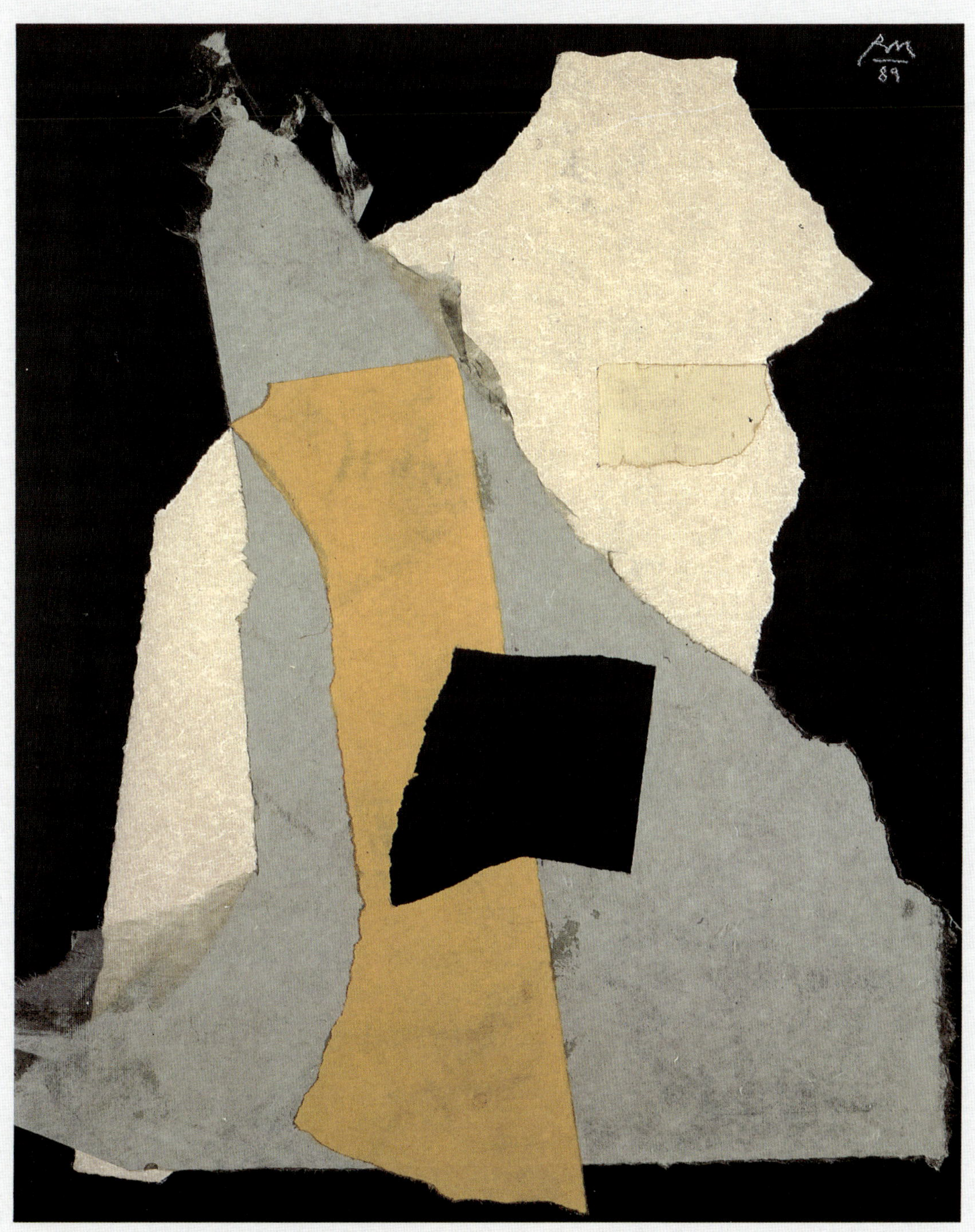

133. *Night Music Opus No. 25*, 1989. Collage and acrylic on canvas panel, 32½ x 25½" (82.6 x 64.8 cm). Cat. no. XI.6

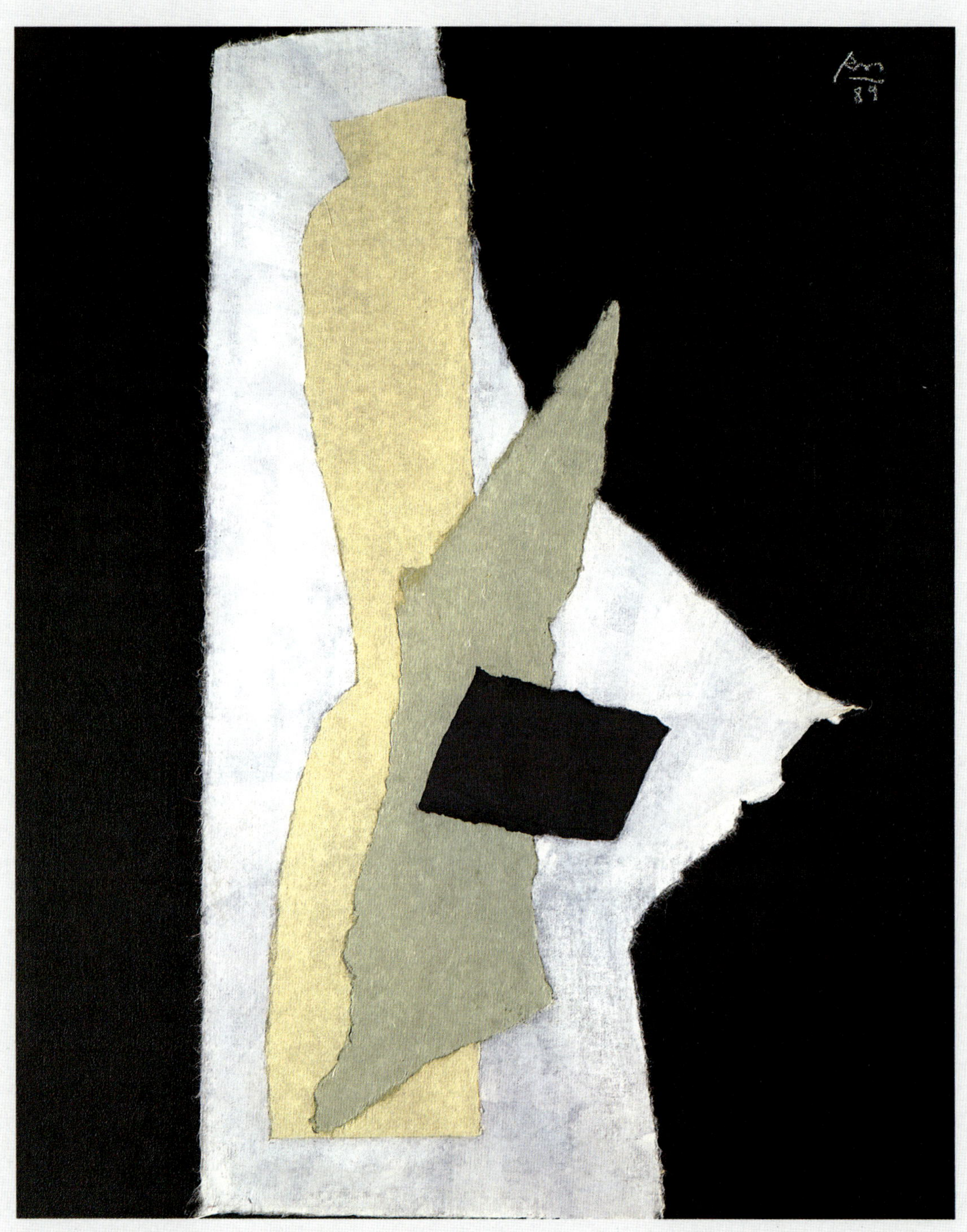

134. *Night Music Opus No. 26*, 1989. Collage and acrylic on canvas panel, 32½ x 25½" (82.6 x 64.8 cm). Cat. no. XI.7

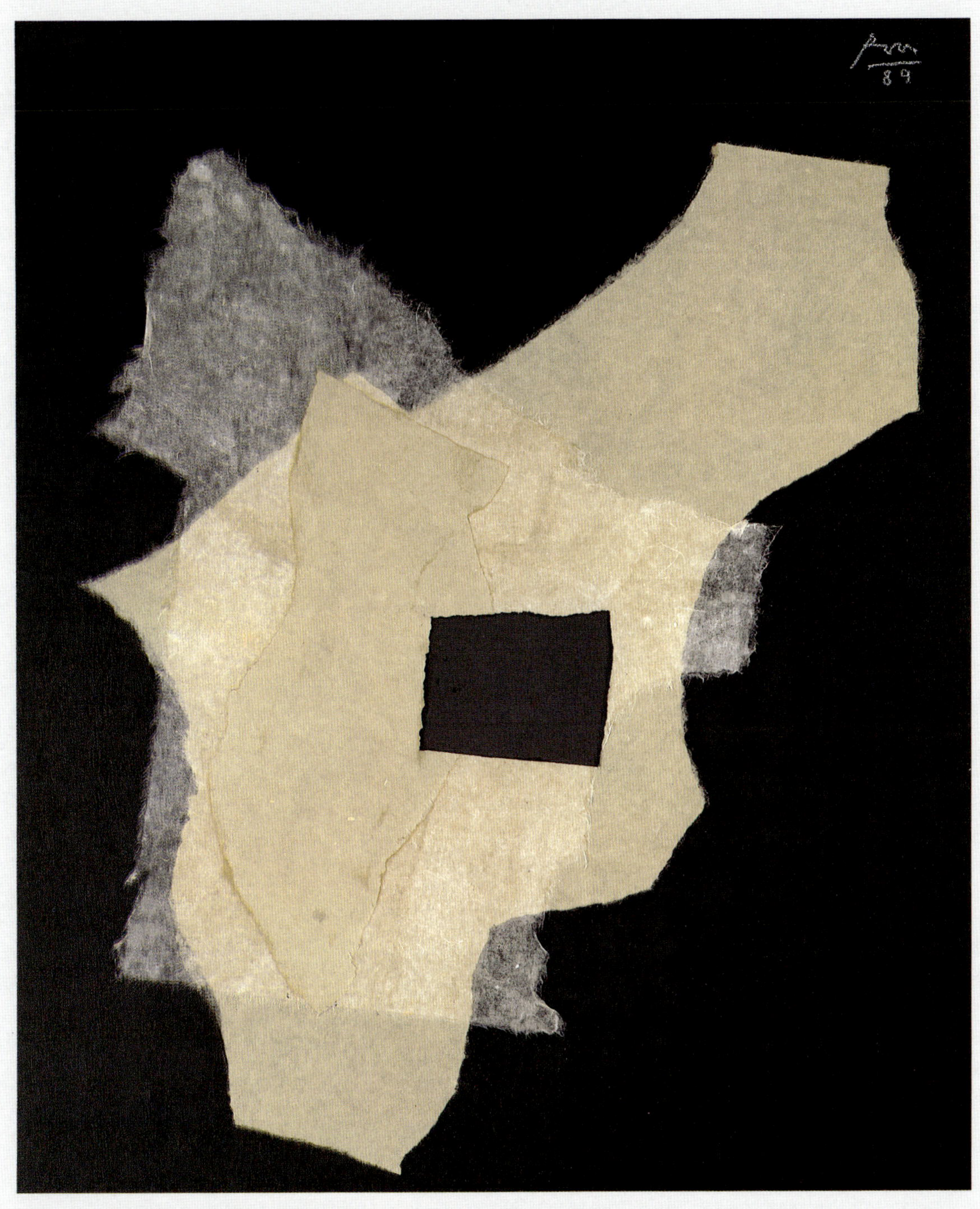

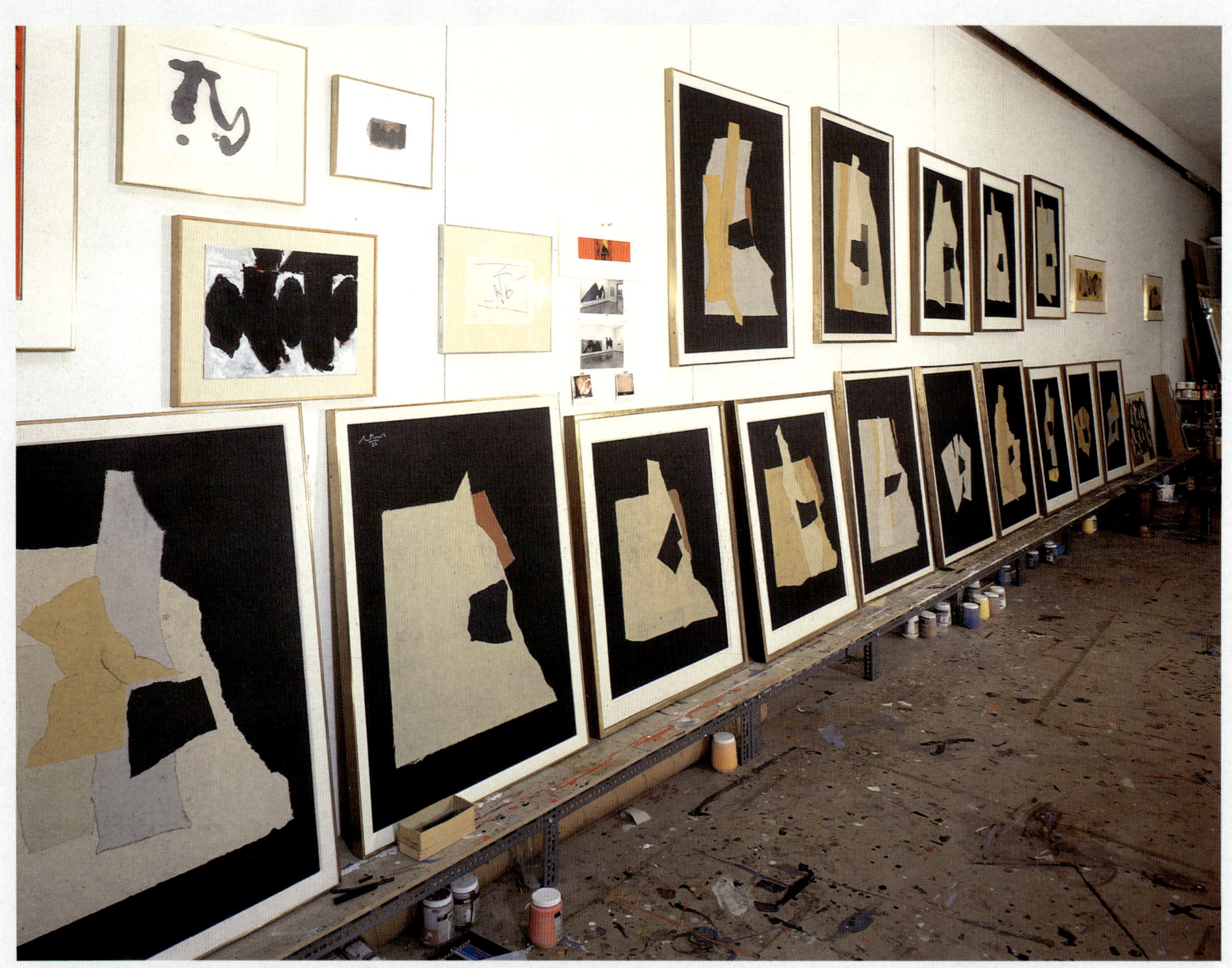

135. *Night Music* collage series in the artist's studio, Greenwich, Connecticut, February 1989. Photograph by Ken Cohen

Catalogue

Unless otherwise noted, all works are from the collection of the Dedalus Foundation, Inc. Works marked with an asterisk are exhibited in New York only. References for the prints are to the "Catalogue Raisonné, 1943–1990" by Dorothy C. Belknap, in Stephanie Terenzio, *The Prints of Robert Motherwell*, 3rd ed., revised and enlarged (New York: Hudson Hills Press in association with the American Federation of Arts, 1991). A glossary note on the printmaking terms used in the catalogue appears on page 202.

I. *Elegies to the Spanish Republic*

1. *Elegy to the Spanish Republic No. 1*, 1948 (frontispiece)*
India ink on paper
10¾ x 8½" (27.3 x 21.8 cm)
The Museum of Modern Art, New York. Gift of the artist

2. *At Five in the Afternoon*, 1949 (plate 1)*
Casein on paperboard
15 x 20" (38.1 x 50.8 cm)
Collection Helen Frankenthaler, New York

3. *Torn Elegy*, 1962 (plate 2)*
Acrylic on cardboard fragment
10⅝ x 15" (27 x 38.1 cm)
(Dedalus no. P62–1954)
Collection Renate Ponsold Motherwell, Greenwich, Connecticut

4. *The Black Wall*, 1980–81 (plate 4)
Lift-ground etching and aquatint from one copper plate printed in black on Hawthorne of Larroque handmade paper (irregular)
Plate: 10⅝ x 27" (27.1 x 68.6 cm)
Paper: 18½ x 35¾" (47.1 x 90.9 cm)
(Belknap no. 242)

5. *Alberti Elegy*, 1981–82 (plate 3)
Lithograph from one aluminum plate printed in black on tan handmade Okawara paper, Chine appliqué
Image (appliqué sheet): 10 x 12¼" (25.4 x 31.2 cm)
Paper: 14 x 15" (35.6 x 38.2 cm)
(Belknap no. 253)

6. *Running Elegy II, Red State*, 1983 (plate 5)
Lift-ground etching and aquatint from one copper plate printed in black; soft ground etching from one copper plate printed in red (blue, yellow) on Hawthorne of Larroque handmade paper
Plates: 11⅝ x 29⅜" (29 x 74.7 cm)
Paper: 18⅜ x 35½" (46.6 x 90.1 cm)
(Belknap no. 295)

7. *Running Elegy II, Blue State*, 1983 (plate 6)

8. *Running Elegy II, Yellow State*, 1983 (plate 7)

II. Automatism

1. *Untitled*, 1957 (plate 8)
Ink and oil on paper
11⅝ x 14¼" (29.5 x 36.2 cm)
Signed with initials lower right in pen; titled "*UNENTITLED*," dated *1957*, and signed *Robert Motherwell* with medium *Ink + oil on rag paper* on reverse in pen
(Dedalus no. D57–32)

2. *In Sepia Ink (Automatism Series)*, 1958 (plate 9)
Ink on paper
14½ x 11½" (36.8 x 29.2 cm)
Signed with initials upper right in ink
(Dedalus no. D58–33)

3. *Sepia Automatism*, 1958 (plate 10)
Ink on paper
14½ x 11½" (36.8 x 29.2 cm)
Signed with initials upper left in ink
(Dedalus no. D58–34)

4. *Sepia Automatism*, 1958 (plate 11)
Ink on paper
14½ x 11½" (36.8 x 29.2 cm)
Signed with initials upper right in ink
(Dedalus no. D58–36)

5. *Sepia Automatism*, 1958 (plate 12)
Ink on paper
14½ x 11" (36.8 x 27.9 cm)
Signed with initials upper right in ink
(Dedalus no. D58–38)

6. *Calligraphy*, 1965–66 (plate 13)
Lithograph from one zinc plate printed in black
Image: 15 x 22" (38.1 x 55.8 cm)
Paper: 19¼ x 26" (48.9 x 66 cm)
(Belknap no. 8)

III. From *Lyric Suite*

1. *Lyric Suite*, 1965 (plate 14)
Black ink with orange bleed and blue ink on rice paper
11 x 9″ (27.9 x 22.9 cm)
Signed with initials upper left in ink
(Dedalus no. D65–103)

2. *Lyric Suite*, 1965 (plate 15)
Black ink on rice paper
9 x 11″ (22.9 x 27.9 cm)
Signed with initials and dated *65* lower left in pencil
(Dedalus no. D65–104)

3. *Lyric Suite*, 1965 (plate 16)
Black and brown ink on rice paper
9 x 11″ (22.9 x 27.9 cm)
Signed with initials lower right in pencil
(Dedalus no. D65–105)

4. *Lyric Suite*, 1965 (plate 17)
Black ink on rice paper
11 x 9″ (27.9 x 22.9 cm)
Signed with initials upper right in pencil
(Dedalus no. D65–113)

5. *Lyric Suite*, 1965 (plate 18)
Black ink on rice paper
11 x 9″ (27.9 x 22.9 cm)
Signed with initials and dated *65* upper right in pencil
(Dedalus no. D65–115)

6. *Lyric Suite*, 1965 (plate 19)
Dark blue/black ink bleeding to olive green on rice paper
9 x 11″ (22.9 x 27.9 cm)
Signed with initials lower right in pencil
(Dedalus no. D65–1611)

7. *Lyric Suite*, 1965 (plate 20)
Dark blue/black ink with olive green cast on rice paper
9 x 11″ (22.9 x 27.9 cm)
Signed with initials upper right in pencil
(Dedalus no. D65–1617)

8. *Lyric Suite*, 1965 (plate 21)
Dark blue/black ink with olive green cast on rice paper
9 x 11″ (22.9 x 27.9 cm)
Signed with initials upper right in pencil
(Dedalus no. D65–1627)

9. *Lyric Suite*, 1965 (plate 22)
Black ink with green bleed, blue ink (appears purple), and royal blue ink on rice paper
11 x 9″ (27.9 x 22.9 cm)
Signed with initials lower left in pencil
(Dedalus no. D65–163)

10. *Lyric Suite*, 1965 (plate 23)
Black ink with orange bleed on rice paper
11 x 9″ (27.9 x 22.9 cm)
Signed with initials upper left in pencil
(Dedalus no. D65–1633)

11. *Lyric Suite*, 1965 (plate 24)
Black ink with orange bleed on rice paper
11 x 9″ (27.9 x 22.9 cm)
Signed with initials lower right in ink
(Dedalus no. D65–1635)

12. *Lyric Suite*, 1965 (plate 25)
Dark blue-green ink on rice paper
9 x 11″ (22.9 x 27.9 cm)
Signed with initials upper right in pencil
(Dedalus no. D65–1652)

13. *Lyric Suite*, 1965 (plate 26)
Blue and black ink on rice paper
9 x 11″ (22.9 x 27.9 cm)
Signed with initials lower center in pencil
(Dedalus no. D65–1692)

14. *Lyric Suite*, 1965 (plate 27)
Black ink with greenish cast on rice paper
9 x 11″ (22.9 x 27.9 cm)
Signed with initials lower right in pencil
(Dedalus no. D65–1695)

15. *Lyric Suite*, 1965 (plate 28)
Black ink with orange bleed and royal blue ink on rice paper
11 x 9″ (27.9 x 22.9 cm)
Signed with initials upper right in pencil
(Dedalus no. D65–1700)

16. *Lyric Suite*, 1965 (plate 29)
Black ink with light yellow bleed on rice paper
11 x 9″ (27.9 x 22.9 cm)
Signed with initials lower right in pencil
(Dedalus no. D65–1703)

17. *Lyric Suite*, 1965 (plate 30)
Black and peacock blue ink on rice paper
11 x 9″ (27.9 x 22.9 cm)
Not signed
(Dedalus no. D65–176)

18. *Lyric Suite*, 1965 (plate 31)
Brown ink with orange bleed on rice paper
9 x 11″ (22.9 x 27.9 cm)
Signed with initials upper left in pencil
(Dedalus no. D65–1782)

19. *Lyric Suite*, 1965 (plate 32)
Royal blue ink (appears purple) on rice paper
11 x 9″ (27.9 x 22.9 cm)
Signed with initials lower right in pencil
(Dedalus no. D65–1846)

20. *Lyric Suite*, 1965 (plate 33)
Ink on rice paper
11 x 9″ (27.9 x 22.9 cm)
Signed with initials lower right in ink
(Dedalus no. D65–1941)

21. *Lyric Suite*, 1965 (plate 34)
Black ink (thins out to appear brown) on rice paper
11 x 9″ (27.9 x 22.9 cm)
Signed with initials upper right in pencil
(Dedalus no. D65–206)

22. *Lyric Suite*, 1965 (plate 35)
Black ink with orange bleed and blue ink (appears purple) on rice paper
11 x 9″ (27.9 x 22.9 cm)
Signed with initials lower right in ink
(Dedalus no. D65–214)

23. *Lyric Suite*, 1965 (plate 36)
Red and blue ink on rice paper
11 x 9″ (27.9 x 22.9 cm)
Signed with initials upper left in pencil
(Dedalus no. D65–2588)

24. *Lyric Suite*, 1965 (plate 37)
Red and blue ink on rice paper
9 x 11″ (22.9 x 27.9 cm)
Signed with initials lower right in pencil
(Dedalus no. D65–2594)

IV. *Je t'aime*

1. *Je t'aime (ce dessin me plait)*, 1956 (plate 38)
Pencil on Strathmore paper
23 x 29″ (58.4 x 73.7 cm)
Signed with initials and dated *56* lower right in pencil
(Dedalus no. D56–2745)

2–11. *Madrid Suite*, 1965–66 (plates 39–48)
Suite of ten lithographs, each from one zinc plate printed in black on Arches Cover paper
Image: 19¾ x 25″ (50.4 x 63.5 cm) (varies)
Paper: 22 x 30″ (55.9 x 76.2 cm)
2. *Madrid Suite* (Belknap no. 9) (plate 39)
3. *Madrid Suite* (Belknap no. 10) (plate 40)
4. *Madrid Suite* (Belknap no. 11) (plate 41)
5. *Madrid Suite* (Belknap no. 12) (plate 42)
6. *Madrid Suite* (Belknap no. 13) (plate 43)
7. *Madrid Suite* (Belknap no. 14) (plate 44)
8. *Madrid Suite* (Belknap no. 15) (plate 45)
9. *Madrid Suite* (Belknap no. 16) (plate 46)
10. *Madrid Suite* (Belknap no. 17) (plate 47)
11. *Madrid Suite* (Belknap no. 18) (plate 48)

12. *Je t'aime*, 1977 (plate 49)
Lithograph from one aluminum plate printed in black on gray Rives BFK paper
Image and paper: 18 x 23″ (45.8 x 58.5 cm)
(Belknap no. 185)

13. *Je t'adore*, 1982 (plate 50)
Sepia ink on paper
8 x 9¾″ (20.3 x 24.8 cm)
Signed with initials upper left in pencil; titled on frame *"JE T'ADORE"* and signed *R. Motherwell* with date *1982* on reverse; titled *"Je t'adore"* and dated *1982* in pencil on reverse
(Dedalus no. D82–2761)

14. *Je t'aime*, 1983 (plate 51)
Brown ink on paper
10⅛ x 7″ (25.8 x 17.8 cm)
Signed with initials and dated *83* upper left in pencil
(Dedalus no. D83–2907)

15. *Untitled*, 1986 (plate 52)
Grayish blue ink on rice paper
9 x 11″ (22.9 x 27.9 cm)
Signed with initials and dated *86* upper left in pencil
(Dedalus no. D86–3457)

V. *Beside the Sea*

1. *Beside the Sea No. 5*, 1962 (plate 53)*
Oil on Strathmore paper
29 x 23" (73.7 x 58.4 cm)
Signed *Motherwell* lower center in charcoal
(Dedalus no. D62–547)
Smith College Museum of Art, Northampton, Massachusetts

2. *Beside the Sea No. 22*, 1962 (plate 54)
Oil on Strathmore paper
29 x 23" (73.7 x 58.4 cm)
Signed with initials and dated *62* upper right in pencil; signed on reverse with title and photography notes
(Dedalus no. D62–548)

3. *Beside the Sea No. 30*, 1962 (plate 55)
Oil on Strathmore paper
29 x 23" (73.7 x 58.4 cm)
Signed with initials and dated *62* upper right in pencil; numbered *30* lower right in pencil
(Dedalus no. D62–551)

4–10. *A Throw of the Dice*, 1962–63 (plates 56–62)
Suite of seven lithographs, each from one stone, printed in black on Rives BFK paper
Image: 18 x 14" (45.8 x 35.5 cm) (varies)
Paper: 30 x 22" (76.2 x 56 cm)

4. *A Throw of the Dice* (Belknap no. 2 bis) (plate 56)
5. *A Throw of the Dice* (Belknap no. 3 bis) (plate 57)
6. *A Throw of the Dice* (Belknap no. 4 bis) (plate 58)
7. *A Throw of the Dice* (Belknap no. 5 bis) (plate 59)
8. *A Throw of the Dice* (Belknap no. 6 bis) (plate 60)
9. *A Throw of the Dice* (Belknap no. 7 bis) (plate 61)
10. *A Throw of the Dice* (Belknap no. 8 bis) (plate 62)

VI. *Open* Studies and Beyond

1. *Black on White No. 6*, 1968 (plate 63)
Acrylic and pencil on paper
6 x 8" (15.2 x 20.3 cm)
Signed with initials and dated *68* lower right in pencil
(Dedalus no. D68–218)

2. *Open Study No. 4*, 1968 (plate 64)
Charcoal on paper
22 x 30½" (55.9 x 77.5 cm)
Signed with initials and dated *68* upper right in pencil
(Dedalus no. D68–412)

3. *Open Study No. 9*, 1968 (plate 65)
Charcoal on paper
22 x 30½" (55.9 x 77.5 cm)
Signed with initials and dated *68* lower left in pencil
(Dedalus no. D68–409)

4. *Untitled (Open)*, 1968 (plate 66)
Charcoal and acrylic on paper
22 x 30" (55.9 x 76.9 cm)
Signed with initials and dated *68* upper left in pencil
(Dedalus no. D68–1497)

5. *Study for "Shem the Penman," No. 9*, 1972 (plate 67)
Acrylic and charcoal on Upson board
8½ x 11½" (62.2 x 48.3 cm)
Signed with initials and dated *72* upper left in charcoal
(Dedalus no. D72–278)

6. *Study for "Shem the Penman," No. 11*, 1972 (plate 68)
Charcoal on tan paper
8½ x 11½" (21.6 x 29.2 cm)
Signed with initials and dated *72* lower left in charcoal
(Dedalus no. D72–279)

7. *Study for "Shem the Penman,"* 1972 (plate 69)
Acrylic on board
8¼ x 11" (21 x 27.9 cm)
Signed with initials and dated *72* upper left in black ink
(Dedalus no. D72–282)

8. *Untitled (Open Study)*, 1974 (plate 70)
Charcoal on tan paper
15 x 7¾" (38.1 x 19.7 cm)
Signed with initials and dated *74* lower right in charcoal; signed *Robert Motherwell* and dated *74* on reverse in marker
(Dedalus no. D74–2859)

VII. Choreographics of *M*

1. *Calligraphic Study I*, 1976 (plate 71)
Lift-ground etching and aquatint from one copper plate printed in black on pale gray-green and white Trent HMP handmade paper
Plate: 6 x 8″ (15.3 x 23 cm)
Paper: 23 x 18″ (58.5 x 45.8 cm)
(Belknap no. 159)

2. *Calligraphic Study II*, 1976 (plate 72)
Lift-ground etching and aquatint from one copper plate printed in black on pale gray-green and white Trent HMP handmade paper
Plate: 6 x 8″ (15.3 x 23 cm)
Paper: 23 x 18″ (58.5 x 45.8 cm)
(Belknap no. 160)

3. *Calligraphic Study III*, 1976 (plate 73)
Lift-ground etching and aquatint from one copper plate printed in black on pale gray-green and white Trent HMP handmade paper
Plate: 9 x 12″ (22.9 x 30.5 cm)
Paper: 23 x 18″ (58.5 x 45.8 cm)
(Belknap no. 161)

4. *Calligraphic Study IV*, 1976 (plate 74)
Lift-ground etching and aquatint from one copper plate printed in black on buff and white Chatham HMP handmade paper
Plate: 9 x 12″ (22.9 x 30.5 cm)
Paper: 23 x 18″ (58.5 x 45.8 cm)
(Belknap no. 162)

5. *Calligraphic Study V*, 1976 (plate 75)
Lift-ground etching and aquatint from one copper plate printed in black on buff Chatham HMP handmade paper
Plate: 9 x 12″ (22.9 x 30.5 cm)
Paper: 23 x 18″ (58.5 x 45.8 cm)
(Belknap no. 163)

6. *Dance I*, 1978 (plate 76)
Lift-ground etching and aquatint from one copper plate printed in black on J. B. Green paper
Plate: 10 x 24″ (25.5 x 61 cm)
Paper: 19½ x 30½″ (49.5 x 77.5 cm)
(Belknap no. 199)

7. *Dance II*, 1978 (plate 77)
Lift-ground etching and aquatint from one copper plate printed in black on J. B. Green paper
Plate: 18 x 36″ (45.8 x 91.5 cm)
Paper: 25½ x 41″ (64.8 x 104.1 cm)
(Belknap no. 200)

8. *Dance III*, 1978 (plate 78)
Lift-ground etching and aquatint from one copper plate printed in black on J. B. Green paper
Plate: 20 x 24″ (50.4 x 61 cm)
Paper: 27½ x 30½″ (69.9 x 77.5 cm)
(Belknap no. 201)

VIII. *Samurai*

1. *Totemic Emblem*, 1967 (plate 79)
Acrylic on board
20 x 16″ (50.8 x 40.6 cm)
Signed and dated lower center *R Motherwell 1967 / acrylic on canvas*; inscribed upper right *Top* with arrow
(Dedalus no. P67–1232)

2. *Samurai*, 1971 (plate 80)
Lithograph from one aluminum plate printed in black on Japanese Suzuki handmade paper
Image: 42 x 35½″ (106.6 x 90.2 cm)
Paper: 73½ x 37″ (186 x 94 cm)
(Belknap no. 75)

3. *Untitled (Samurai)*, 1972 (plate 81)
Acrylic on paper
22 x 11¾″ (55.9 x 28.9 cm)
Signed with initials and dated *72* upper right
(Dedalus no. D72–3254)

4. *Untitled*, 1972 (plate 82)
Lithograph from one stone printed in black on Jeff Goodman handmade paper
Image: 7 x 14″ (17.8 x 35 cm)
Paper: 24 x 18″ (61 x 45.7 cm)
(Belknap no. 81)

5. *Samurai No. 5*, 1974 (plate 83)
Acrylic on Upson board
48 x 36″ (121.9 x 91.4 cm)
Signed *Motherwell* and dated *74* upper left in black crayon
(Dedalus no. P74–1553)

6. *Samurai No. 6*, 1974 (plate 84)
Acrylic on board
48 x 36″ (121.9 x 91.4 cm)
Signed *Motherwell* and dated *74* lower right in pencil
(Dedalus no. P74–1554)

7. *Untitled*, 1978 (plate 85)
Lithograph from one aluminum plate printed in black on buff handmade Kitakata paper, Chine collé
Image (collé sheet): 22 x 16″ (56 x 40.6 cm)
Paper: 30 x 22¼″ (76.2 x 56.5 cm)
(Belknap no. 195)

8. *Samurai II*, 1979–80 (plate 86)
Lithograph from one stone printed in black on handmade natural Sekishu paper, Chine appliqué
Image (appliqué sheet): 39 x 24½″ (99 x 62.2 cm)
Paper: Two joined sheets of Napal handmade paper with overall dimensions 57 x 24½″ (144.7 x 62.2 cm)
(Belknap no. 213)

9. *Primal Sign I*, 1979–80 (plate 87)
Aquatint from one zinc plate printed in brown; lift-ground etching and aquatint from one copper plate printed in black on Whatman paper
Plates: 23½ x 18″ (59.7 x 45.2 cm) (black) and 23½ x 8″ (59.7 x 20.3 cm) (brown)
Paper: 28½ x 21½″ (71.9 x 54.6 cm)
(Belknap no. 223)

10. *Primal Sign II*, 1979–80 (plate 88)
Aquatint from one copper plate printed in brown; lift-ground etching and aquatint from one copper plate printed in black on German Etching paper
Plates: 23 x 10″ (58.5 x 25.4 cm) (aquatint plate slanted)
Paper: 30 x 21″ (76.2 x 53.4 cm) (varies)
(Belknap no. 235)

11. *Primal Sign III*, 1979–80 (plate 89)
Aquatint from one copper plate printed in brown; lift-ground etching and aquatint from one copper plate printed in black on Arches Cover paper
Plates: 23 x 10″ (58.5 x 25.4 cm)
Paper: 28¾ x 20¾″ (73.1 x 52.9 cm) (varies)
(Belknap no. 236)

12. *Primal Sign IV*, 1979–80 (plate 90)
Aquatint from one zinc plate printed in brown; lift-ground etching and aquatint from one copper plate printed in black on German Etching paper
Plates: 23 x 11⅝″ (58.5 x 29.6 cm)
Paper: 30 x 21″ (76.2 x 53.4 cm)
(Belknap no. 237)

IX. *Drunk with Turpentine*

1. *Drunk with Turpentine Series*, 1979 (plate 91)
Oil on paper
29 x 23″ (73.7 x 58.4 cm)
Signed with initials and dated *1979* upper right in pen
(Dedalus no. D79–2300)

2. *Drunk with Turpentine No. 47*, 1979 (plate 92)
Oil on rag board
20 x 30″ (50.8 x 76.2 cm)
Signed with initials and dated *79* upper left in pen
(Dedalus no. D79–2335)

3. *Drunk with Turpentine No. 51*, 1979 (plate 93)
Oil on rag paper
23 x 29″ (58.4 x 73.7 cm)
Signed with initials and dated *17 Aug 79* upper left in charcoal
(Dedalus no. D79–2389)

4. *Drunk with Turpentine Series*, 1979 (plate 94)
Oil on rag paper
20 x 30″ (50.8 x 76.2 cm)
Signed with initials and dated *79* lower right in pen
(Dedalus no. D79–2392)

X. Literary Figures

1. *Stephen's Iron Crown Etched*, 1981–82 (plate 95)
Aquatint from one copper plate printed in cream; lift-ground etching and aquatint from one copper plate printed in black on German Etching paper
Plates: 15¾ x 19¾" (40.1 x 50.3 cm)
Paper: 25 x 28" (63.5 x 71.2 cm)
(Belknap no. 257)

2. *Mulligan's Tower*, 1982–83 (plate 96)
Etching from one copper plate printed with plate tone in sepia on German Etching paper
Plate: 9¾ x 6⅞" (24.8 x 17.5 cm)
Paper: 17 x 13" (43.2 x 33.1 cm)
(Belknap no. 263)

3. *Athena*, 1982–83 (plate 97)
Lift-ground etching and aquatint from one copper plate printed in ochre on Auvergne à la Main handmade paper
Plate: 7¾ x 9¾" (19.7 x 24.8 cm)
Paper: 19⅞ x 17¾" (50.6 x 45.1 cm)
(Belknap no. 264)

4. *Wind*, 1982–83 (plate 98)
Lift-ground etching and aquatint from one copper plate printed in ochre on Auvergne à la Main handmade paper
Plate: 7⅞ x 9¾" (20.1 x 24.8 cm)
Paper: 20 x 17½" (50.9 x 44.5 cm)
(Belknap no. 265)

5. *Wanderers*, 1985 (plate 99)
Aquatint from one copper plate printed in light salmon; lift-ground etching and aquatint from one copper plate in black on Whatman paper
Plates: 15¾ x 19⅝" (40.1 x 50 cm)
Paper: 23¼ x 27" (59.1 x 68.6 cm)
(Belknap no. 332)

6–12. *Hollow Men Suite*, 1985–86 (plates 100–106)
Suite of seven lift-ground etchings with aquatint from one copper plate printed in black on handmade cream Moriki paper, Chine collé
Paper: 11¼ x 12" (28.7 x 30.5 cm)

6. *Hollow Men Suite* (plate 100)
Plate (collé sheet): 4½ x 5⅞" (11.5 x 15 cm)
(Belknap no. 336)

7. *Hollow Men Suite* (plate 101)
Plate (collé sheet): 4 x 5⅞" (10.2 x 15 cm)
(Belknap no. 337)

8. *Hollow Men Suite* (plate 102)
Plate (collé sheet): 3¾ x 4⅞" (9.6 x 12.5 cm)
(Belknap no. 338)

9. *Hollow Men Suite* (plate 103)
Plate (collé sheet): 3⅝ x 4⅞" (9.3 x 12.5 cm)
(Belknap no. 339)

10. *Hollow Men Suite* (plate 104)
Plate (collé sheet): 4 x 5⅞" (10.2 x 15 cm)
(Belknap no. 340)

11. *Hollow Men Suite* (plate 105)
Plate (collé sheet): 3⅝ x 4⅞" (9.3 x 12.5 cm)
(Belknap no. 341)

12. *Hollow Men Suite* (plate 106)
Plate (collé sheet): 5 x 6⅞" (12.8 x 17.7 cm)
(Belknap no. 342)

13–33. *From the "Joyce Sketchbook"* (plates 107–127)

13. *Ulysses Drawings*, 1986 (plate 107)
Pencil, China marker, and ink wash on paper
3 x 5" (7.6 x 12.7 cm)
Signed with initials lower left in pencil
(Dedalus no. D85–3147)

14. *Ulysses Drawings*, 1985 (plate 108)
Pencil, ink, and China marker on paper
3 x 5" (7.6 x 12.7 cm)
Signed with initials upper right in pencil
(Dedalus no. D85–3150)

15. *Joyce Sketchbook II*, 1985 (plate 109)
Pencil and ink on paper
3 x 5" (7.6 x 12.7 cm)
Signed with initials upper right in pencil
(Dedalus no. D85–3151)

16. *Joyce Sketchbook II*, 1985 (plate 110)
Ink wash and China marker on paper
3 x 5" (7.6 x 12.7 cm)
Signed with initials and dated *85* upper right in pencil
(Dedalus no. D85–3152)

17. *Joyce Sketchbook II*, 1985 (plate 111)
Pencil, ink wash, and China marker on paper
5 x 3" (12.7 x 7.6 cm)
Signed with initials lower right in pencil
(Dedalus no. D85–3156)

18. *Untitled*, 1985 (plate 112)
Ink and China marker on paper
3 x 5″ (7.6 x 12.7 cm)
Signed with initials and dated *85* upper left in pencil
(Dedalus no. D85–3163)

19. *Untitled*, 1985 (plate 113)
Ink, pencil, and China marker on paper
3 x 5″ (7.6 x 12.7 cm)
Signed with initials lower right in pencil
(Dedalus no. D85–3165)

20. *Church*, 1985 (plate 114)
Ink, pencil, and China marker on paper
3 x 5″ (7.6 x 12.7 cm)
Signed with initials lower right in pencil
(Dedalus no. D85–3169)

21. *Untitled (Elegy Study)*, 1985 (plate 115)
Pencil on paper
3 x 5″ (7.6 x 12.7 cm)
Signed with initials upper right in pencil
(Dedalus no. D85–3171)

22. *Untitled (Open Forms)*, 1985 (plate 116)
Ink on paper
3 x 5″ (7.6 x 12.7 cm)
Signed with initials upper right in pencil
(Dedalus no. D85–3176)

23. *Untitled*, 1985 (plate 117)
Pencil, ink, and wash on paper
3 x 5″ (7.6 x 12.7 cm)
Signed with initials upper right in pencil
(Dedalus no. D85–3179)

24. *Untitled*, 1985 (plate 118)
Ink and China marker on paper
3 x 5″ (7.6 x 12.7 cm)
Signed with initials upper left in pencil
(Dedalus no. D85–3187)

25. *Untitled*, 1985 (plate 119)
Ink and China marker on paper
3 x 5″ (7.6 x 12.7 cm)
Signed with initials upper left in pencil
(Dedalus no. D85–3188)

26. *Untitled*, 1985 (plate 120)
Ink on paper
3 x 5″ (7.6 x 12.7 cm)
Signed with initials upper left in pencil
(Dedalus no. D85–3189)

27. *Untitled (Elegy Forms)*, 1985 (plate 121)
Brown ink on paper
3 x 5″ (7.6 x 12.7 cm)
Signed with initials upper right in ink
(Dedalus no. D85–3194)

28. *Untitled*, 1985 (plate 122)
Ink on paper
3 x 5″ (7.6 x 12.7 cm)
Signed with initials upper right in pencil
(Dedalus no. D85–3197)

29. *Untitled*, 1985 (plate 123)
Ink and China marker on paper
3 x 5″ (7.6 x 12.7 cm)
Signed with initials upper right in pencil
(Dedalus no. D85–3198)

30. *Untitled*, 1985 (plate 124)
Black ink on paper
3 x 5″ (7.6 x 12.7 cm)
Signed with initials upper right in pencil
(Dedalus no. D85–3202)

31. *Ulysses Drawing*, 1985 (plate 125)
Ink wash, pencil, and China marker on paper
3 x 5″ (7.6 x 12.7 cm)
Signed with initials upper right in pencil
(Dedalus no. D85–3207)

32. *Ulysses Drawing*, 1985 (plate 126)
Ink, wash, and China marker on paper
3 x 5″ (7.6 x 12.7 cm)
Signed with initials upper left in pencil
(Dedalus no. D85–3211)

33. *Untitled*, 1985 (plate 127)
Ink wash, pencil, and China marker on paper
3 x 5″ (7.6 x 12.7 cm)
Signed with initials upper right in pencil
(Dedalus no. D85–3697)

XI. *Night Music*

1. *Black Refracts Heat*, 1974 (plate 128)*
Collage and acrylic on Upson board
48 x 36" (121.9 x 91.4 cm)
Signed with initials and dated *74* upper right in white conté crayon
(Dedalus no. C74–1454)
Walker Art Center, Minneapolis

2. *Night Music Opus No. 14*, 1989 (plate 129)
Collage of rice paper and acrylic on canvas panel
33¼ x 25" (84.5 x 63.5 cm)
(Dedalus no. C89–3489)

3. *Night Music Opus No. 16*, 1989 (plate 130)
Collage of rice paper and acrylic on canvas panel
32½ x 25¼" (82.6 x 64.1 cm)
Signed with initials and dated *89* lower left in white chalk
(Dedalus no. C89–3495)

4. *Night Music Opus No. 17*, 1989 (plate 131)
Collage of rice paper and acrylic on canvas panel
32¼ x 25½" (81.9 x 64.8 cm)
Signed with initials and dated *89* upper left in white crayon
(Dedalus no. C89–3493)

5. *Night Music Opus No. 24*, 1989 (plate 132)
Collage and acrylic on canvas panel
32½ x 25½" (82.6 x 64.8 cm)
Signed with initials and dated *89* upper right in white chalk
(Dedalus no. C89–3514)

6. *Night Music Opus No. 25*, 1989 (plate 133)
Collage with acrylic on canvas panel
32½ x 25½" (82.6 x 64.8 cm)
Signed with initials and dated *89* upper right in white chalk
(Dedalus no. C89–3664)

7. *Night Music Opus No. 26*, 1989 (plate 134)
Collage and acrylic on canvas panel
32½ x 25½" (82.6 x 64.8 cm)
Signed with initials and dated *89* upper right in white chalk
(Dedalus no. C89–3679)

Glossary Note on the Prints

Aquatint
A technique for producing an overall tone of granulated texture by etching through a porous ground consisting of particles of resin that have been fused to the plate and resist the bite of the acid.

Chine appliqué
A method of gluing an already printed sheet of paper to another under pressure, usually by running them together through the press a second time.

Chine collé
A thin sheet of rice paper printed and mounted simultaneously on a larger, heavier sheet of paper.

Etching
The intaglio process in which acid is used to corrode a design into metal. The plate is first covered with a protective ground into which the design is drawn with an etching needle; the metal thus exposed is subject to the corrosive action of acid.

Lift-ground (sugar-lift) etching
The design is brushed freely and directly onto the plate with a water-soluble pigment (often a mixture of sugar and India ink). The plate is varnished and immersed in water; as the sugar swells, it lifts the varnish off the plate, exposing the original drawing as bare copper, which is then prepared and etched as aquatint.

Lithography
A planographic method that depends upon the mutual repellence of water and grease. The drawing is made directly on the stone or plate with a greasy medium; the plate is dampened with water, which remains only on the unmarked areas. Printing ink is then rolled over the surface and adheres only to the greasy medium of the drawing.

Soft ground
The plate is prepared with a ground to which tallow has been added to prevent it from hardening. A piece of paper is placed directly on that surface, on which a drawing is made, usually with pencil. The soft ground adheres to the paper, which is then removed, exposing the metal for etching. The technique preserves the texture of the original drawn line.

Bibliographical Note

On Robert Motherwell

The critical literature on Robert Motherwell followed and grew with his career, without, however, quite keeping up with it. A catalogue raisonné of the artist's work is in preparation, under the direction of Joan Banach, curator of the Dedalus Foundation, and will be published under the auspices of the foundation. In its third edition, Dorothy C. Belknap's catalogue raisonné of the prints has been brought up to date (1991). Motherwell's own extensive writings—articles and reviews, lectures, correspondence—which afford the most eloquent commentary on his art, have recently been published, although not exhaustively, in the anthology edited by Stephanie Terenzio (1992). The catalogues of retrospective exhibitions and the monographs on the artist offer summaries up to date, including bibliographies and chronologies. What follows, then, is a guide to that essential literature, which should be consulted for further bibliography:

1965 Frank O'Hara, *Robert Motherwell, with Selections from the Artist's Writings*, exhibition catalogue (New York: The Museum of Modern Art, 1965).

1972 E. A. Carmean, Jr., *The Collages of Robert Motherwell: A Retrospective Exhibition*, exhibition catalogue (Houston: The Museum of Fine Arts, 1972).

1973 *Robert Motherwell: Recent Work*, exhibition catalogue with essays by Sam Hunter et al. (Princeton: The Art Museum, Princeton University, 1973).

1975 Robert C. Hobbs, "Motherwell's Concern with Death in Painting: An Investigation of His Elegies to the Spanish Republic, including an Examination of His Philosophical and Methodological Considerations," Ph.D. dissertation (University of North Carolina, Chapel Hill, 1975).

1976 *Robert Motherwell*, exhibition catalogue with essays by Robert C. Hobbs (Düsseldorf: Städtische Kunsthalle, 1976).

1979 *Robert Motherwell: Drawings—A Retrospective, 1941 to the Present*, exhibition catalogue with text by Jack Flam (Houston: Janie C. Lee Gallery, 1979).

1980 E. A. Carmean, Jr., ed., *Robert Motherwell: Reconciliation Elegy* (Geneva: Skira; New York: Rizzoli, 1980).

Stephanie Terenzio, *Robert Motherwell and Black* (Storrs: William Benton Museum of Art, University of Connecticut, 1980).

1982 H. H. Arnason, *Robert Motherwell*, second edition, new and revised, with an introduction by Dore Ashton and an interview by Barbaralee Diamonstein (New York: Harry N. Abrams, 1982).

1983 *Robert Motherwell*, exhibition catalogue, Albright-Knox Art Gallery, Buffalo, with essays by Dore Ashton and Jack D. Flam and an introduction by Robert T. Buck (New York: Abbeville Press, 1983).

1984 Gabriella Drudi, *Note romane a Robert Motherwell* (Milan: Multhipla Edizioni, 1984).

1985 E. A. Carmean, Jr., *Robert Motherwell: "Stephen's Iron Crown" and Related Works*, exhibition catalogue (Fort Worth Art Museum, 1985).

1986 Robert Saltonstall Mattison, *Robert Motherwell: The Formative Years* (Ann Arbor and London: UMI Research Press, 1986).

1990 Marcelin Pleynet, *Robert Motherwell*, trans. Mary Ann Caws (Paris: Editions Daniel Papierski, 1990).

1991 Stephanie Terenzio, *The Prints of Robert Motherwell*, with a catalogue raisonné, 1943–1990, by Dorothy C. Belknap, third revised edition (New York: Hudson Hills Press in association with the American Federation of Arts, 1991).

Jack Flam, *Motherwell* (Oxford: Phaidon Press, 1991).

Robert Motherwell 1915/1991: La Puerta abierta/The Open Door, exhibition catalogue with essays by Joan Banach, Teresa del Conde, and Dore Ashton (Mexico City and Fort Worth: InterCultura, 1991).

1992 *The Collected Writings of Robert Motherwell*, edited by Stephanie Terenzio (New York and Oxford: Oxford University Press, 1992).

1996 Mary Ann Caws, *Robert Motherwell: What Art Holds* (New York: Columbia University Press, 1996).

On Abstract Expressionism

The literature on the surrounding and sustaining context of Motherwell's early achievement as an artist also grew during the decades of his career. Sympathetic critics in the late forties and fifties, direct witnesses to the development of Abstract Expressionism and participants in the New York art world, sought to define and interpret the new painting with a sense of shared excitement. That enthusiasm, the direct involvement of their response, was tempered by younger generations of critics, themselves more involved with post–Abstract Expressionist developments, and, more recently still, by art historians for whom Abstract Expressionism seems a purely historical phenomenon of a distant past—indeed, half a century away. As historians, they have done their research, uncovering with greater precision the details of the artists' lives (and libraries) and of the response to their art; they have concentrated on the rhetoric of the artists and on their cultural values and defenses. Also, with the objectivity of distance, they have sought to locate the phenomenon within the historical moments of America, focusing on the sociopolitical and the economic during the hard times of the Depression, of World War II, and of the postwar era. Several of these studies began life as doctoral dissertations, perhaps the surest sign that the subject has been thoroughly historicized. Studies of critical reception, they seem often to focus more on words than pictures—understandably, perhaps, but also unfortunately: such indirect critical response is not likely to prove a particularly reliable guide into the meaning of these pictures.

The words themselves, of the painters and of the contemporaneous critics, are of course crucial for an understanding of the cultural moment. Three voices in particular, participants in and commentators on that culture, are especially important; many of their critical essays have been made available in collected volumes:

Clement Greenberg, *The Collected Essays and Criticism*, ed. John O'Brian, 4 vols. (Chicago: University of Chicago Press, 1986–93).

Harold Rosenberg, *The Tradition of the New* (New York: Horizon Press, 1959; reprint, Chicago and London: University of Chicago Press, 1982), and *The Anxious Object: Art Today and Its Audience* (New York: Horizon Press, 1964; reprint, Chicago and London: University of Chicago Press, 1982).

Meyer Schapiro, *Modern Art, Nineteenth and Twentieth Centuries*, vol. 2 of his selected papers (New York: George Braziller, 1978).

Without pretending to be exhaustive, the following bibliography offers some of the basic titles in the literature on Abstract Expressionism:

1955 William C. Seitz, *Abstract Expressionist Painting in America* (Cambridge, Mass., and London: Harvard University Press for the National Gallery of Art, 1983). Originally submitted as a Ph.D. dissertation, Princeton University, 1955.

1970 Irving Sandler, *The Triumph of American Painting: A History of Abstract Expressionism* (New York: Harper & Row, 1970).

1973 Dore Ashton, *The New York School: A Cultural Reckoning* (New York: Viking Press, 1973).

1980 Stephen C. Foster, *The Critics of Abstract Expressionism* (Ann Arbor: UMI Research Press, 1980).

1981 Stewart Buettner, *American Art Theory, 1945–1970* (Ann Arbor: UMI Research Press, 1981).

1982 Annette Cox, *Art-as-Politics: The Abstract Expressionist Avant-Garde and Society* (Ann Arbor and London: UMI Research Press, 1982).

1983 Serge Guilbaut, *How New York Stole the Idea of Modern Art: Abstract Expressionism, Freedom and the Cold War*, trans. Arthur Goldhammer (Chicago and London: University of Chicago Press, 1983).

1985 Francis Frascina, ed., *Pollock and After: The Critical Debate* (London: Harper & Row, 1985).

1987 Michael Auping, ed., *Abstract Expressionism: The Critical Developments* (New York: Harry N. Abrams in association with the Albright-Knox Art Gallery, 1987).

1989 Alwynne Mackie, *Art/Talk: Theory and Practice in Abstract Expressionism* (New York: Columbia University Press, 1989).

1990 David Anfam, *Abstract Expressionism* (London: Thames & Hudson, 1990).

Ann Eden Gibson, *Issues in Abstract Expressionism: The Artist-Run Periodicals* (Ann Arbor and London: UMI Research Press, 1990).

Clifford Ross, *Abstract Expressionism: Creators and Critics—An Anthology* (New York: Harry N. Abrams, 1990).

David Shapiro and Cecile Shapiro, *Abstract Expressionism: A Critical Record* (Cambridge and New York: Cambridge University Press, 1990).

1991 Stephen Polcari, *Abstract Expressionism and the Modern Experience* (Cambridge and New York: Cambridge University Press, 1991).

1992 April Kingsley, *The Turning Point: The Abstract Expressionists and the Transformation of American Art* (New York: Simon & Schuster, 1992).

1993 Michael Leja, *Reframing Abstract Expressionism: Subjectivity and Painting in the 1940s* (New Haven and London: Yale University Press, 1993).

Index

Page numbers in *italics* refer to illustrations. Titles refer to writings and works of art by Robert Motherwell unless otherwise indicated.

Photograph Credits

Photographs of works of art reproduced in this volume were generally provided by the Dedalus Foundation, Inc., or by the other owners or custodians cited in the captions. The following list applies to photographs for which an additional acknowledgment is due. Numbers refer to pages. Unless otherwise indicated, a cited page number includes all of the photographs reproduced on that page.

Courtesy Stephen Addiss: 64, 66, 70, 76
Courtesy Brooke Alexander: 147
Joan Banach: 178, 179, 180 bottom, 181–83, 184 top, 184 center
Geoffrey Clements: 129
Ken Cohen: 98, 103, 110 top left, 111 bottom left, 112 bottom right, 186, 187, 189
Courtesy Knoedler & Company, New York: 97
© Renate Ponsold Motherwell: 6, 12, 26, 68, 81, 94
Doug Munson: 146
© 1996 The Museum of Modern Art, New York: 2, 15–18, 46
Stephen Petegorsky: 127
R. Petersen: 118 top, 119 bottom
Eric Pollitzer: 107, 124, 130, 131 left, 132 right, 142–45, 148, 149
Steven Sloman: 22, 99, 100, 118 bottom, 119 top, 120–23, 131 right, 132 left, 133–35, 139, 150, 153, 154, 159–63, 166–77
Oren Slor: 101, 102, 104–6, 108, 109, 110 top right, 110 bottom left, 110 bottom right, 111 top left, 111 top right, 111 bottom right, 112 top left, 112 top right, 112 bottom left, 113–15, 125, 126, 136–38, 140, 141, 151, 152, 155–58, 164, 165, 180 top, 180 center, 184 bottom, 188, 190, 191
Zindman/Fremont: 116, 117, 128